MOMO

LEGENDARY WA

[脚本] 小林雄次

[作画] Z-ONE

①

TABLE OF CONTENTS

Chapter 1 Momo and Taro

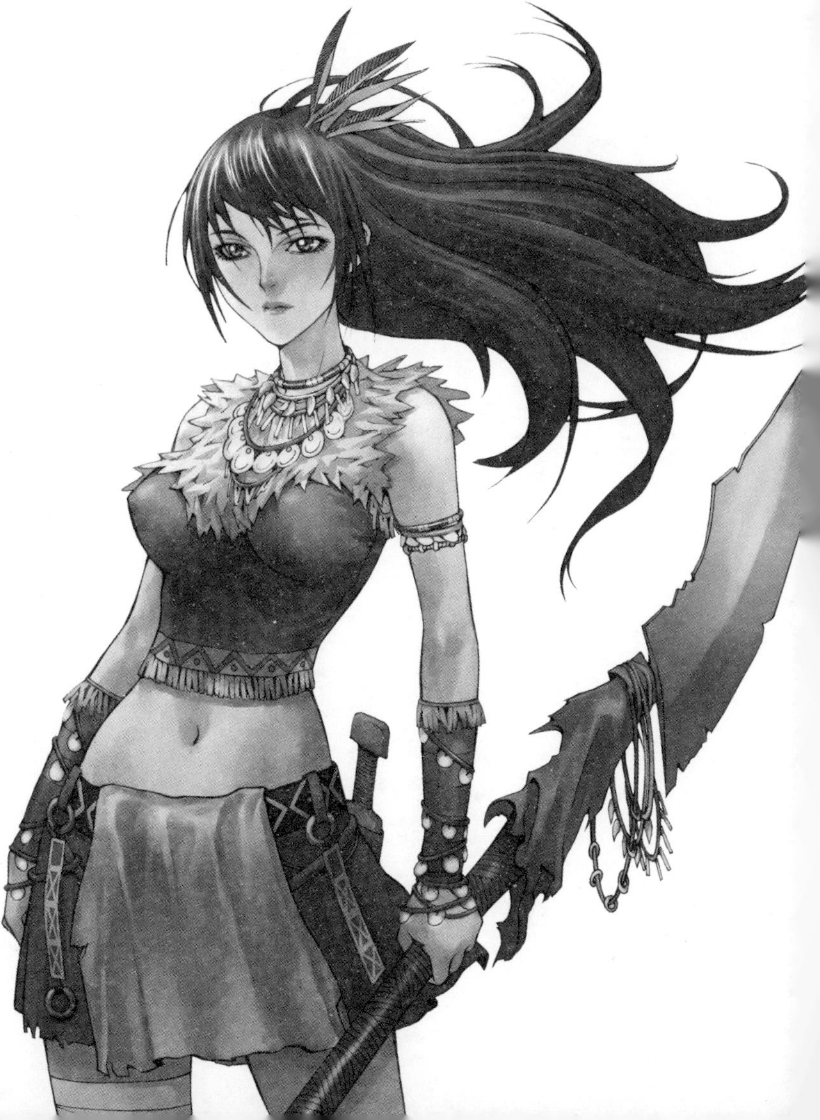

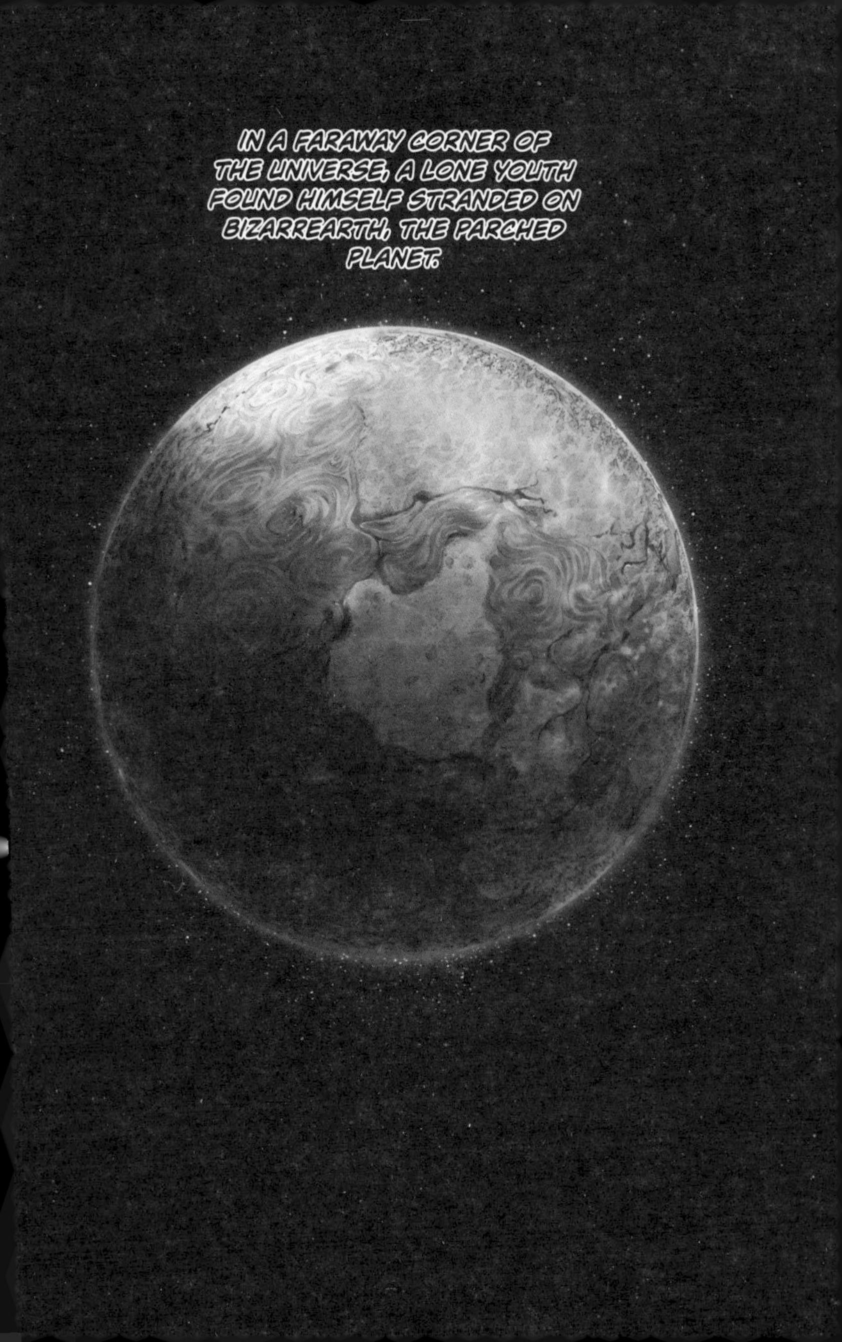
IN A FARAWAY CORNER OF THE UNIVERSE, A LONE YOUTH FOUND HIMSELF STRANDED ON BIZARREARTH, THE PARCHED PLANET.

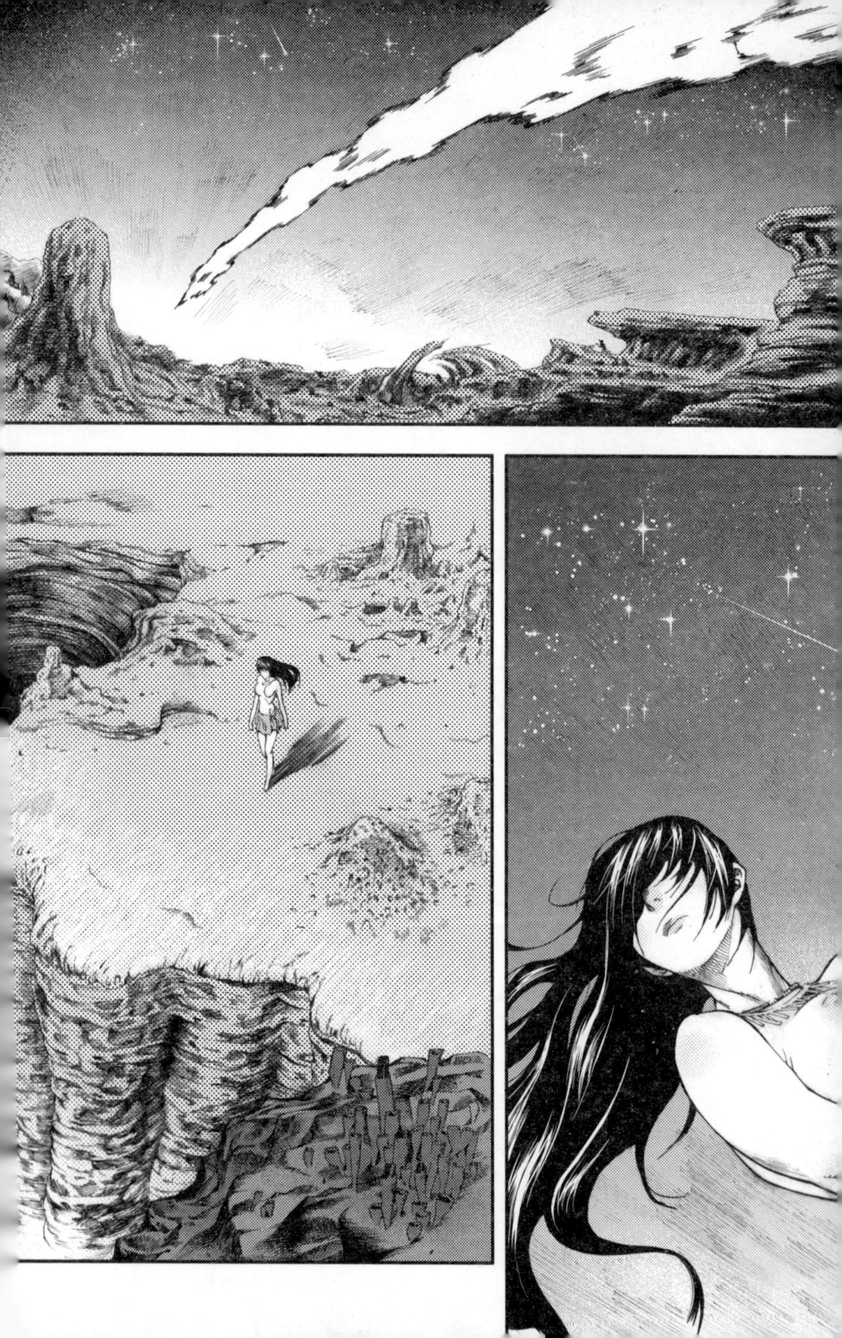

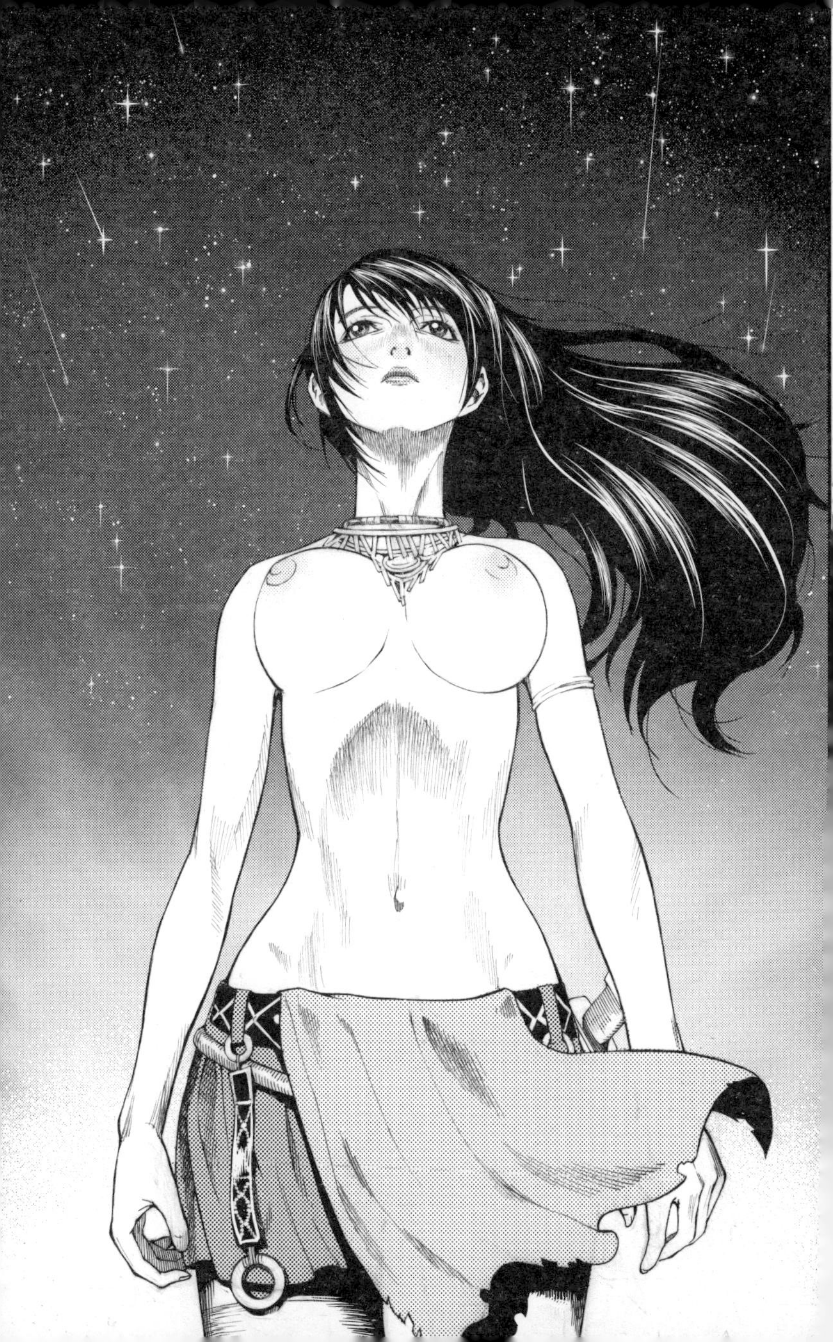

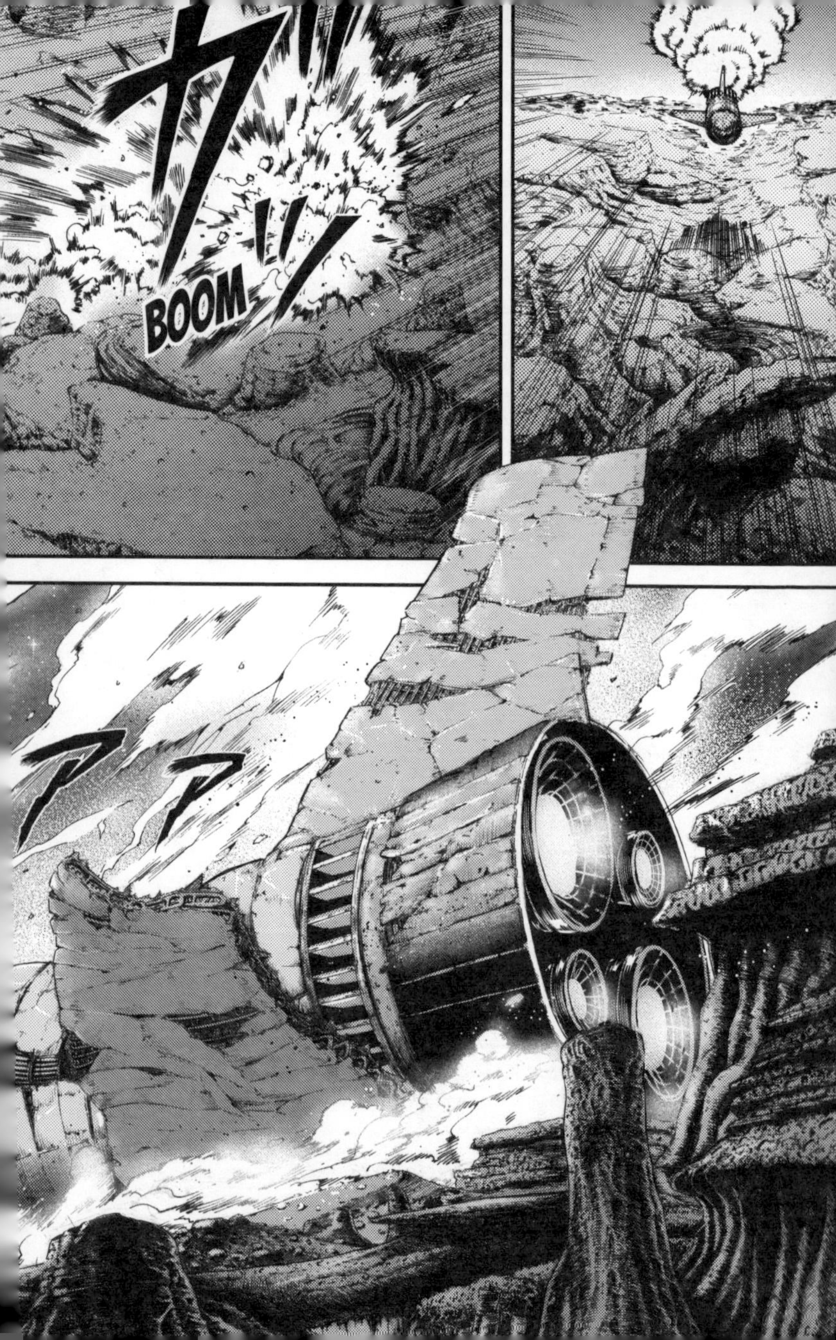
BOOM

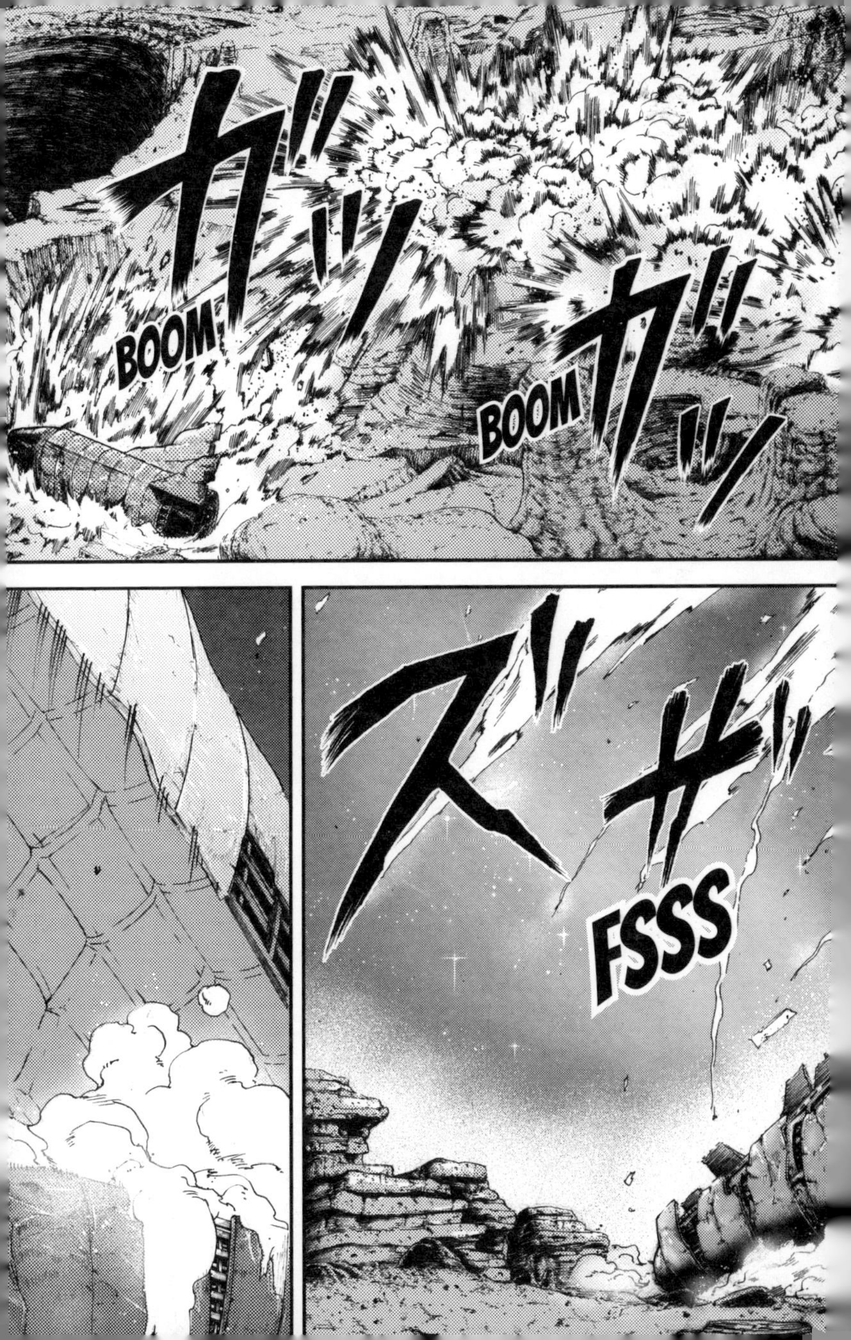

ガッ
BOOM
ガッ
BOOM
ズザッ
FSSS

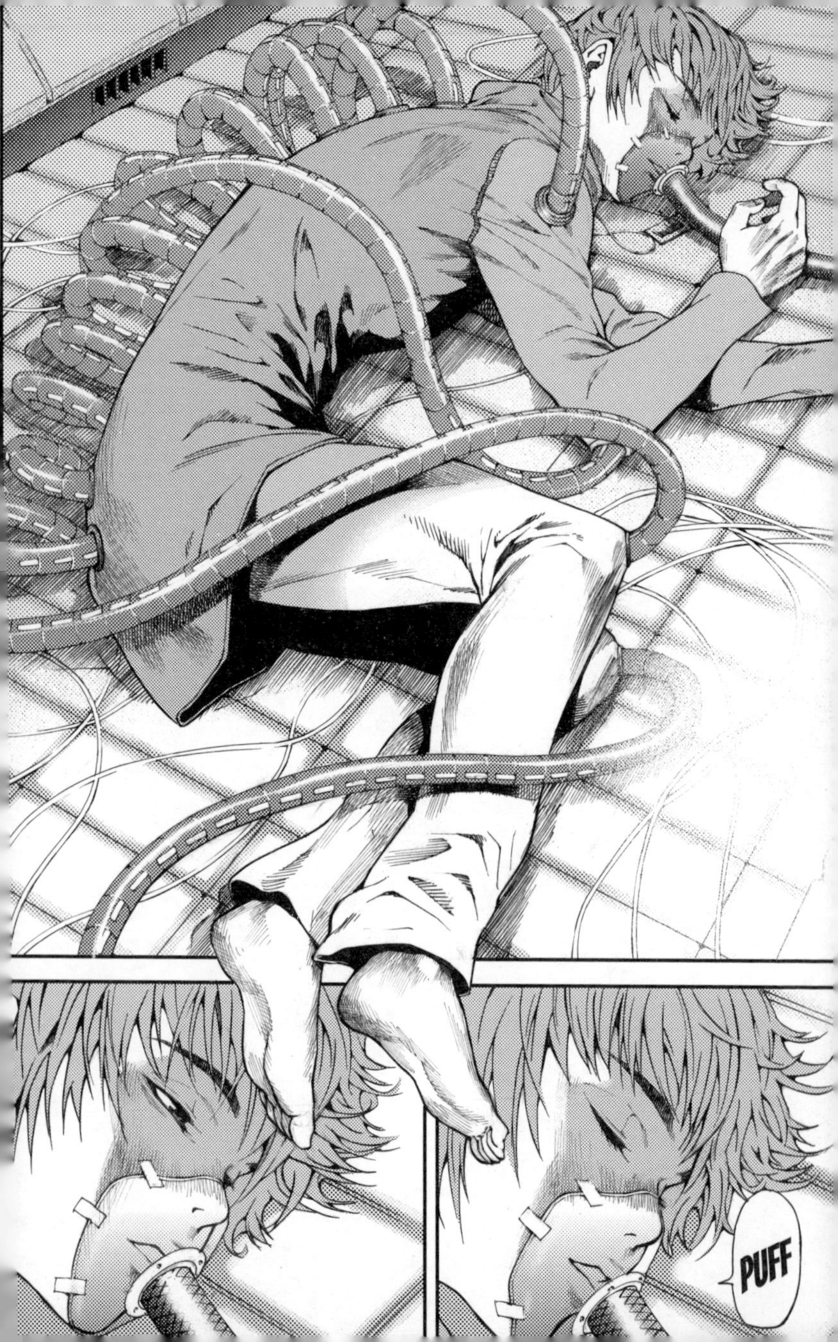
PUFF

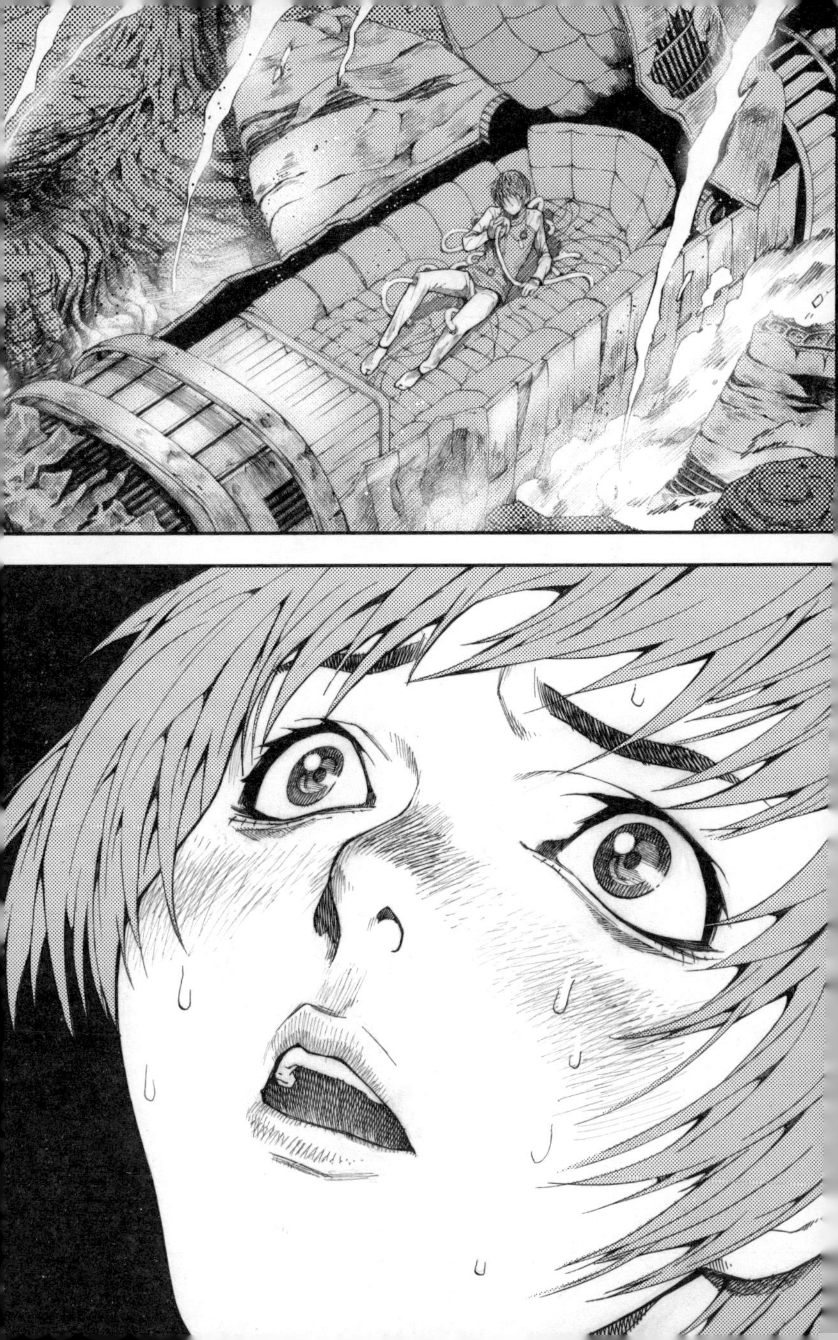

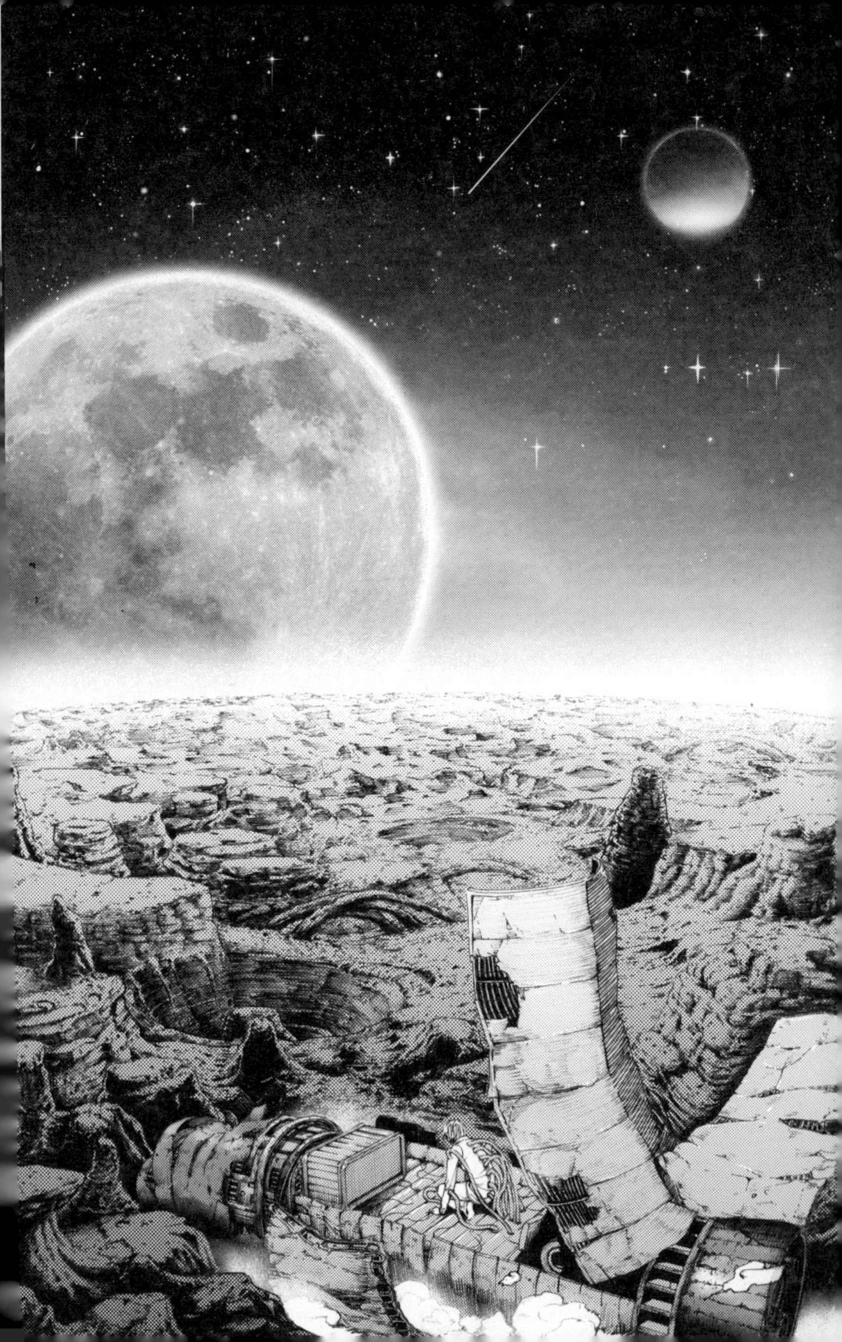

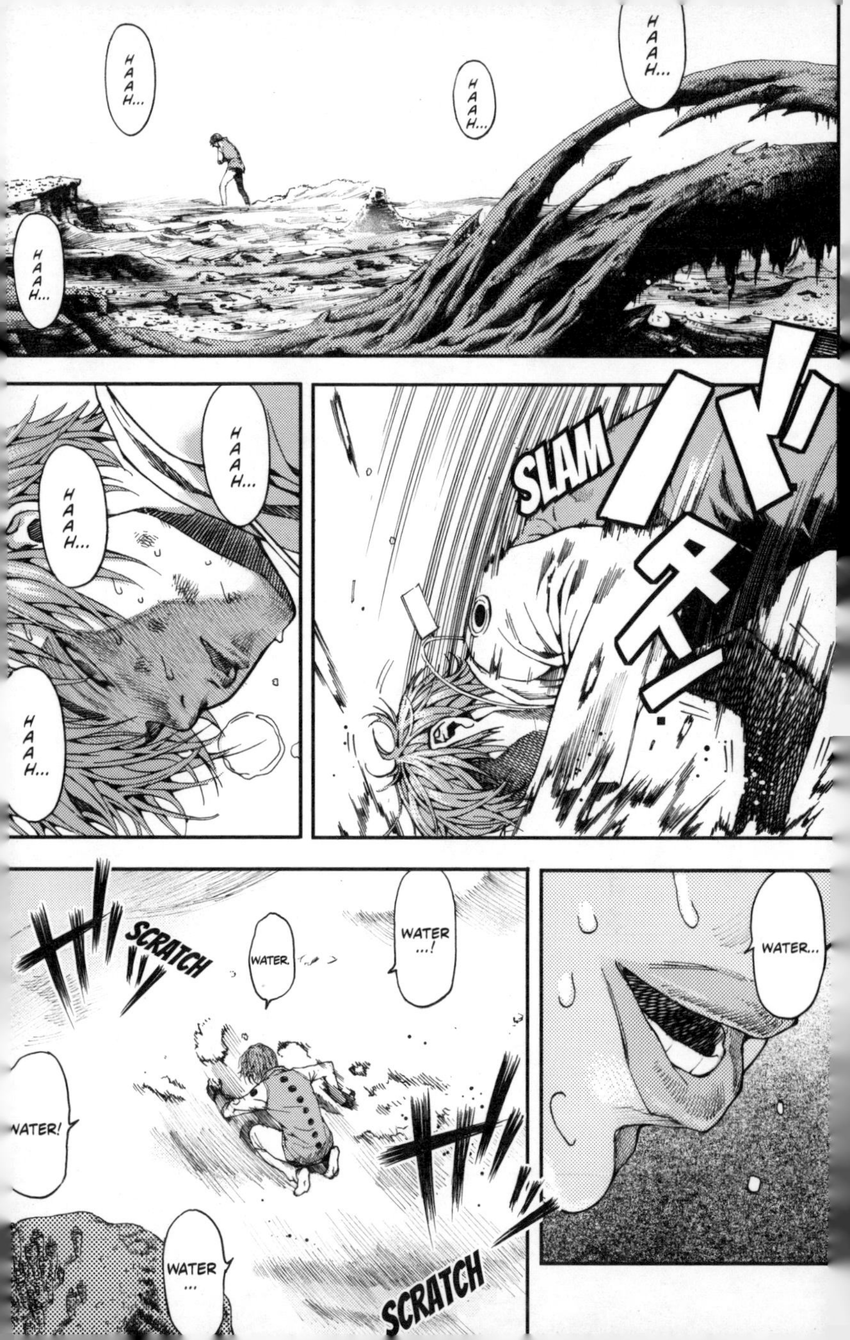
HAAAH...
HAAAH...
HAAAH...
HAAAH...
SLAM
HAAAH...
HAAAH...
HAAAH...
WATER...
WATER ...!
WATER.
SCRATCH
WATER!
WATER ...
SCRATCH

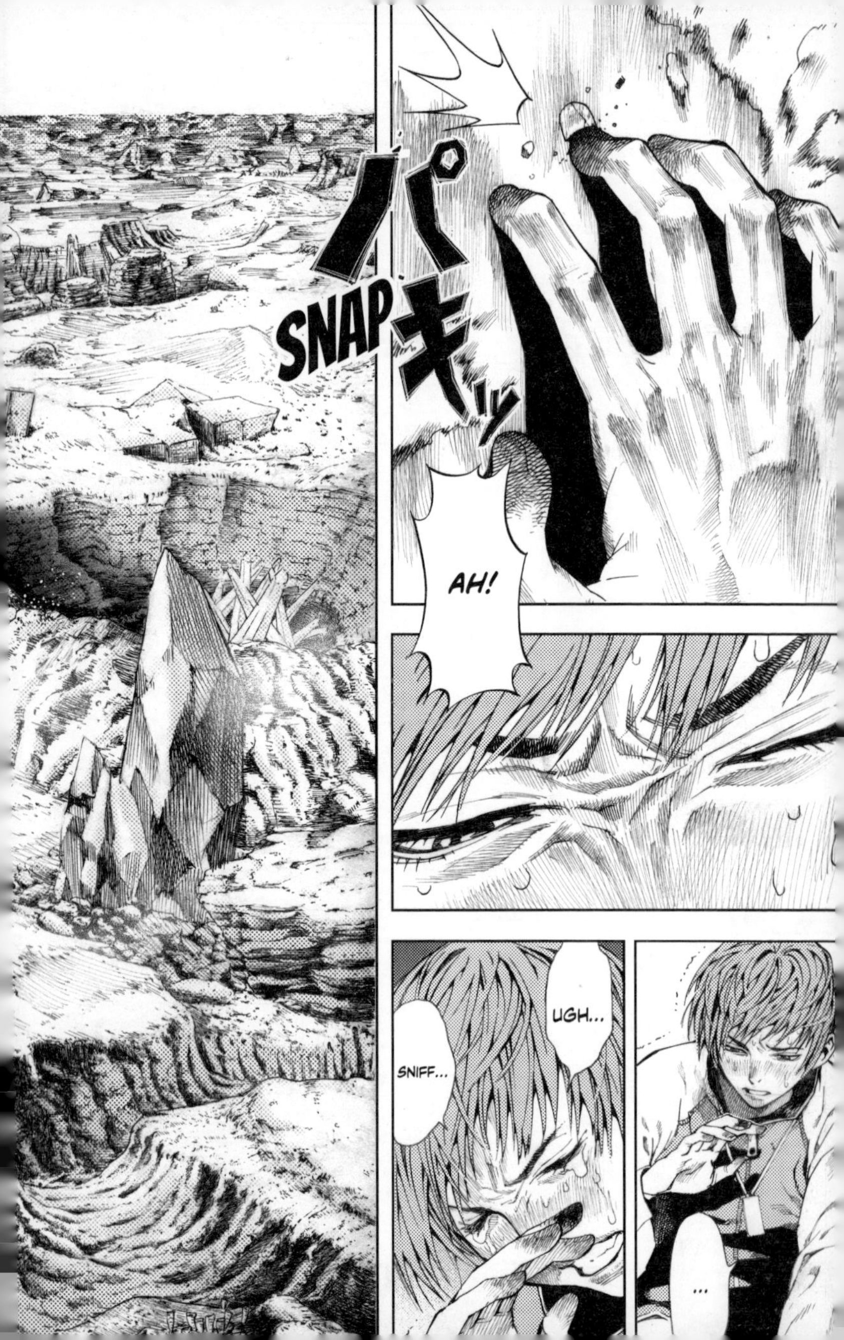
パキッ
SNAP
AH!
...
UGH...
SNIFF...

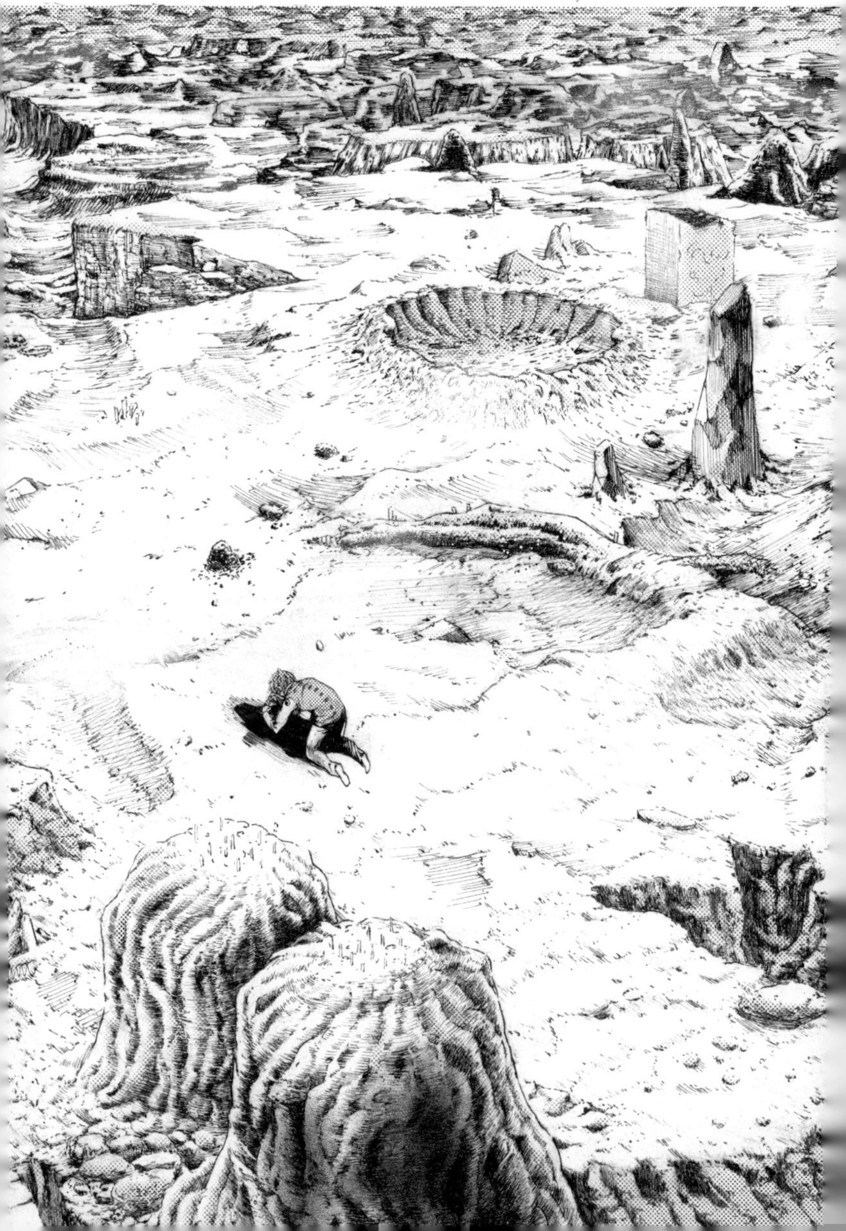

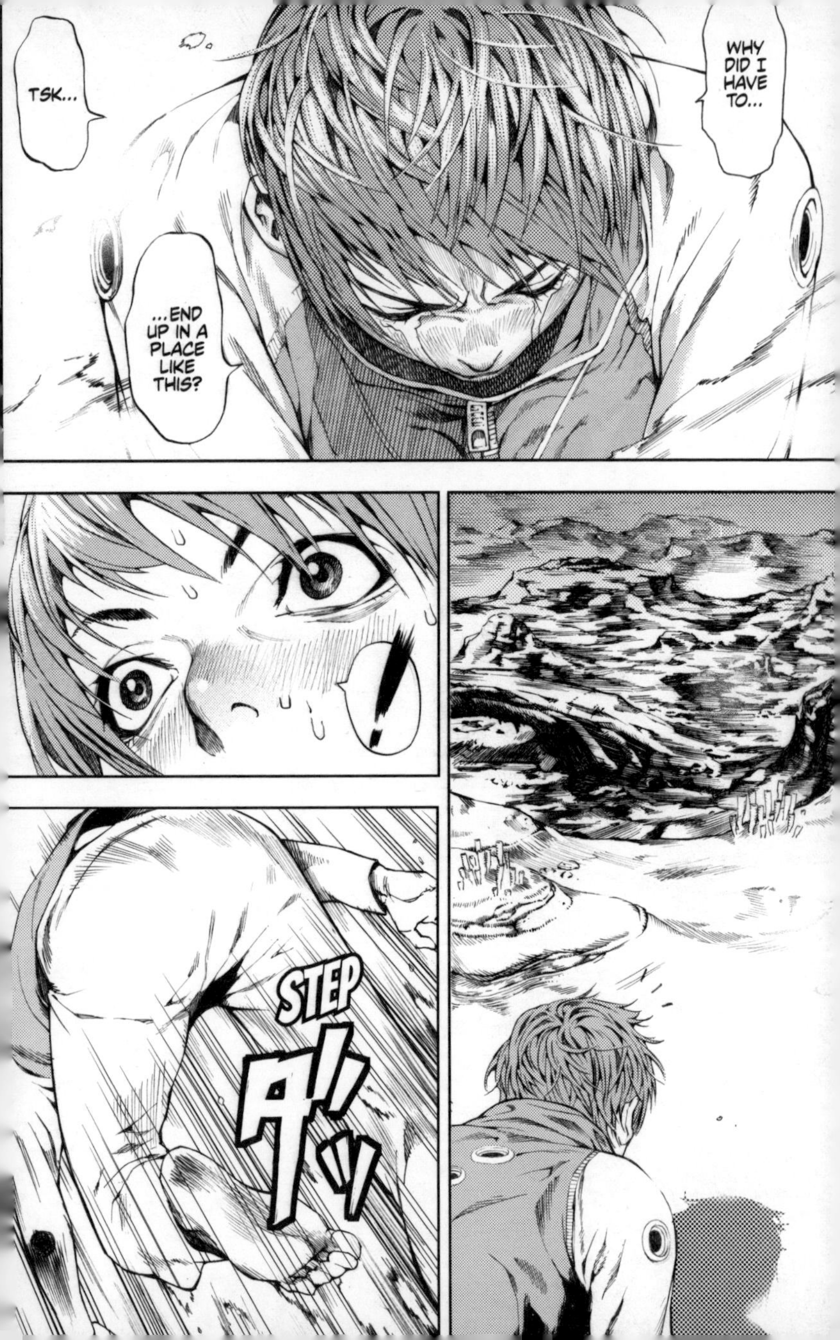
WHY DID I HAVE TO...
TSK...
...END UP IN A PLACE LIKE THIS?
!
STEP
ダッ

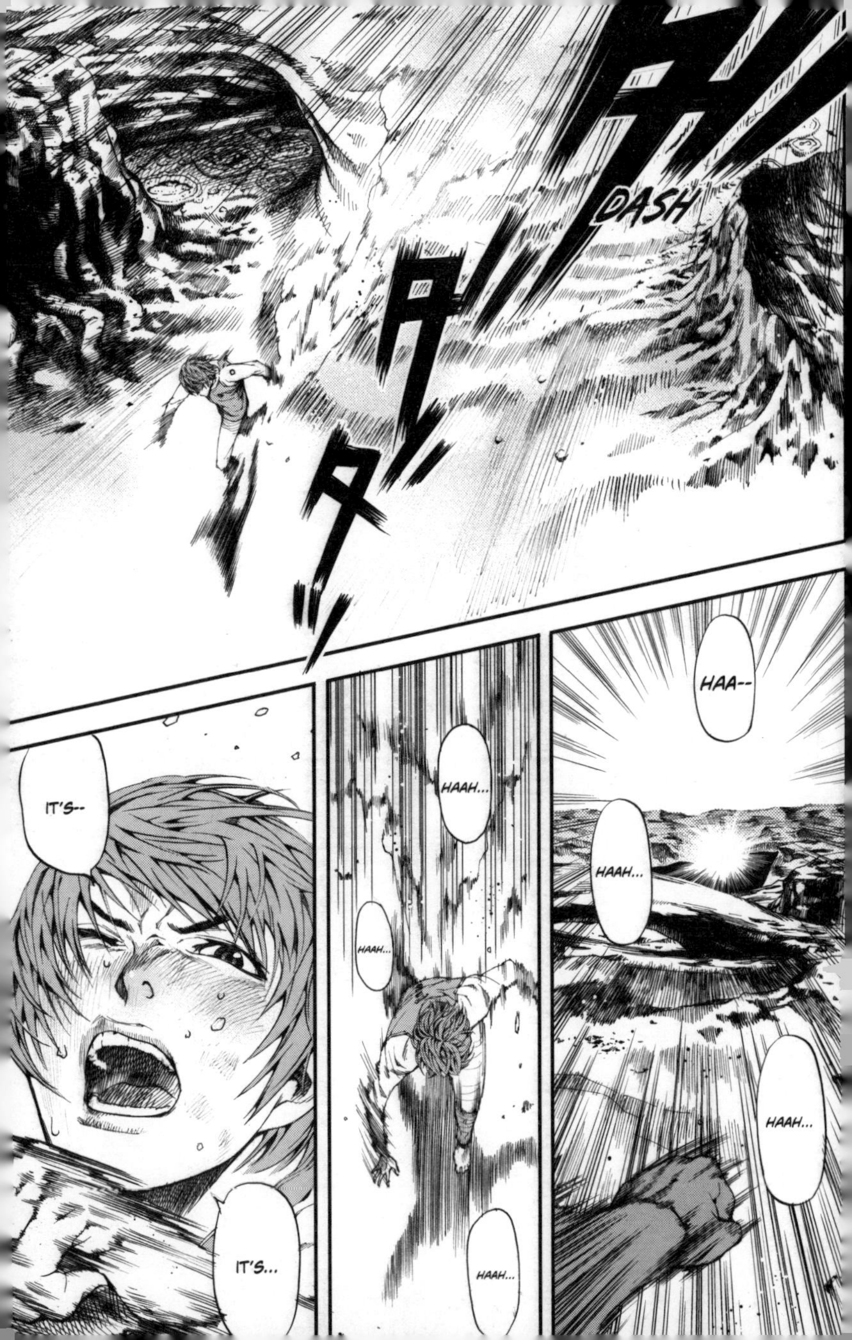
DASH
HAA--
HAAH...
HAAH...
HAAH...
HAAH...
HAAH...
IT'S--
IT'S...

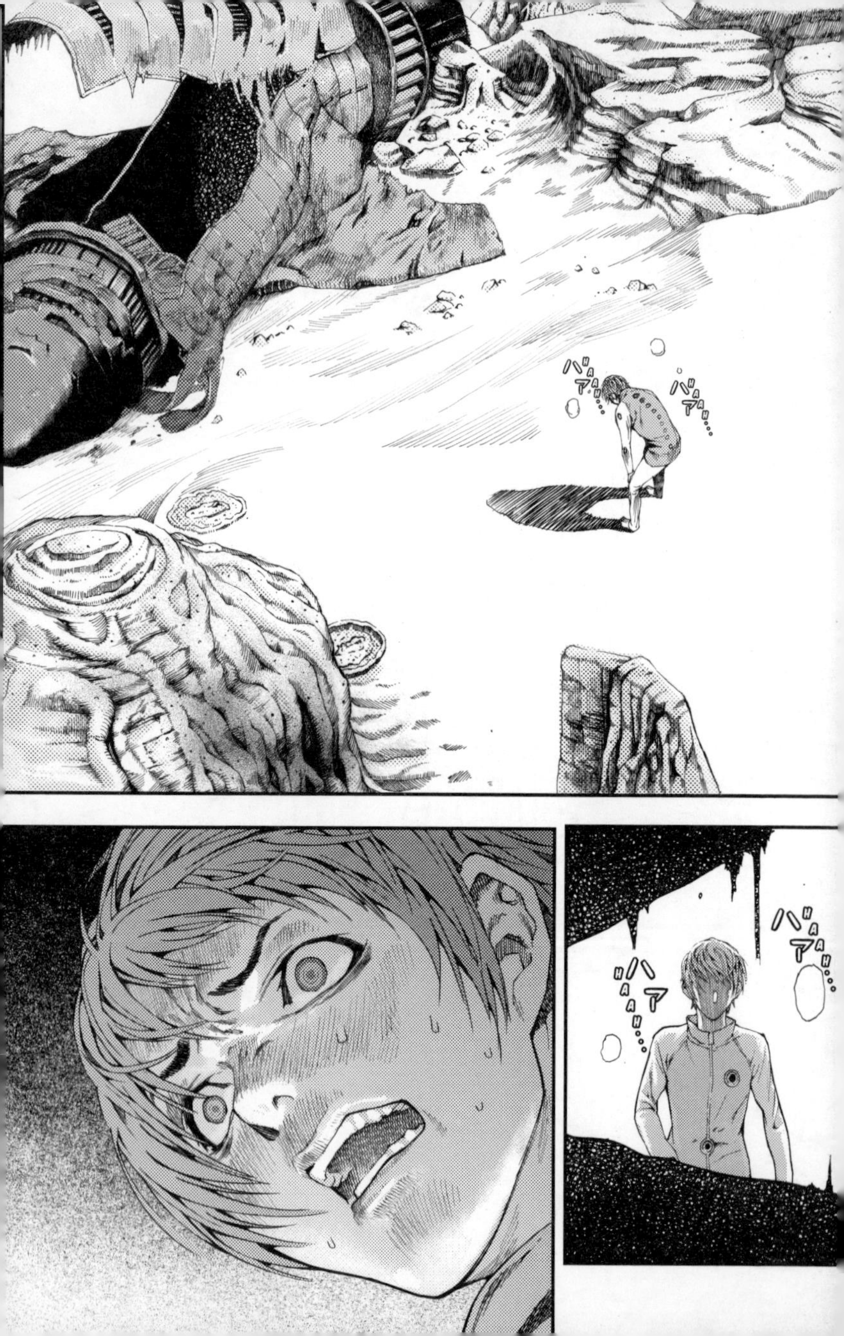
ハァ HAAH...
ハァ HAAH...
ハァ HAAH...
ハァ HAAH...

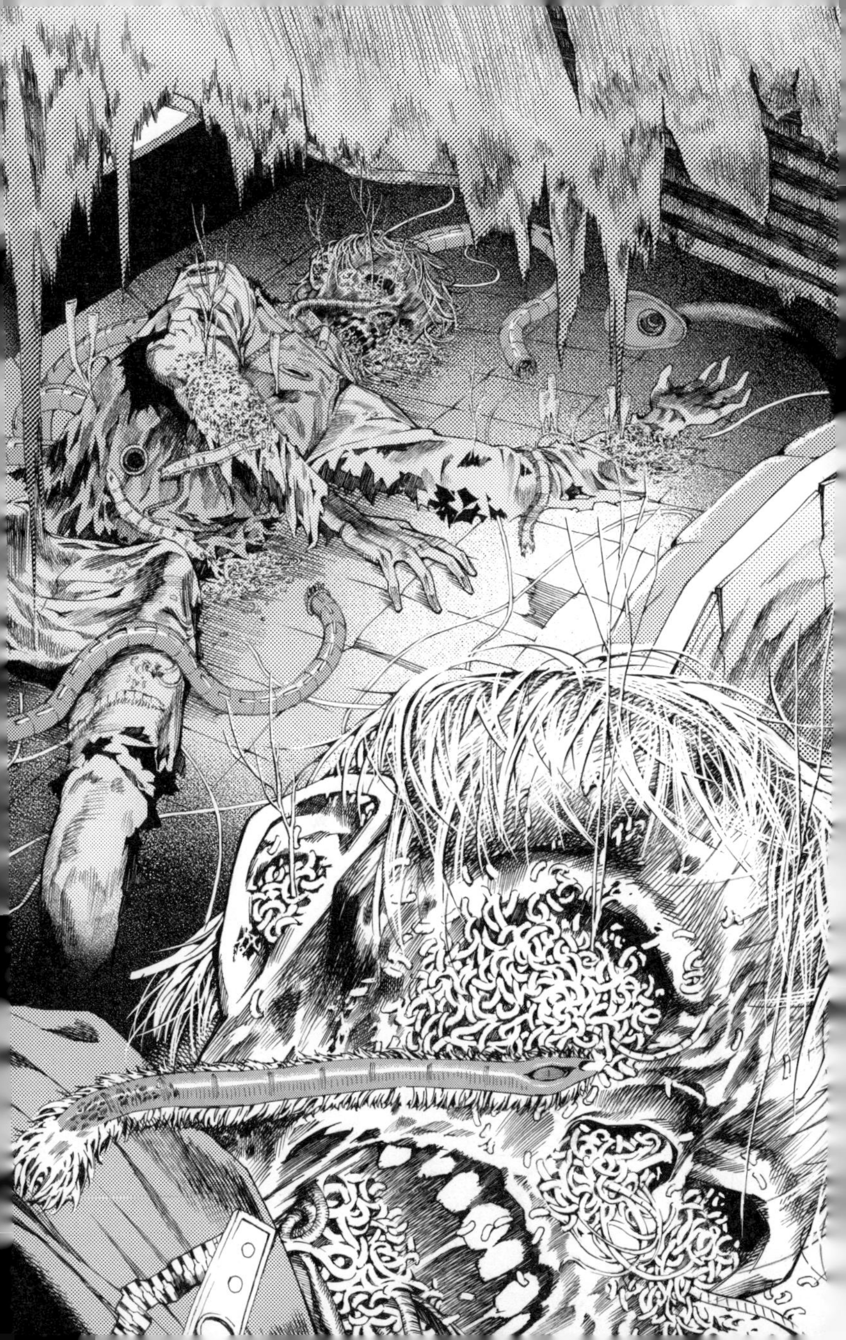

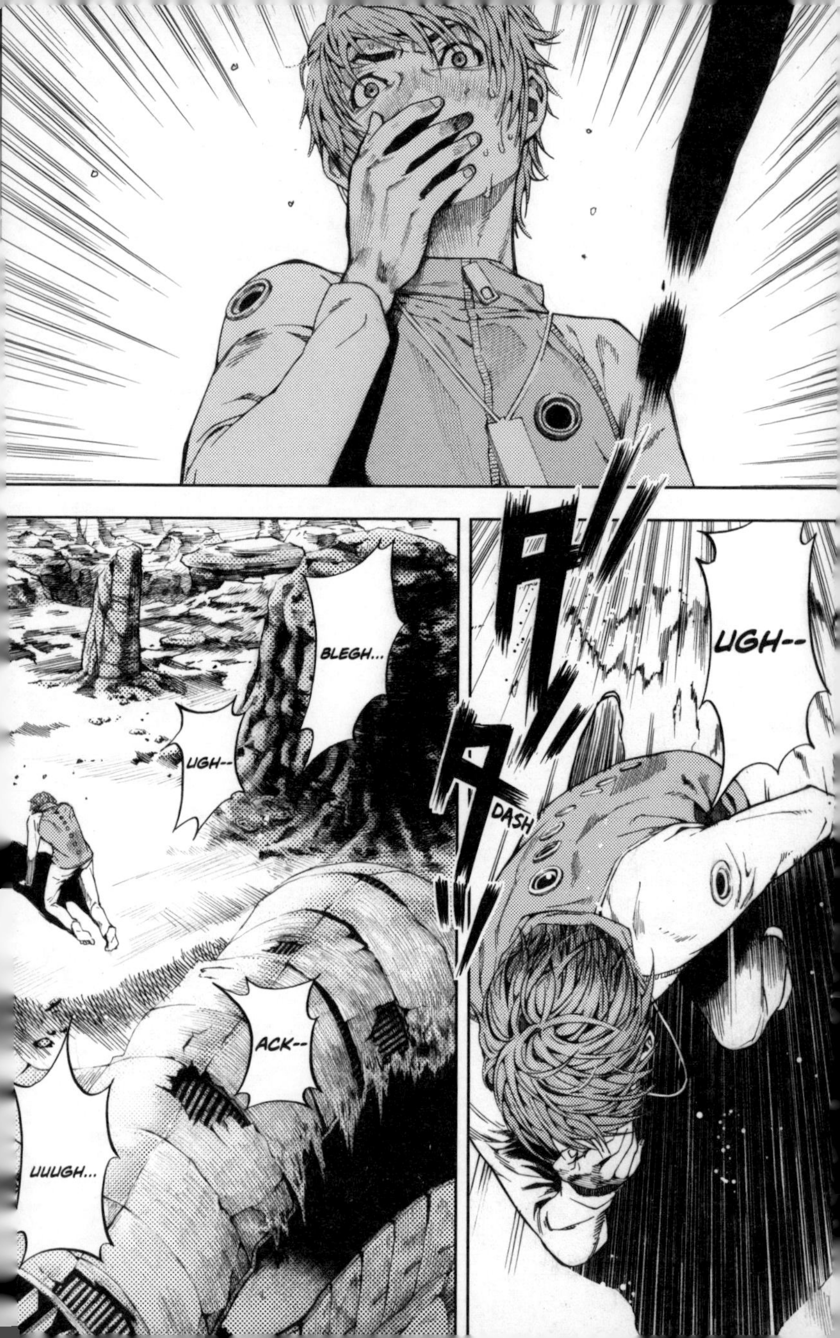
UGH--
DASH
BLEGH...
UGH--
ACK--
UUUGH...

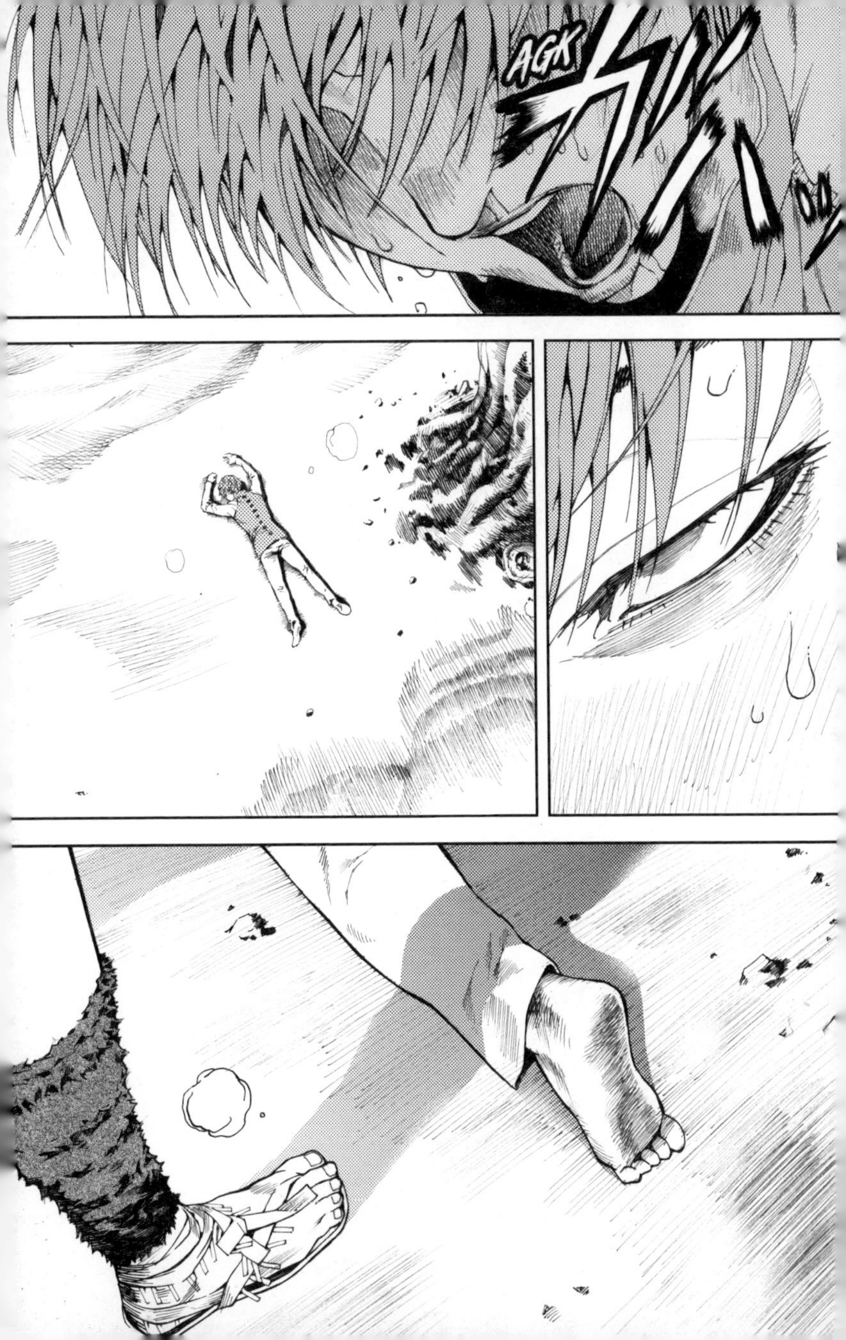
AGK

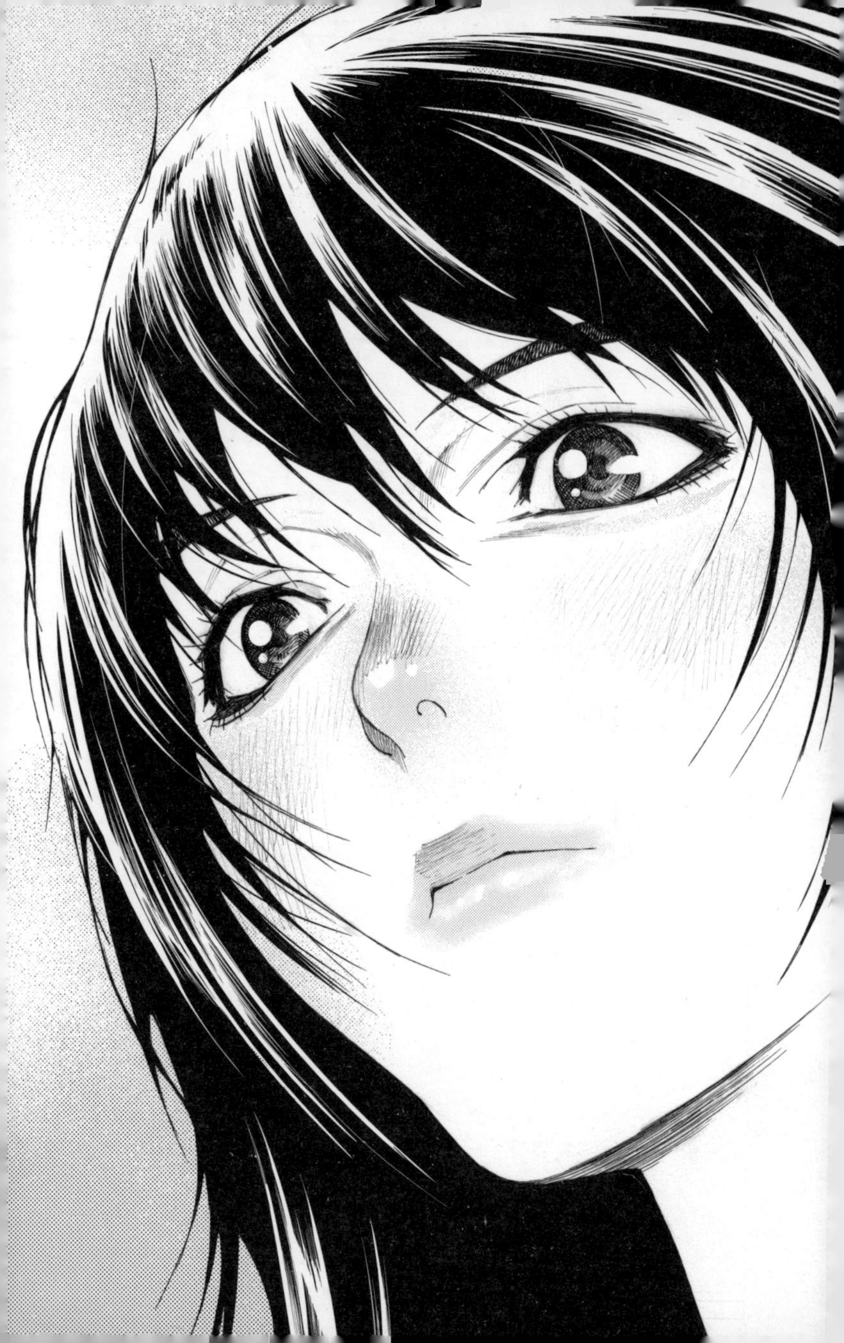

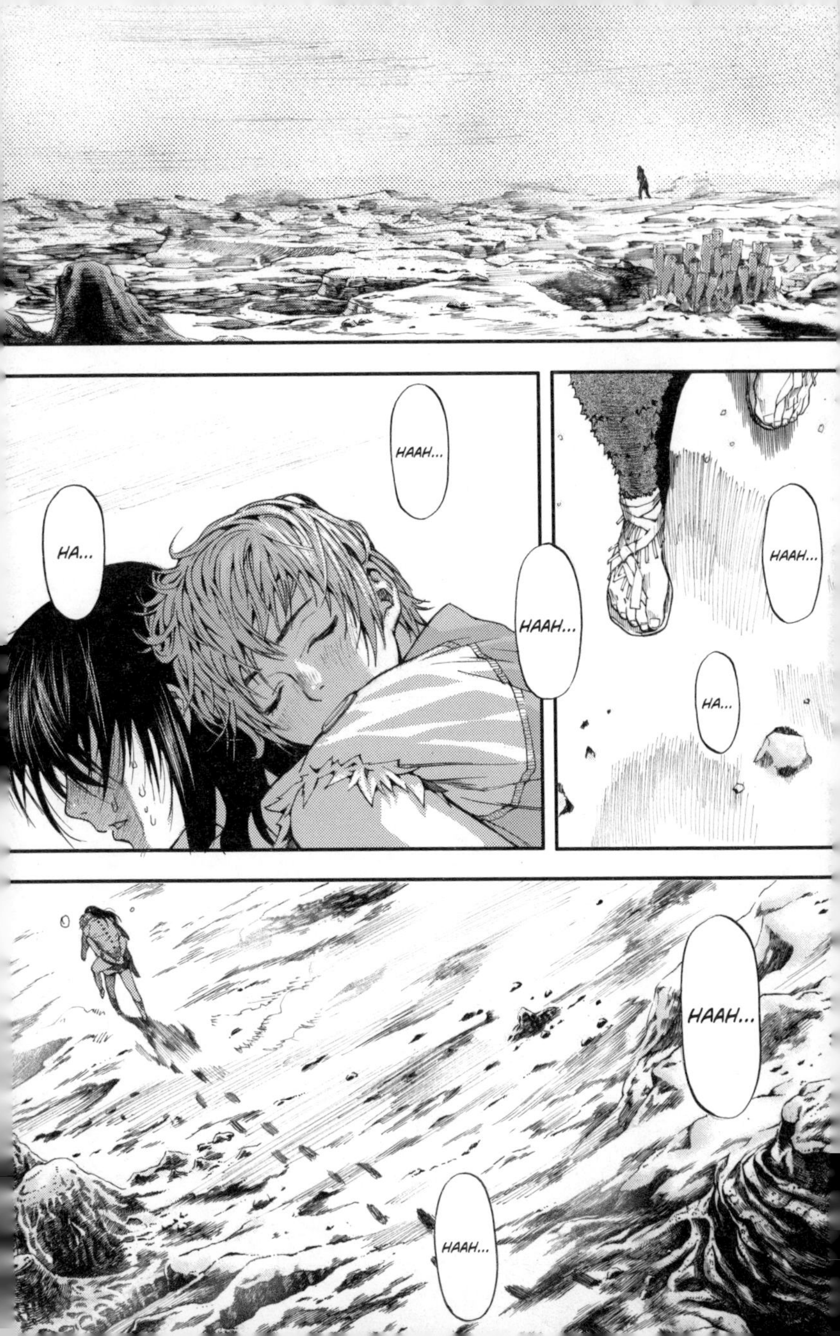
HAAH...
HA...
HAAH...
HAAH...
HA...
HAAH...
HAAH...

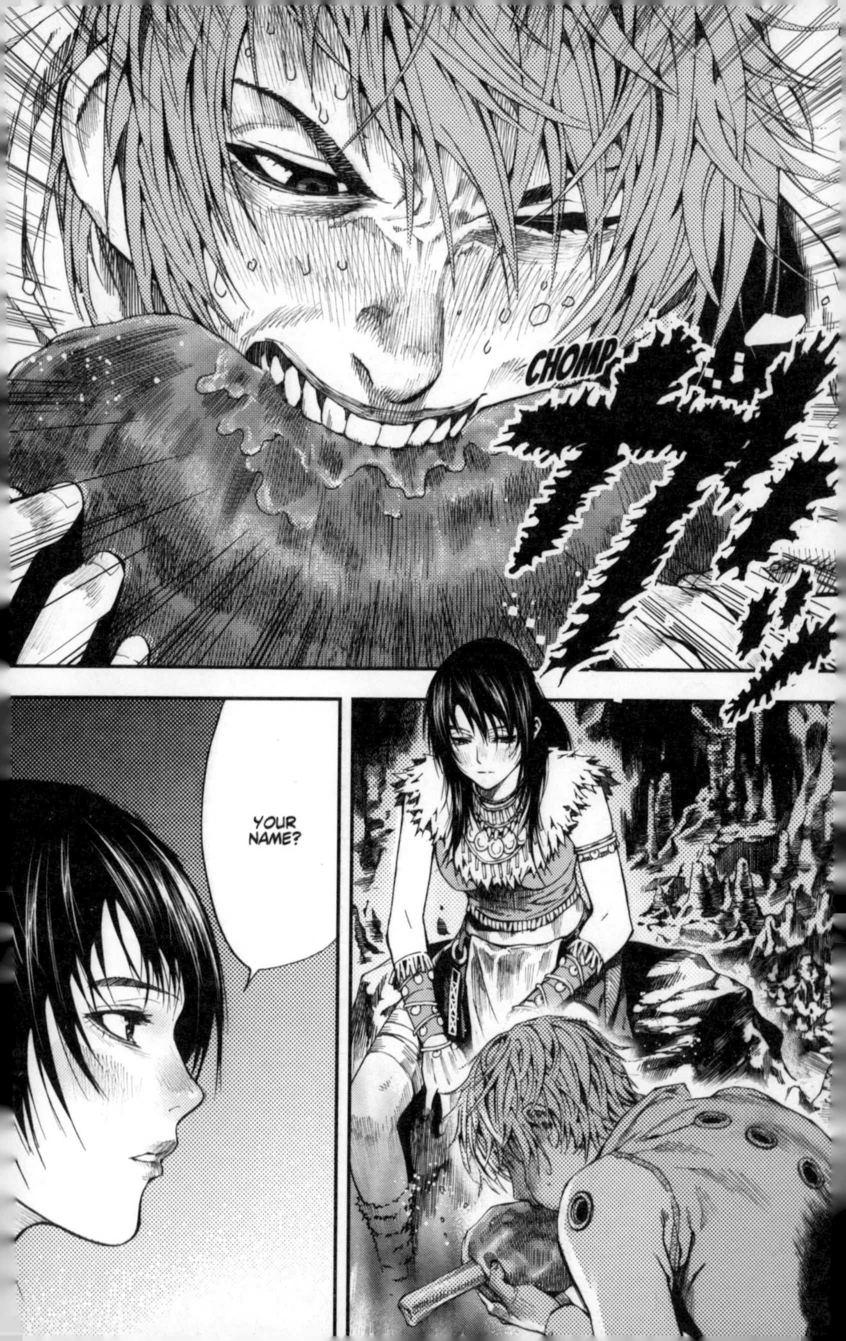
CHOMP
YOUR NAME?

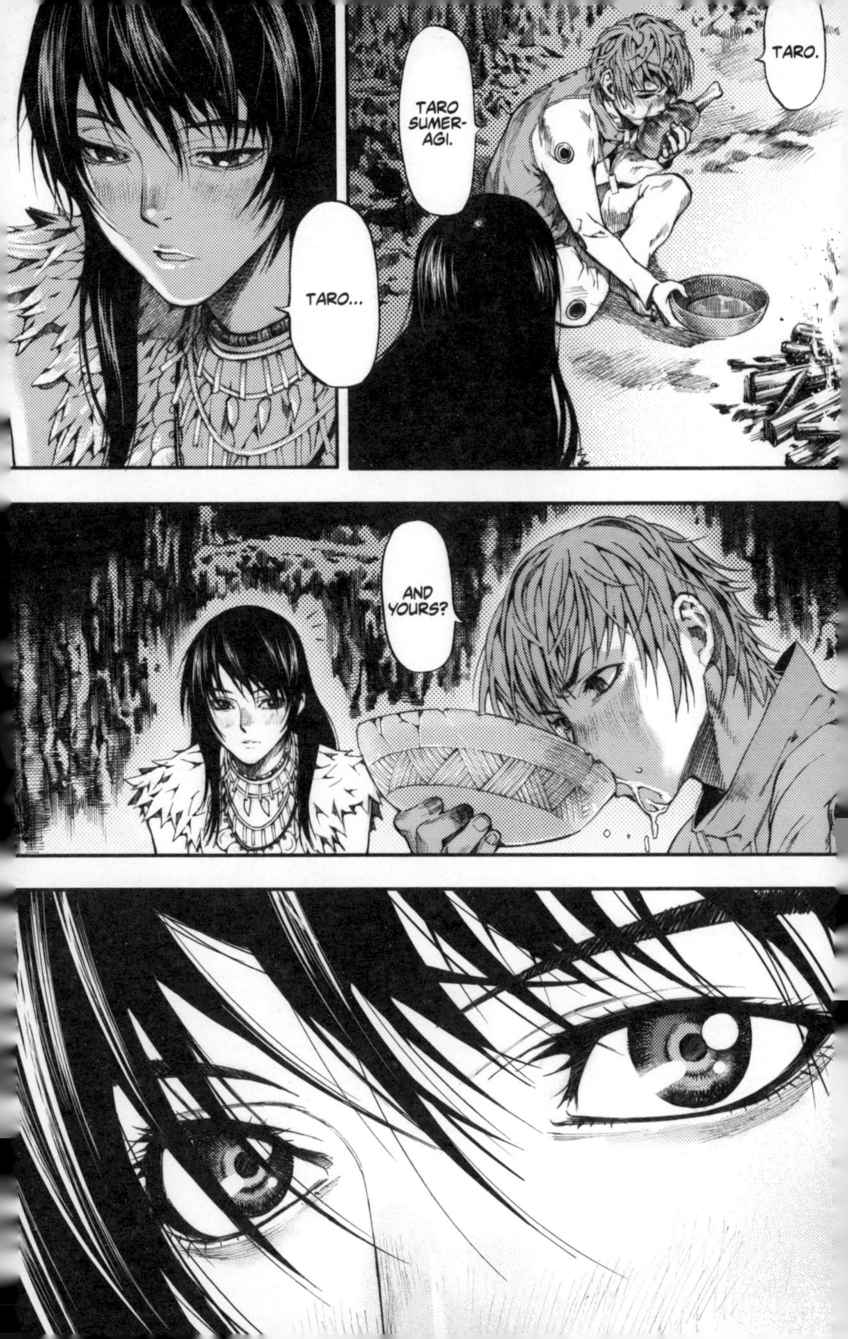
TARO.
TARO SUMER-AGI.
TARO...
AND YOURS?

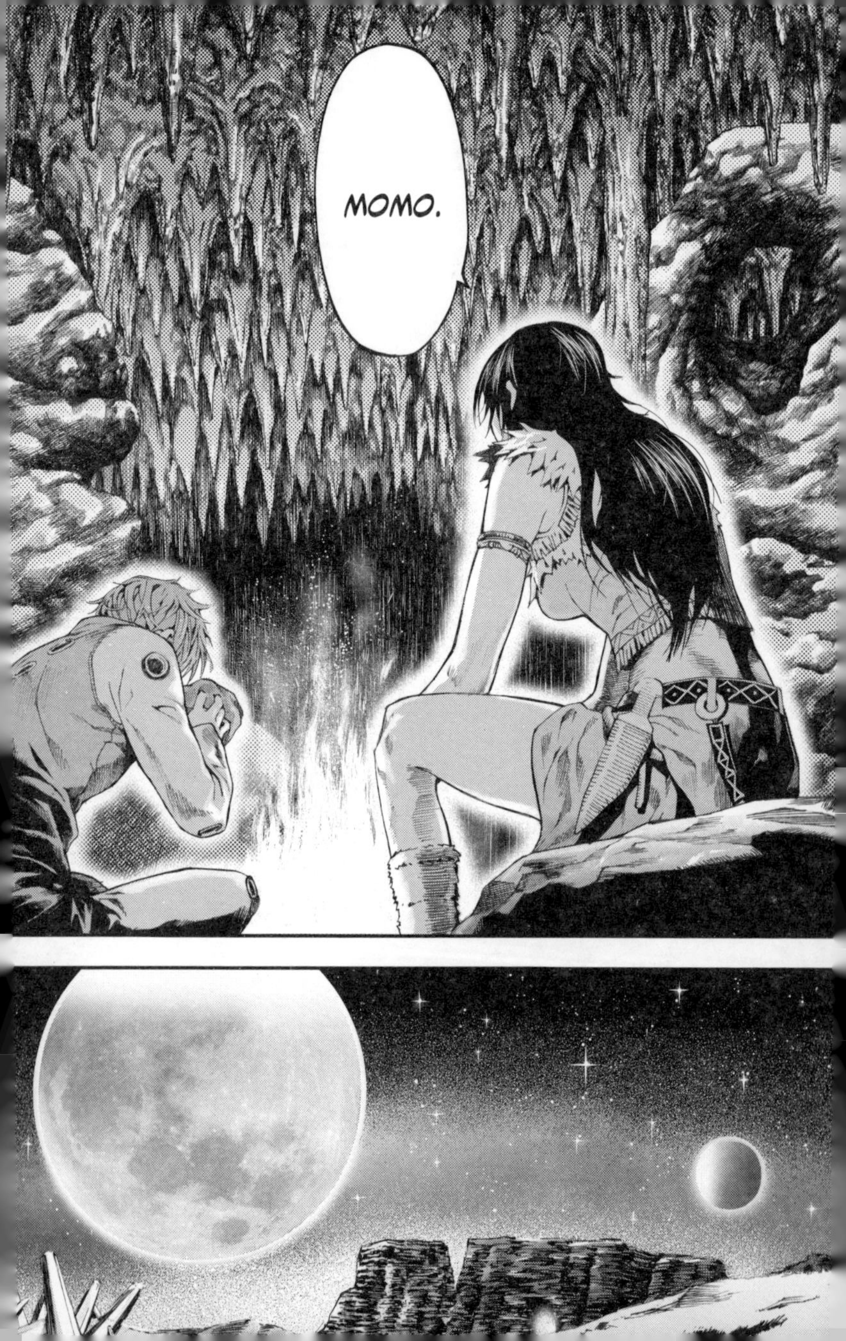
MOMO.

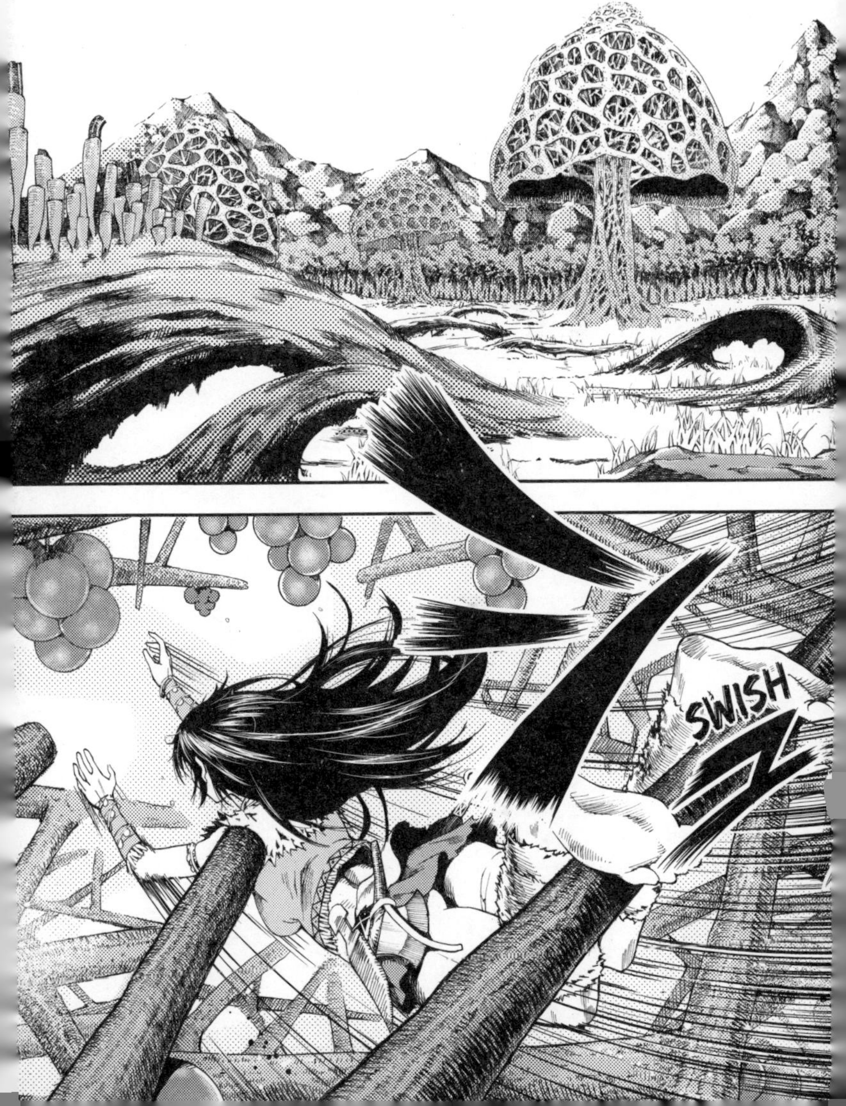
SWISH

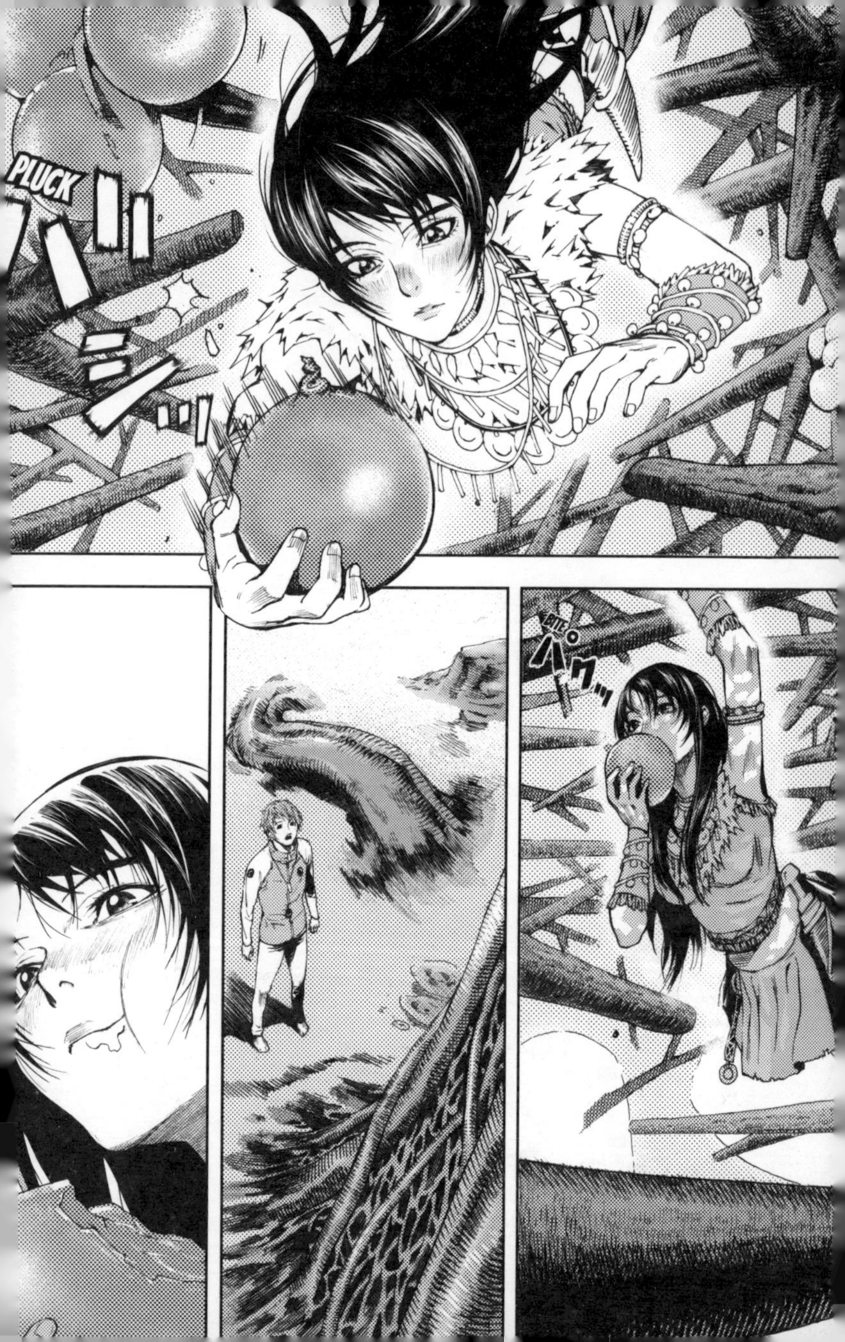
PLUCK
BITE

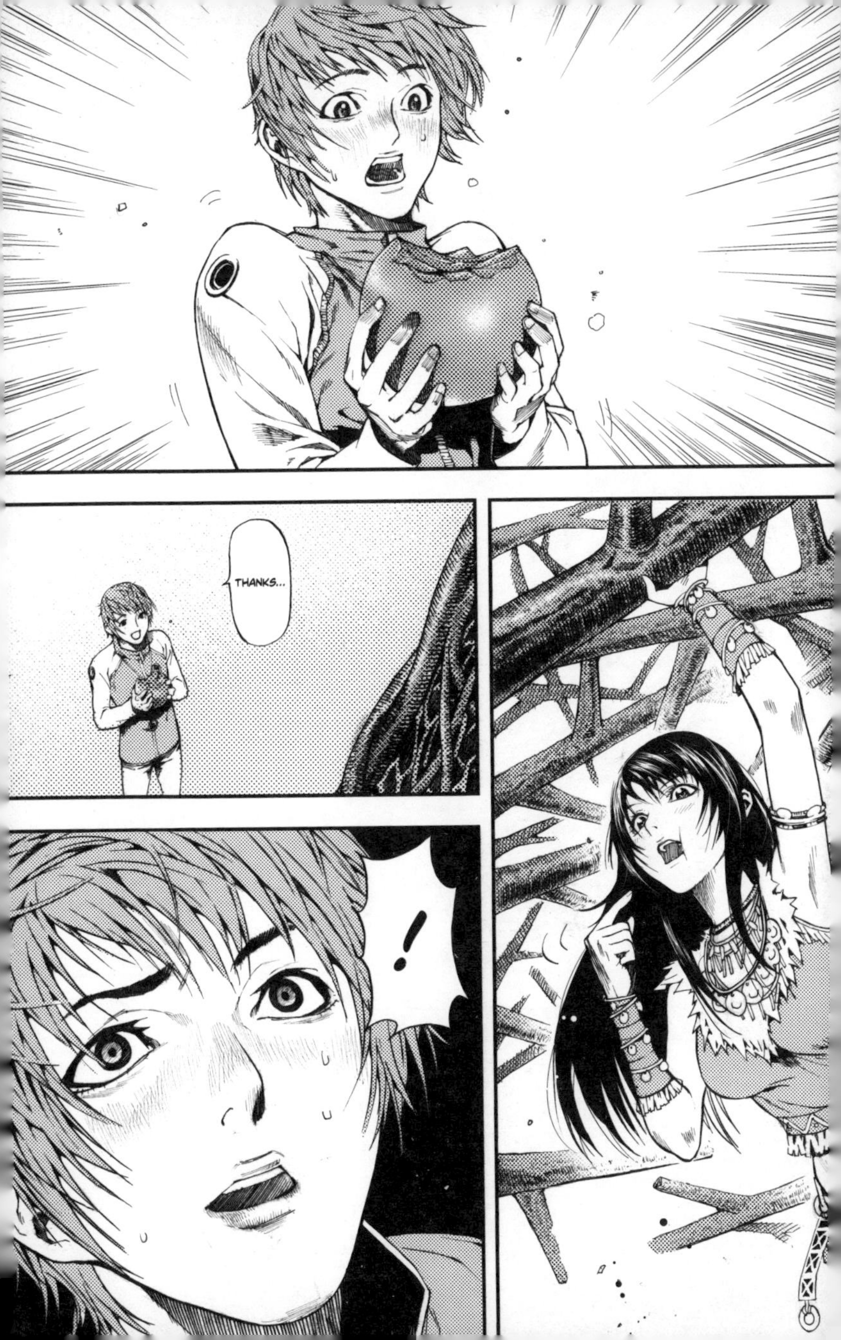
THANKS...
!

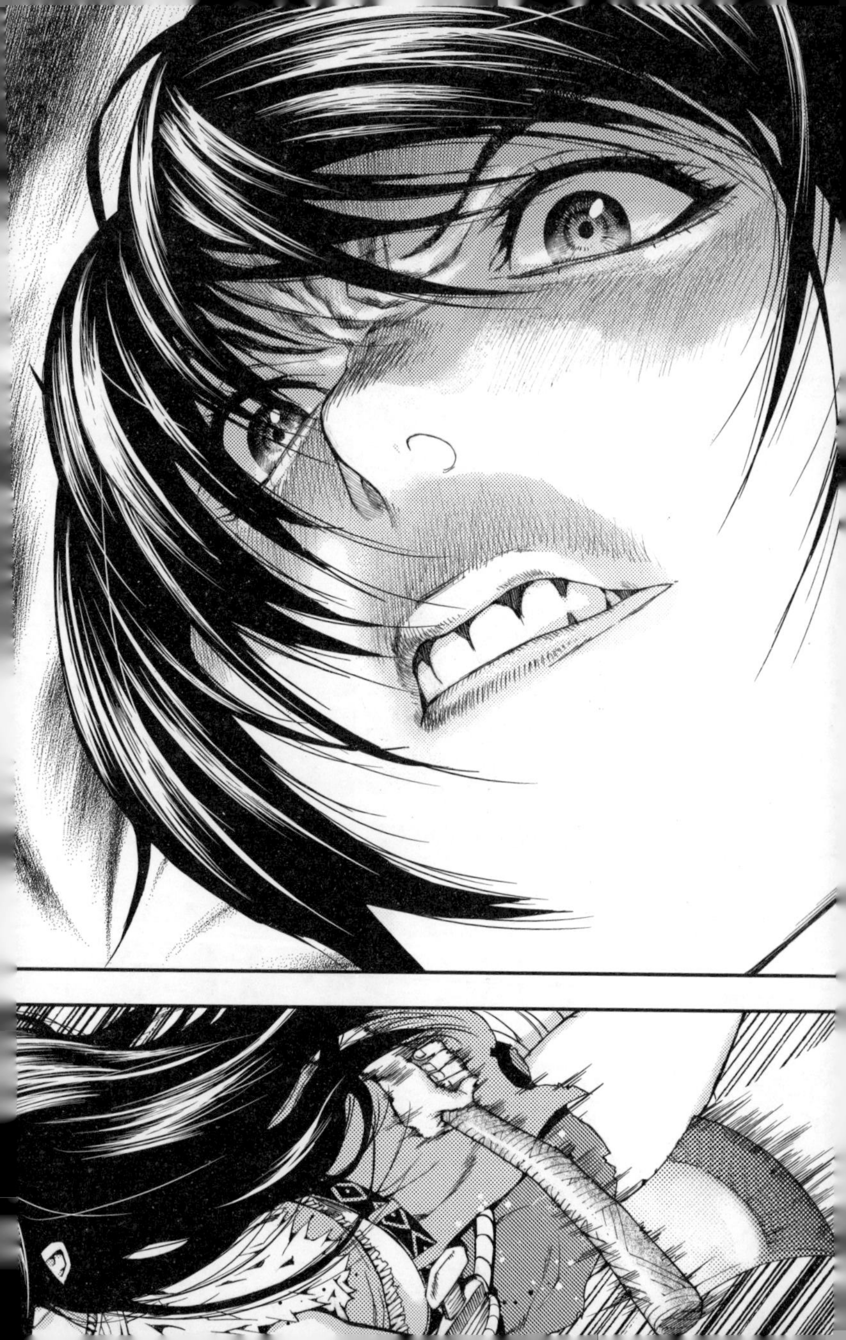

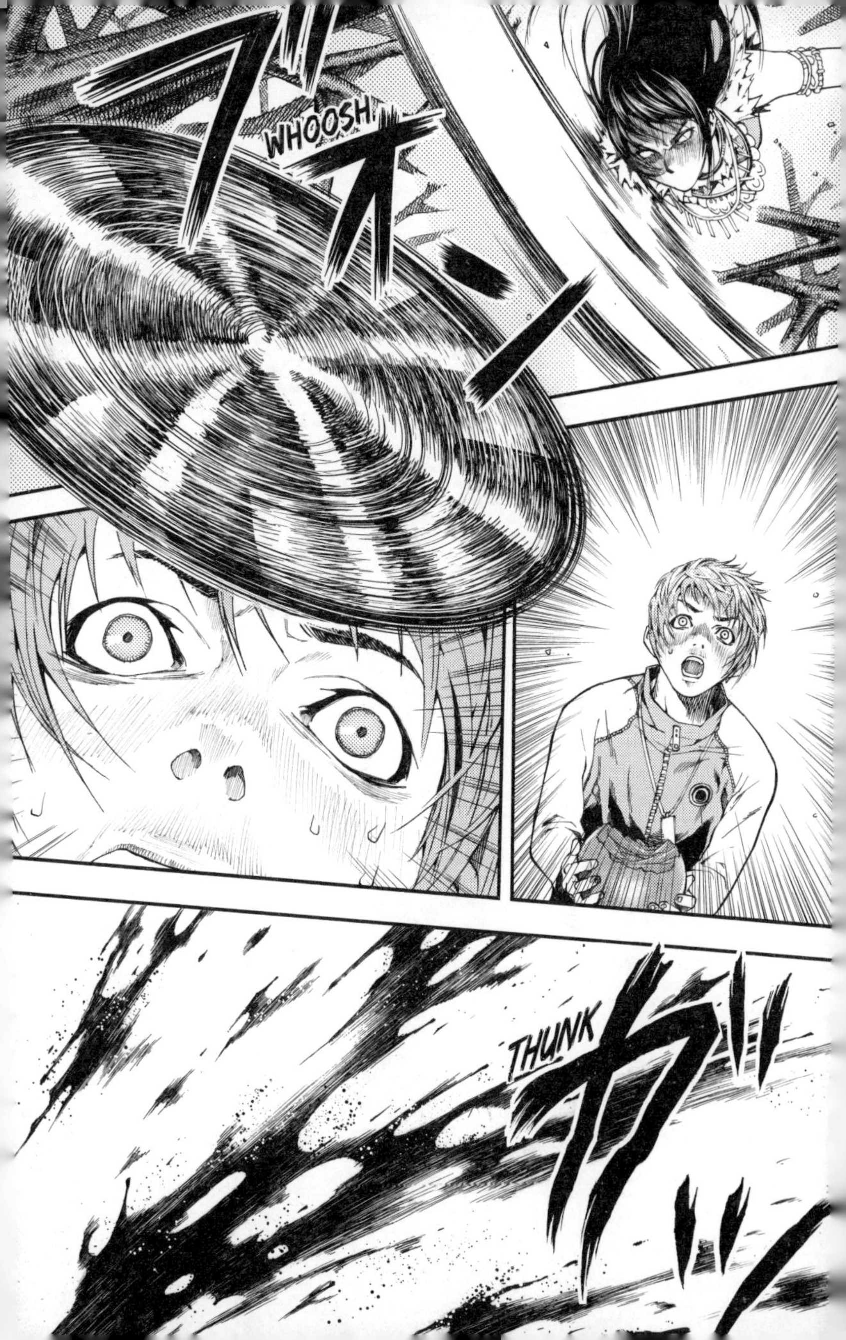
WHOOSH
THUNK

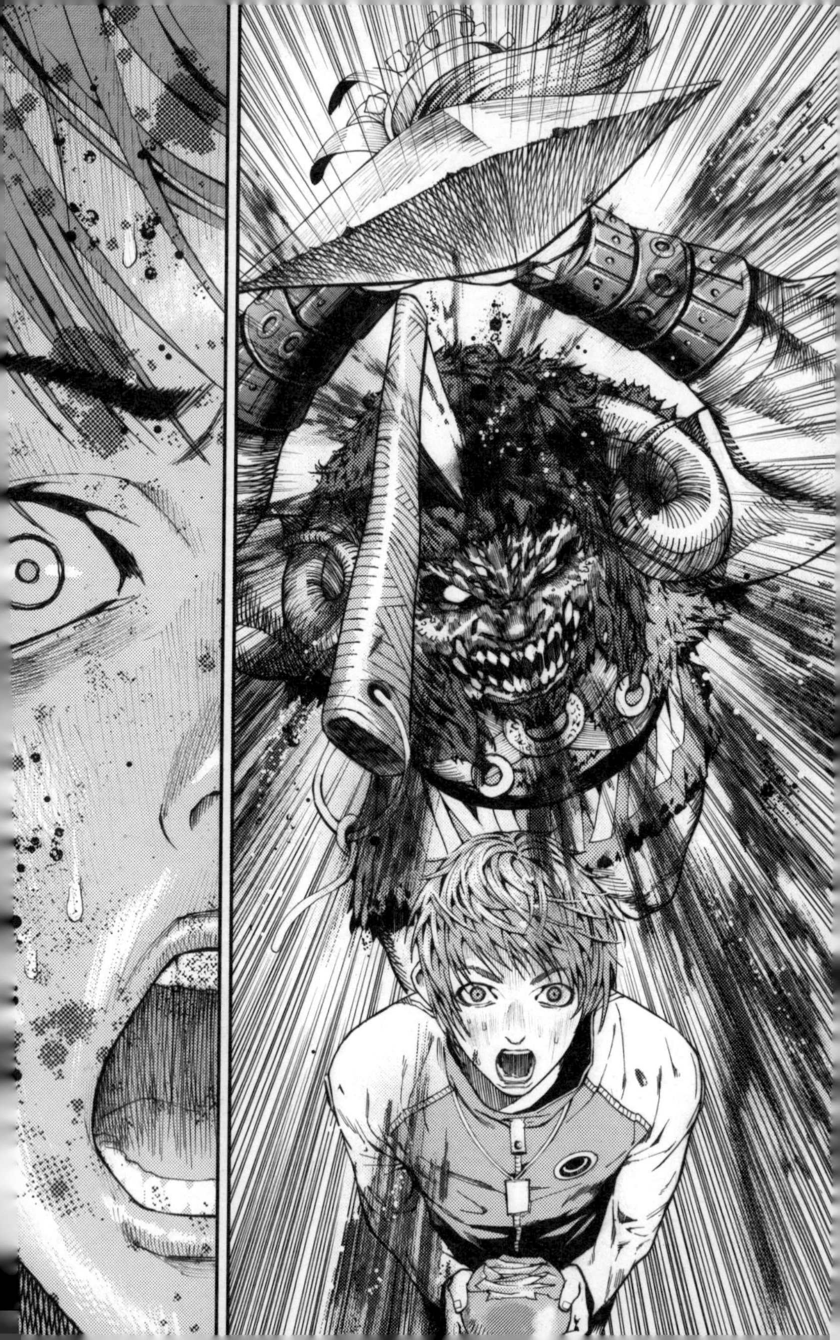

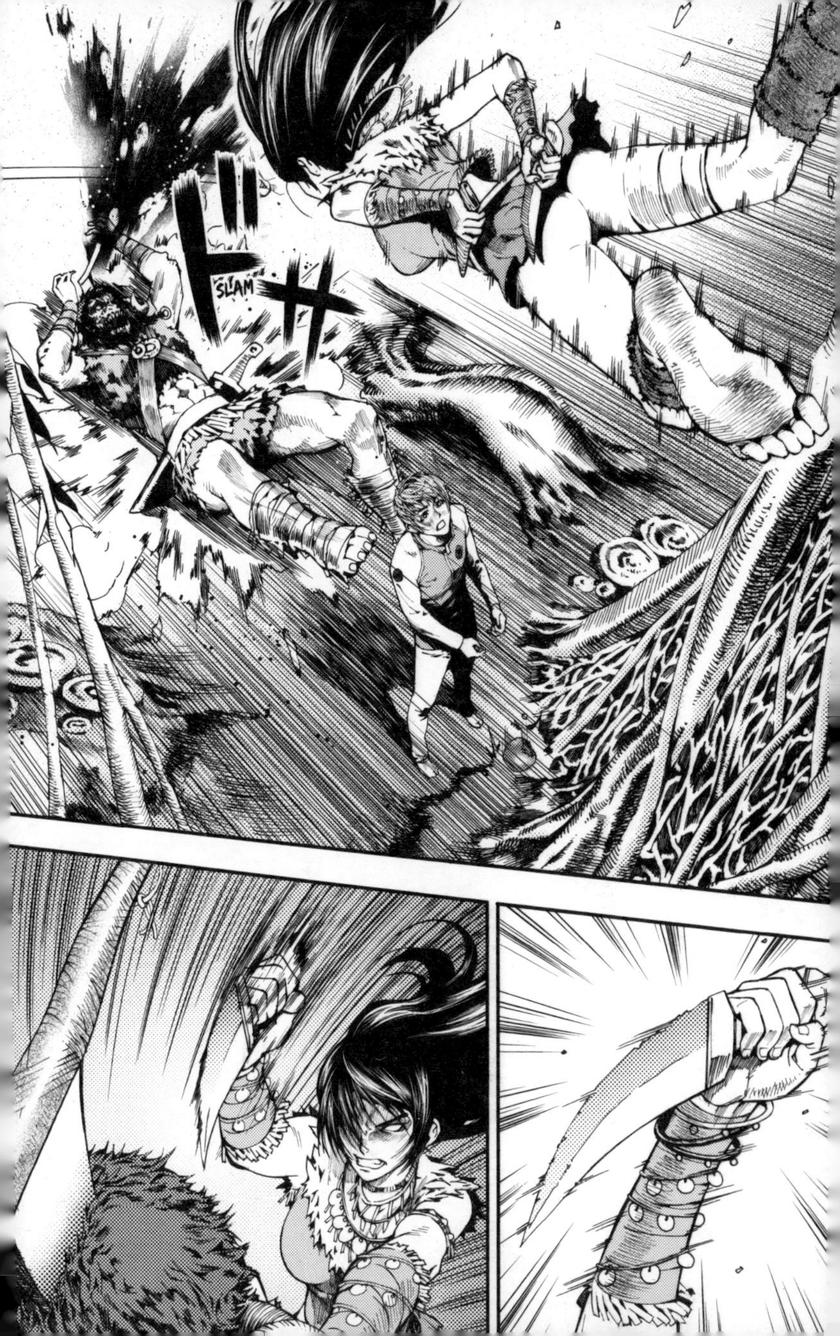
SLAM

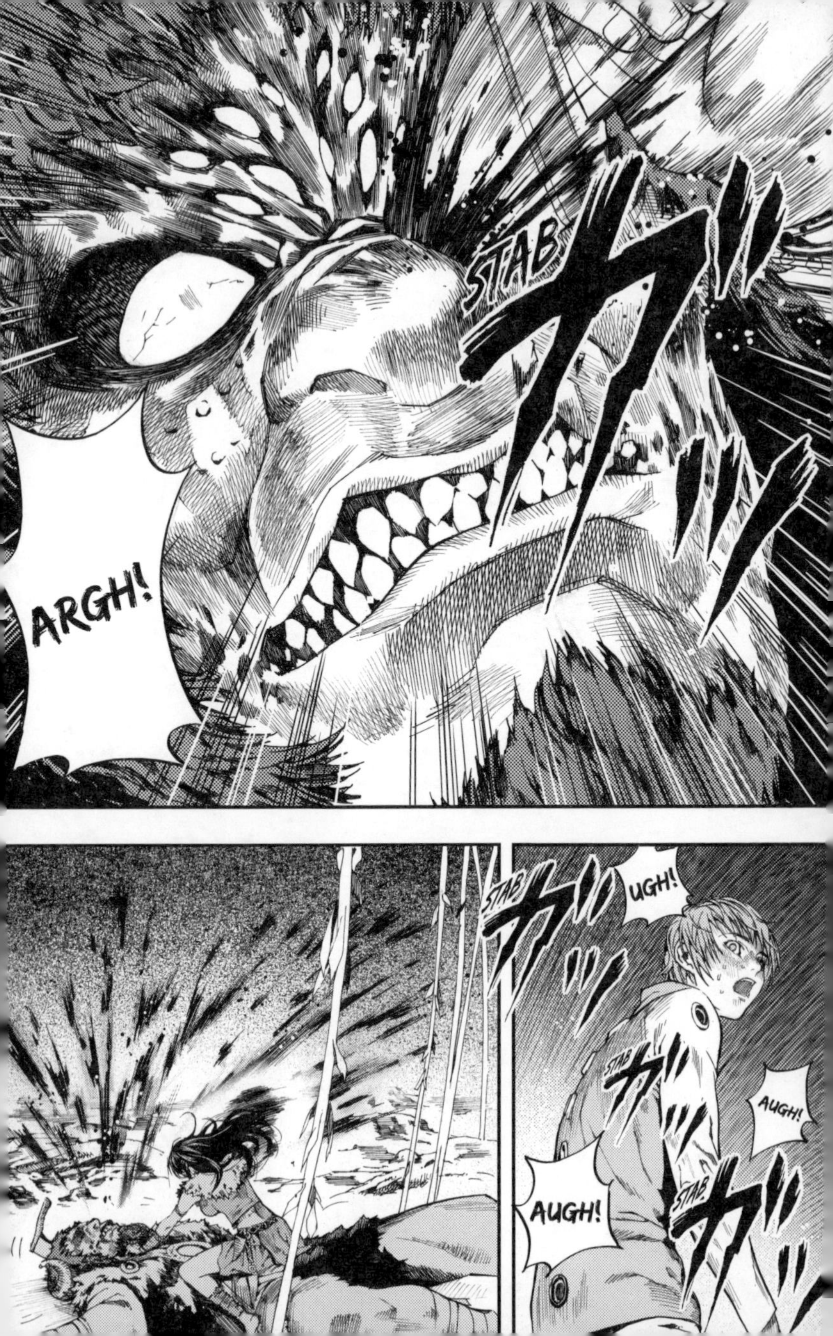
STAB
ARGH!
UGH!
STAB
AUGH!
STAB
STAB
AUGH!

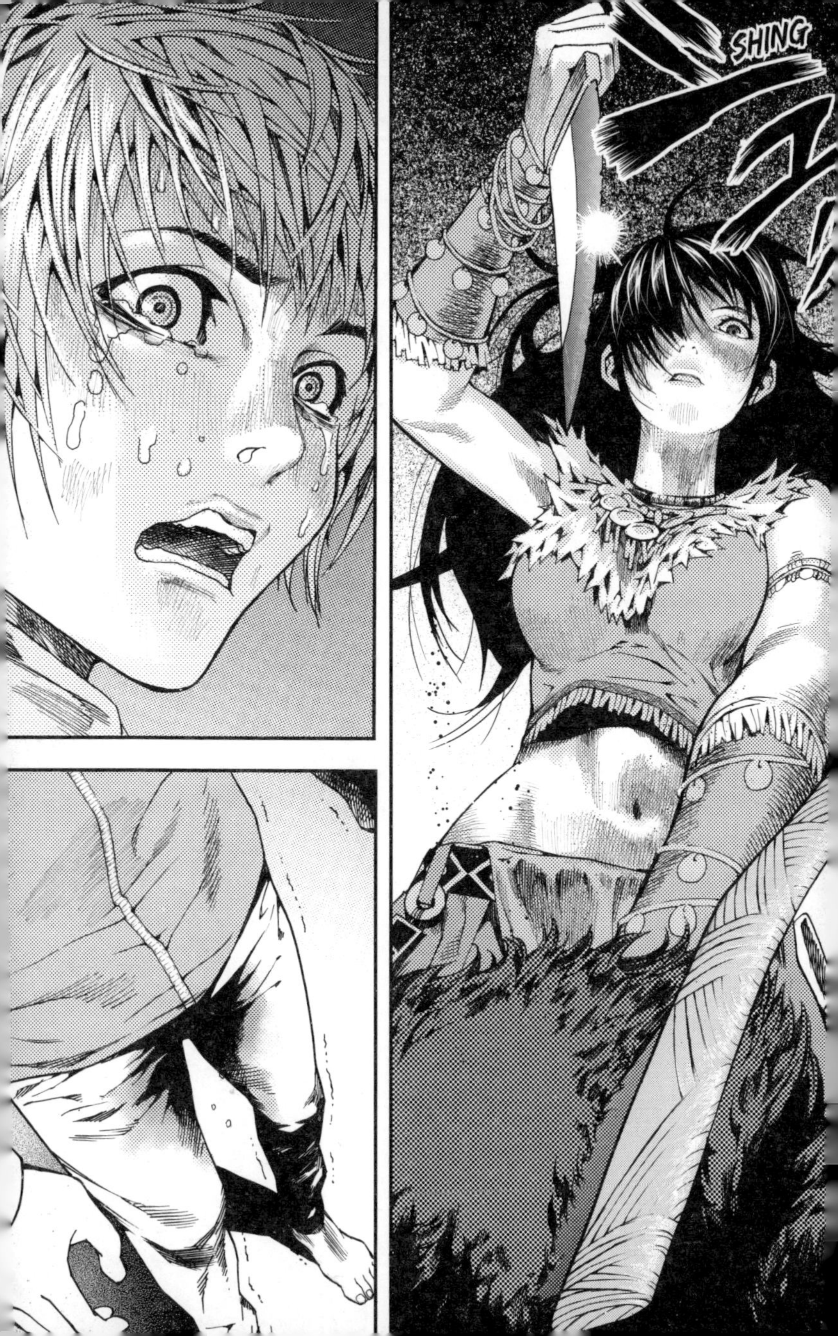
SHING

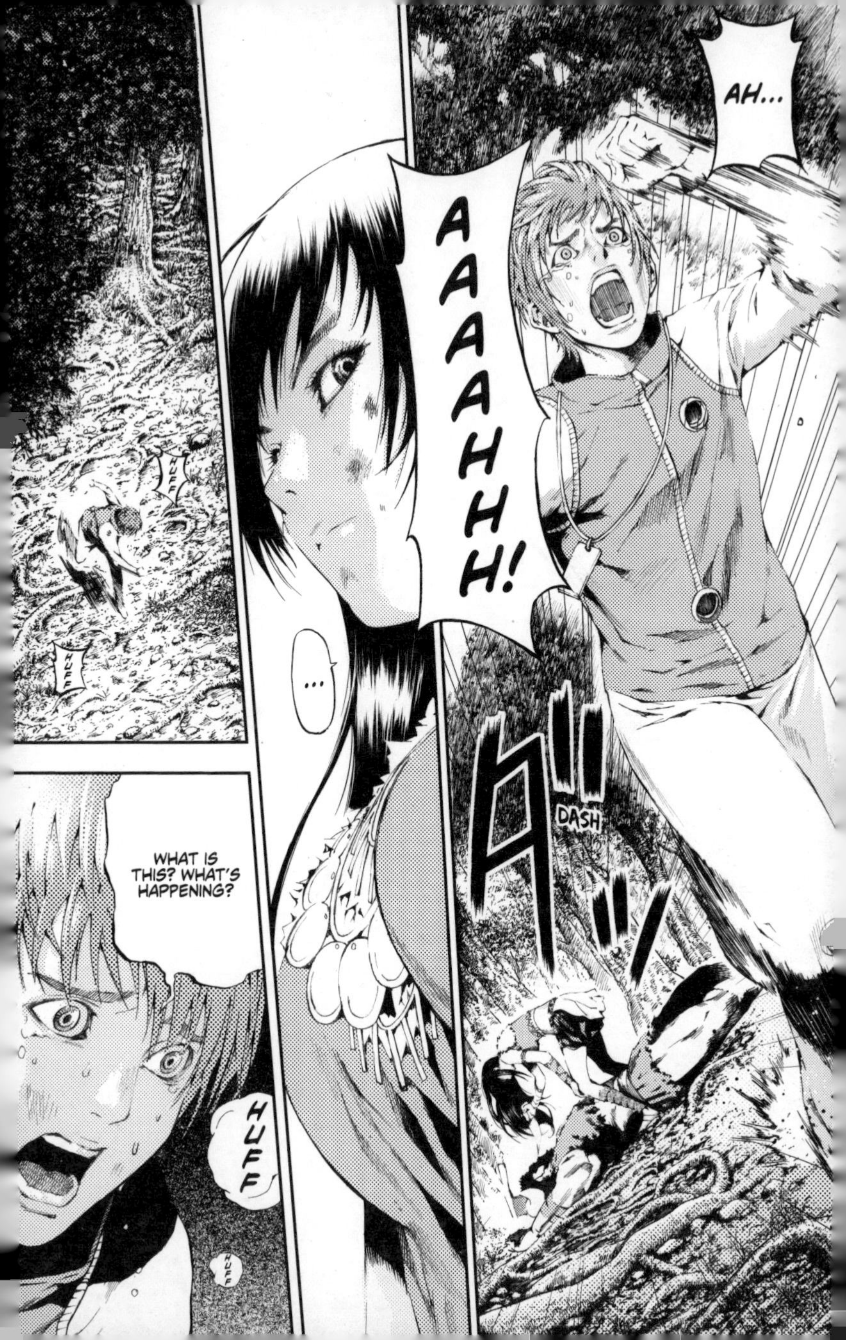
AH...
AAAAHHH!
DASH
...
HUFF
HUFF
WHAT IS THIS? WHAT'S HAPPENING?
HUFF
HUFF

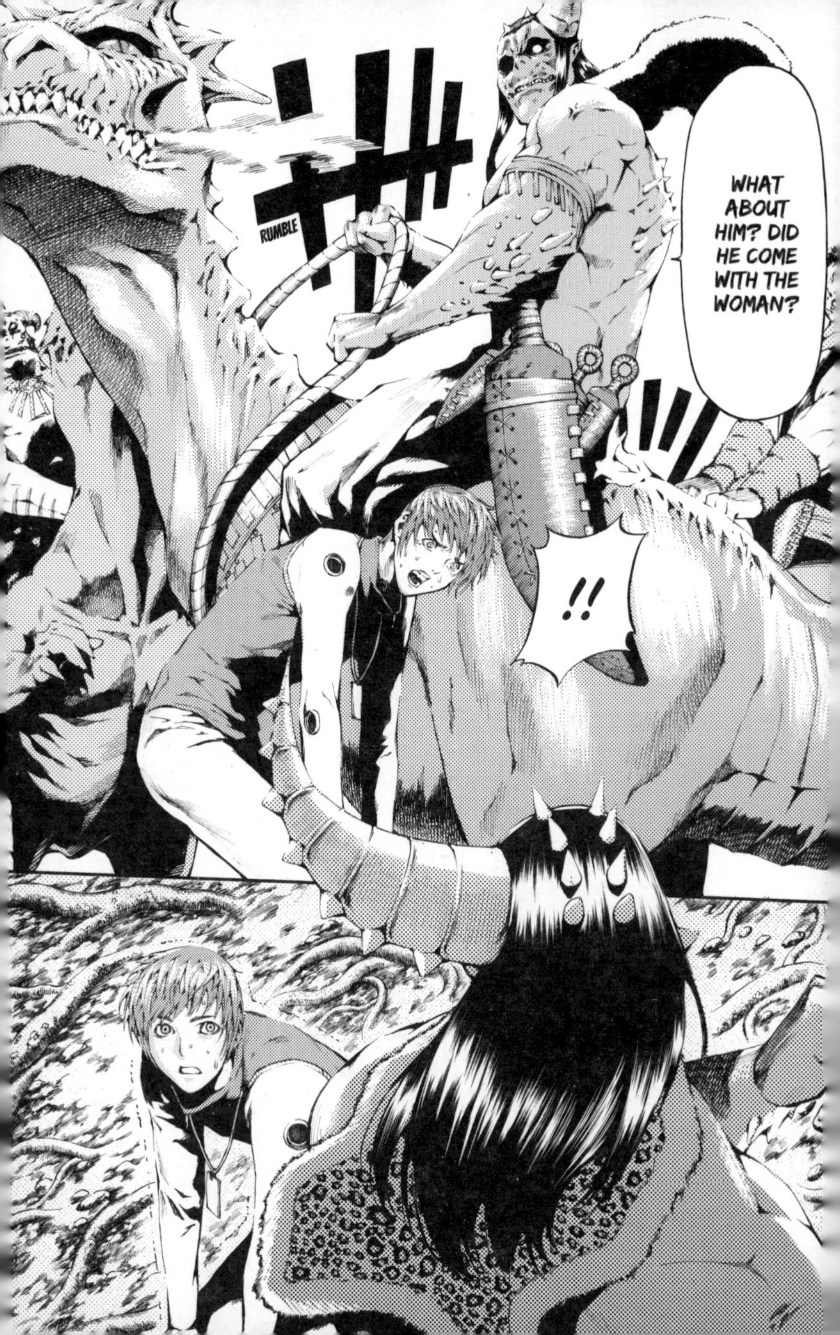
RUMBLE
WHAT ABOUT HIM? DID HE COME WITH THE WOMAN?
!!

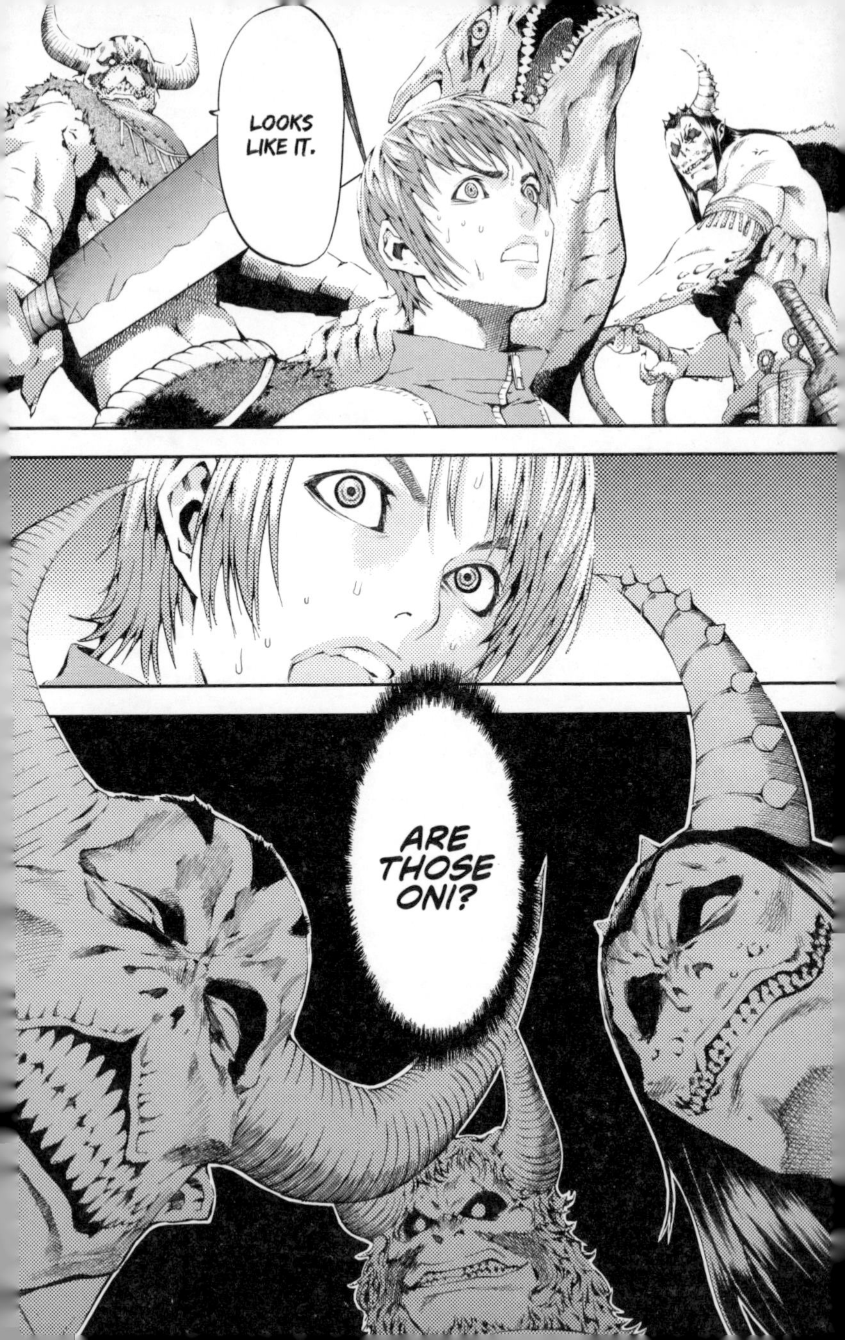
LOOKS LIKE IT.
ARE THOSE ONI?

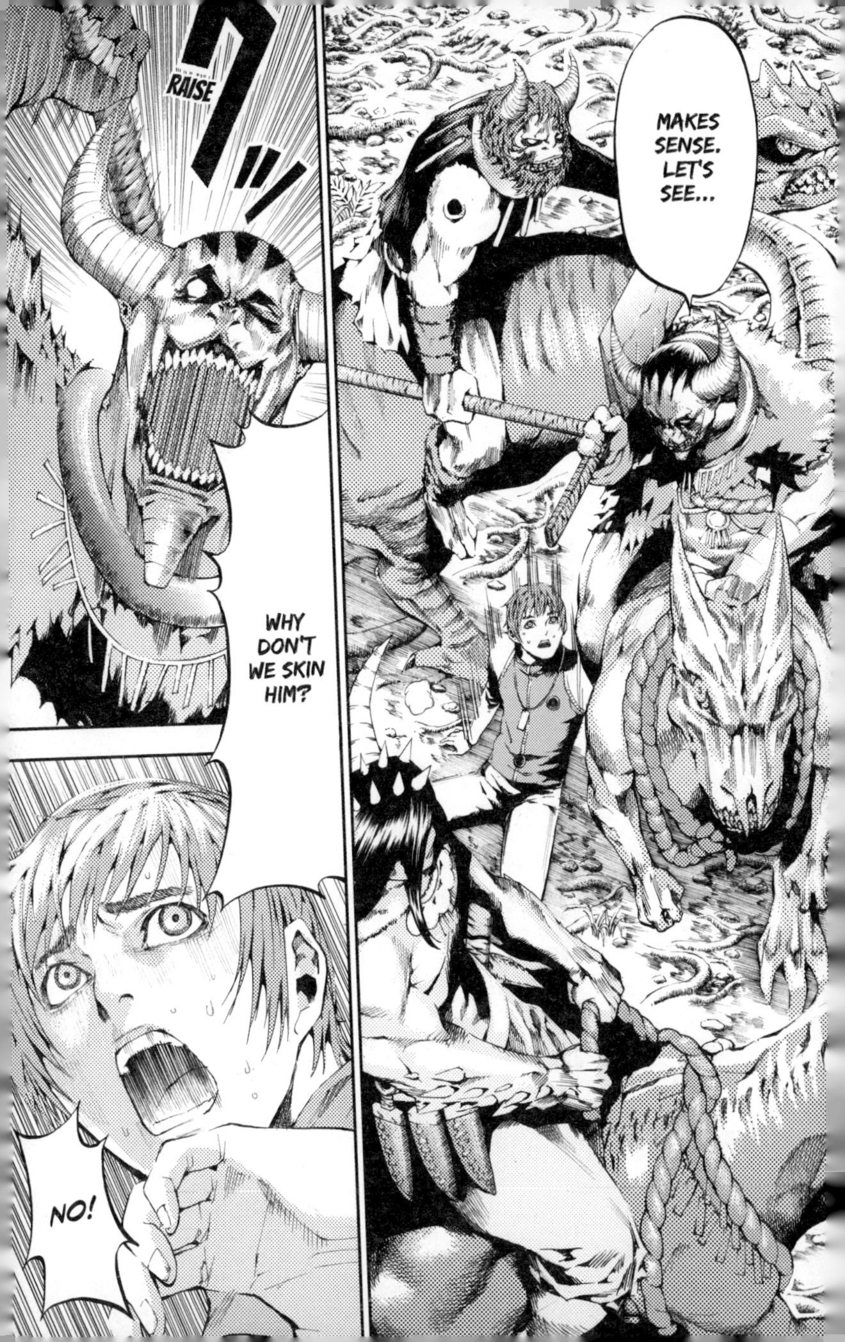
MAKES SENSE. LET'S SEE...
RAISE
WHY DON'T WE SKIN HIM?
NO!

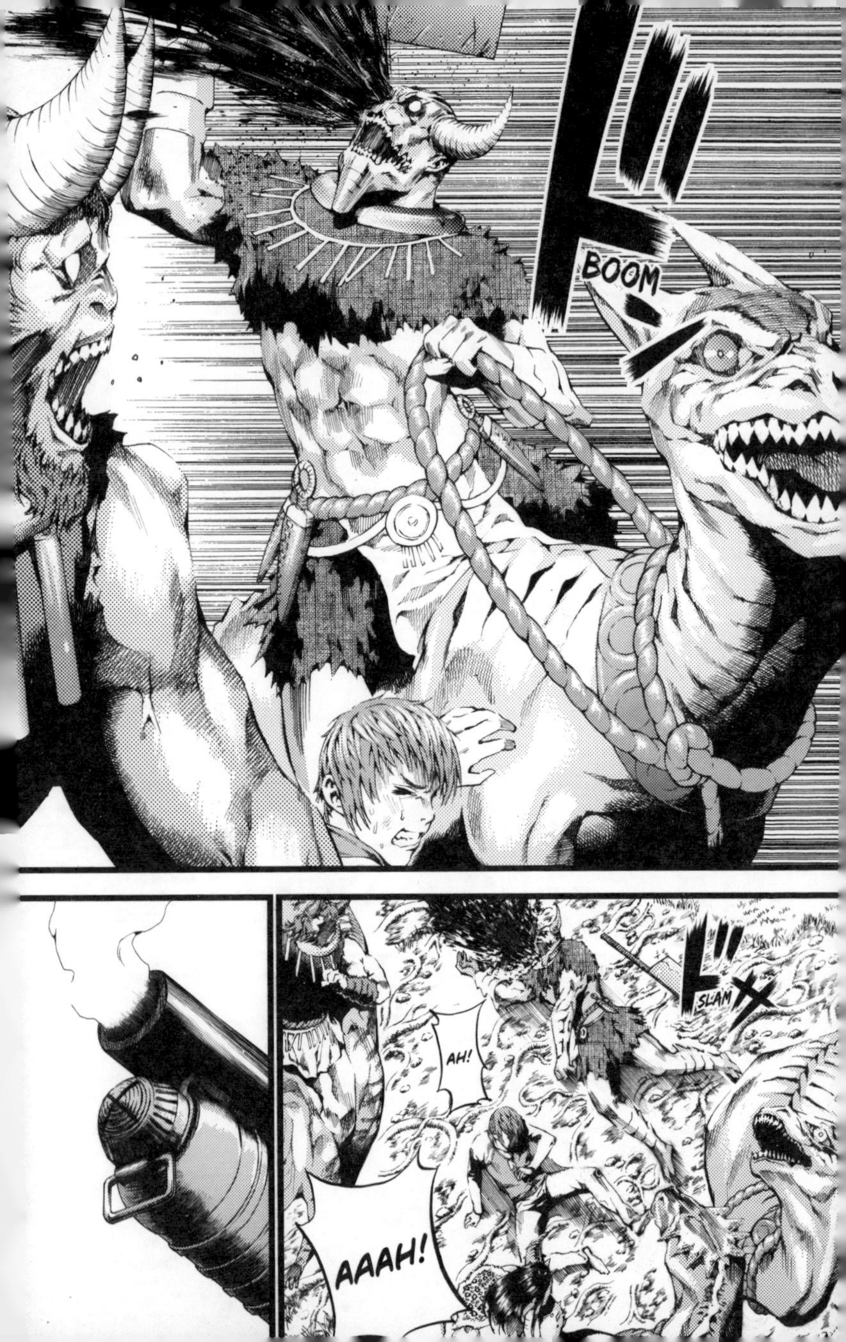
BOOM
SLAM
AH!
AAAH!

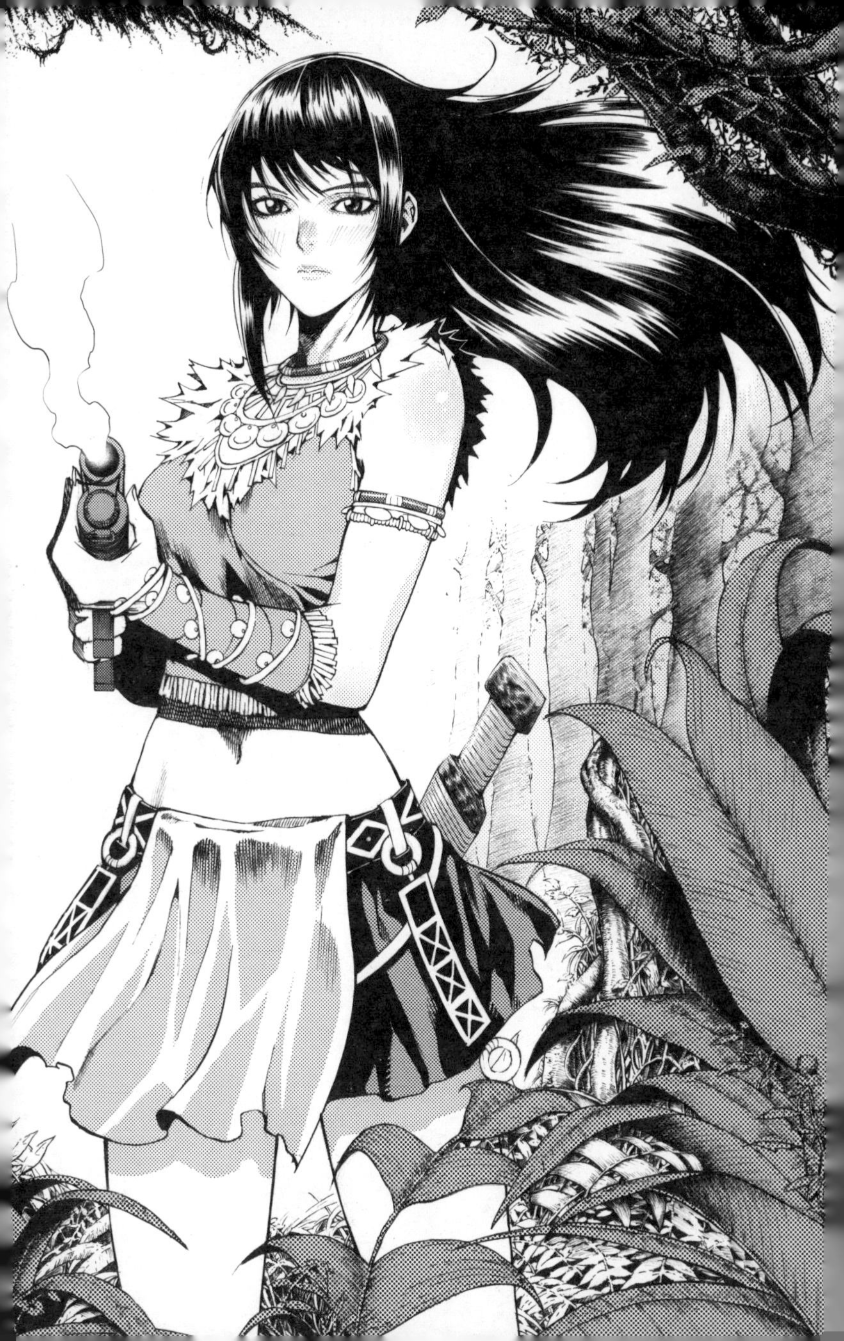

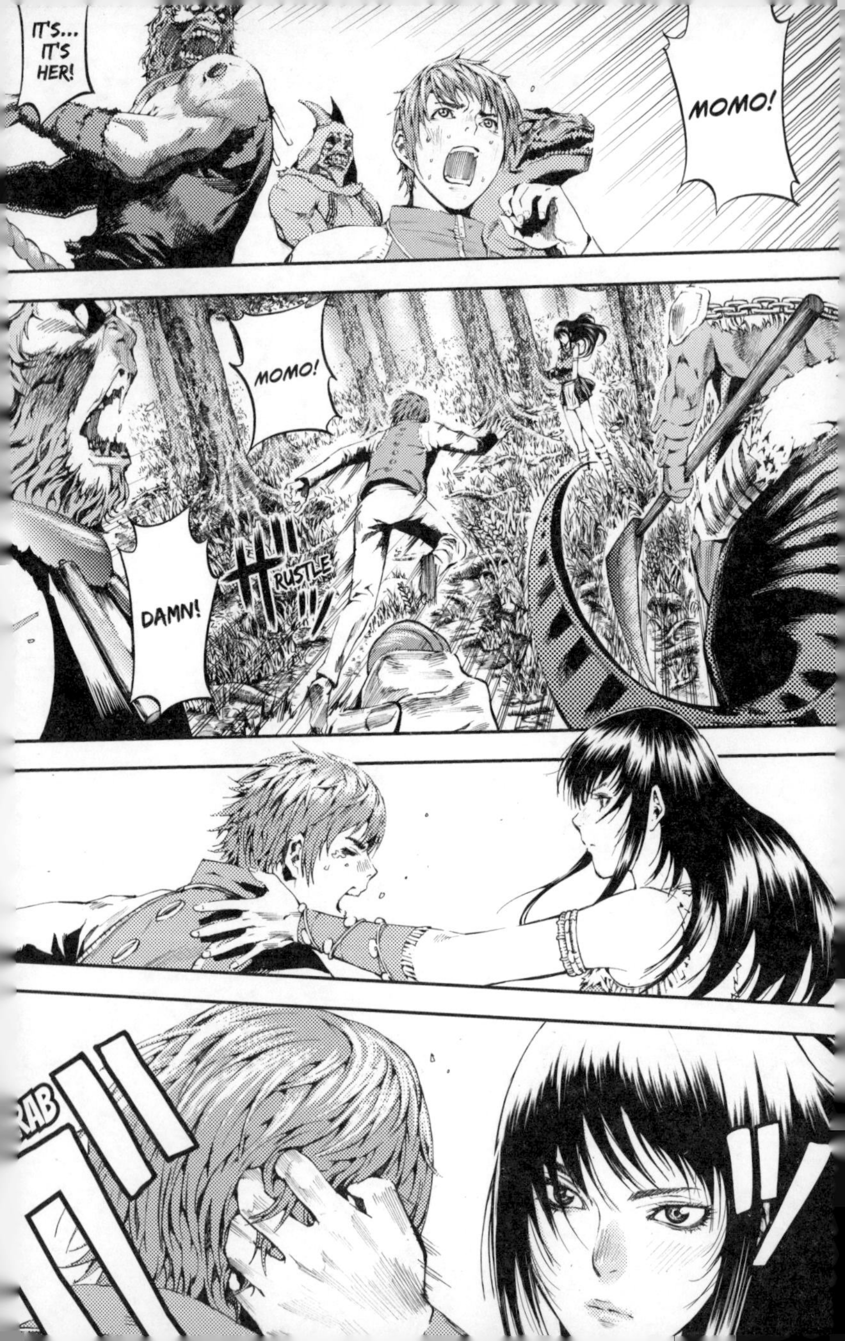
MOMO!
IT'S... IT'S HER!
MOMO!
RUSTLE
DAMN!
RAB

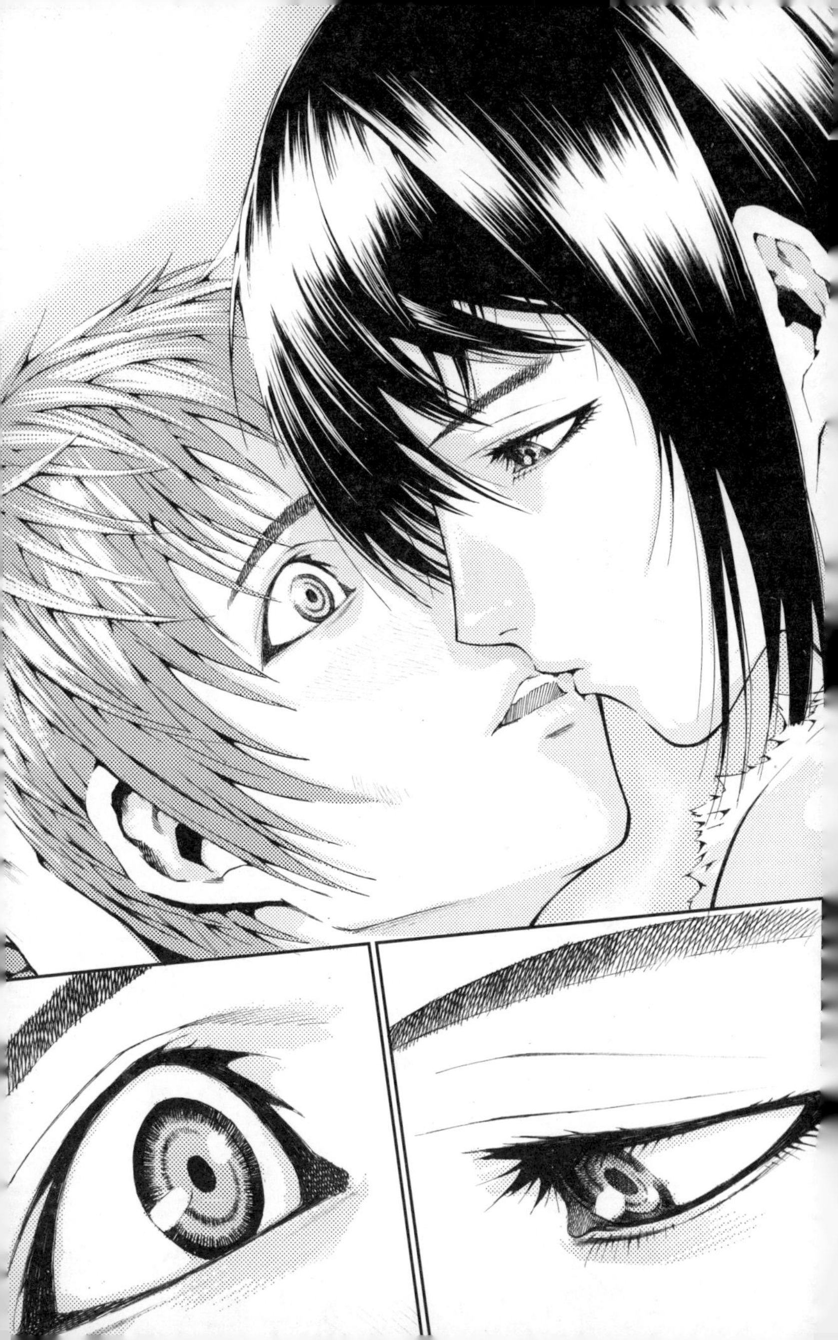

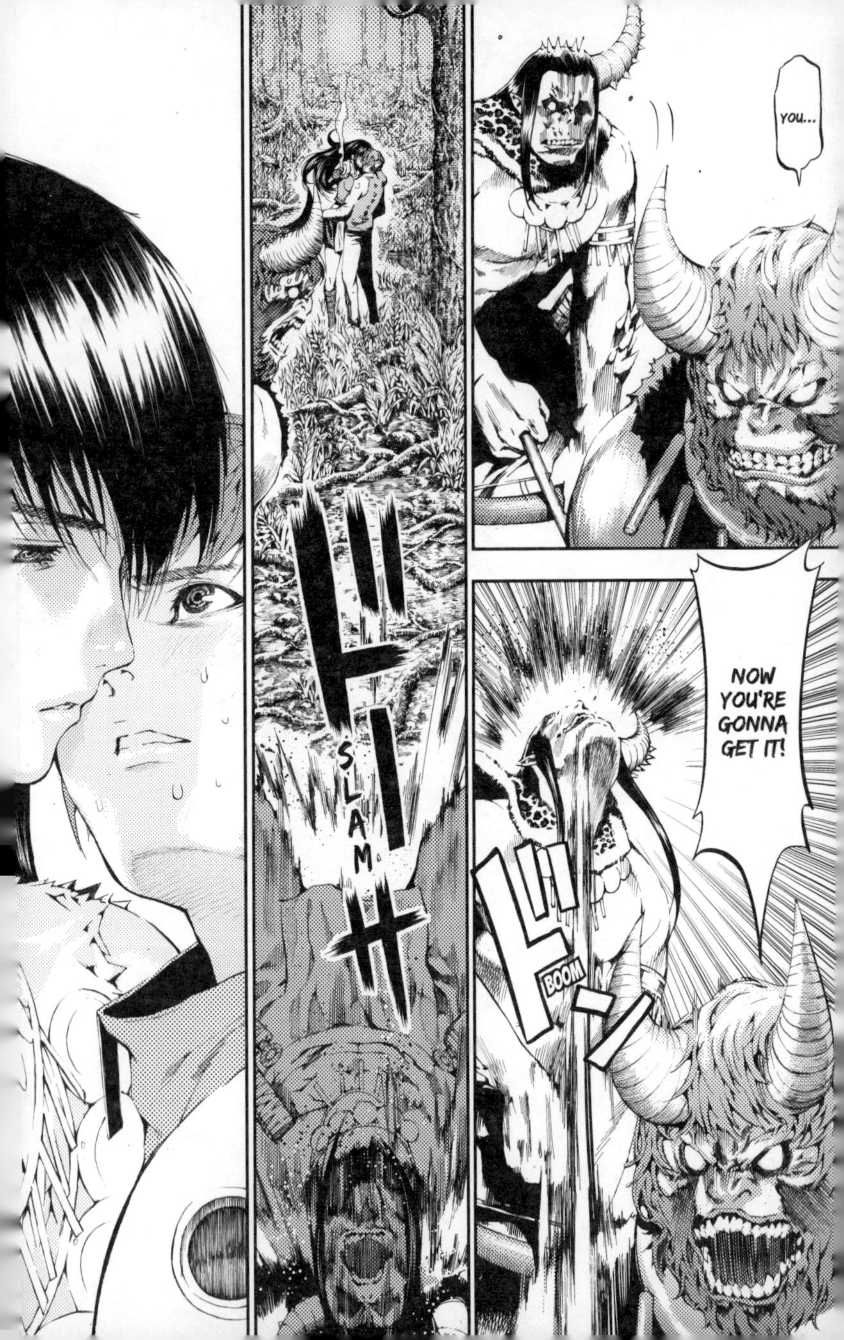
YOU...
NOW YOU'RE GONNA GET IT!
BOOM
SLAM

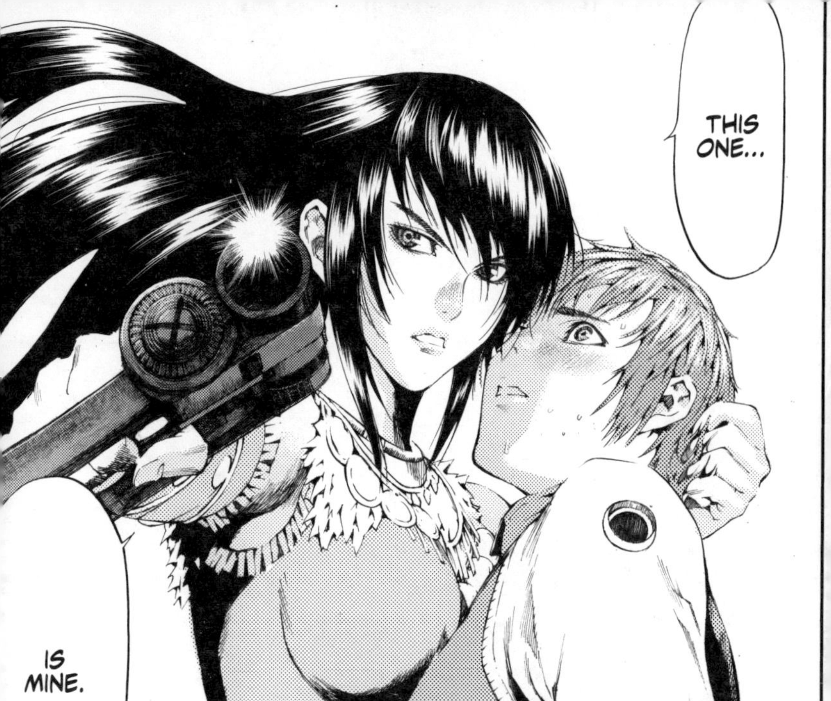
THIS ONE...
IS MINE.

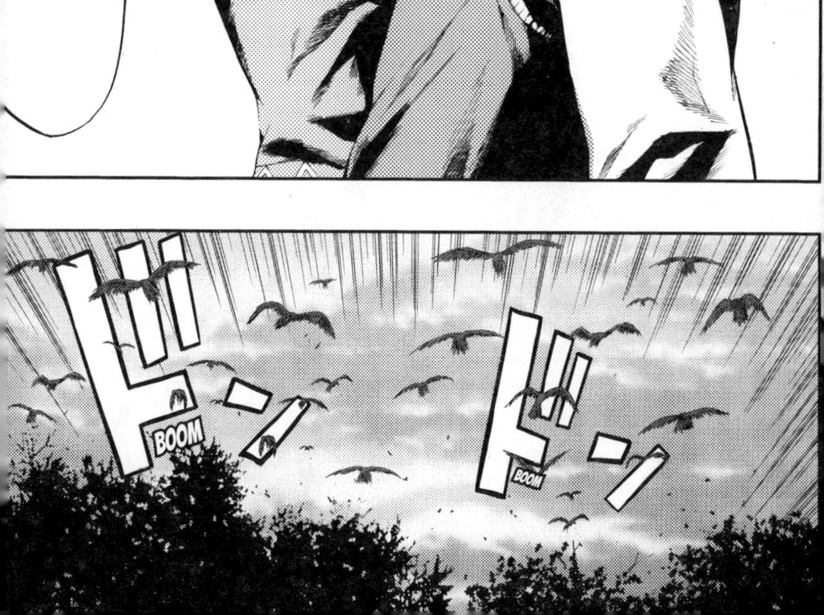
BOOM
BOOM

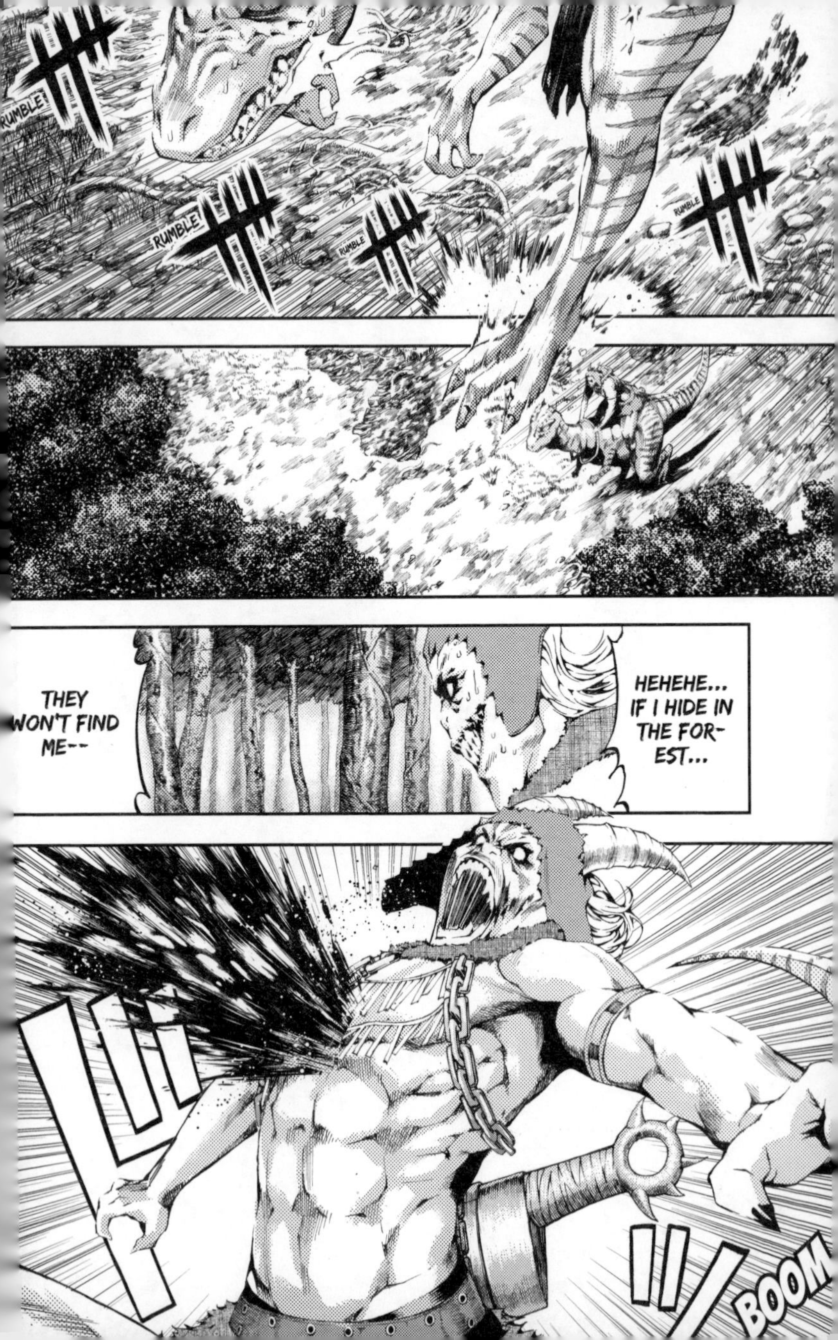
RUMBLE
RUMBLE
RUMBLE
RUMBLE
HEHEHE... IF I HIDE IN THE FOR-EST...
THEY WON'T FIND ME--
BOOM

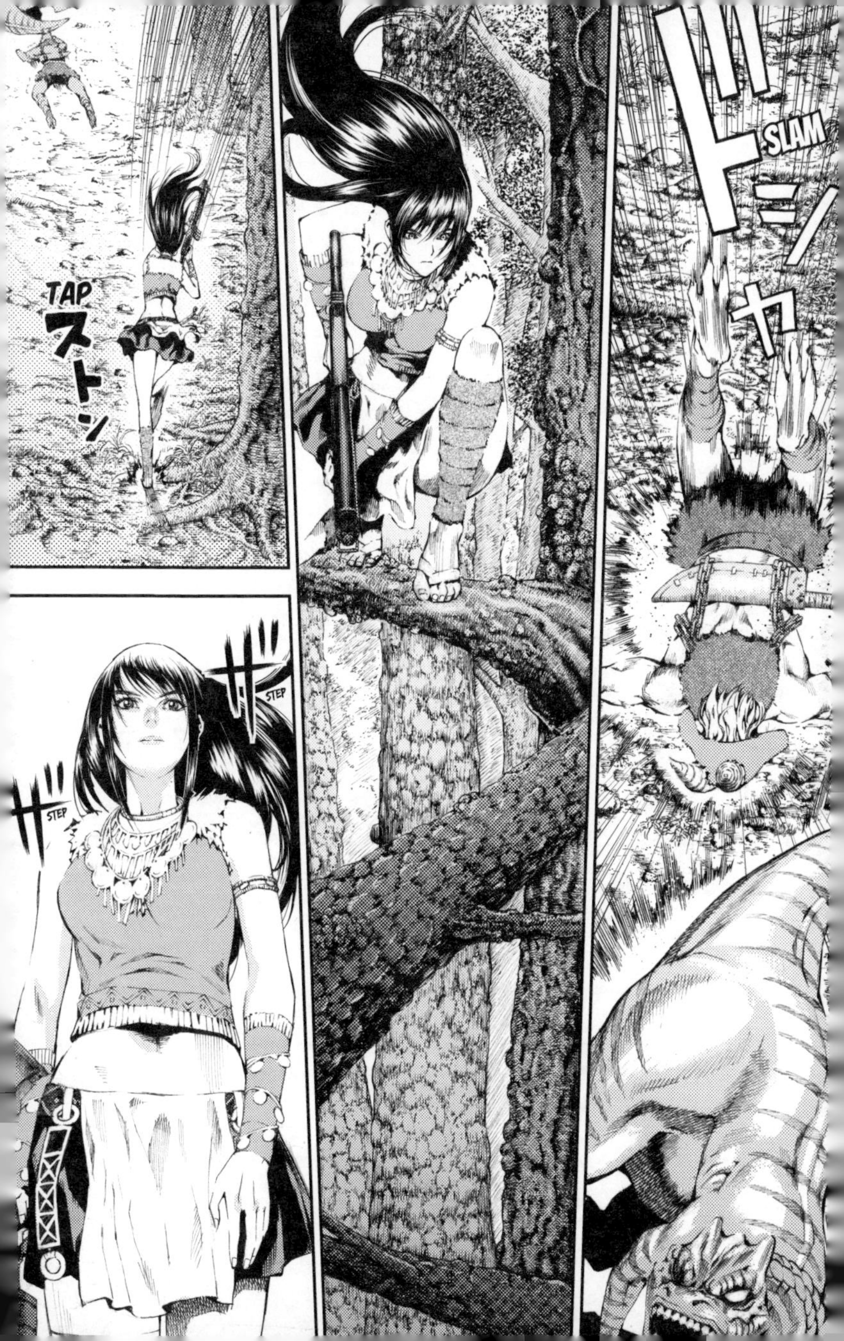
ドシャ
SLAM
TAP
ストッ
ザ
STEP
ザ
STEP

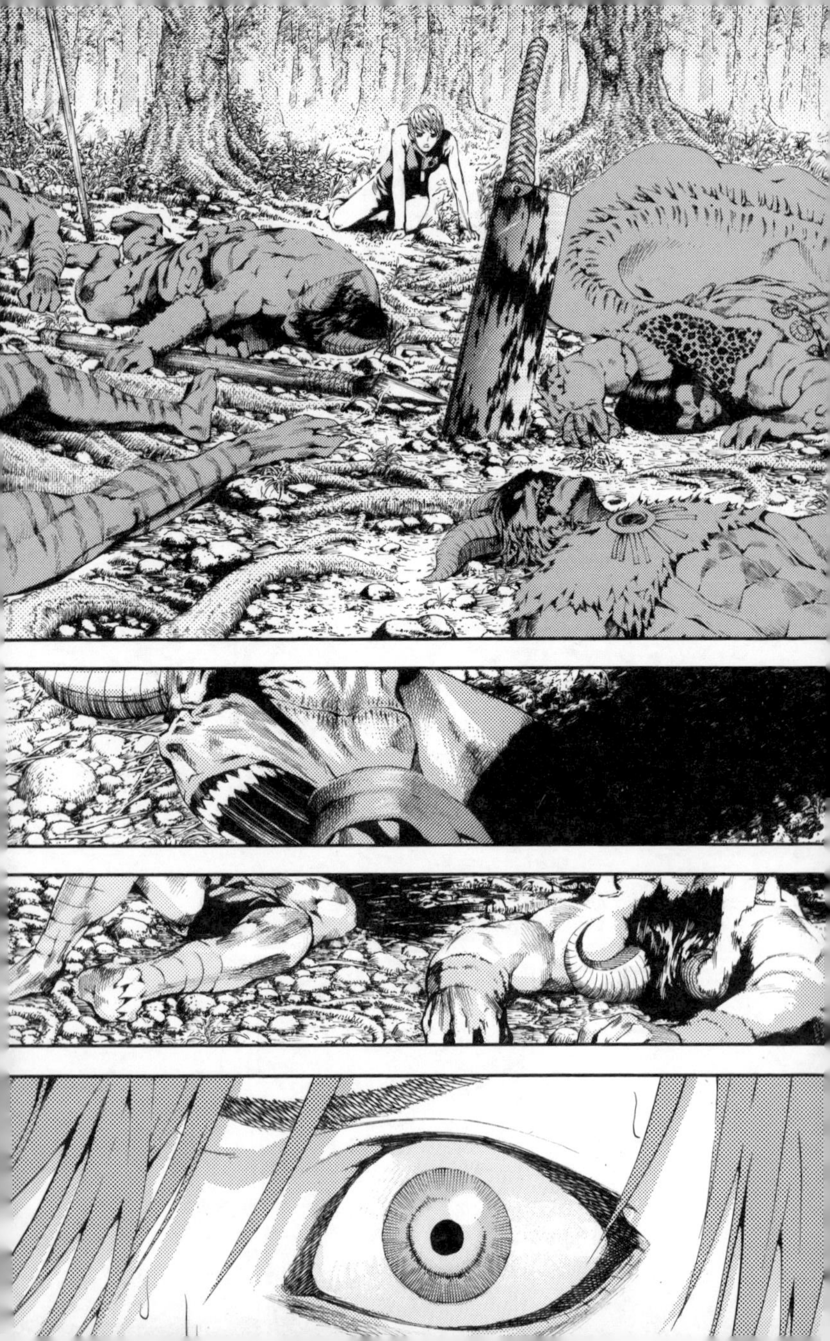

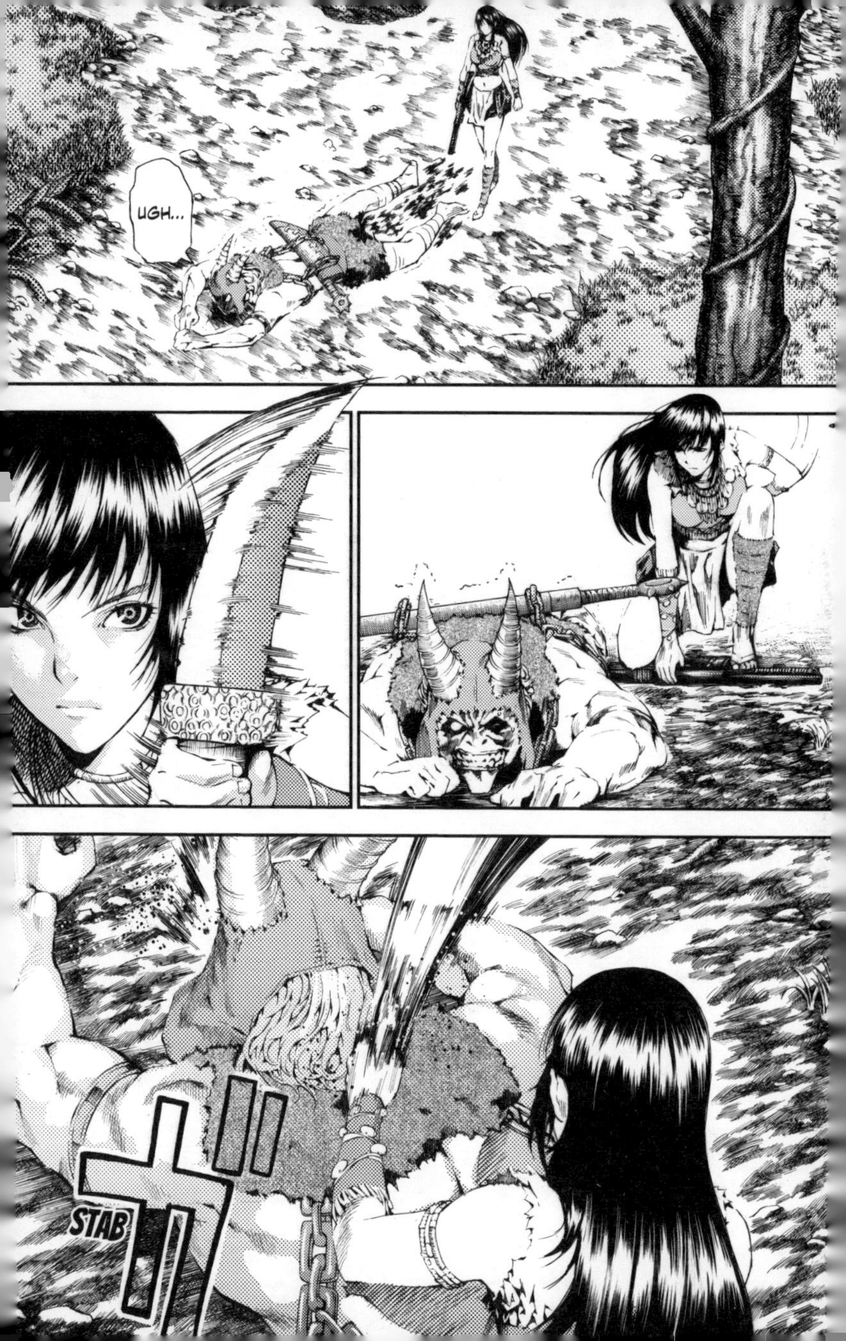
UGH...
STAB

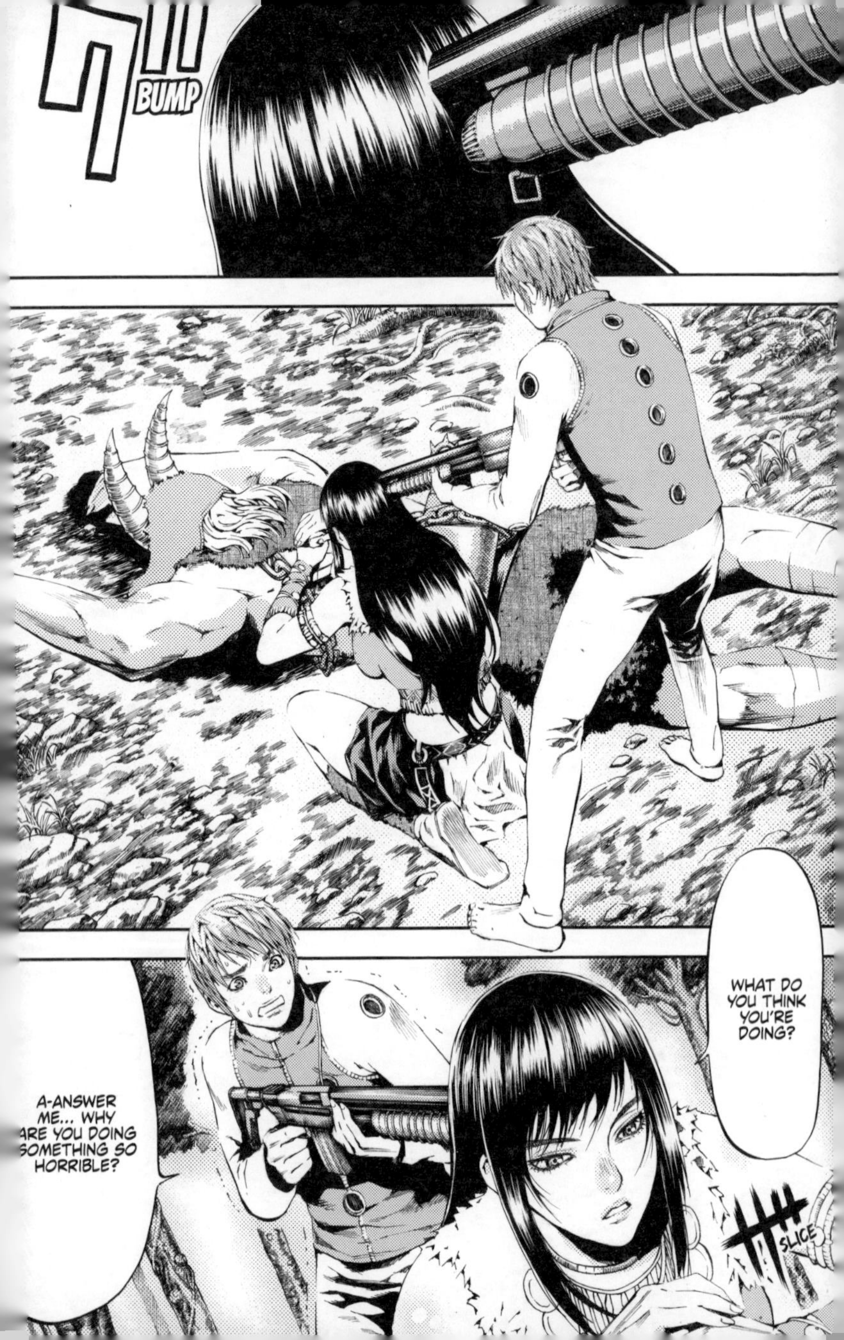
BUMP
WHAT DO YOU THINK YOU'RE DOING?
A-ANSWER ME... WHY ARE YOU DOING SOMETHING SO HORRIBLE?
SLICE

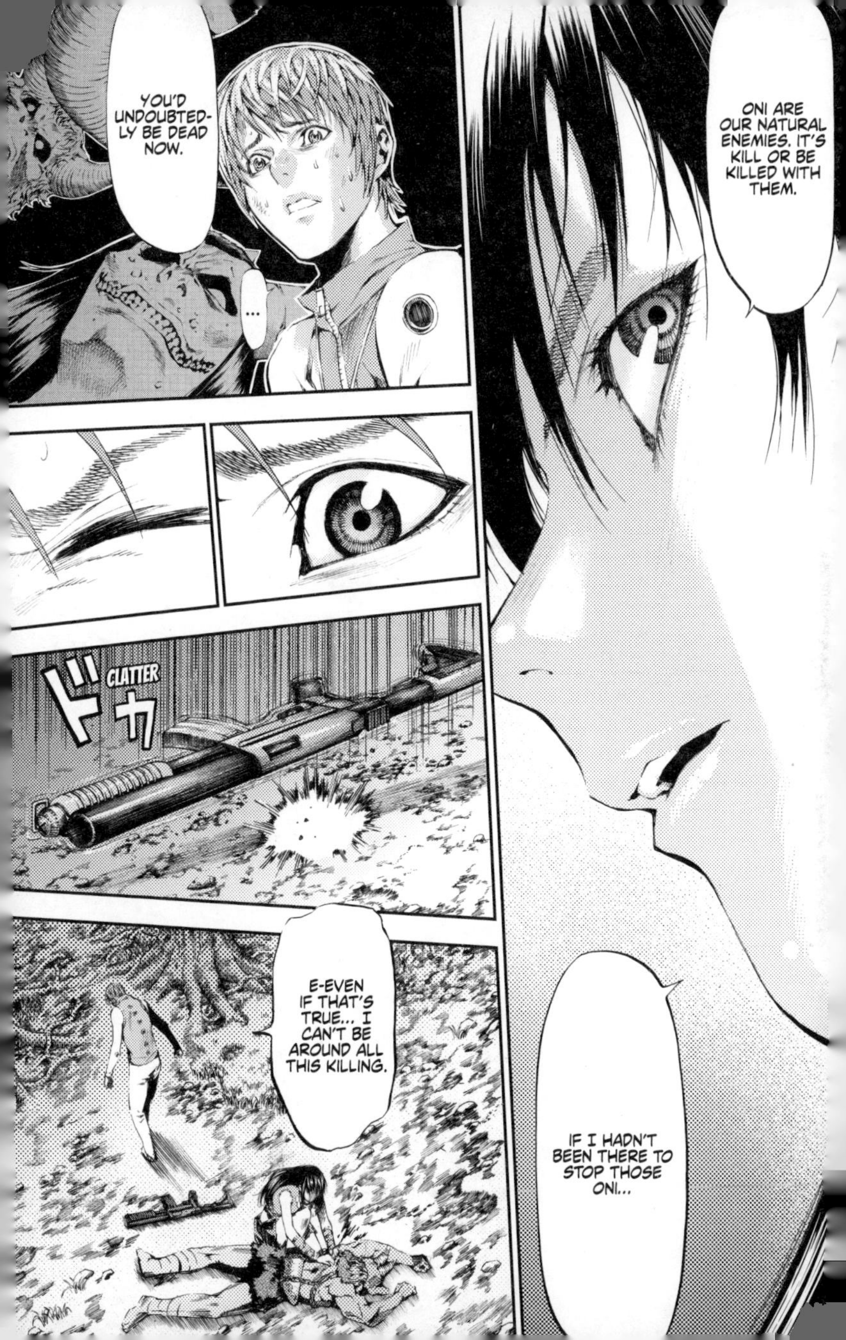
ONI ARE OUR NATURAL ENEMIES. IT'S KILL OR BE KILLED WITH THEM.
IF I HADN'T BEEN THERE TO STOP THOSE ONI...
YOU'D UNDOUBTED-LY BE DEAD NOW.
...
ドカ
CLATTER
E-EVEN IF THAT'S TRUE... I CAN'T BE AROUND ALL THIS KILLING.

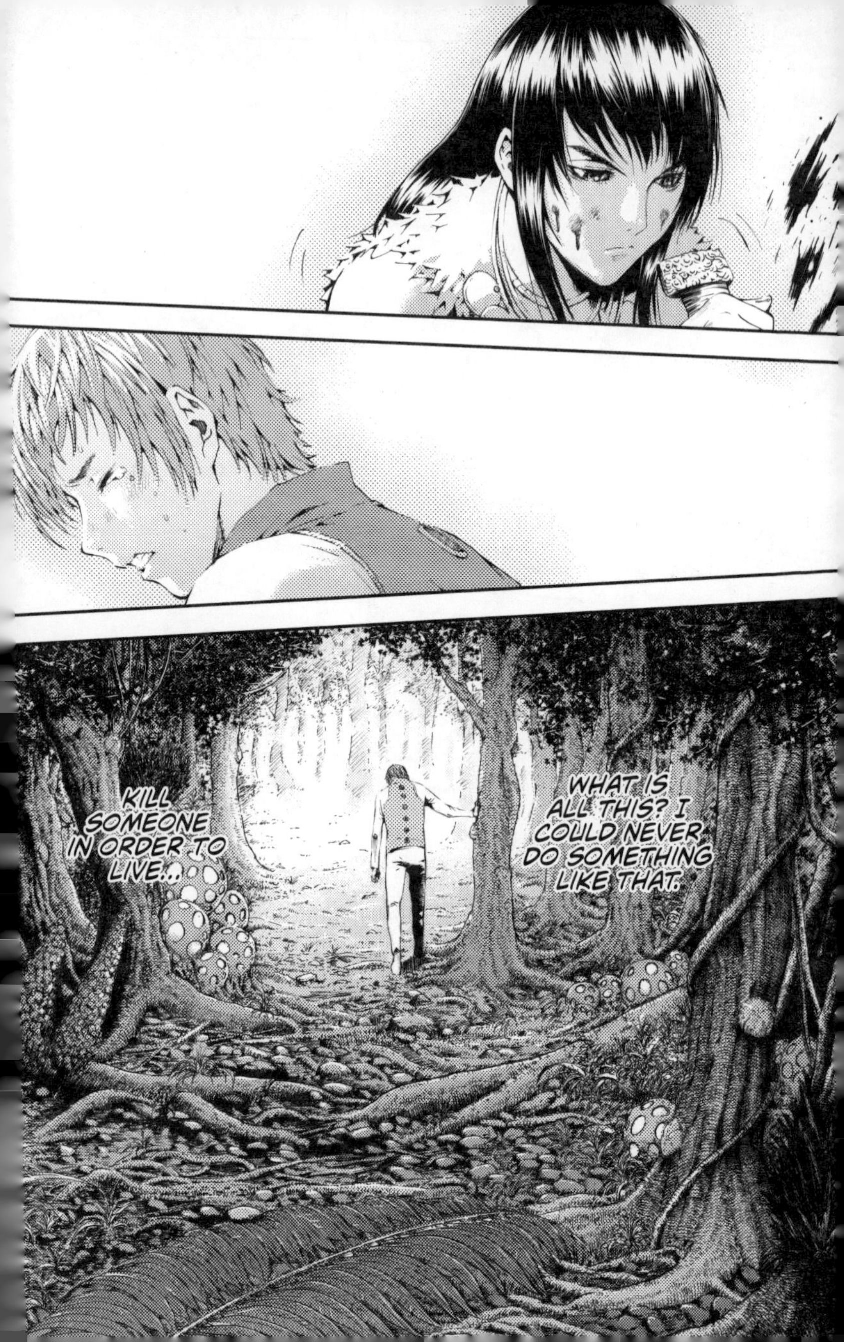
WHAT IS ALL THIS? I COULD NEVER DO SOMETHING LIKE THAT.
KILL SOMEONE IN ORDER TO LIVE...

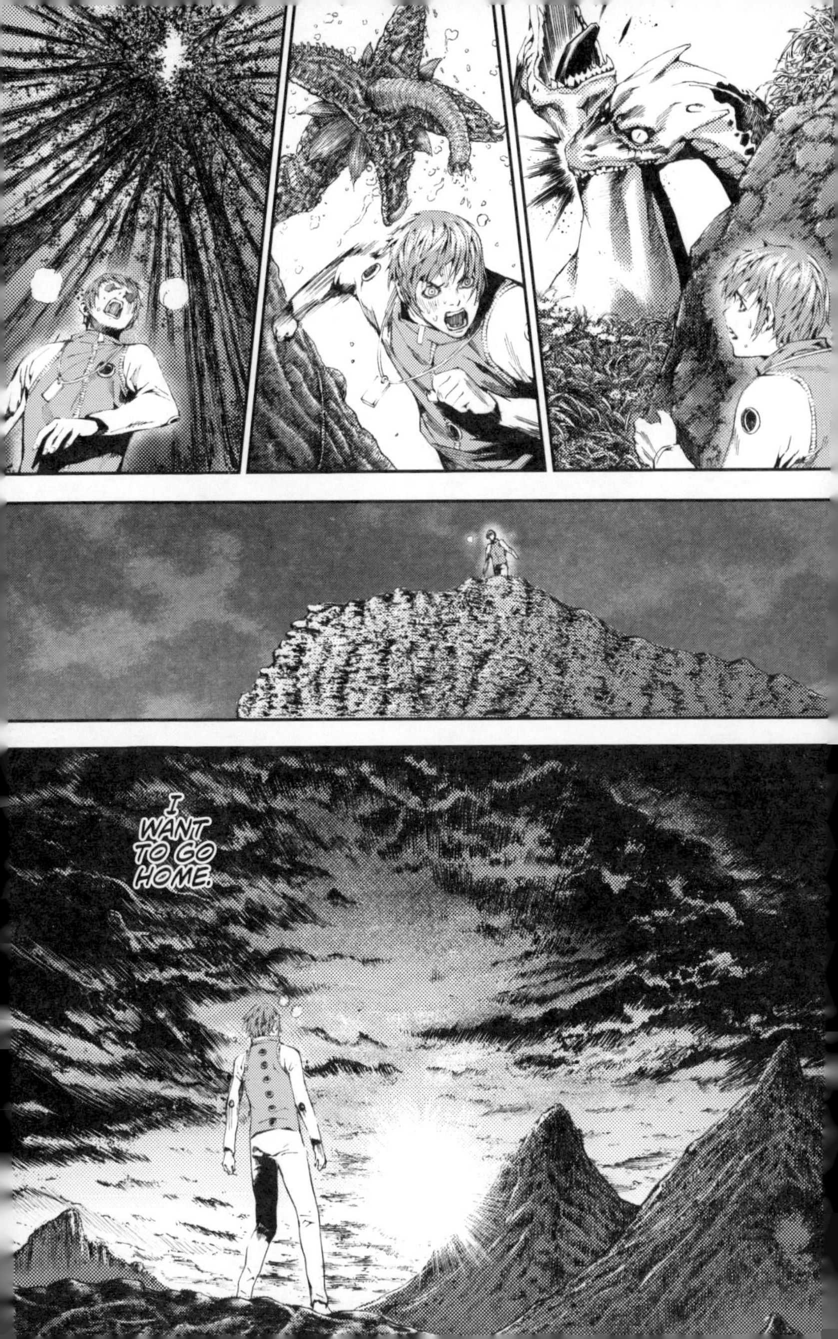
I WANT TO GO HOME.

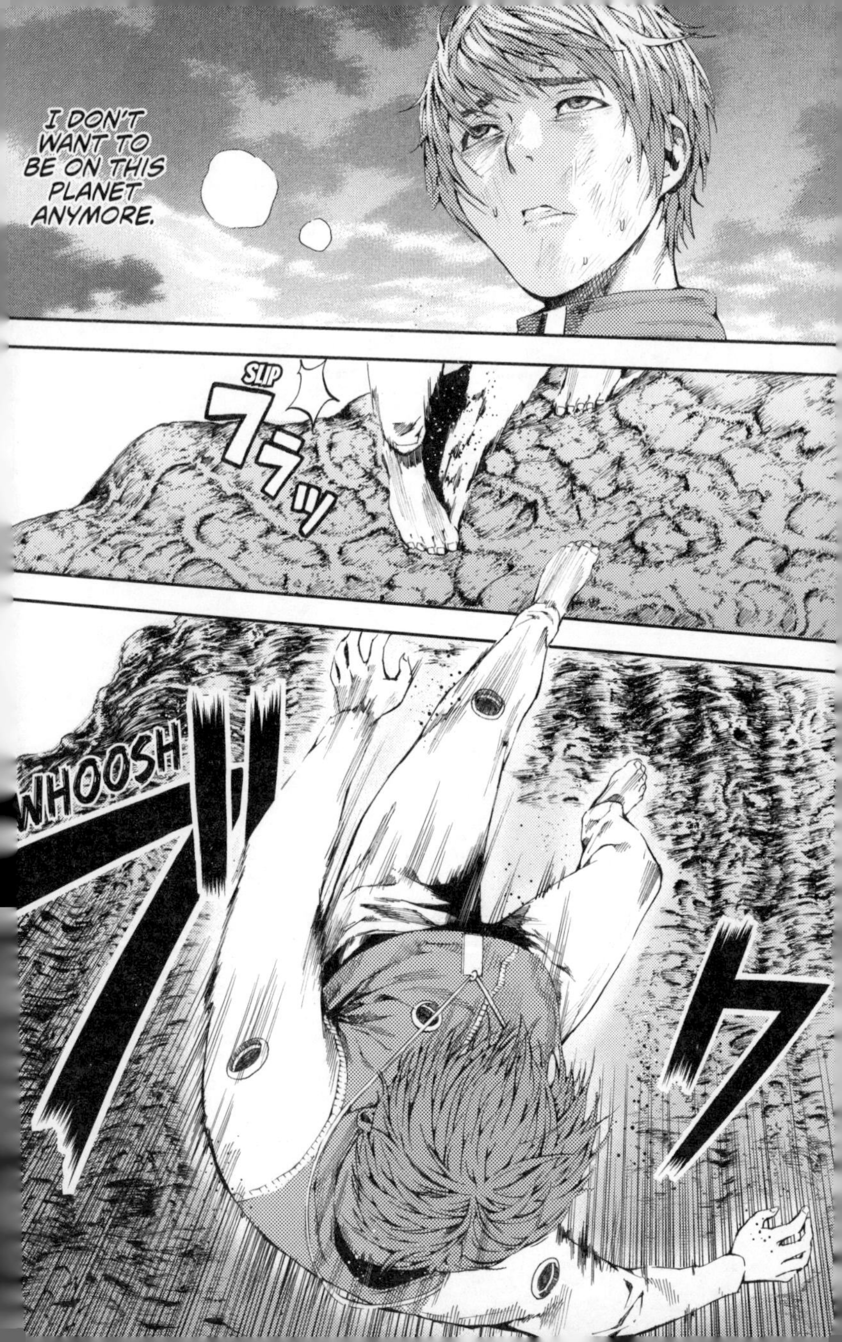
I DON'T WANT TO BE ON THIS PLANET ANYMORE.
SLIP
フラッ
WHOOSH
ゴッ

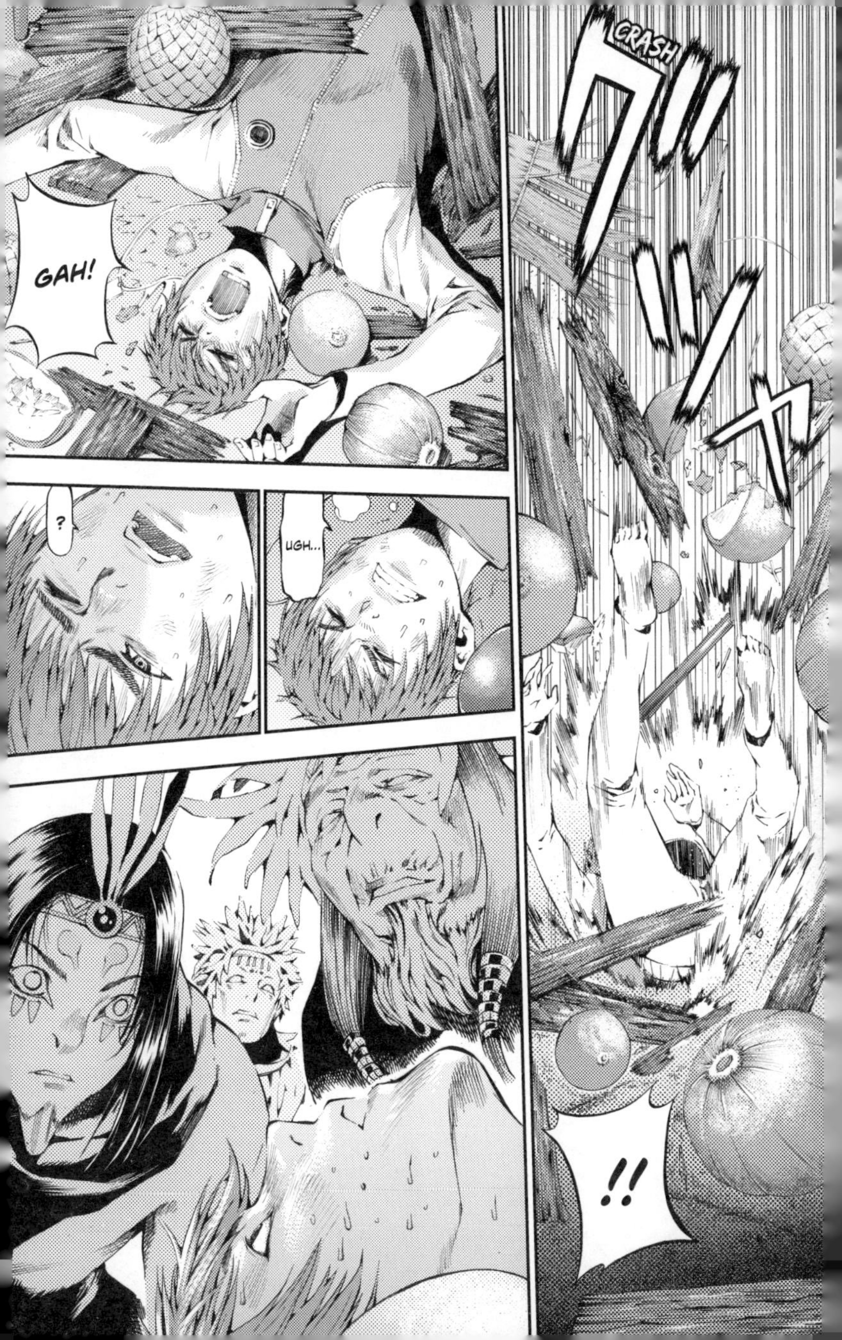
CRASH
!!
GAH!
UGH...
?

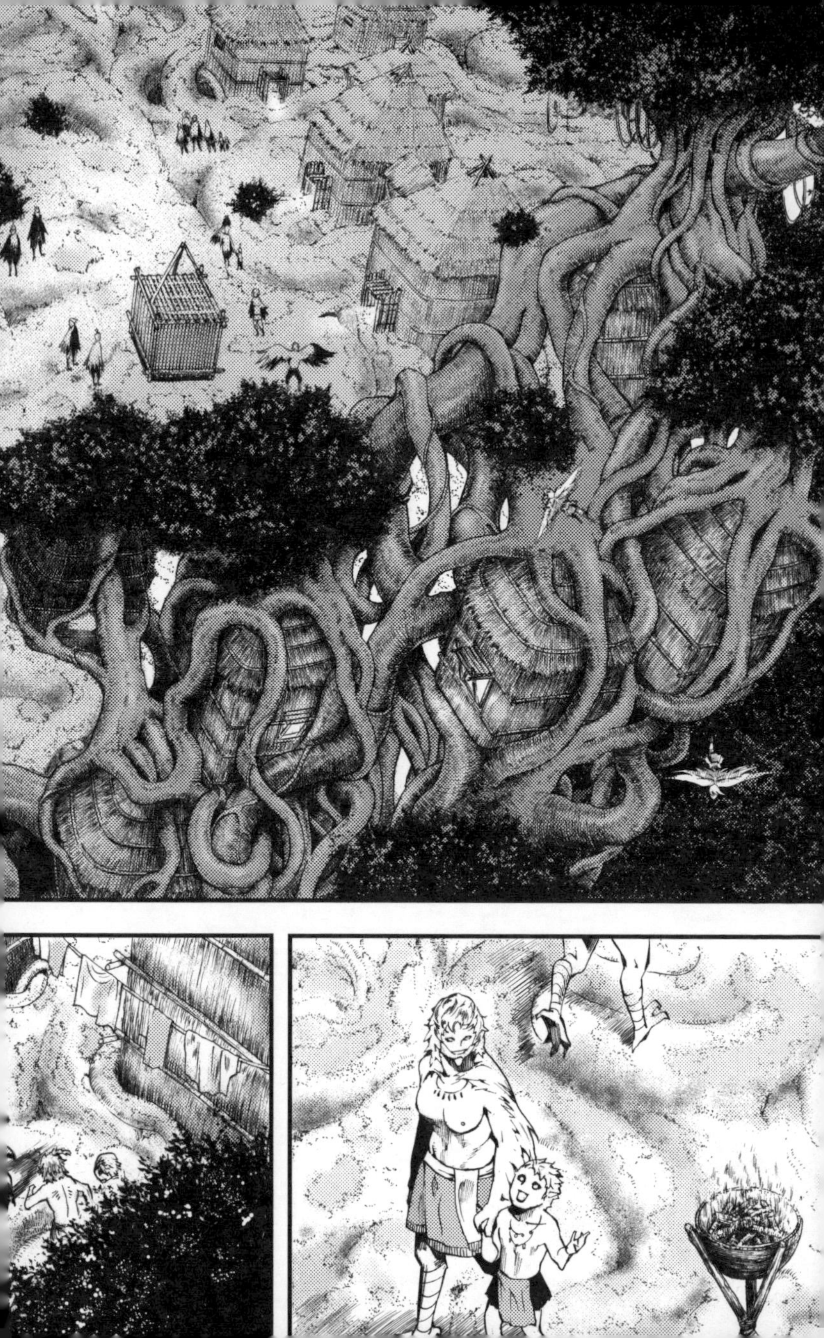

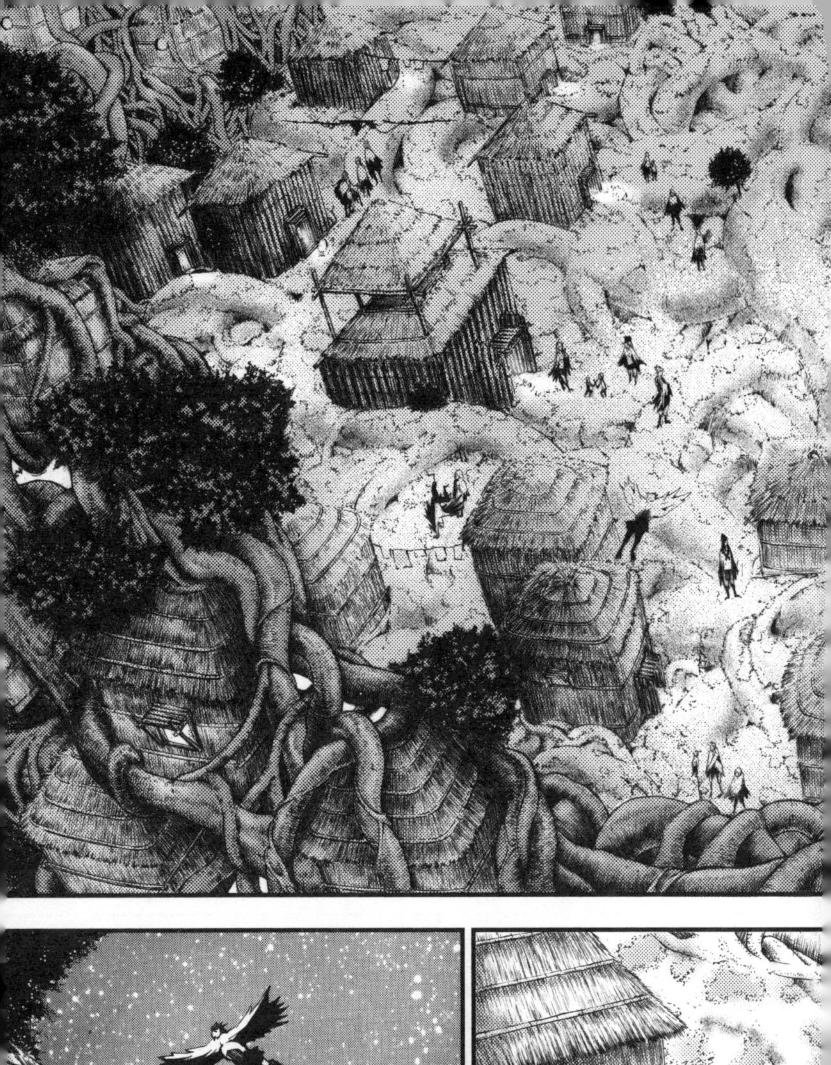
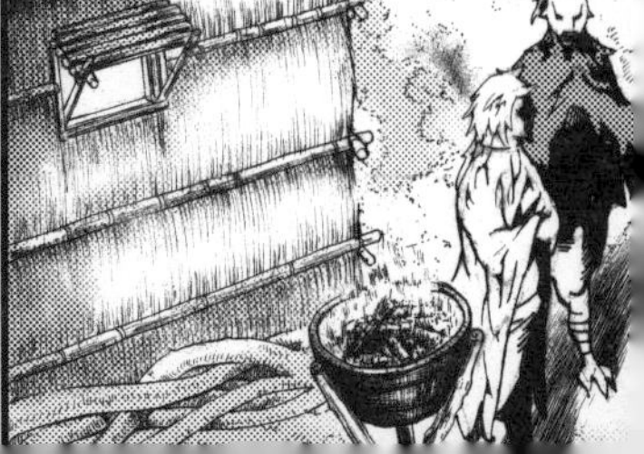
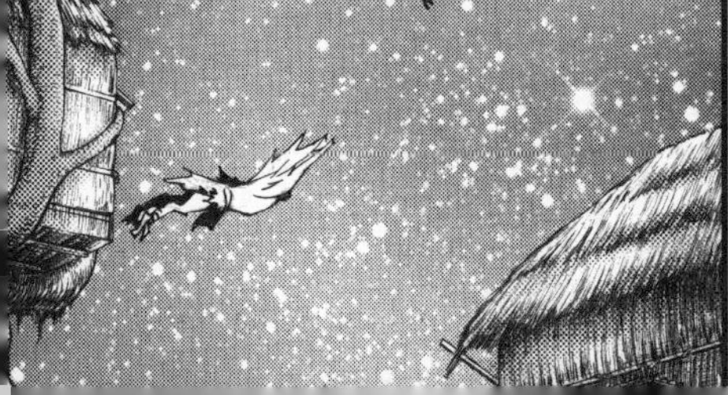

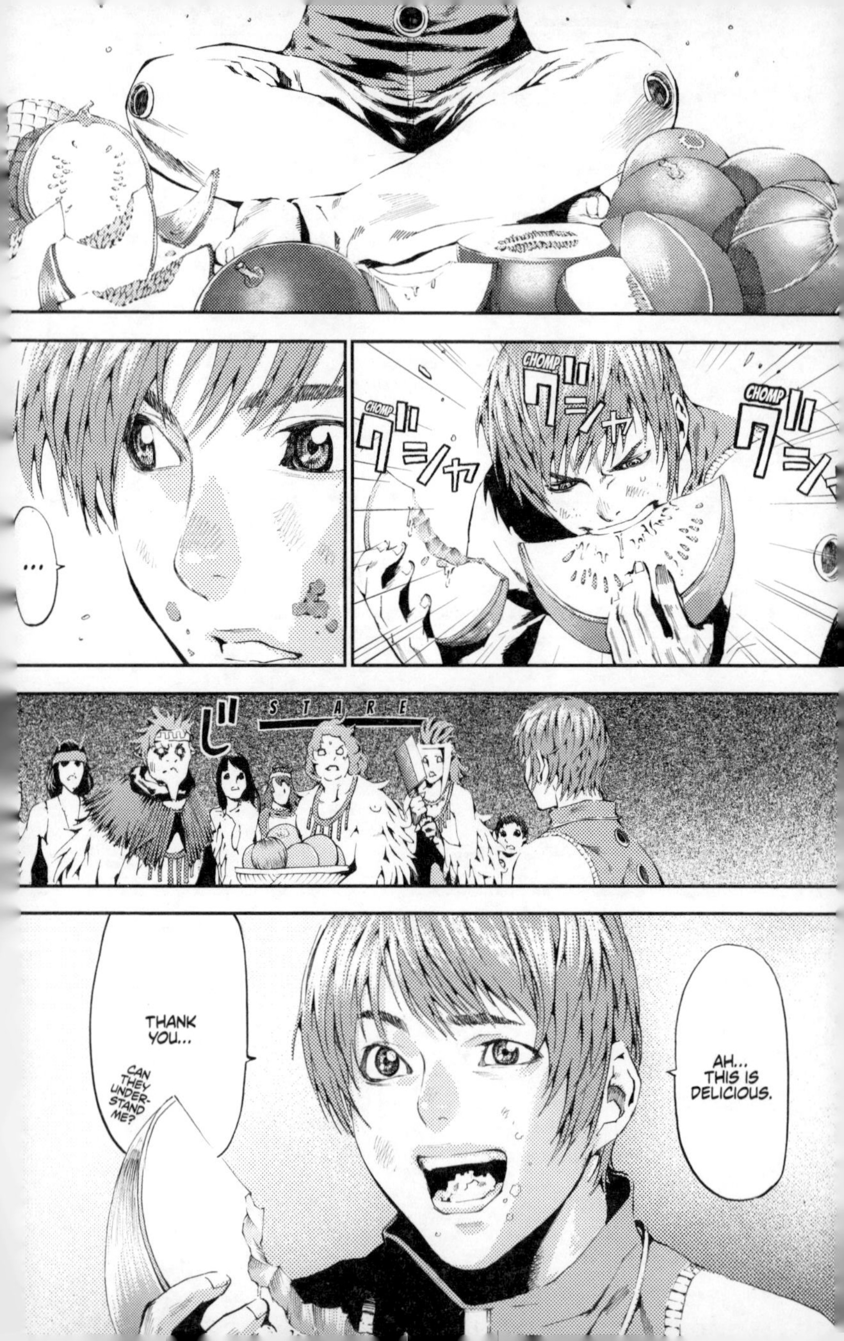

CHOMP
CHOMP
グシャ
CHOMP
グシャ
...
じ
S T A R E
AH... THIS IS DELICIOUS.
THANK YOU...
CAN THEY UNDER-STAND ME?

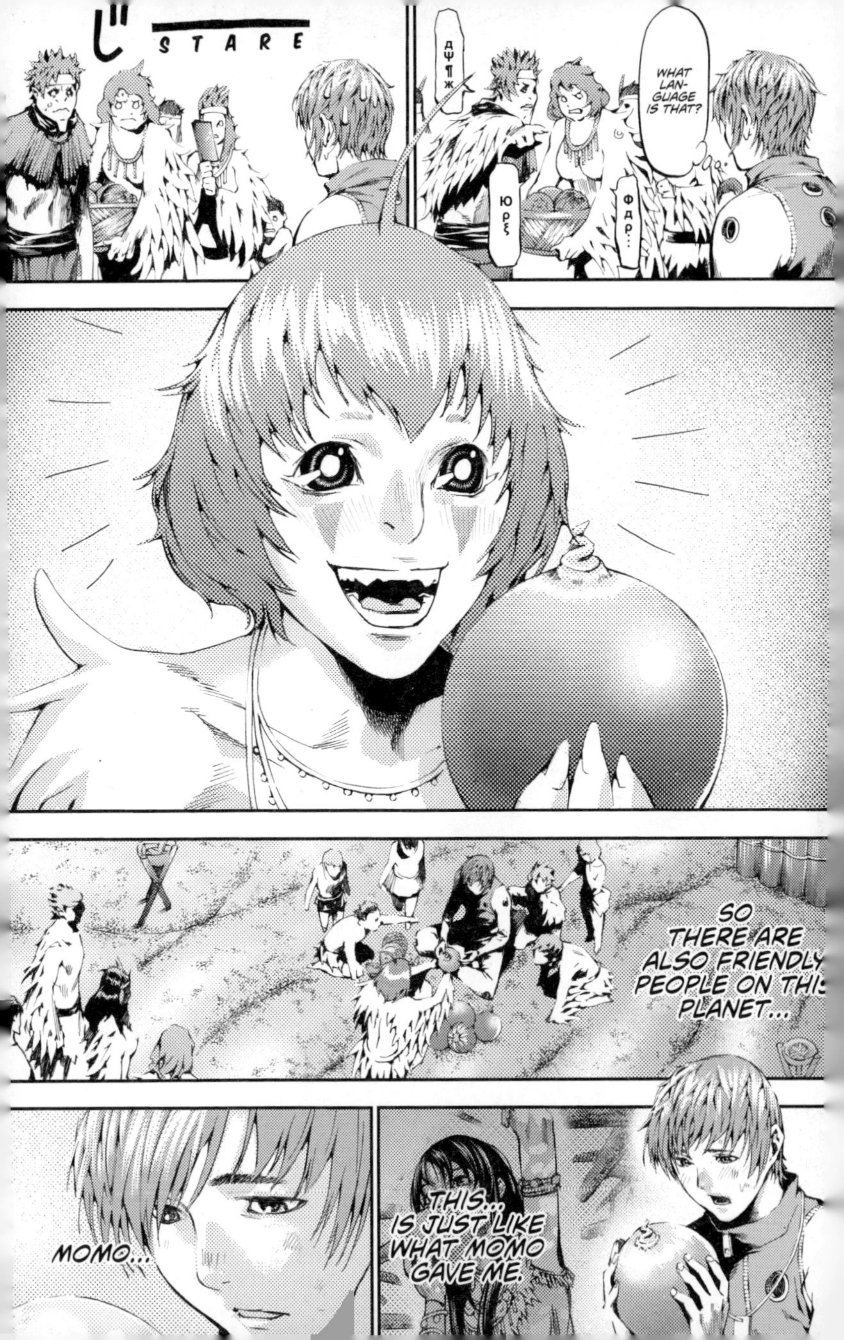
WHAT LAN-GUAGE IS THAT?
Дψ¶ж
Фдр..
Юρξ
じ
STARE
SO THERE ARE ALSO FRIENDLY PEOPLE ON THIS PLANET...
THIS... IS JUST LIKE WHAT MOMO GAVE ME.
MOMO...

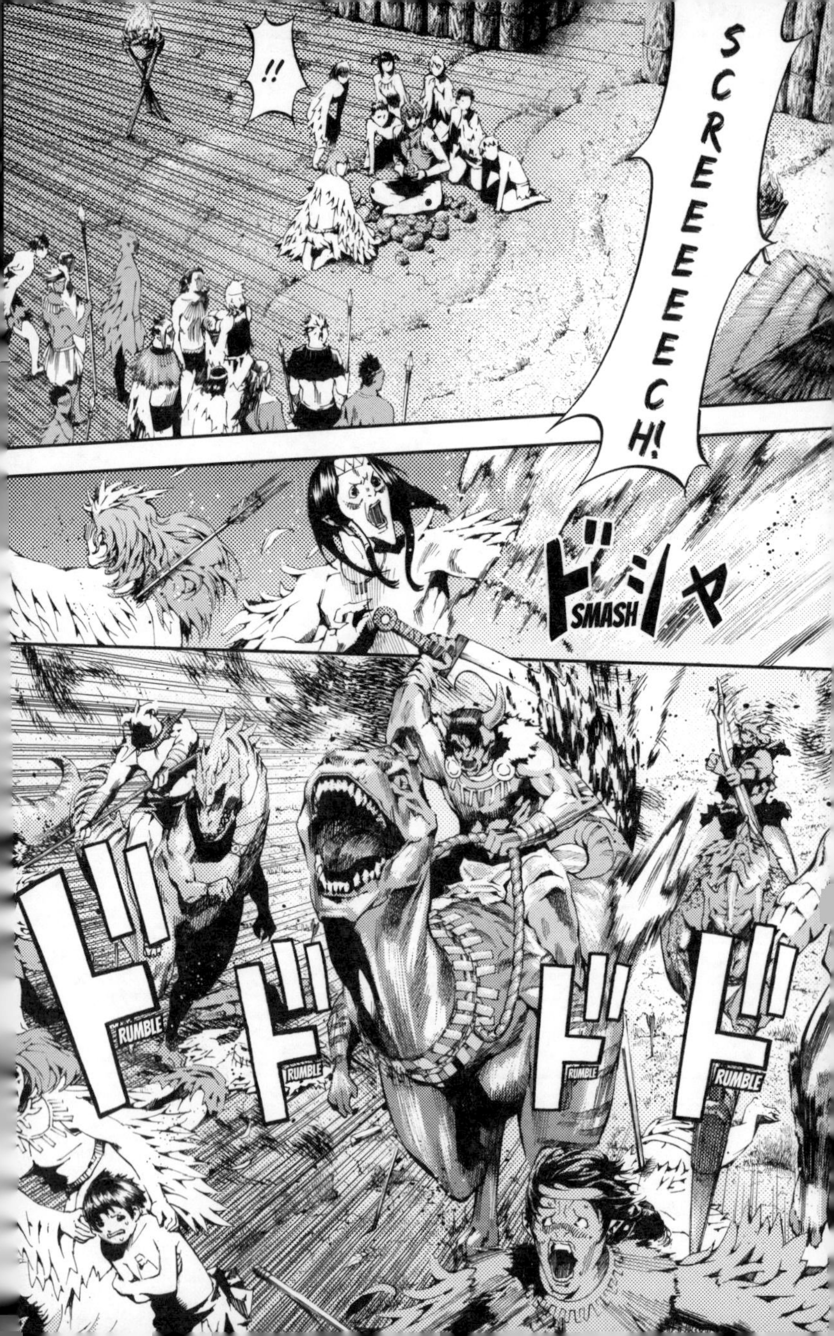
SCREEEEECH!
!!
ドシャ
SMASH
ドドドドドドドド
RUMBLE
RUMBLE
RUMBLE
RUMBLE

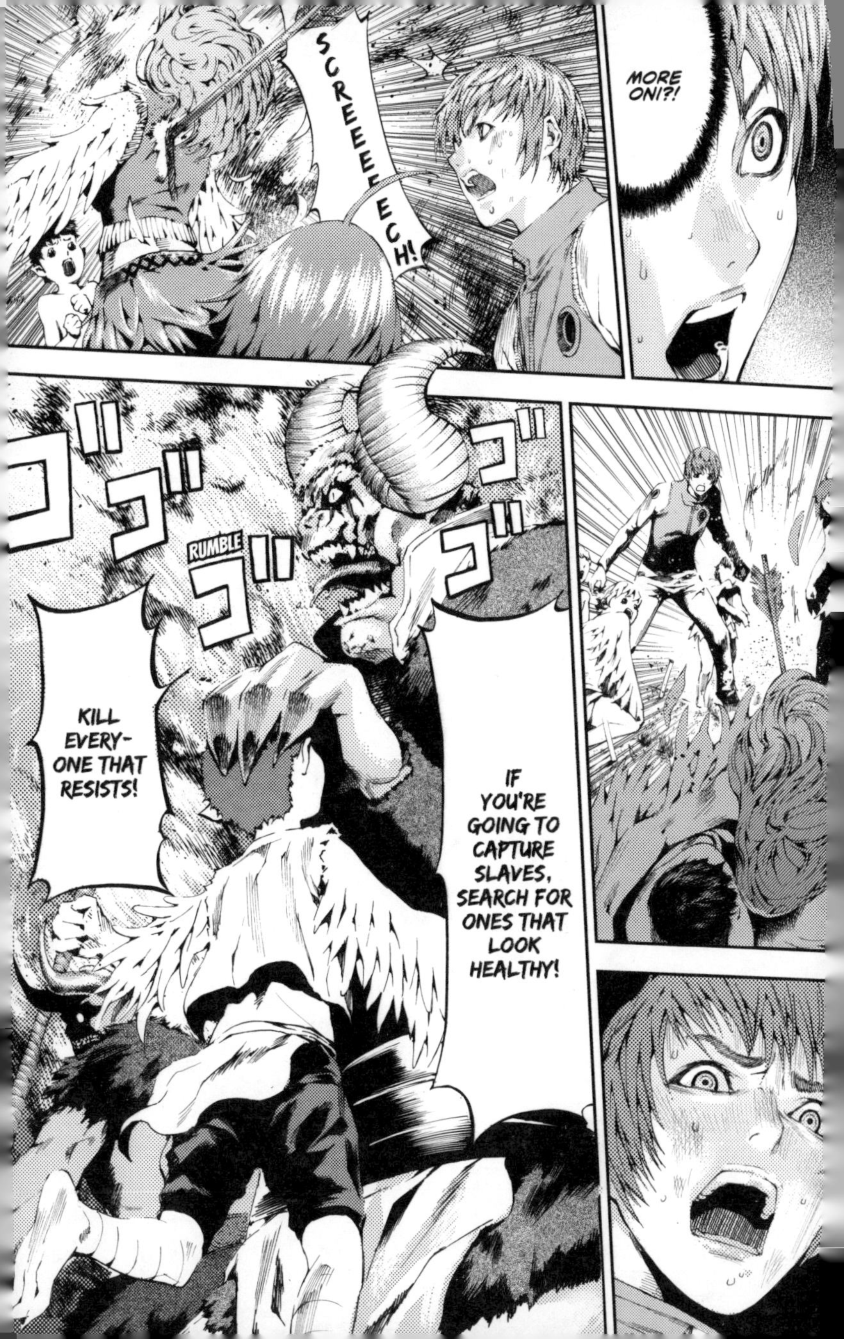
MORE ONI?!
SCREEEEEECH!
ゴゴ
ゴゴ
RUMBLE
ゴ
IF YOU'RE GOING TO CAPTURE SLAVES, SEARCH FOR ONES THAT LOOK HEALTHY!
KILL EVERY-ONE THAT RESISTS!

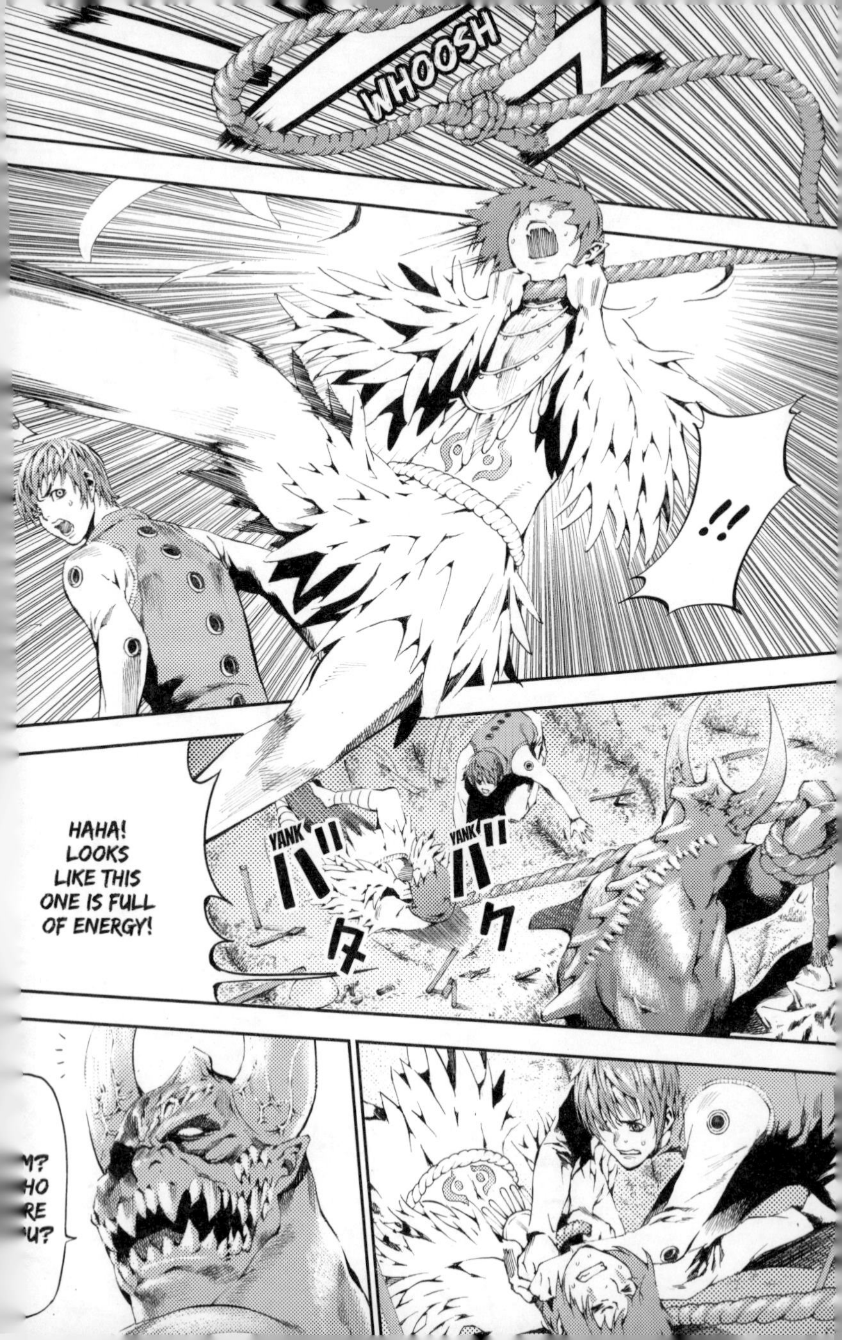
WHOOSH
!!
YANK
YANK
HAHA! LOOKS LIKE THIS ONE IS FULL OF ENERGY!
M? HO RE U?

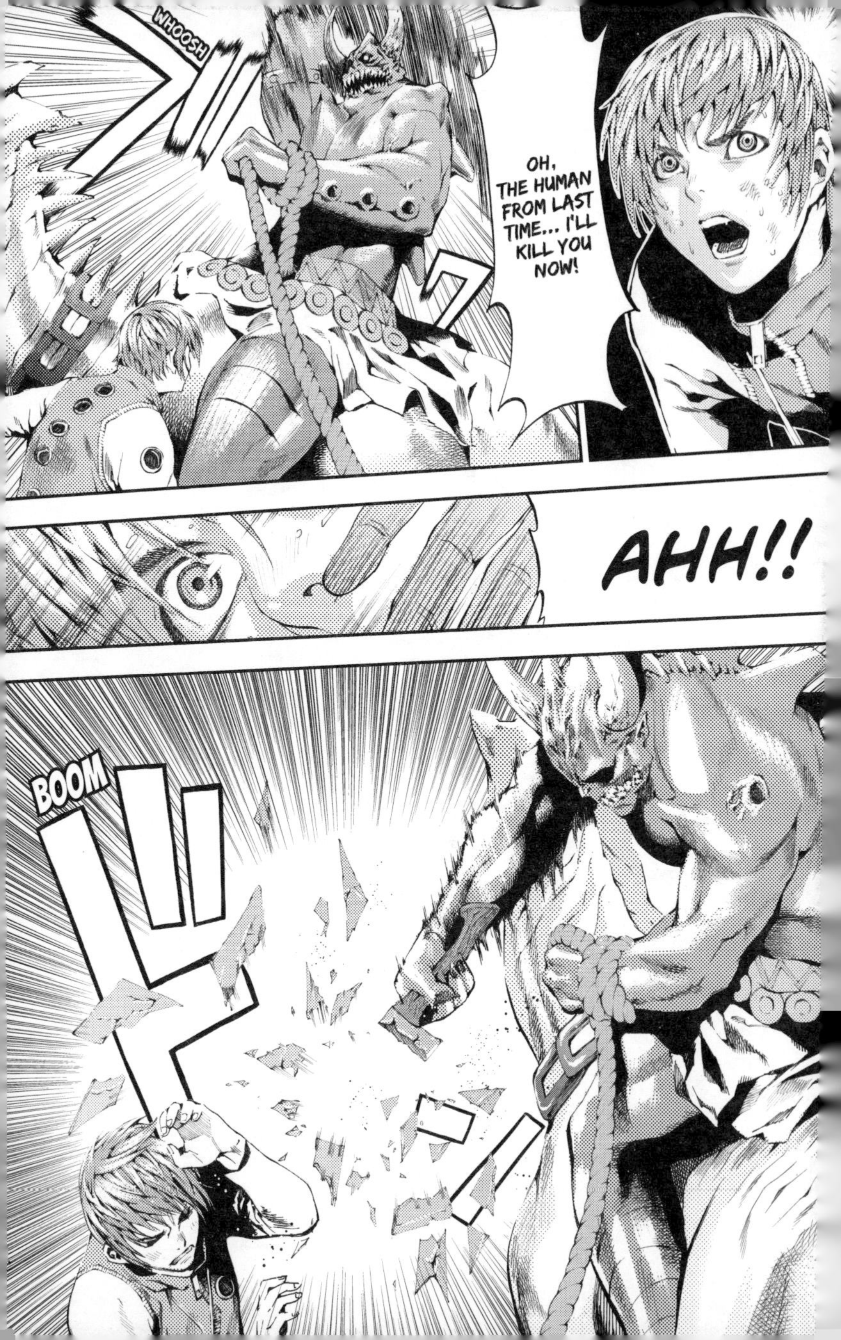

OH, THE HUMAN FROM LAST TIME... I'LL KILL YOU NOW!
WHOOSH
AHH!!
BOOM

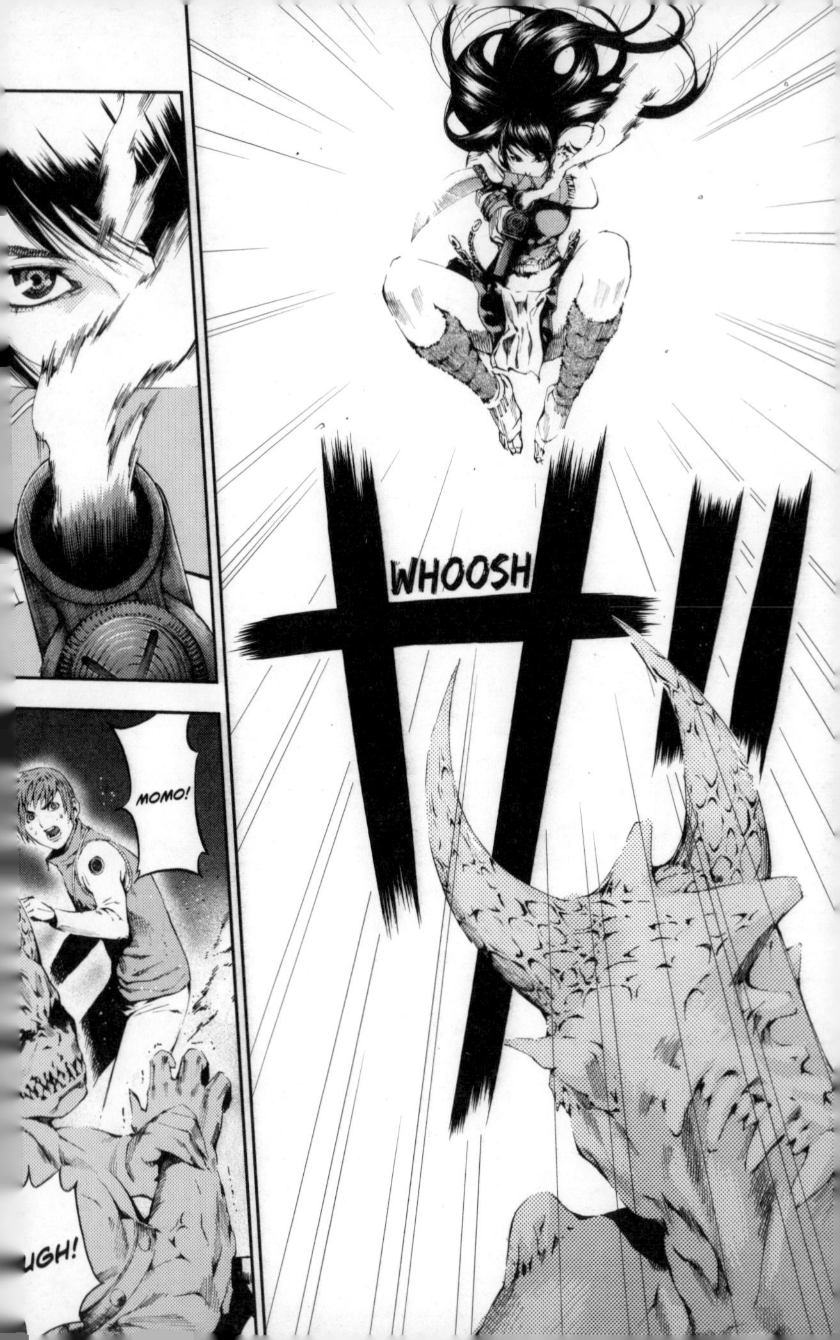
WHOOSH
MOMO!
UGH!

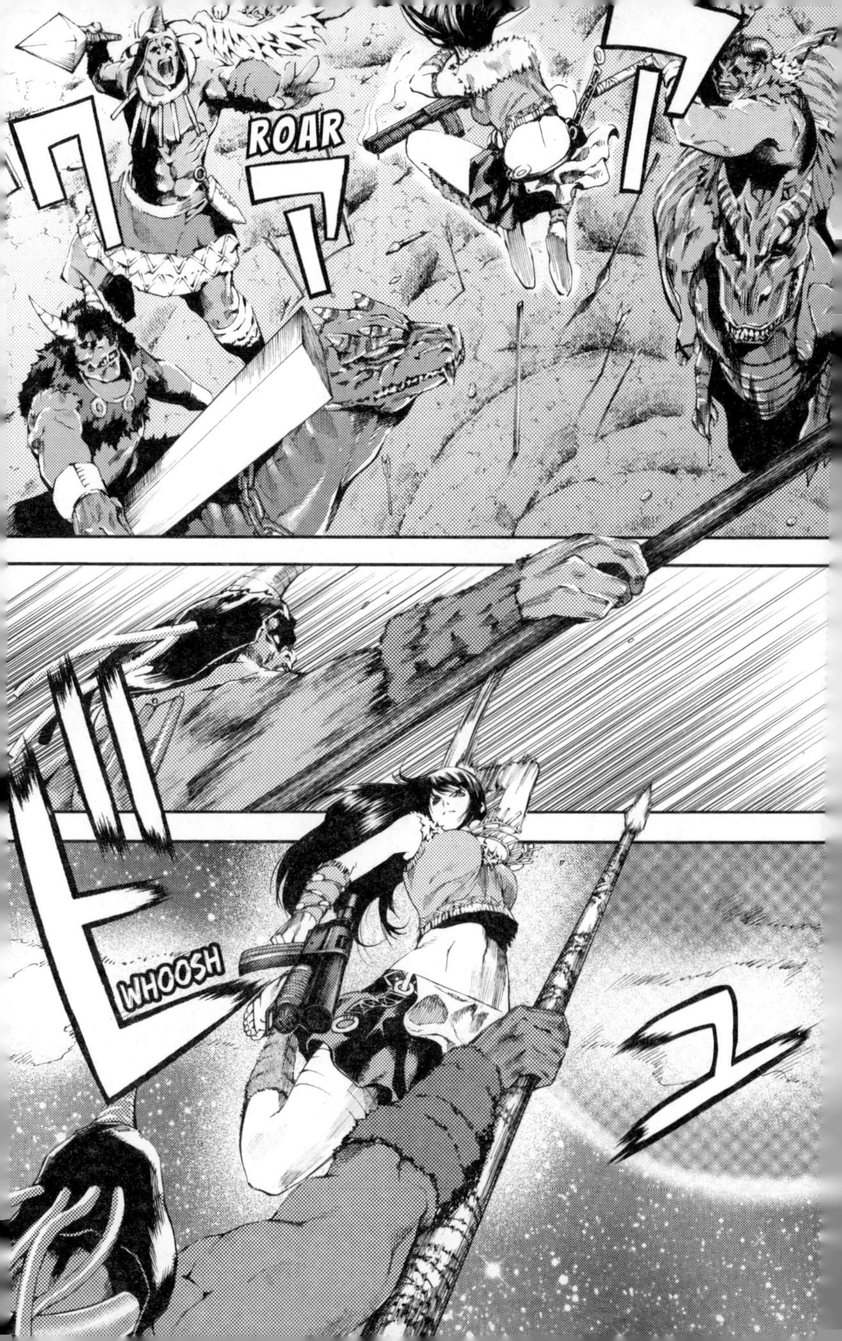
ROAR
WHOOSH

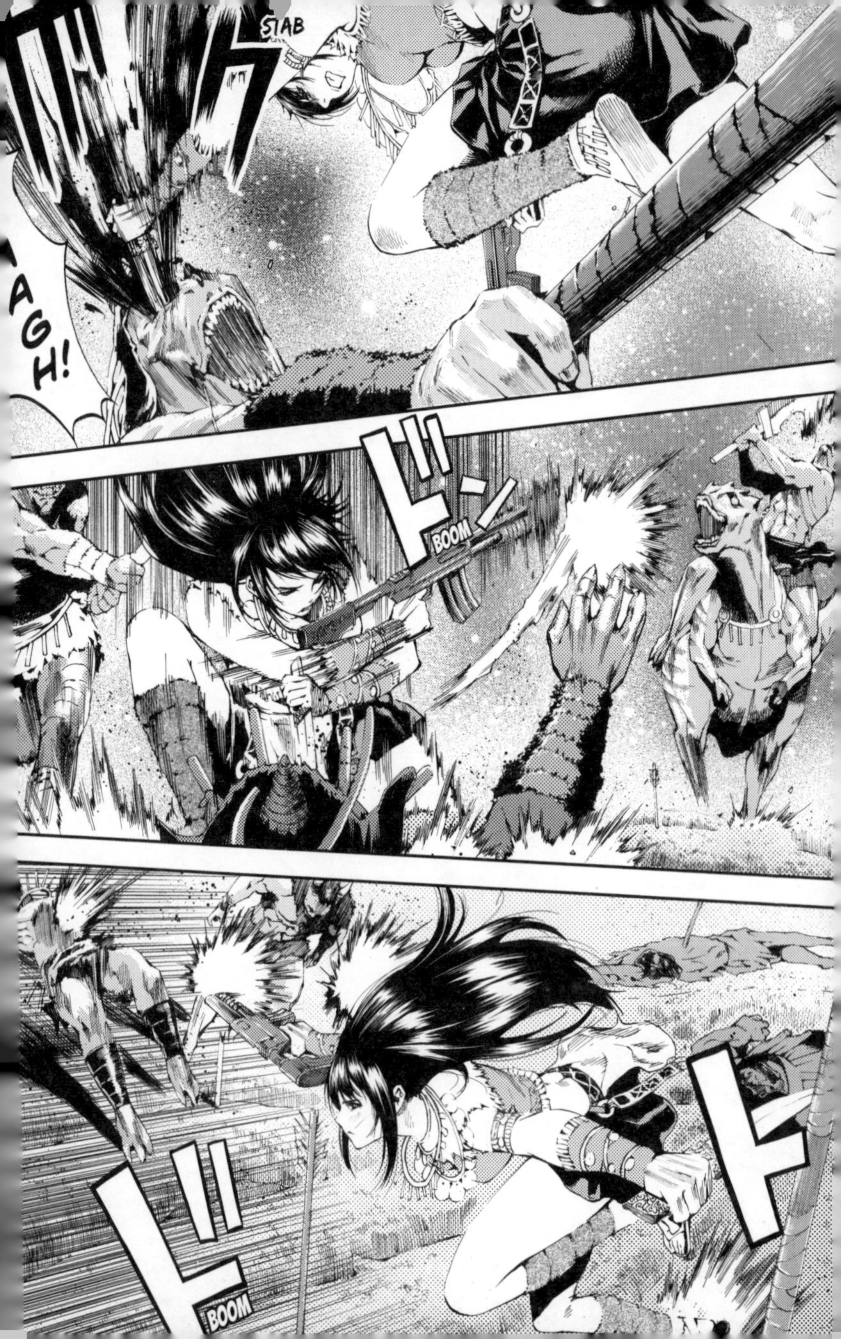
STAB
AGH!
ドーン
BOOM
ド
ドド
BOOM

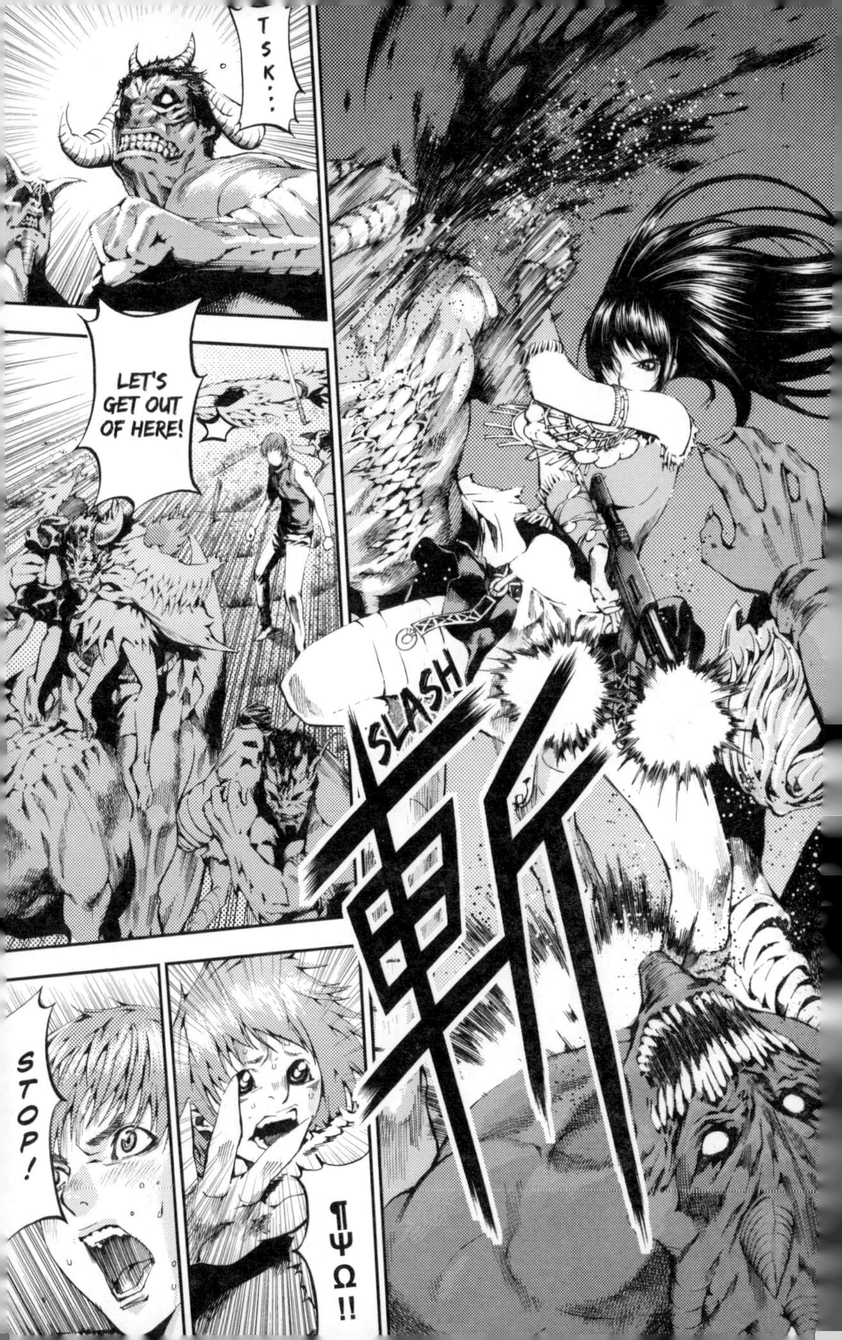
SLASH
斬
TSK...
LET'S GET OUT OF HERE!
¶ΨΩ!!
STOP!

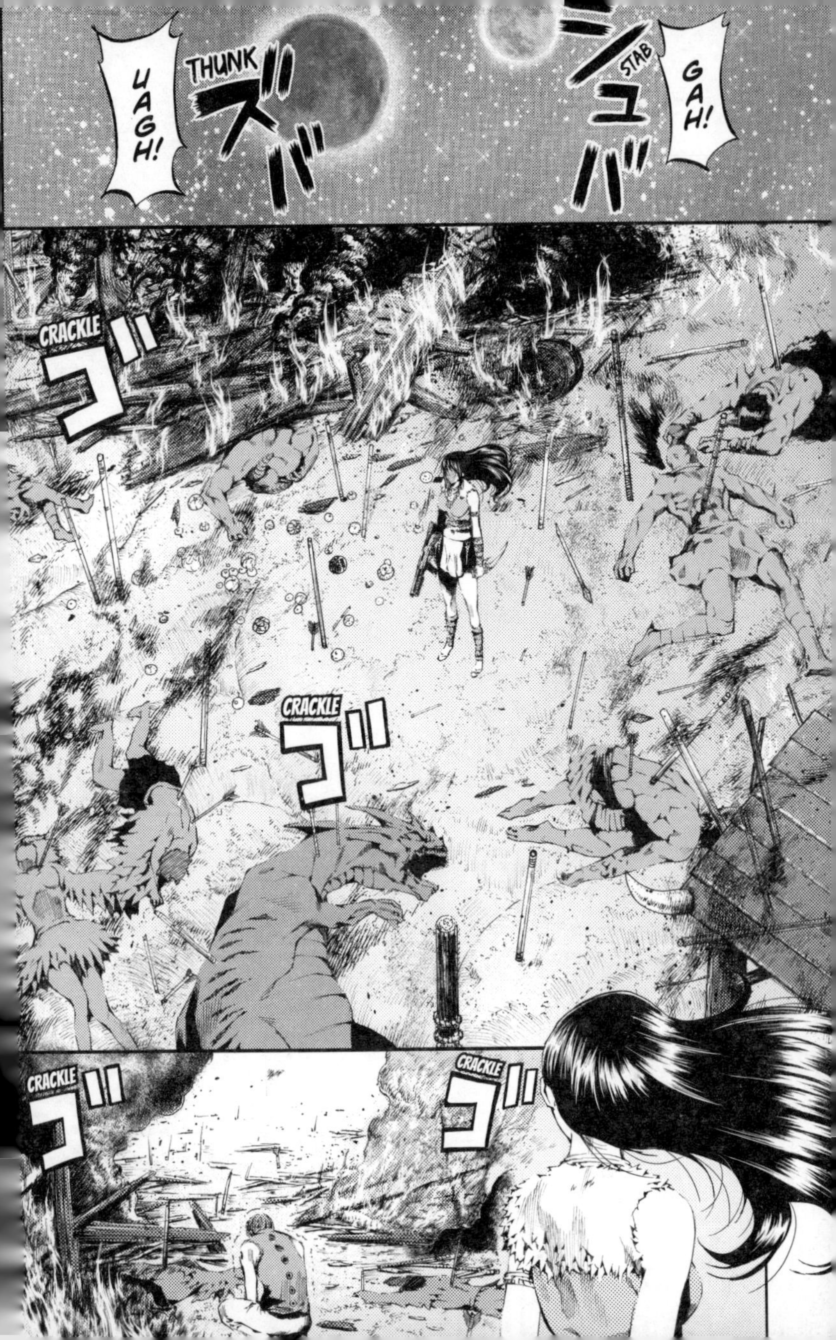
GAH!
STAB
THUNK
UAGH!
CRACKLE
CRACKLE
CRACKLE
CRACKLE

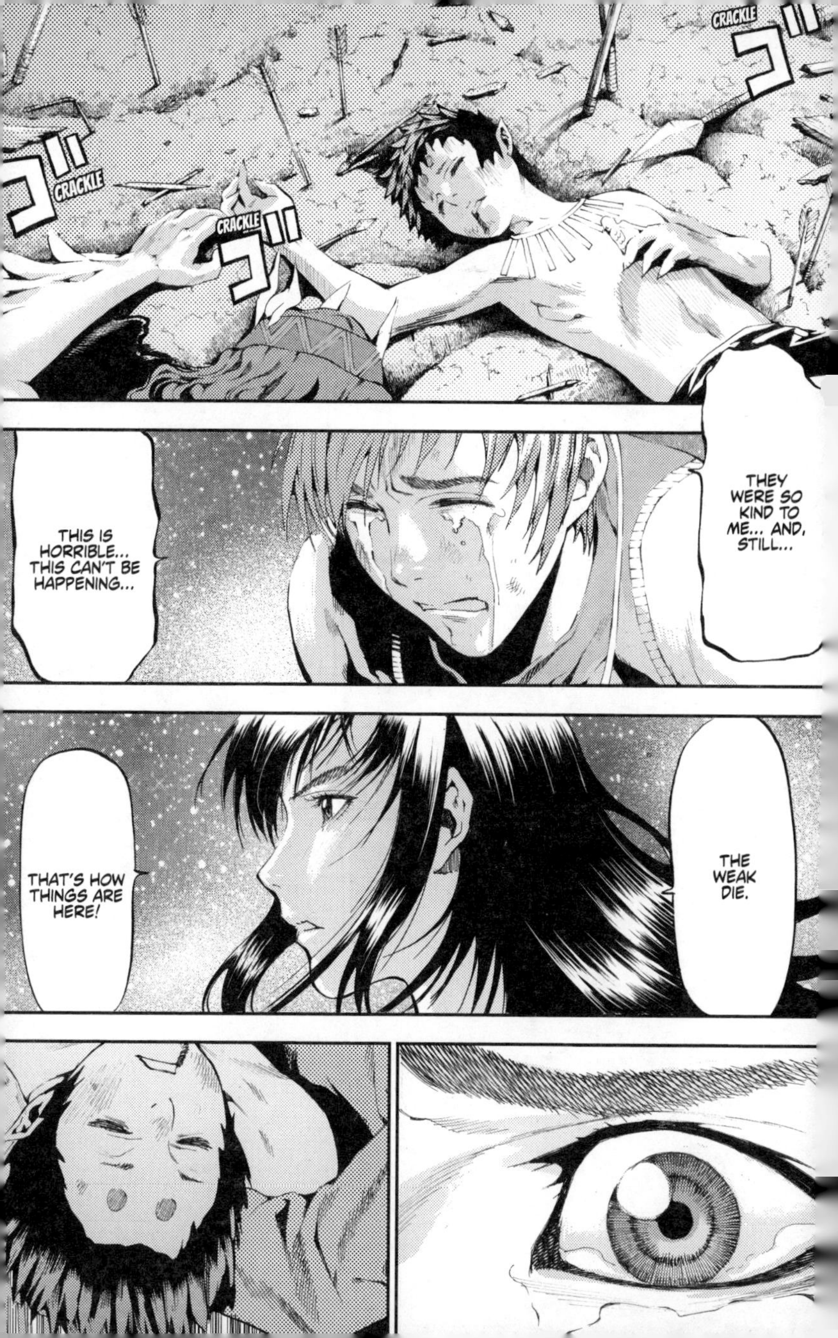

CRACKLE
ゴ
CRACKLE
ゴ
CRACKLE
ゴ
THEY WERE SO KIND TO ME... AND, STILL...
THIS IS HORRIBLE... THIS CAN'T BE HAPPENING...
THE WEAK DIE.
THAT'S HOW THINGS ARE HERE!

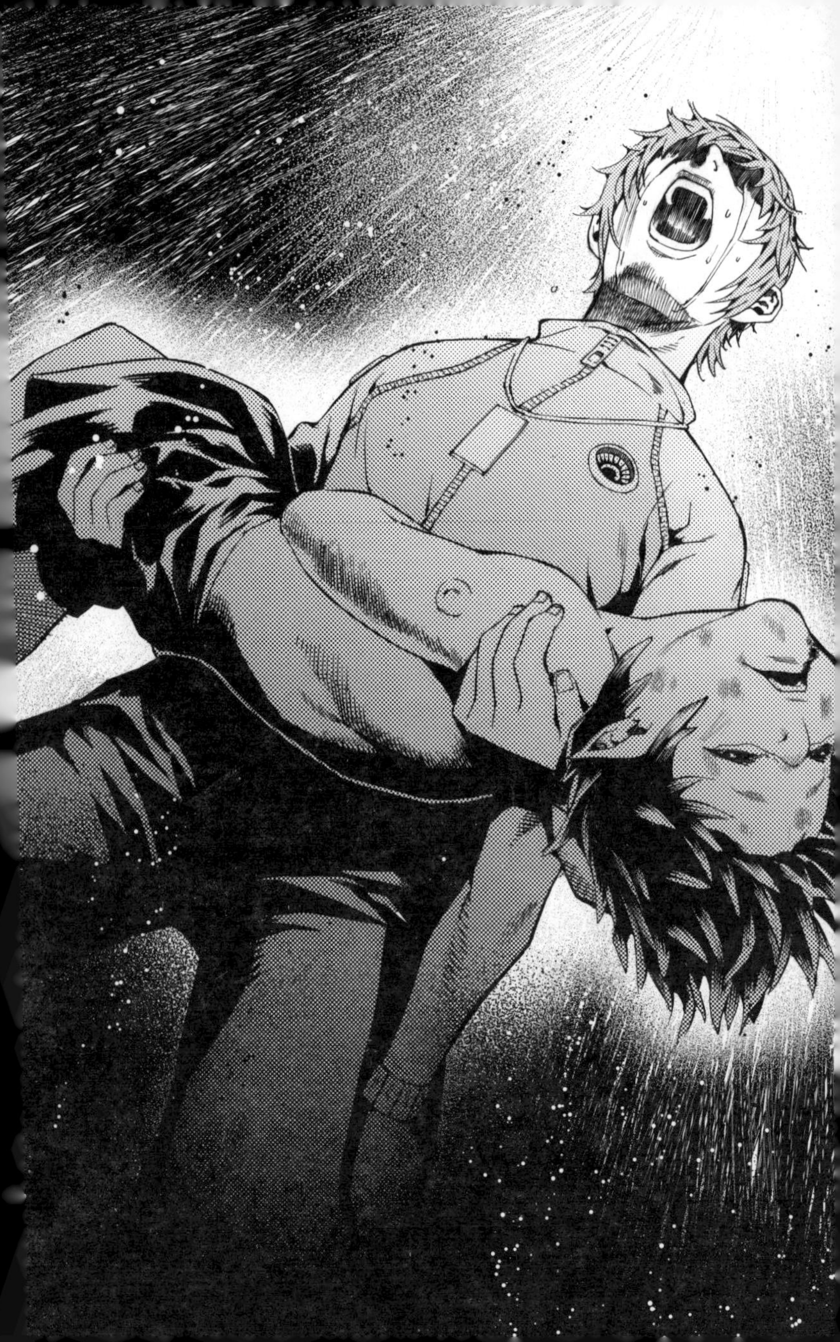

MOMO
LEGENDARY WARRIOR

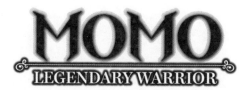

MOMO

LEGENDARY WARRIOR

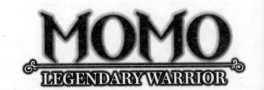

Chapter 2 Desolation and Hope

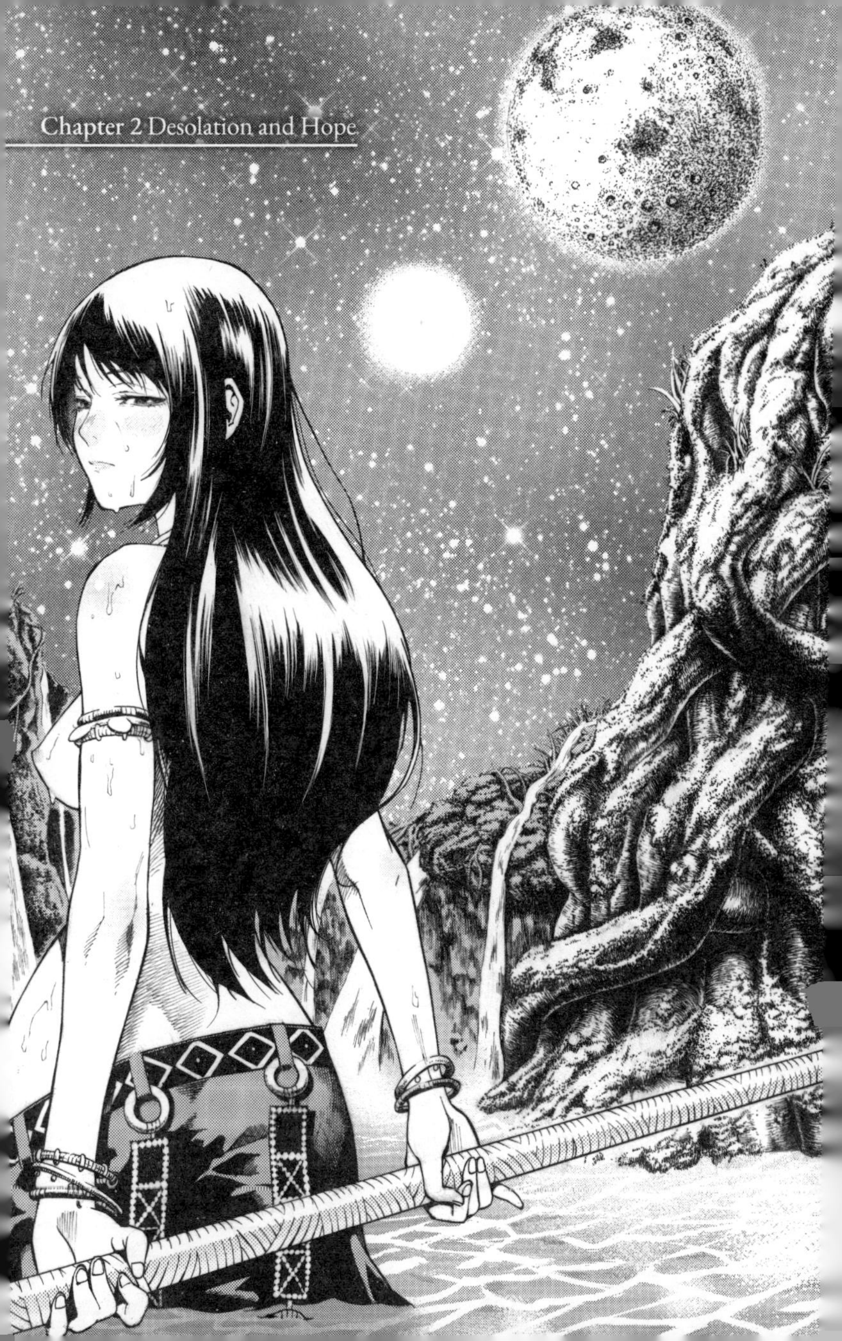

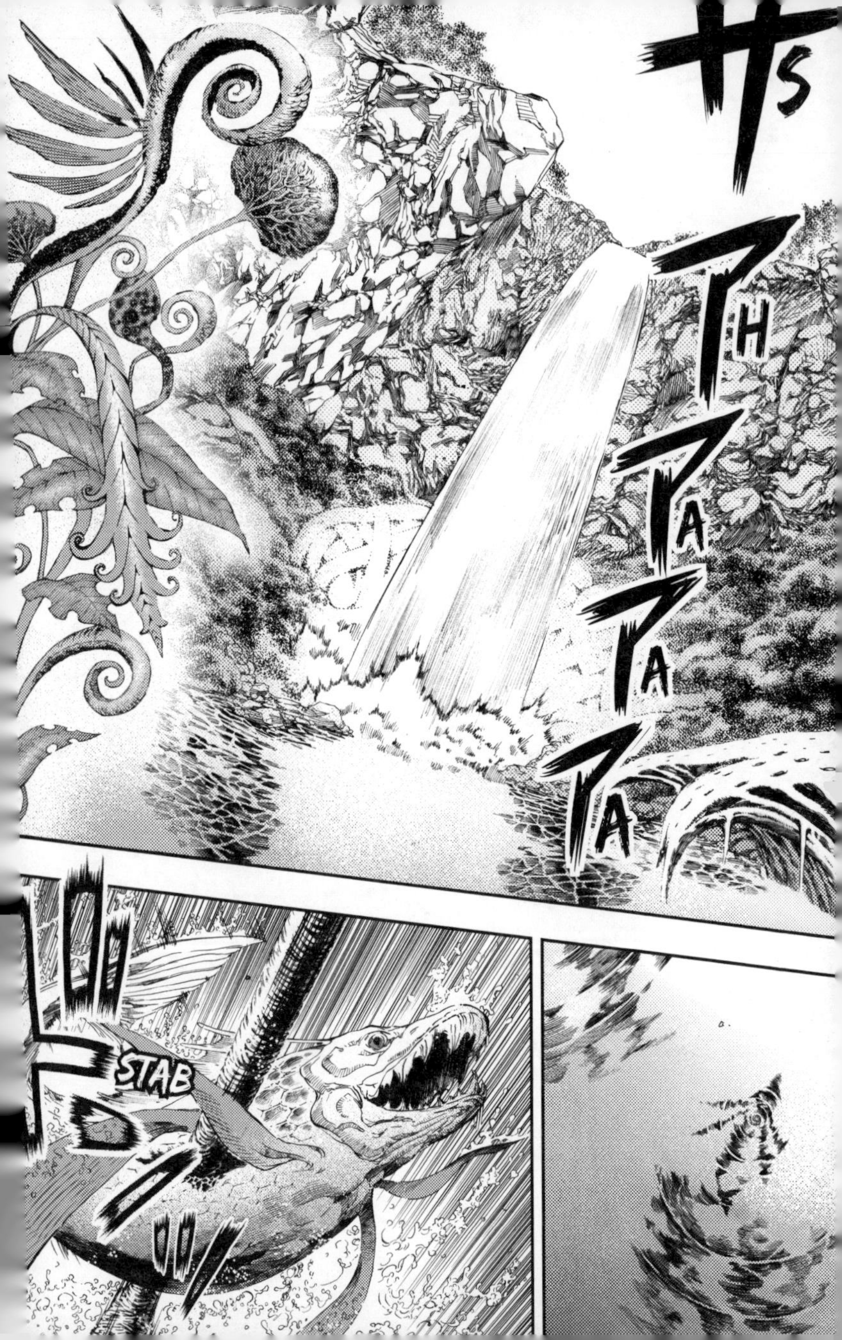
S
TH
STAB

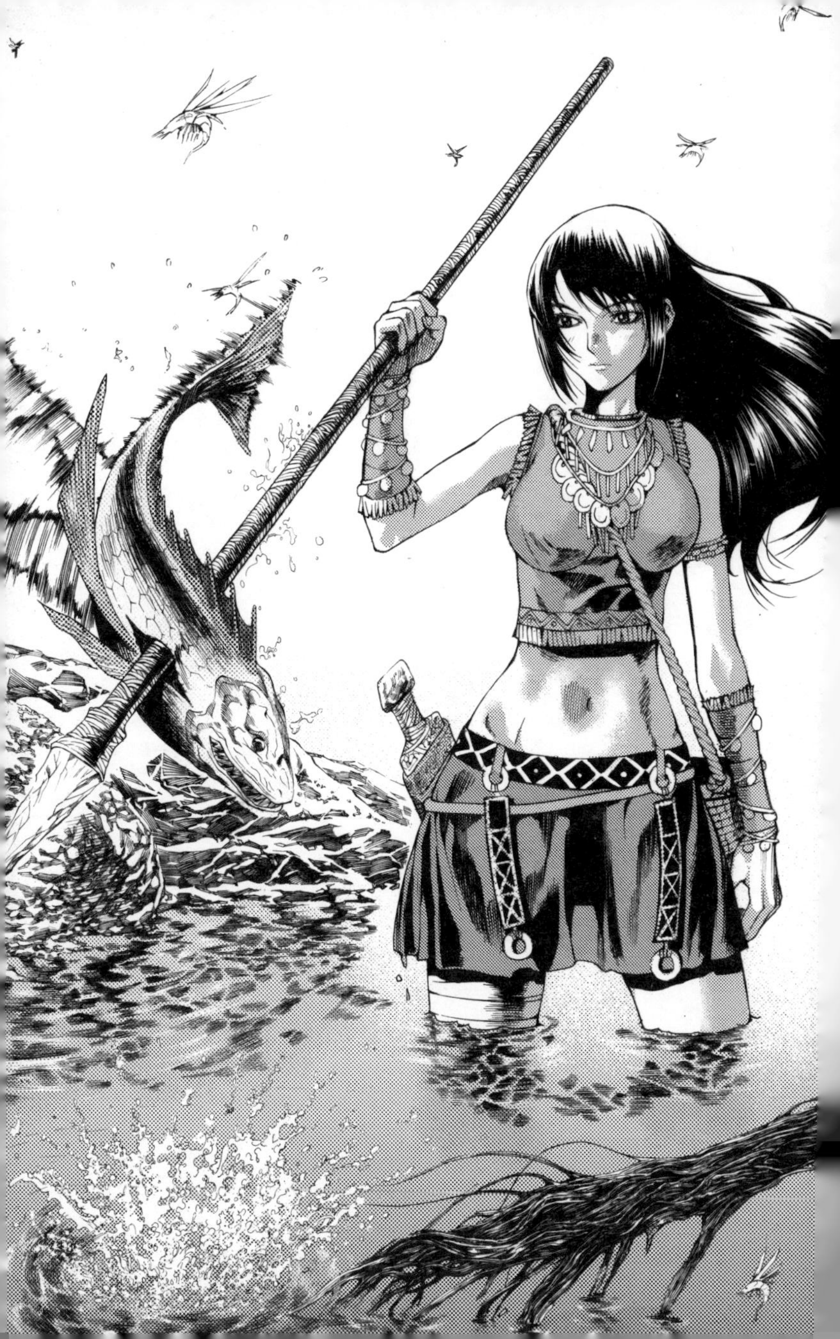

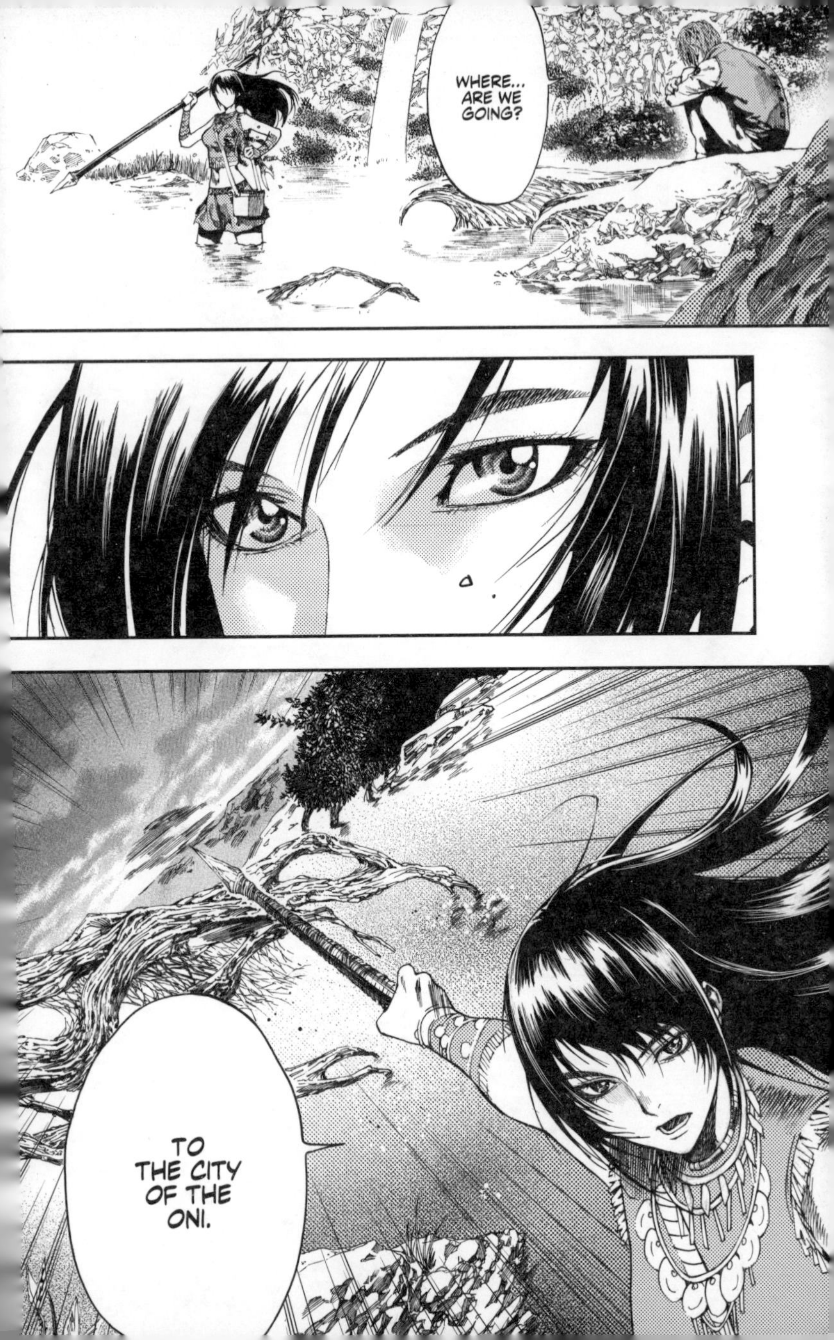
WHERE... ARE WE GOING?
TO THE CITY OF THE ONI.

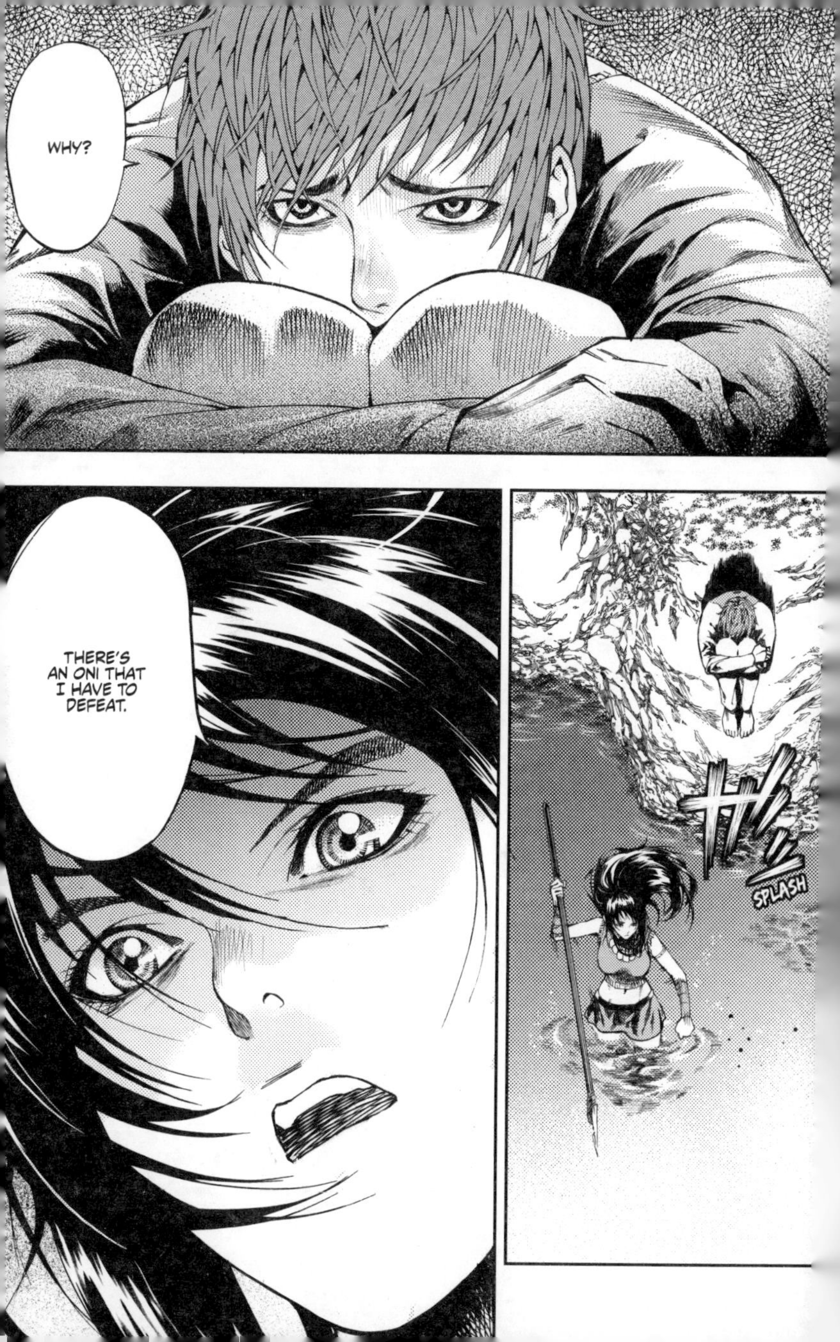
WHY?
SPLASH
THERE'S AN ONI THAT I HAVE TO DEFEAT.

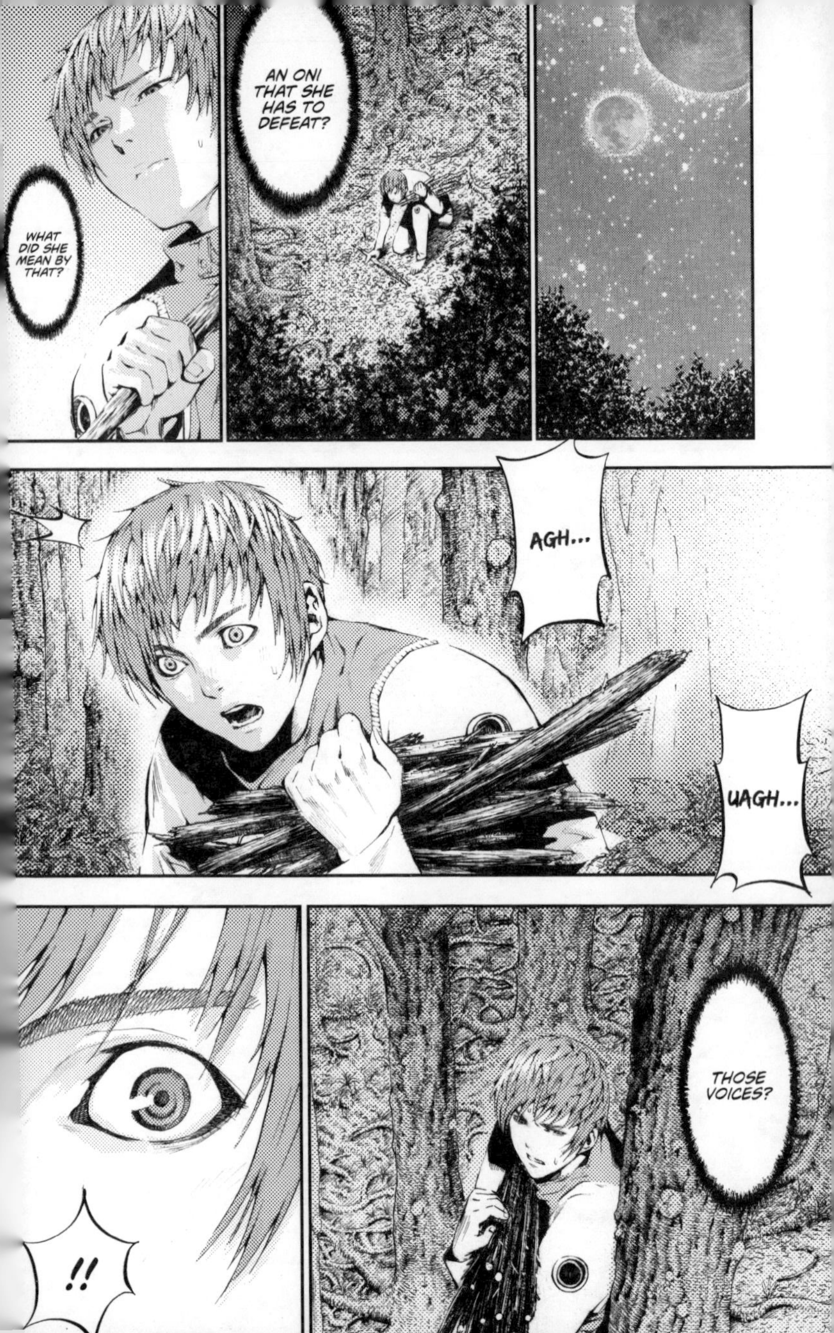
AN ONI THAT SHE HAS TO DEFEAT?
WHAT DID SHE MEAN BY THAT?
AGH...
UAGH...
THOSE VOICES?
!!

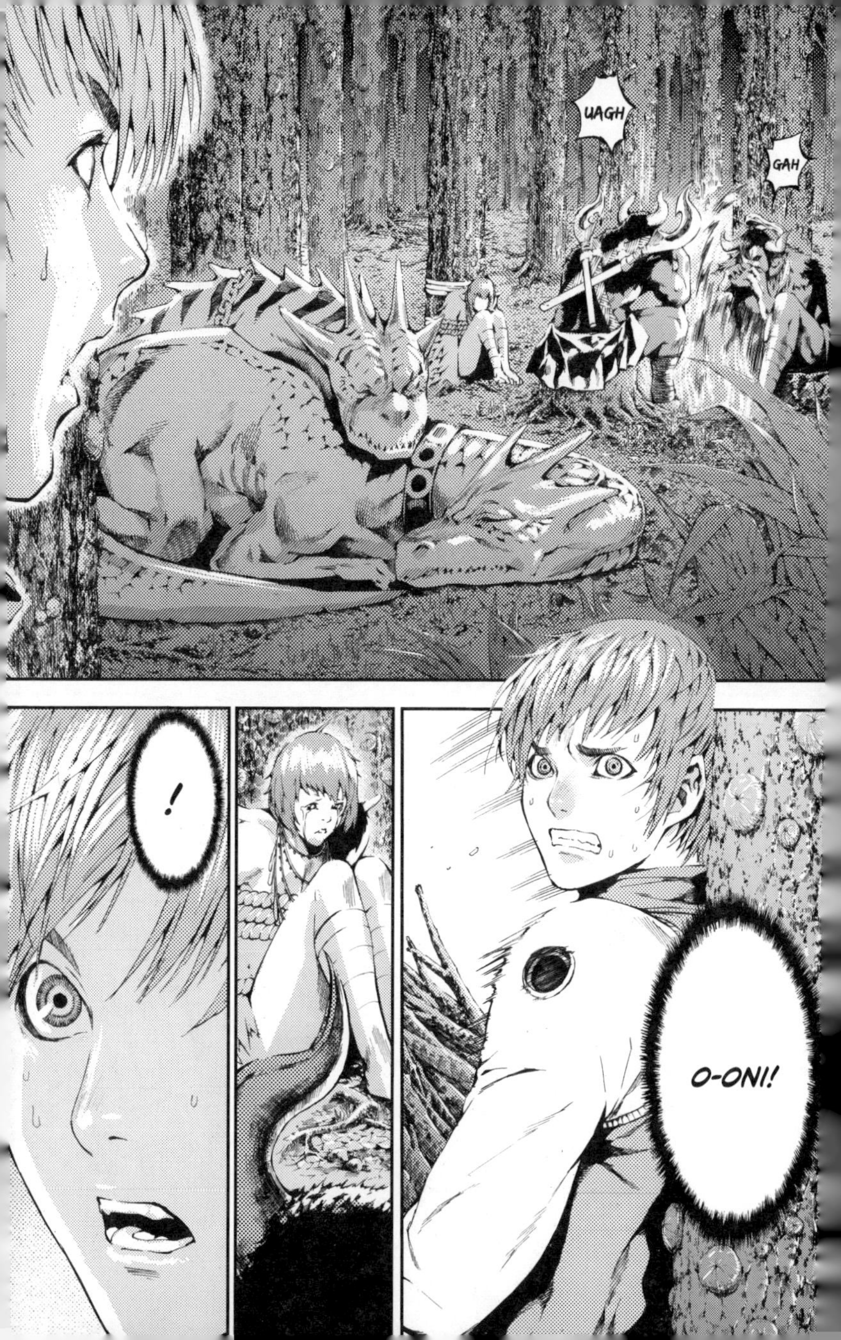
GAH
UAGH
O-ONI!
!

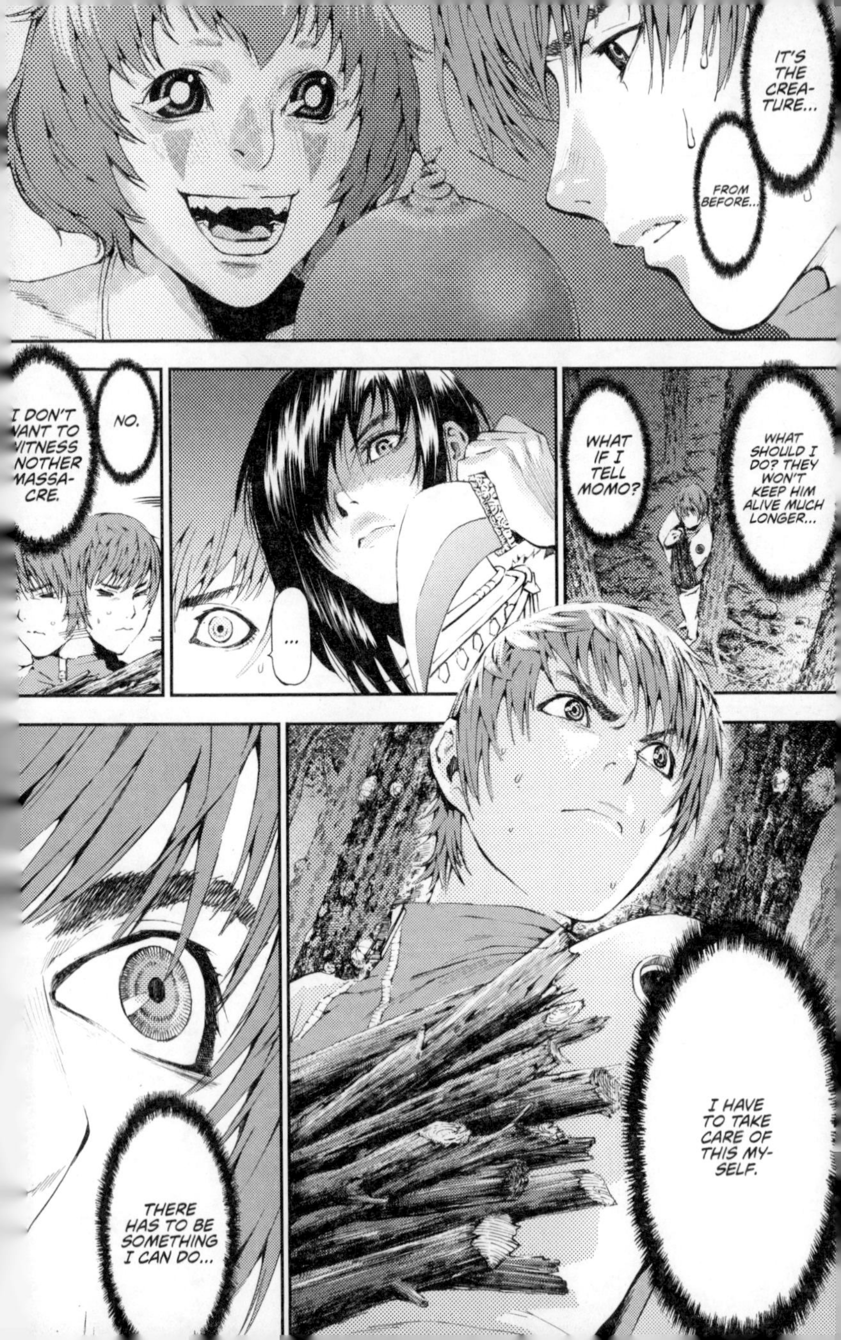
IT'S THE CREATURE...
FROM BEFORE...
WHAT SHOULD I DO? THEY WON'T KEEP HIM ALIVE MUCH LONGER...
WHAT IF I TELL MOMO?
...
NO.
I DON'T WANT TO WITNESS ANOTHER MASSACRE.
I HAVE TO TAKE CARE OF THIS MYSELF.
THERE HAS TO BE SOMETHING I CAN DO...

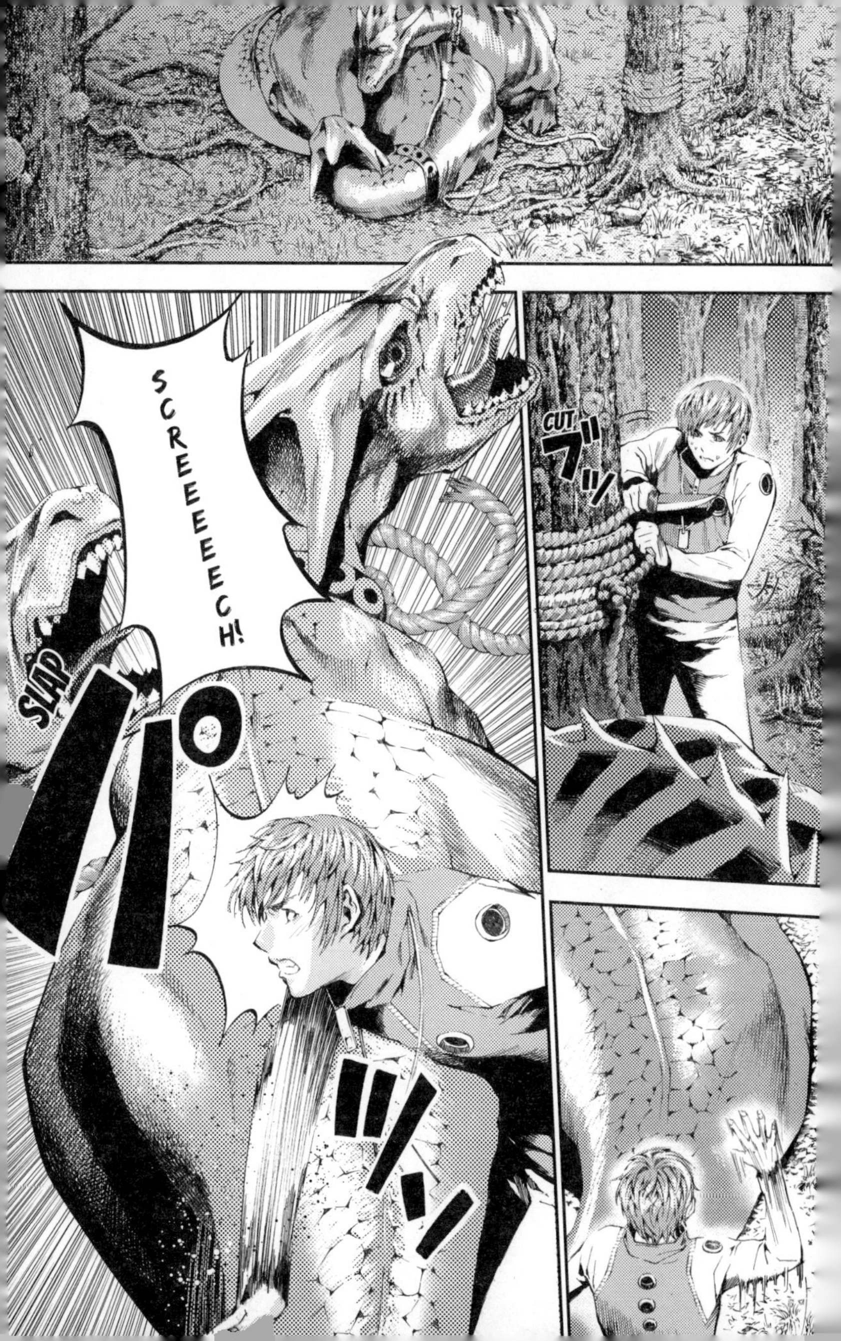
CUT
ブッ
SCREEEEECH!
SLAP

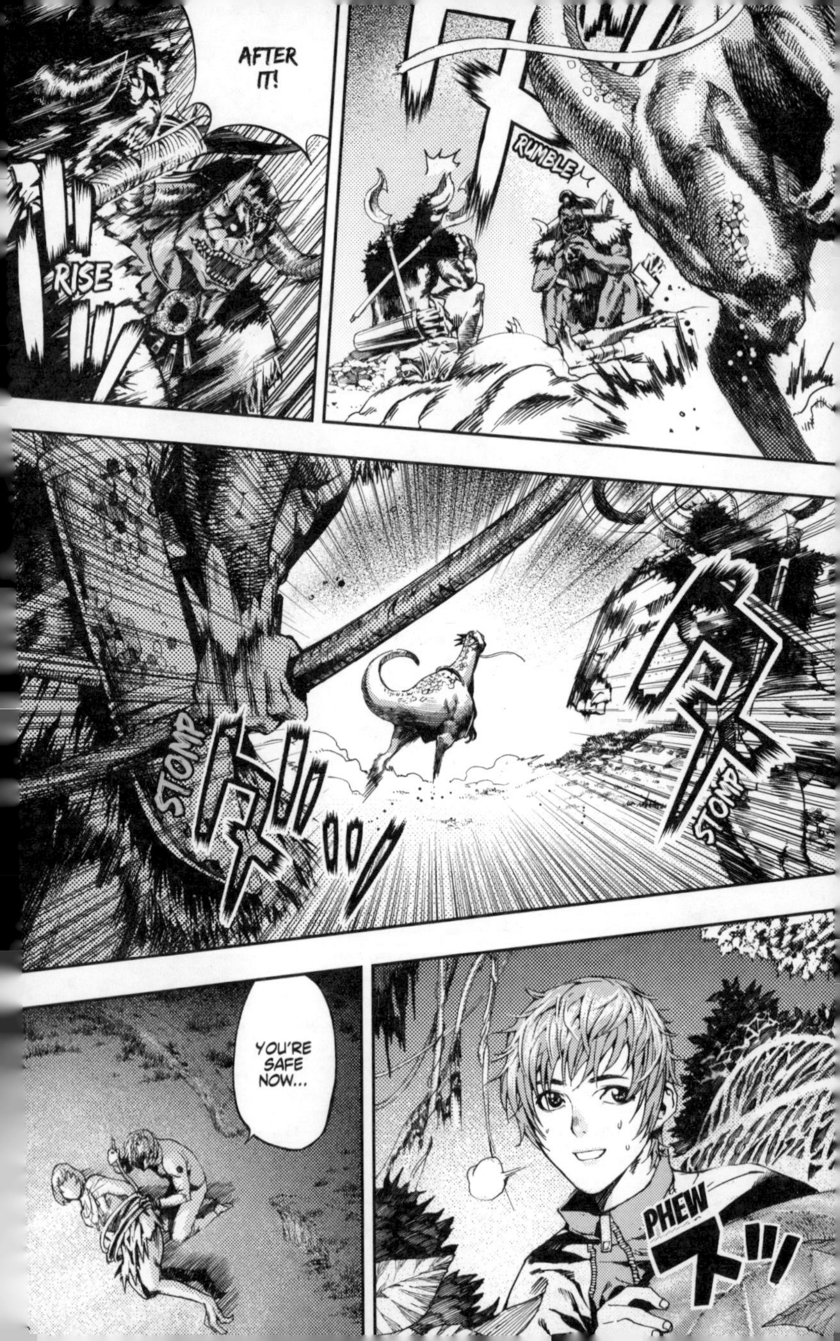
RUMBLE
AFTER IT!
RISE
STOMP
STOMP
PHEW
YOU'RE SAFE NOW...

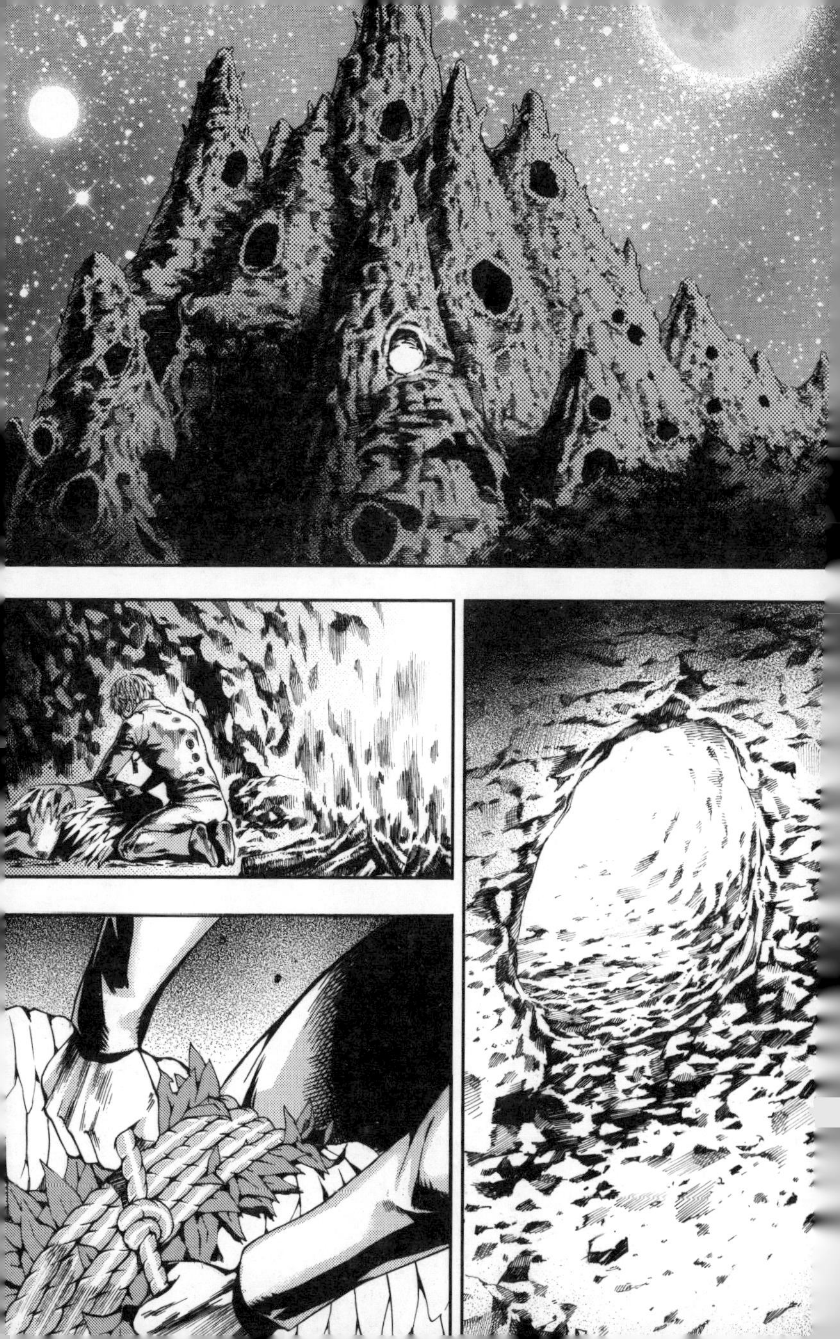

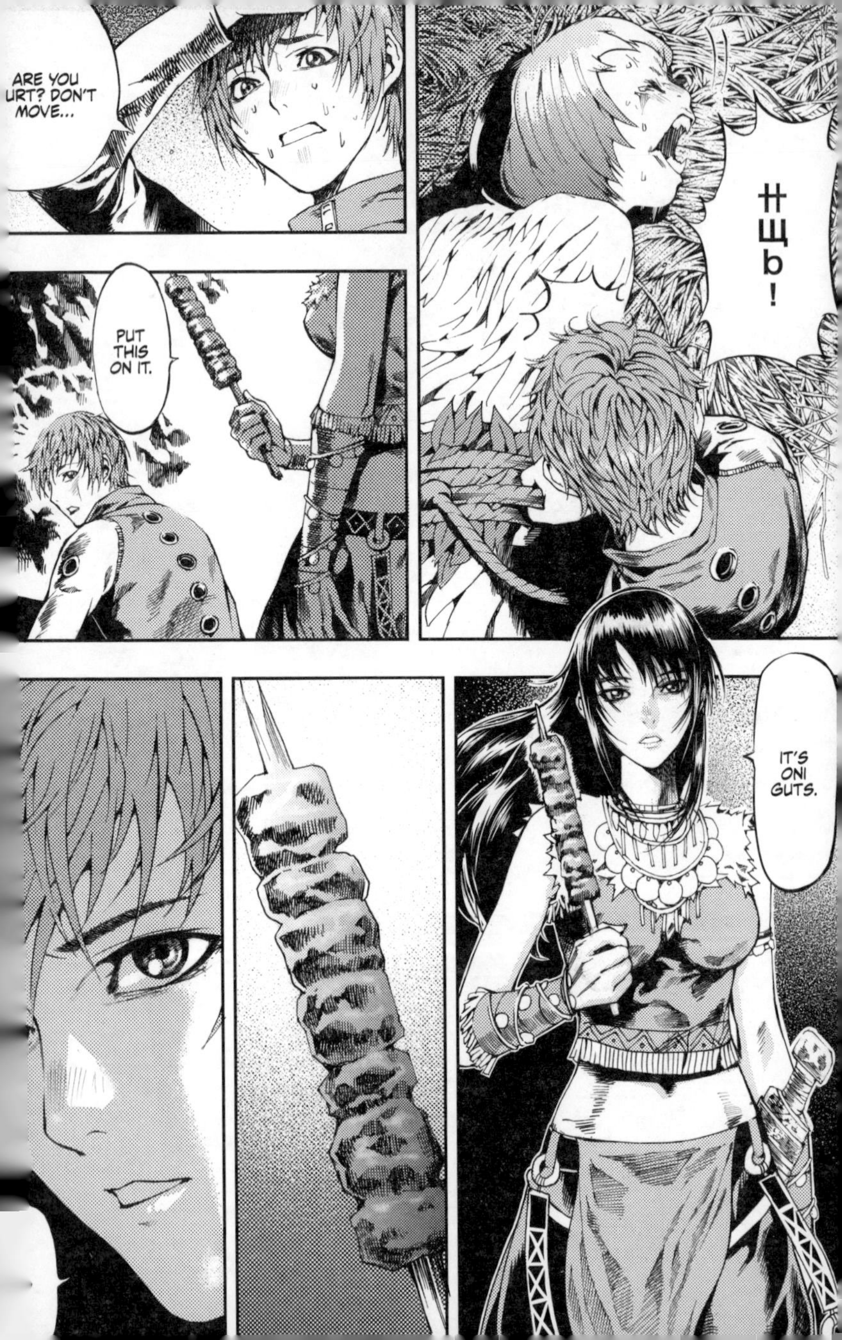
ARE YOU URT? DON'T MOVE...
PUT THIS ON IT.
IT'S ONI GUTS.

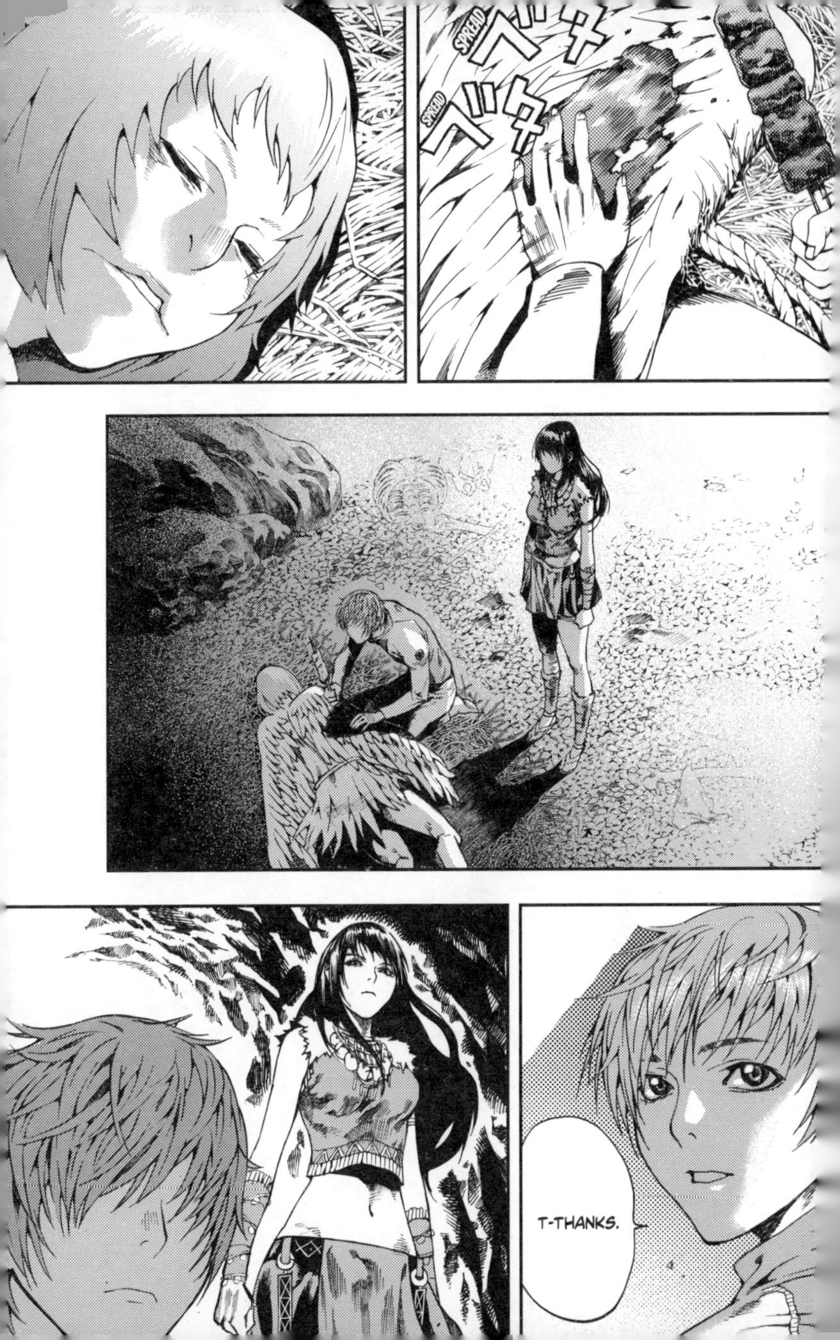
SPREAD
SPREAD
T-THANKS.

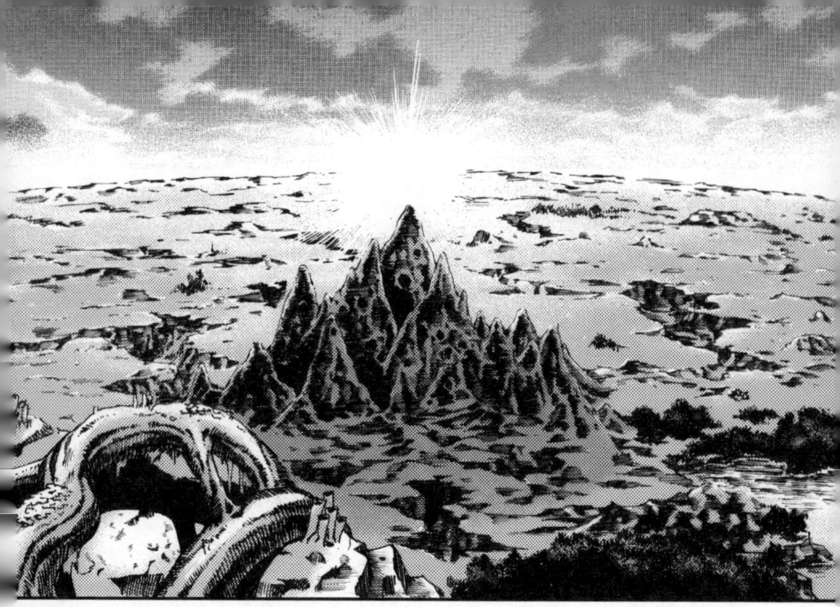

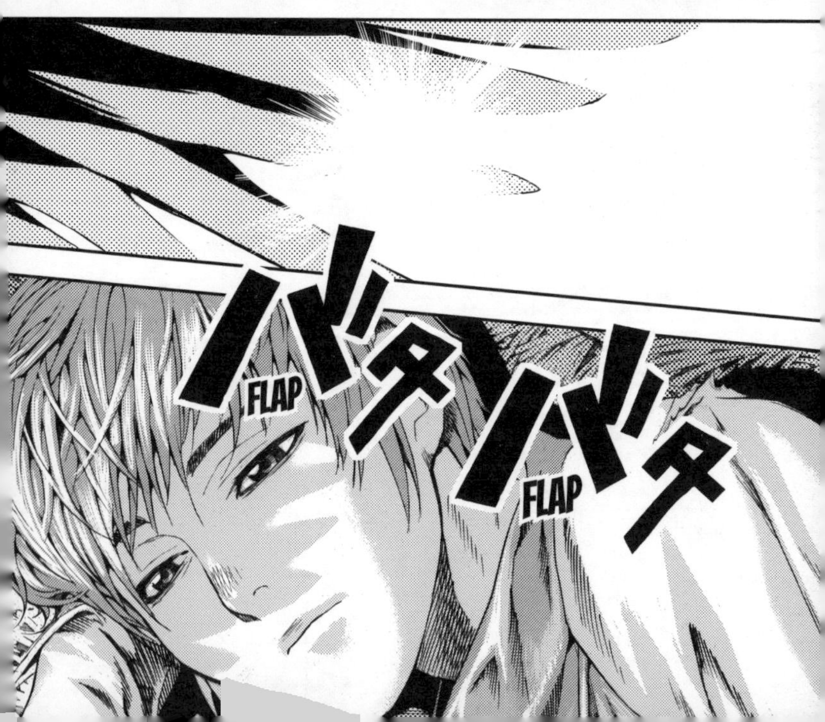
ハタ
FLAP
ハタ
FLAP

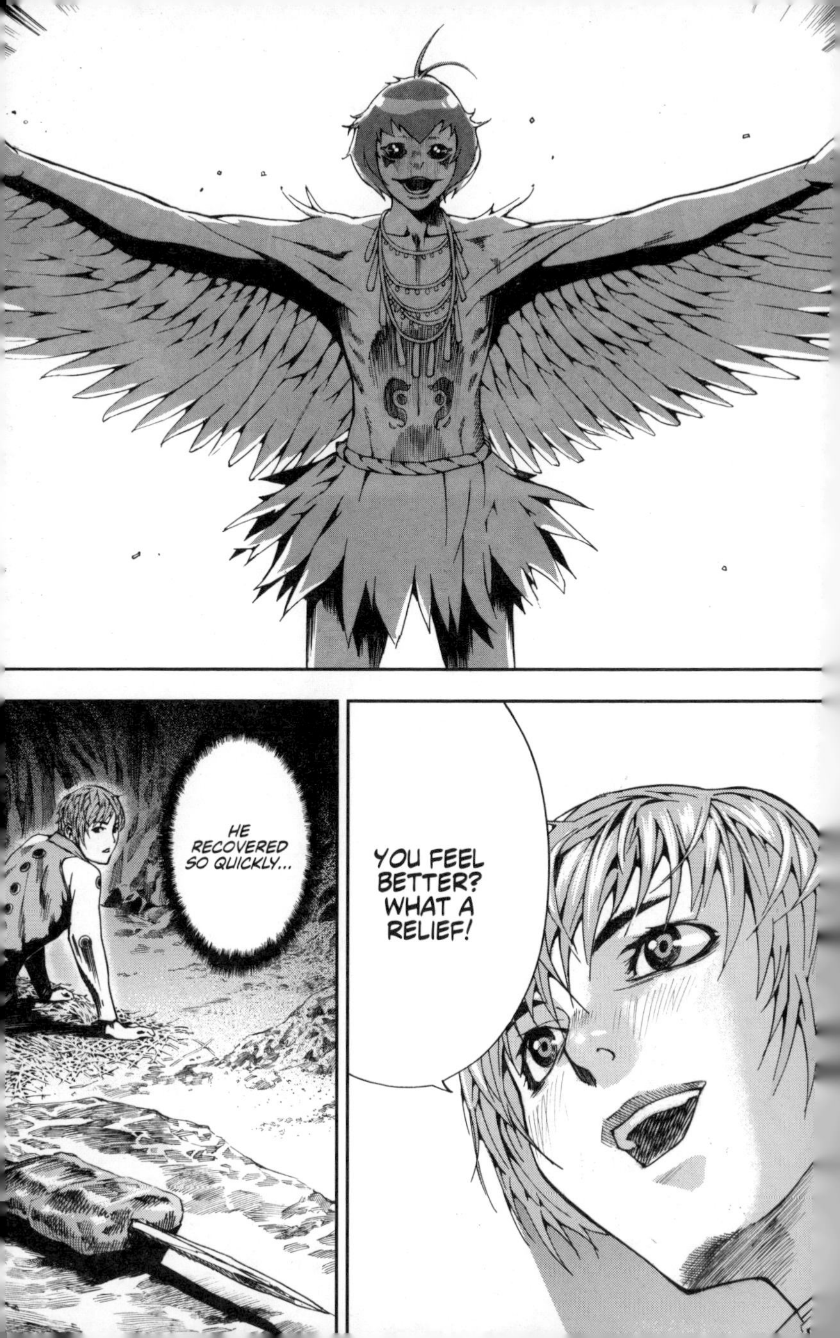
YOU FEEL BETTER? WHAT A RELIEF!
HE RECOVERED SO QUICKLY...

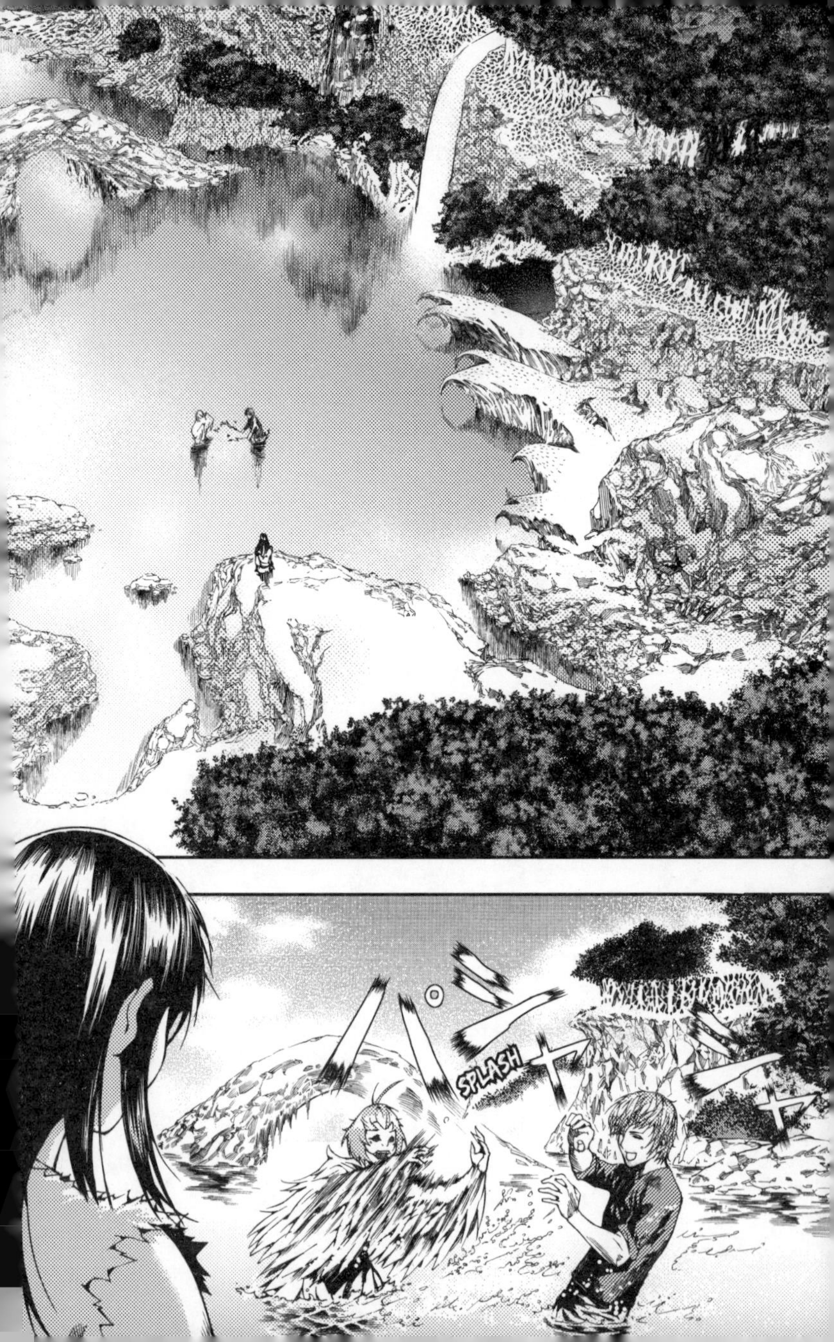
SPLASH

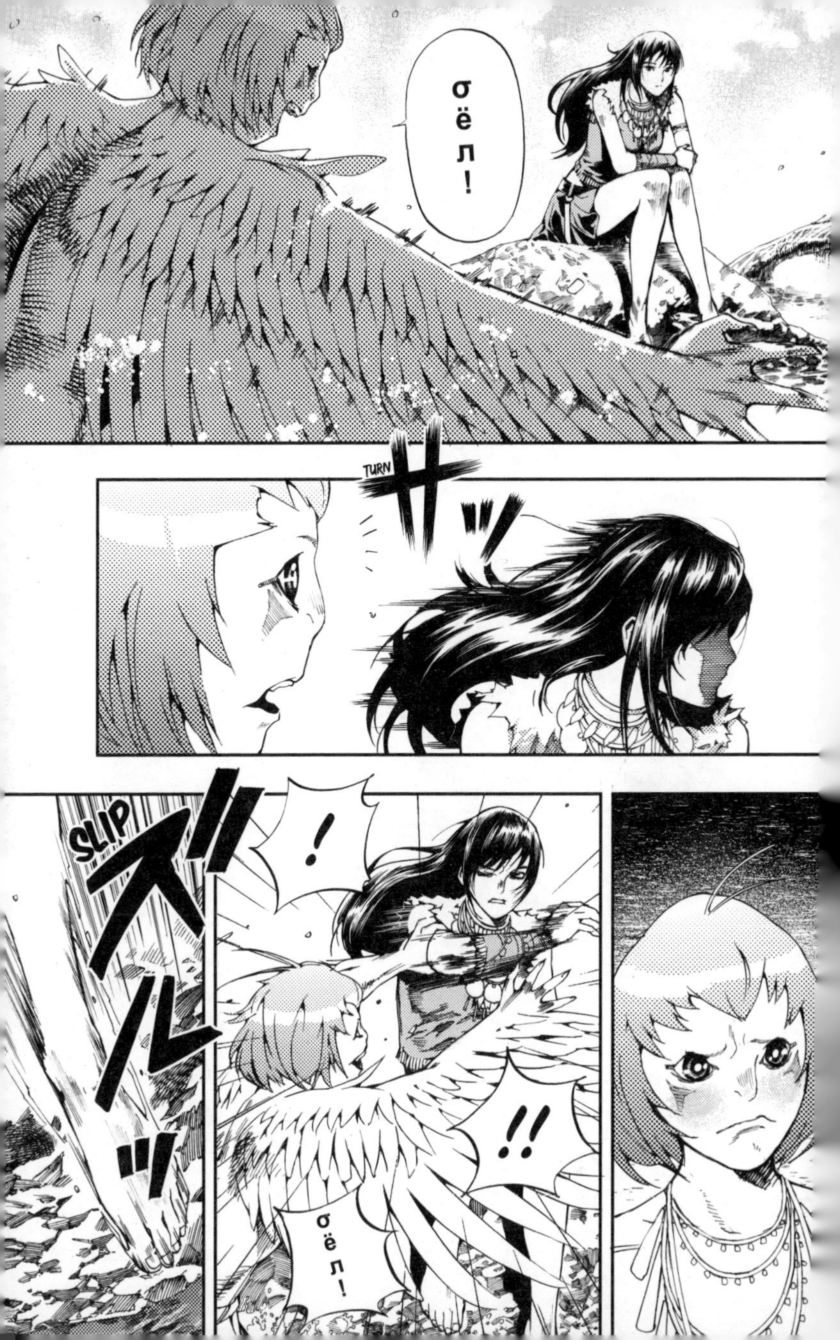
σёл!
TURN
ザッ
!
!!
σёл!
SLIP
ズルッ

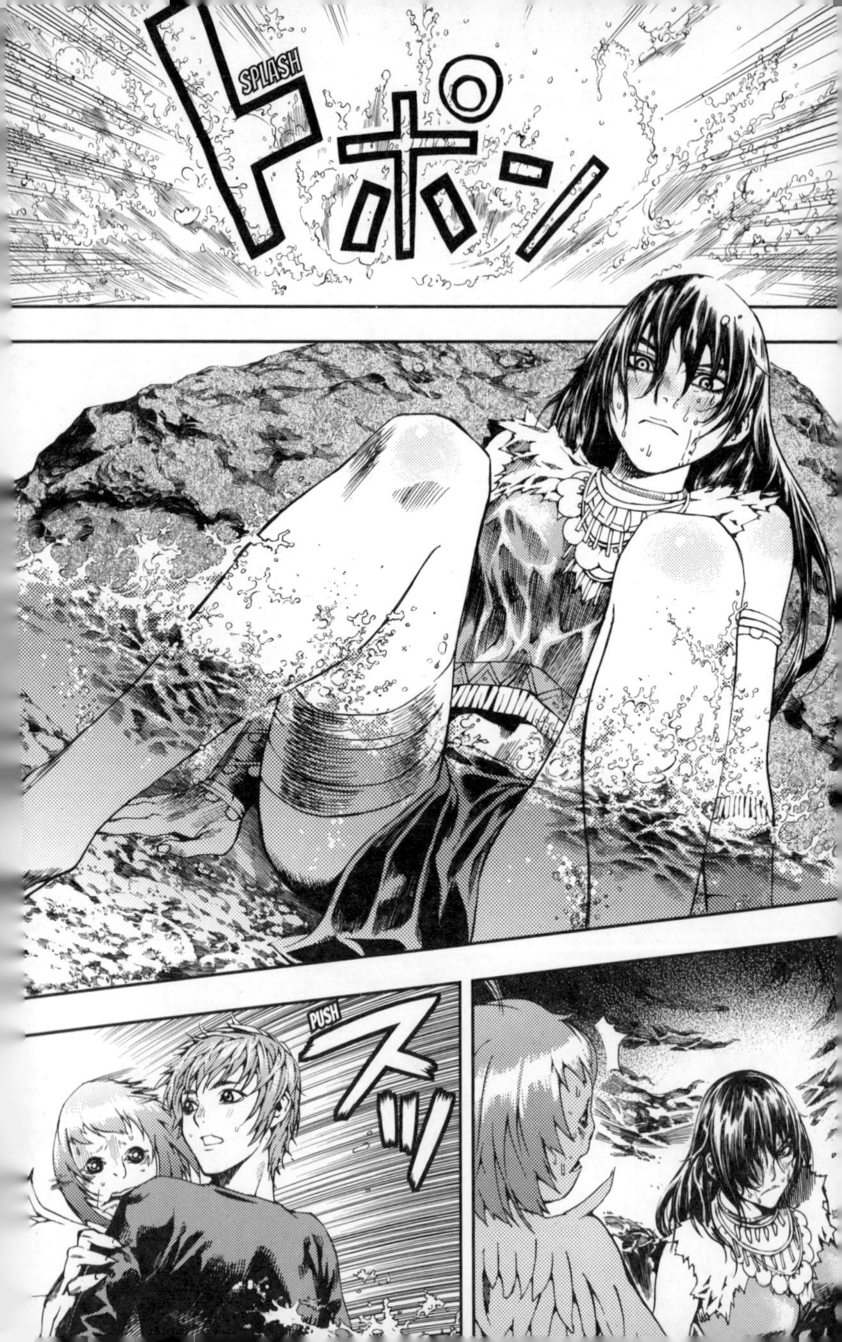
ドポーン
SPLASH
スッ
PUSH

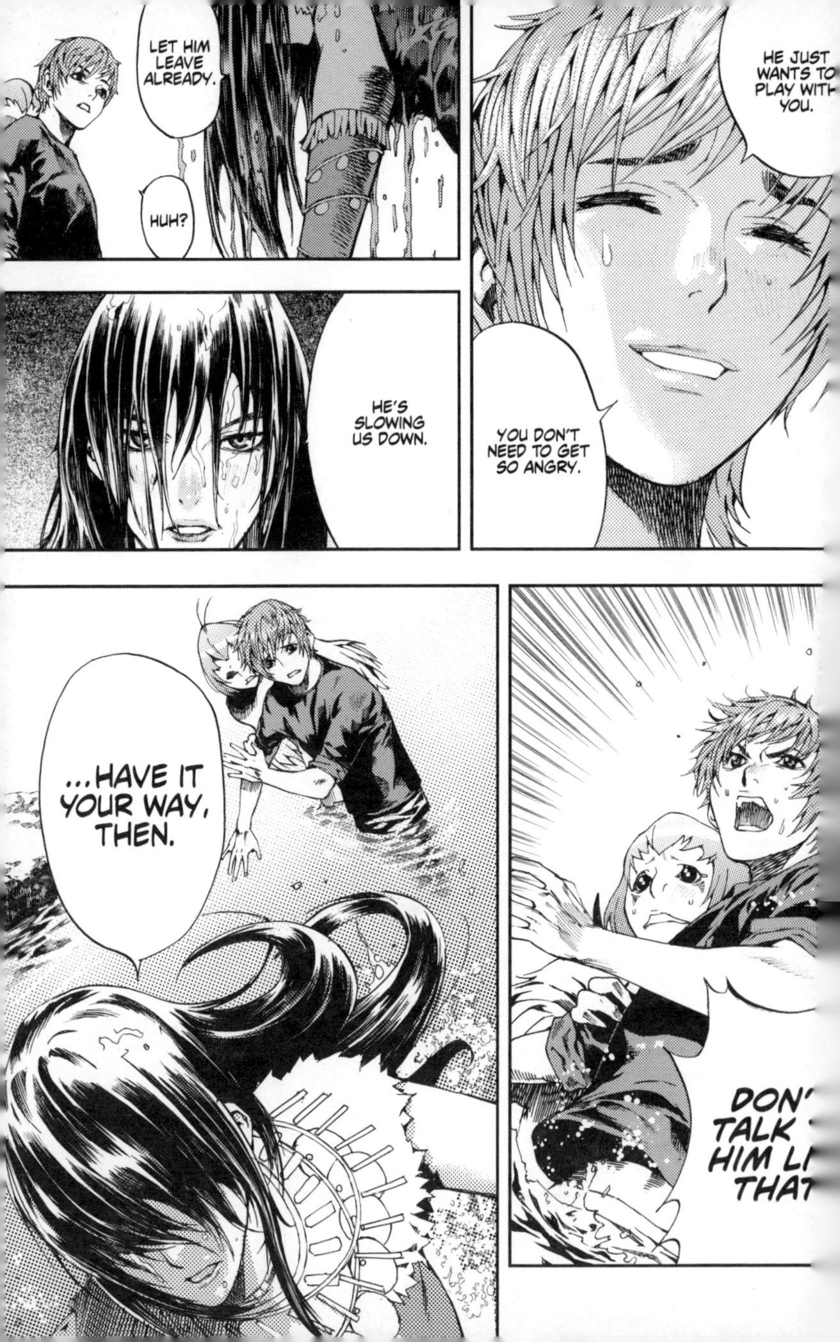
HE JUST WANTS TO PLAY WITH YOU.
YOU DON'T NEED TO GET SO ANGRY.
LET HIM LEAVE ALREADY.
HUH?
HE'S SLOWING US DOWN.
DON' TALK HIM LI THAT
...HAVE IT YOUR WAY, THEN.

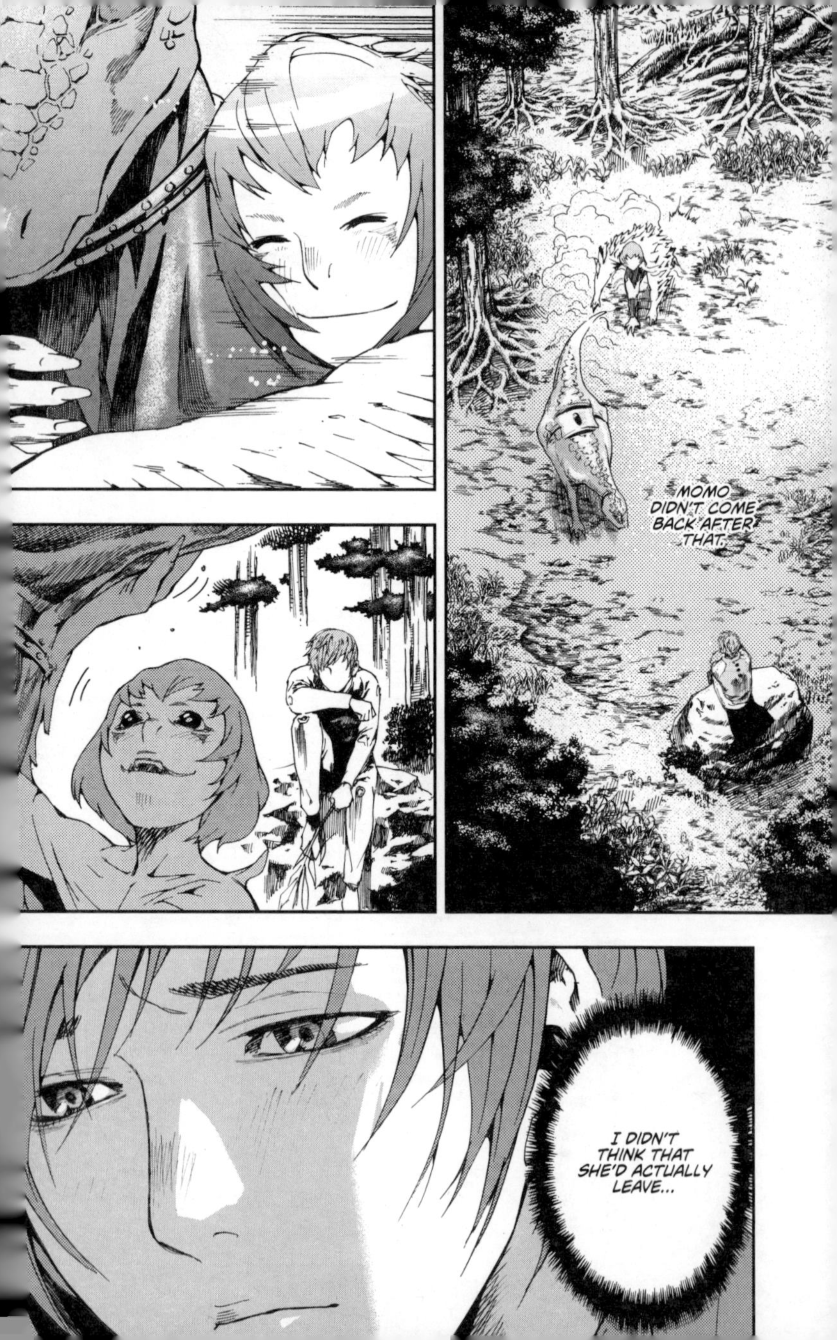
MOMO DIDN'T COME BACK AFTER THAT.
I DIDN'T THINK THAT SHE'D ACTUALLY LEAVE...

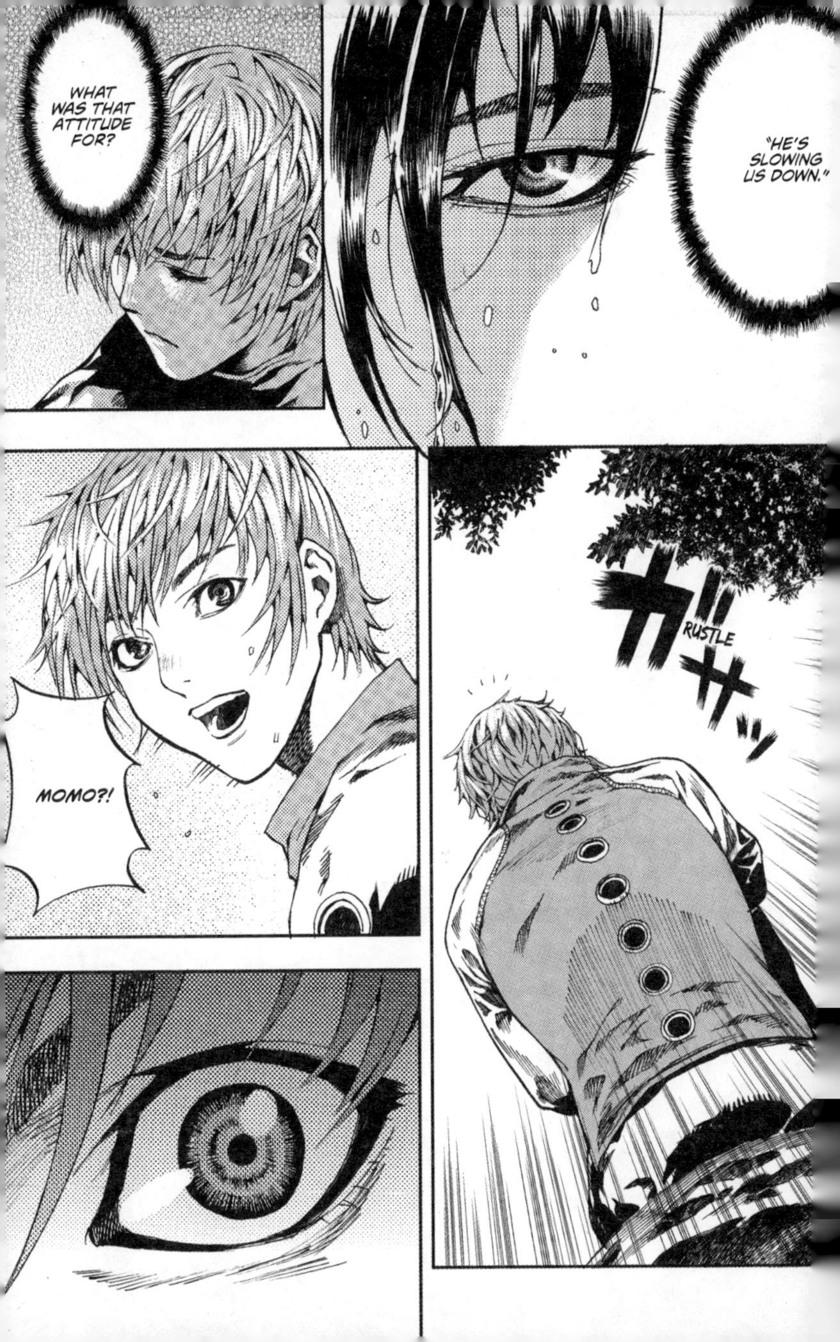
"HE'S SLOWING US DOWN."
WHAT WAS THAT ATTITUDE FOR?
RUSTLE
MOMO?!

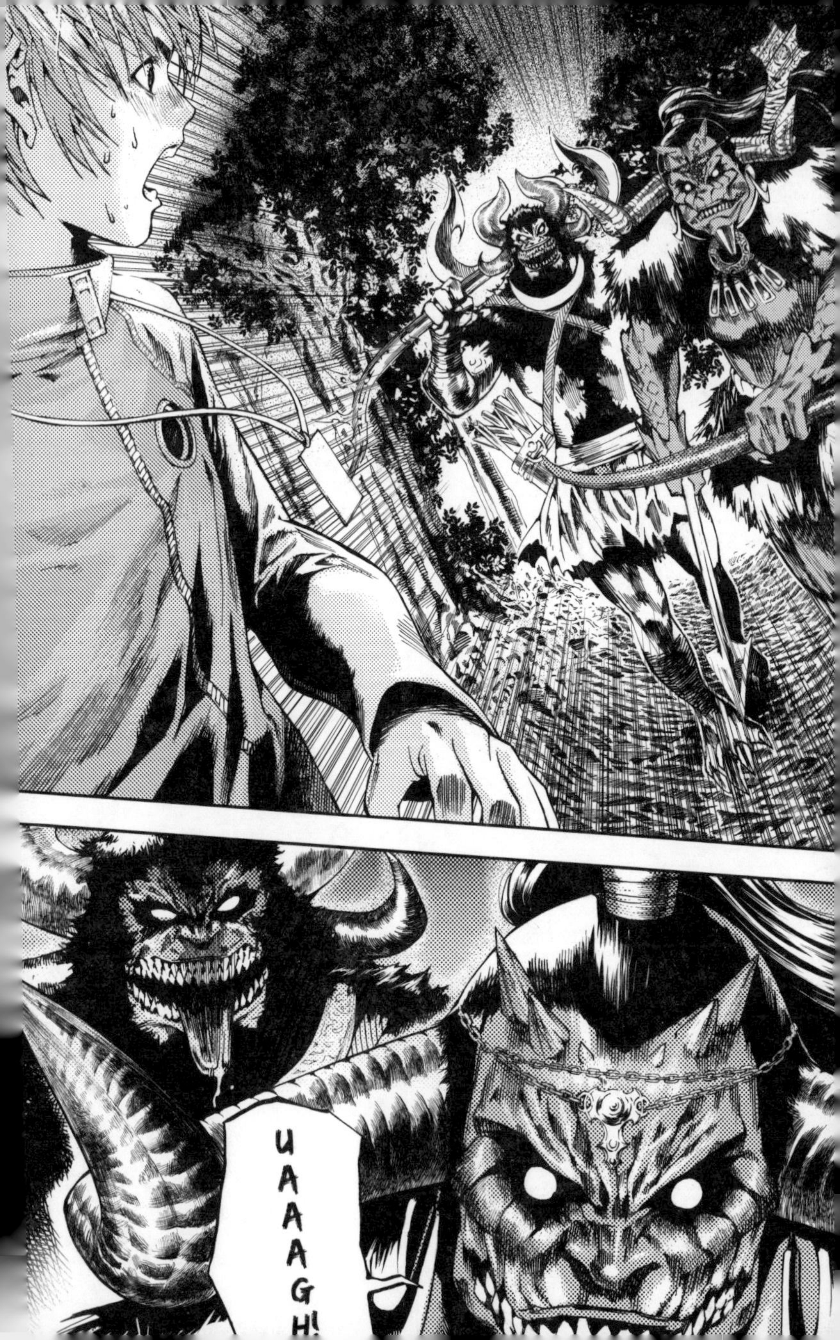
UAAAGH!

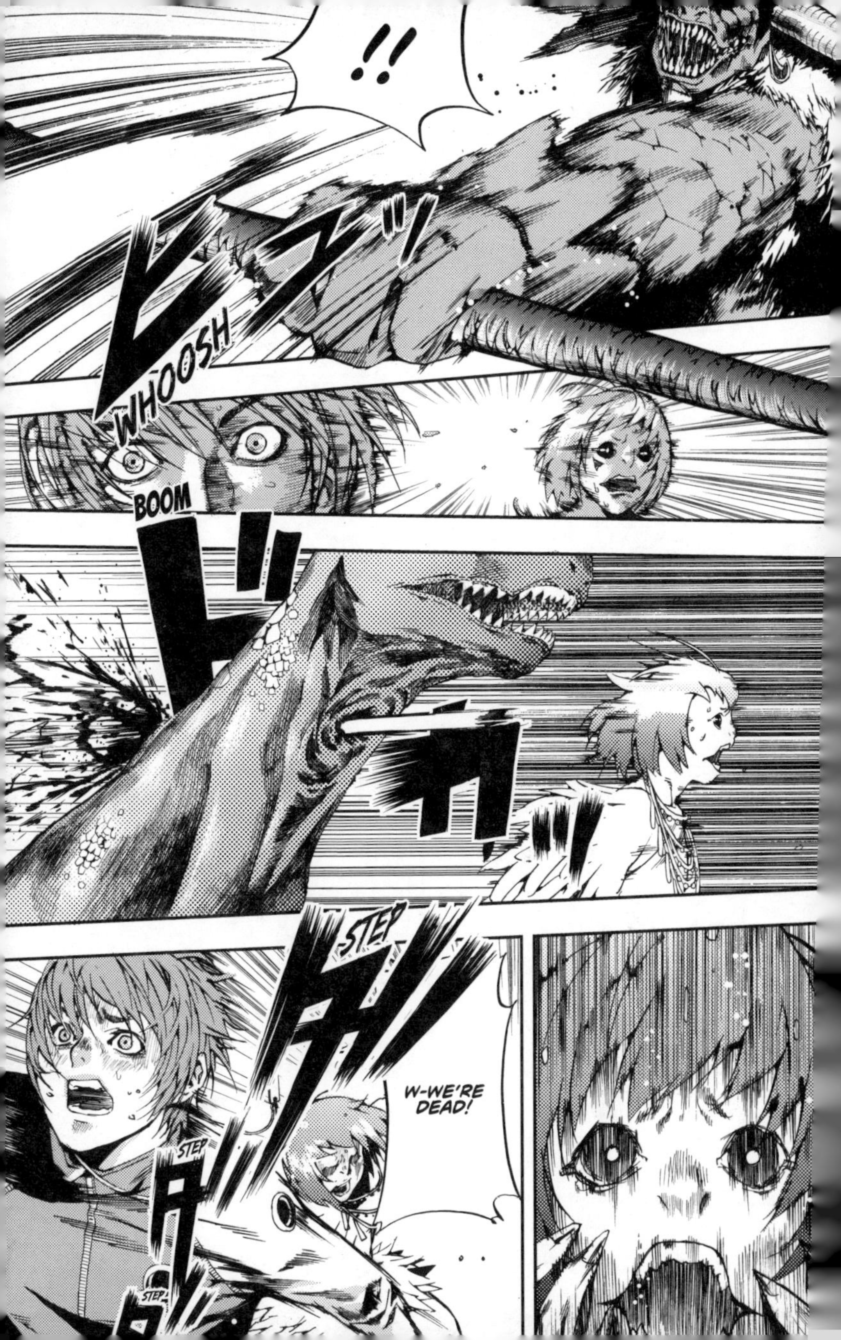

!!
WHOOSH
BOOM
STEP
W-WE'RE DEAD!
STEP
STEP

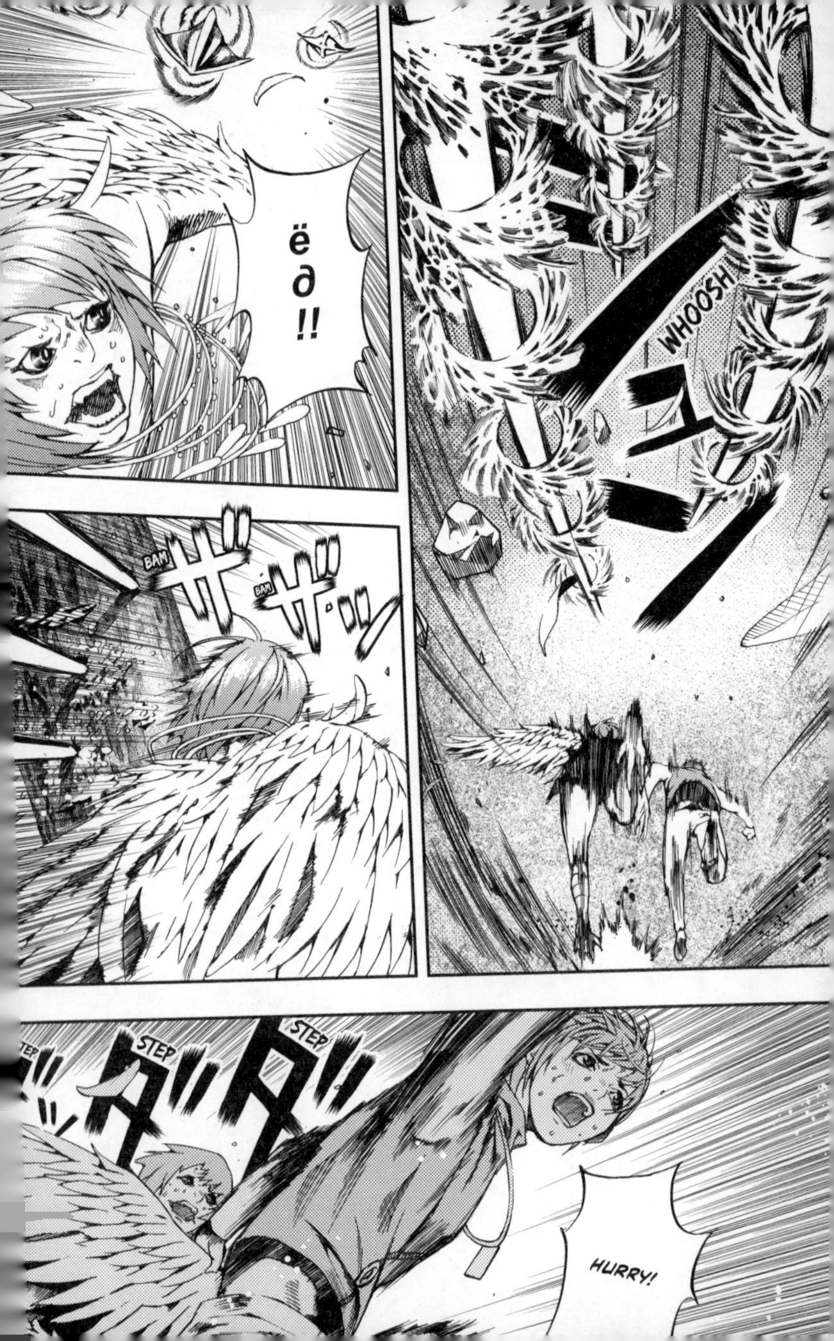
WHOOSH
ë∂!!
BAM
BAM
STEP
STEP
HURRY!

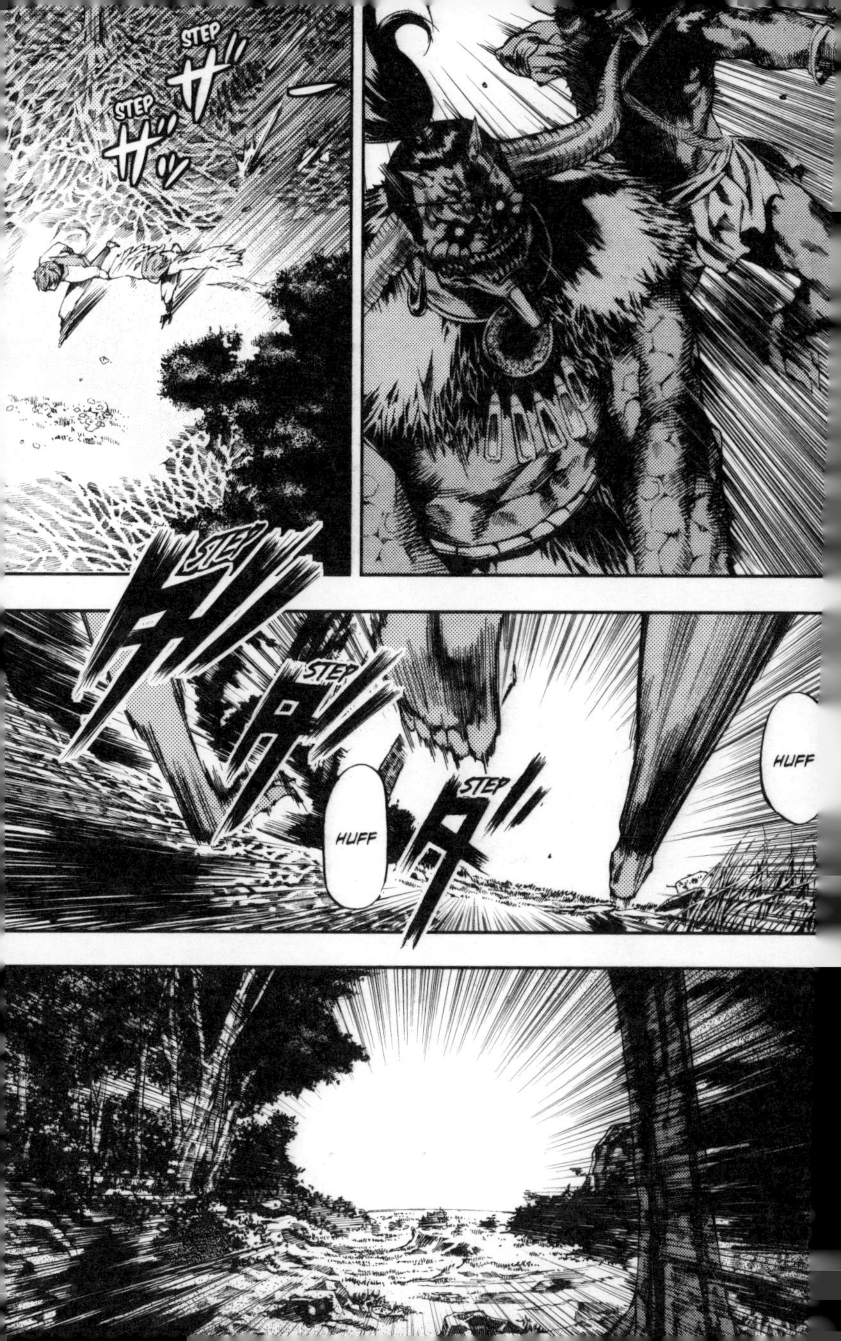
STEP
STEP
HUFF
STEP
STEP
HUFF
STEP

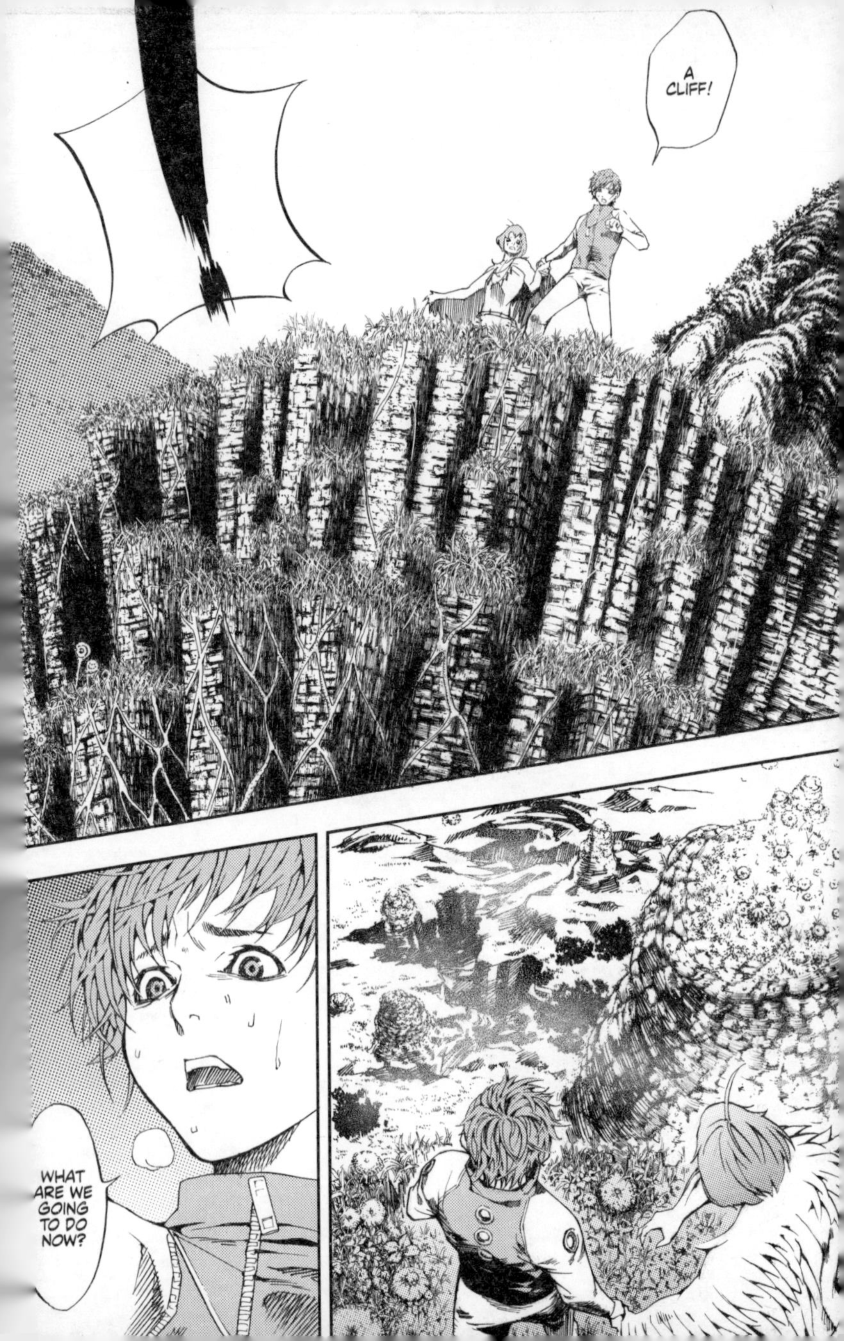
A CLIFF!
WHAT ARE WE GOING TO DO NOW?

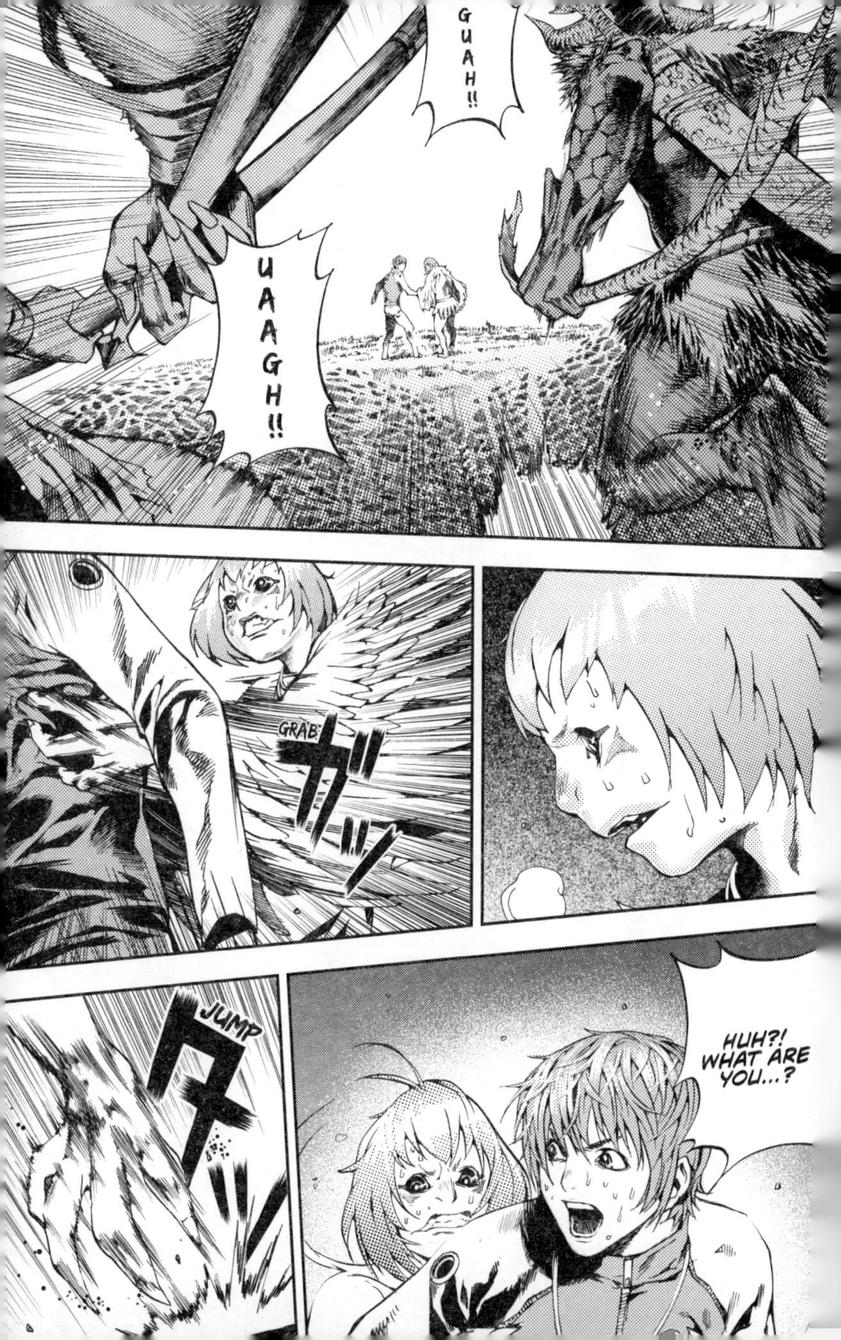
GUAH!!
UAAGH!!
GRAB
HUH?! WHAT ARE YOU...?
JUMP

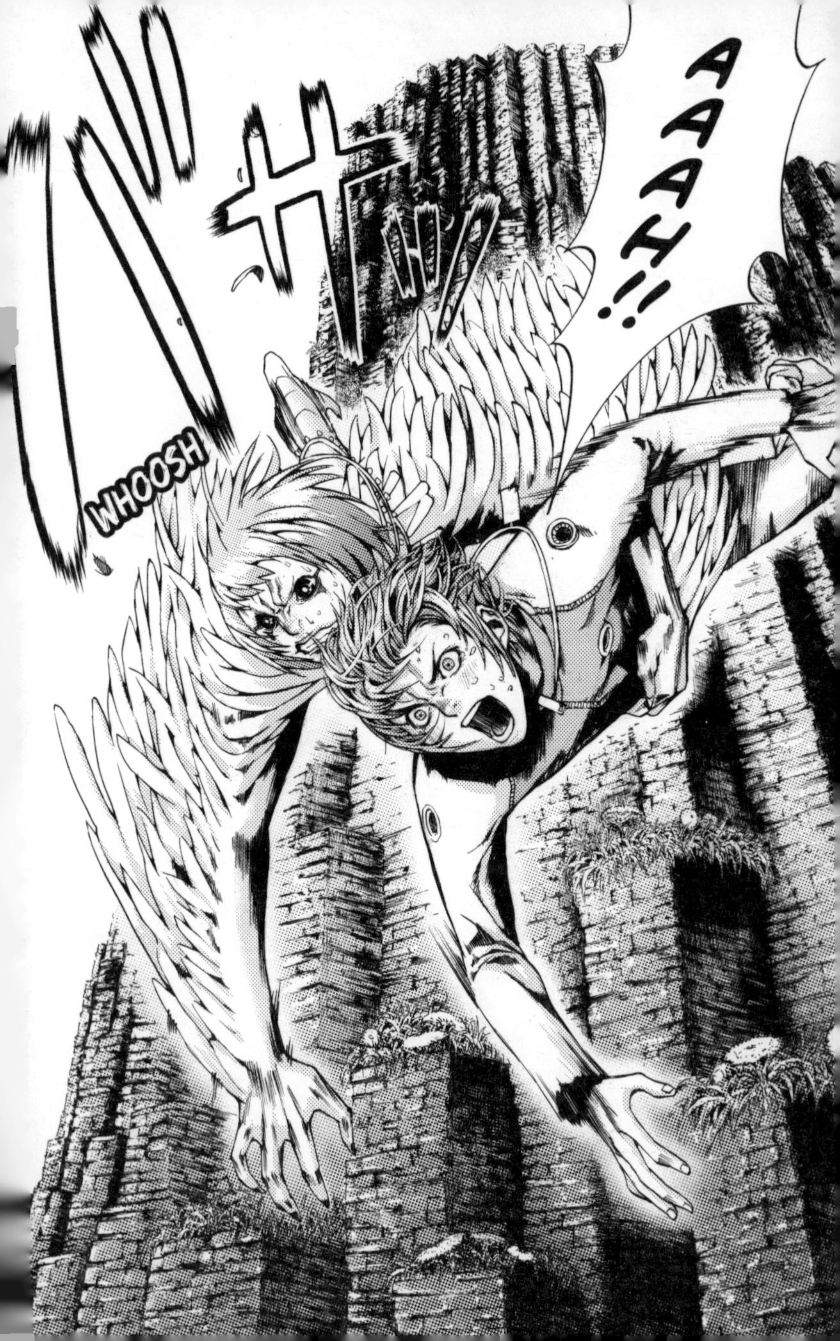
AAAAH!!!
WHOOSH

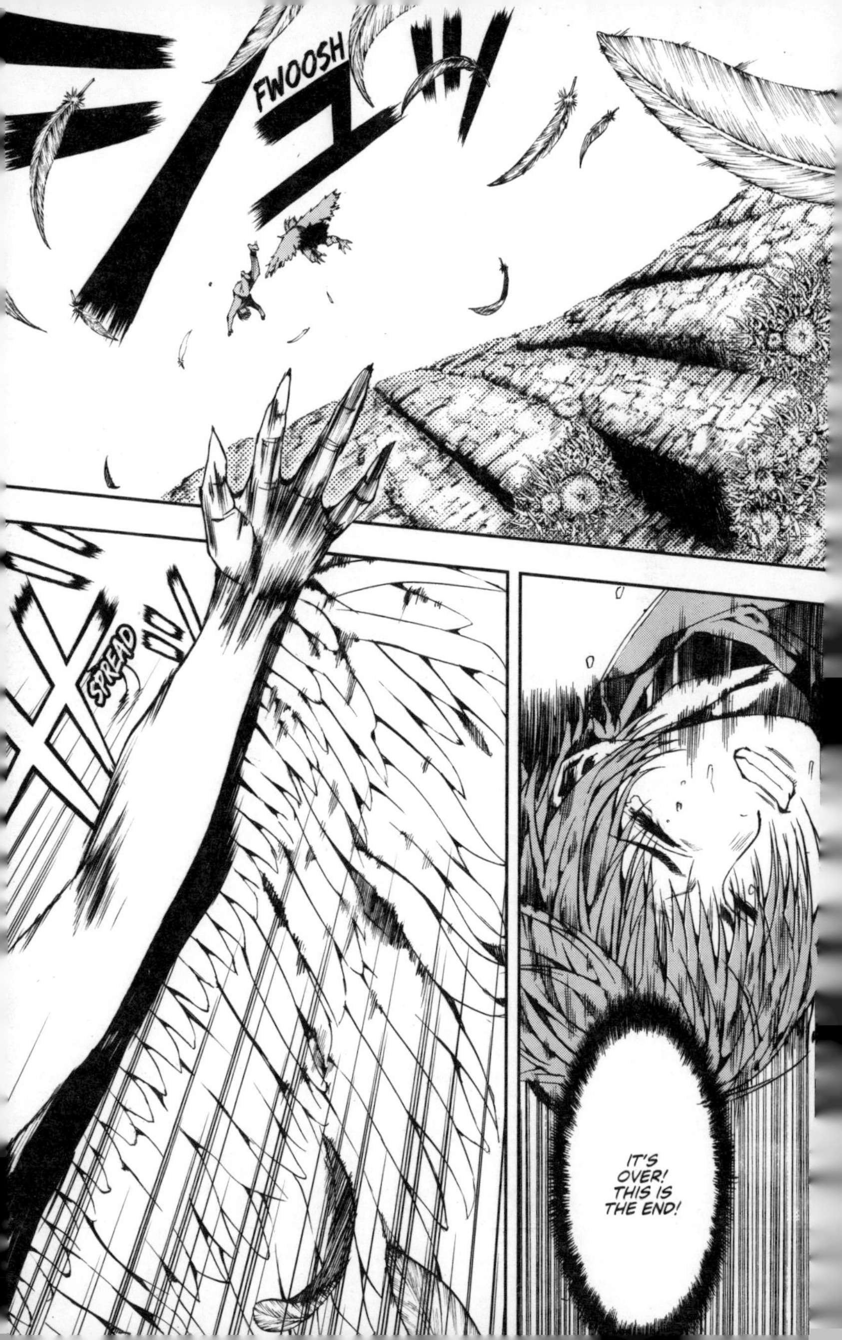
FWOOSH
SPREAD
IT'S OVER! THIS IS THE END!

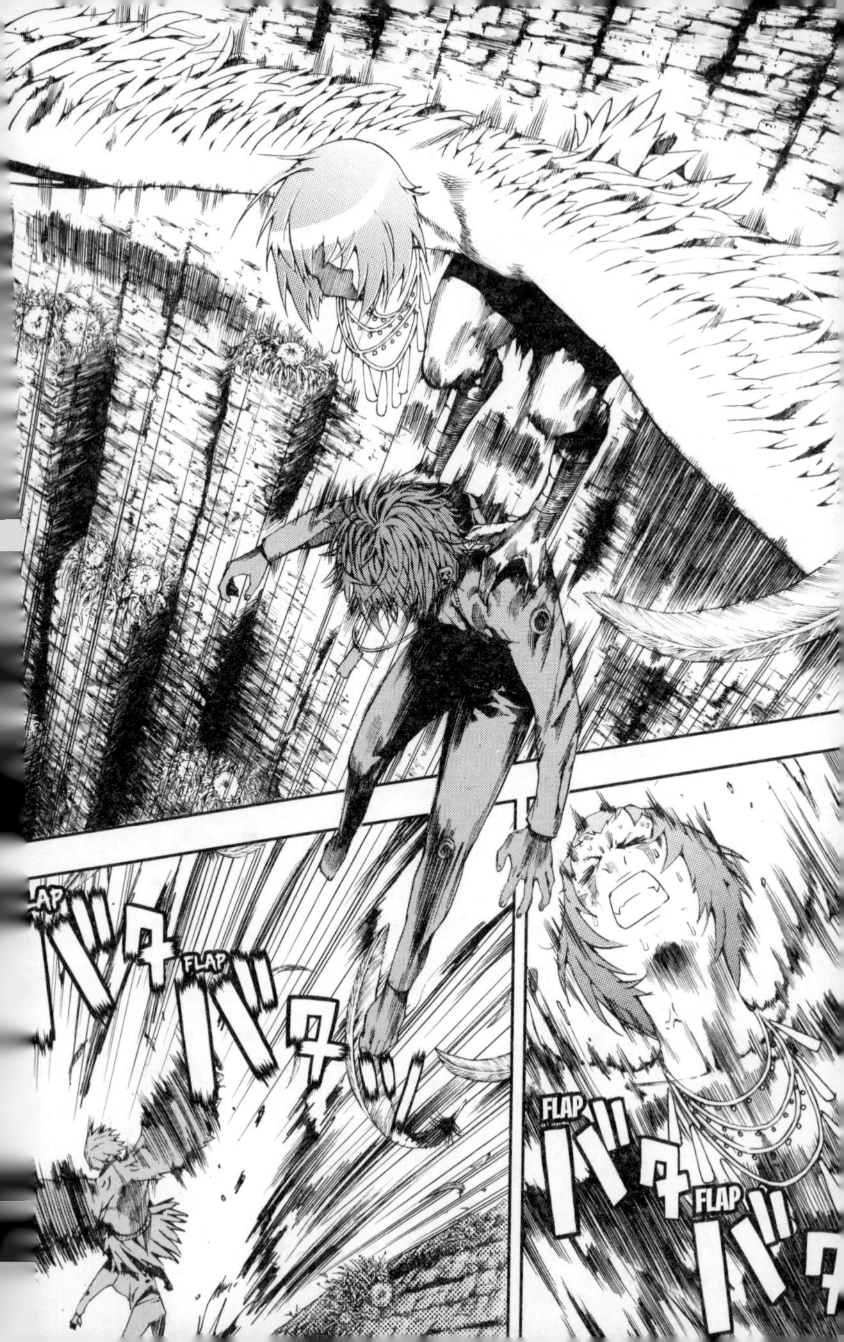
FLAP
バタ
FLAP
バタ
FLAP
バタ
FLAP
バタ

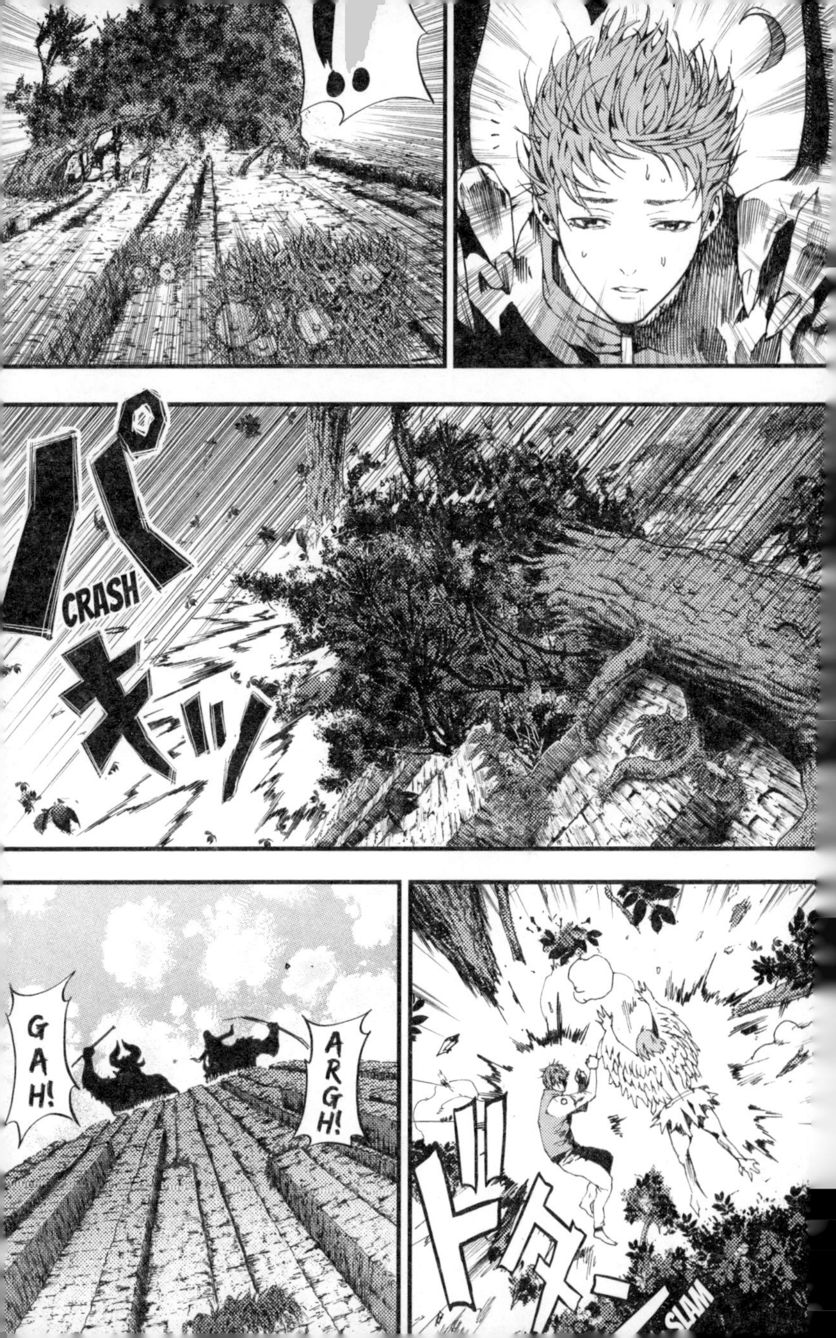
パ
CRASH
ドター
SLAM
ARGH!
GAH!

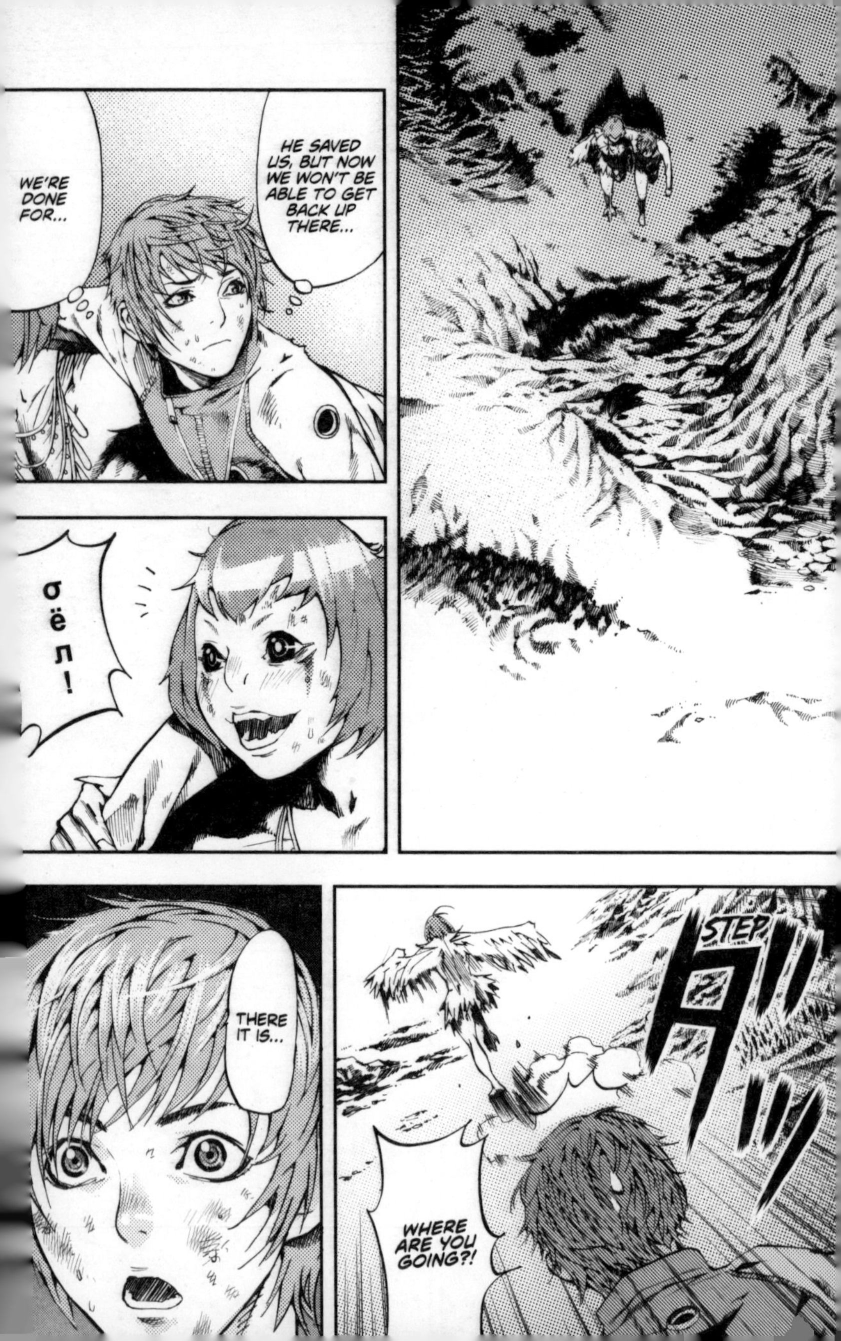
HE SAVED US, BUT NOW WE WON'T BE ABLE TO GET BACK UP THERE...
WE'RE DONE FOR...
σёл!
STEP
WHERE ARE YOU GOING?!
THERE IT IS...

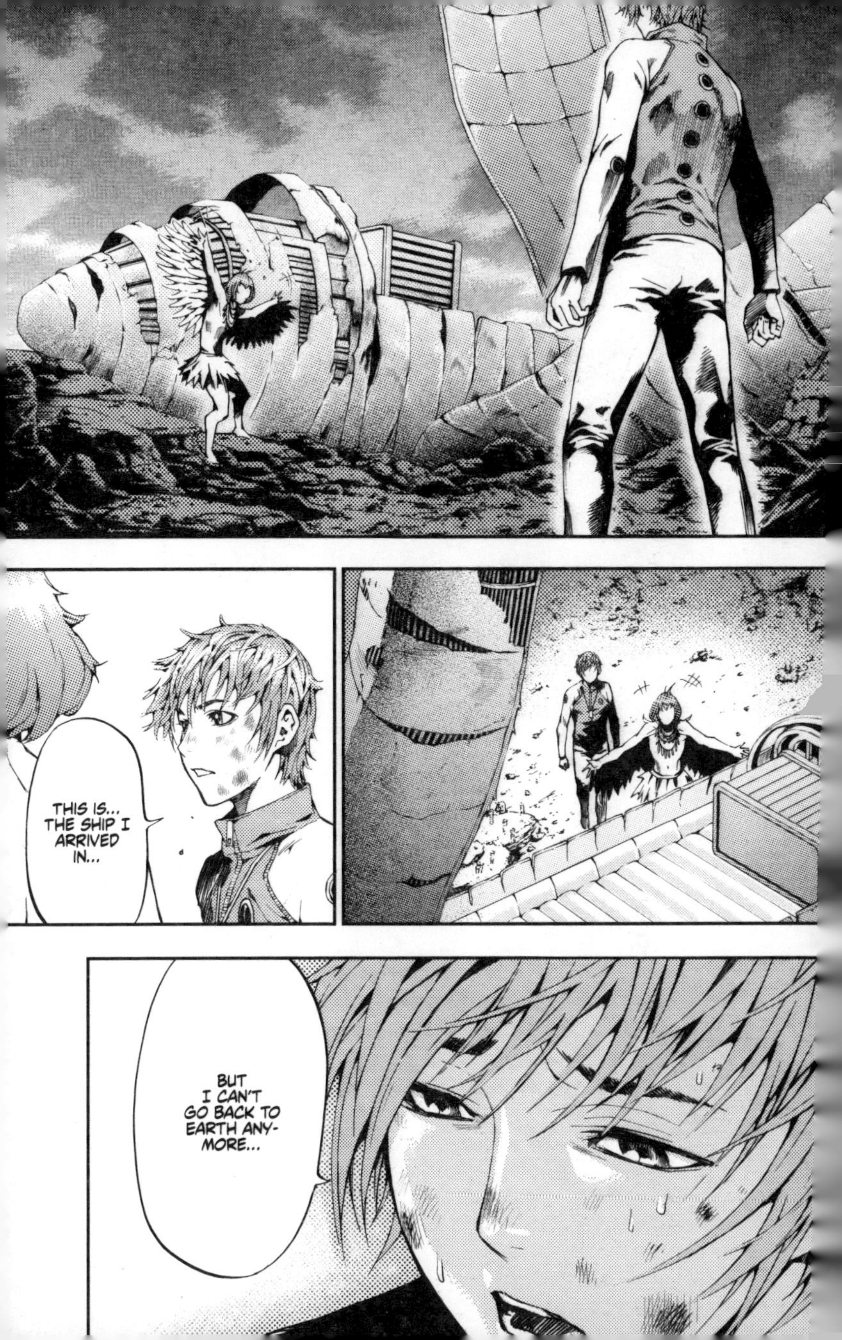
THIS IS... THE SHIP I ARRIVED IN...
BUT I CAN'T GO BACK TO EARTH ANY-MORE...

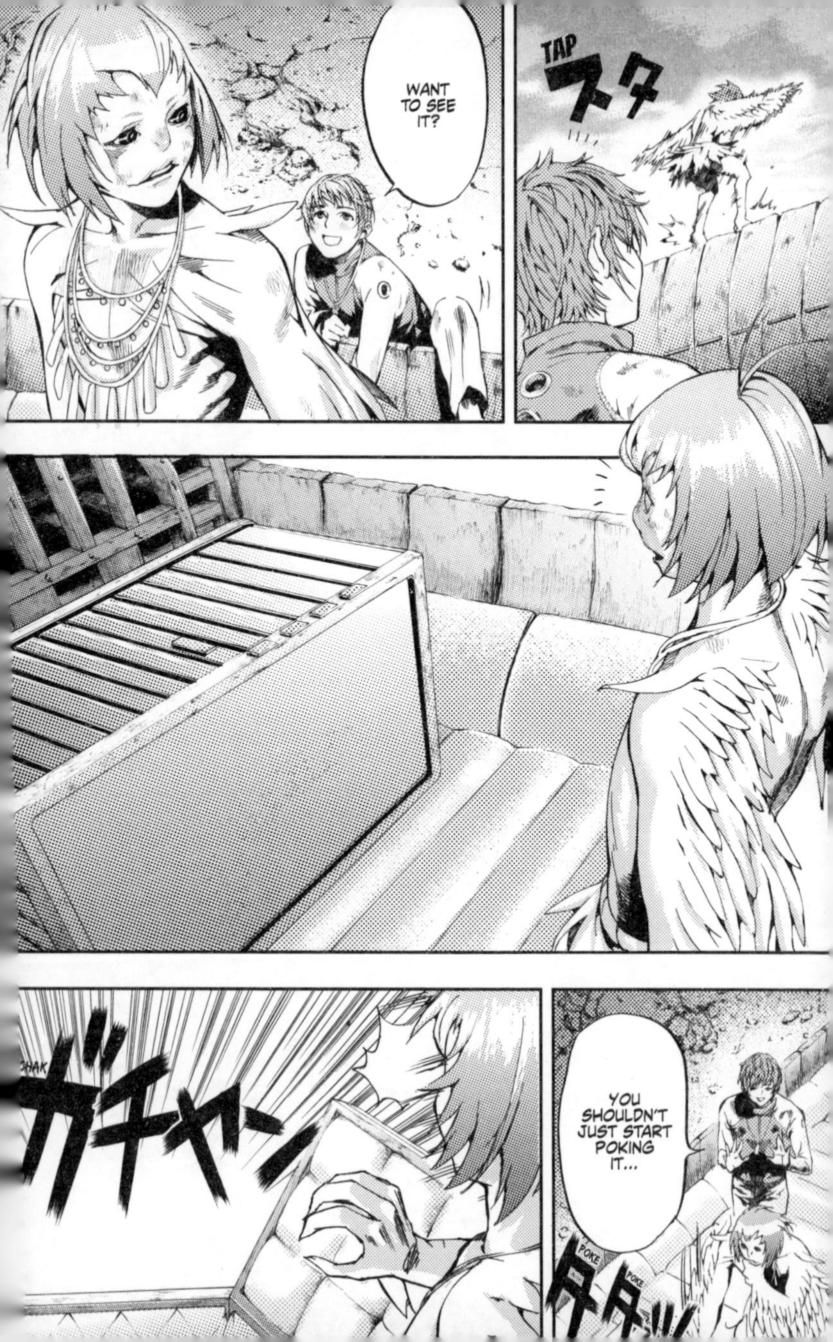
TAP
WANT TO SEE IT?
YOU SHOULDN'T JUST START POKING IT...
POKE
POKE
SHAK

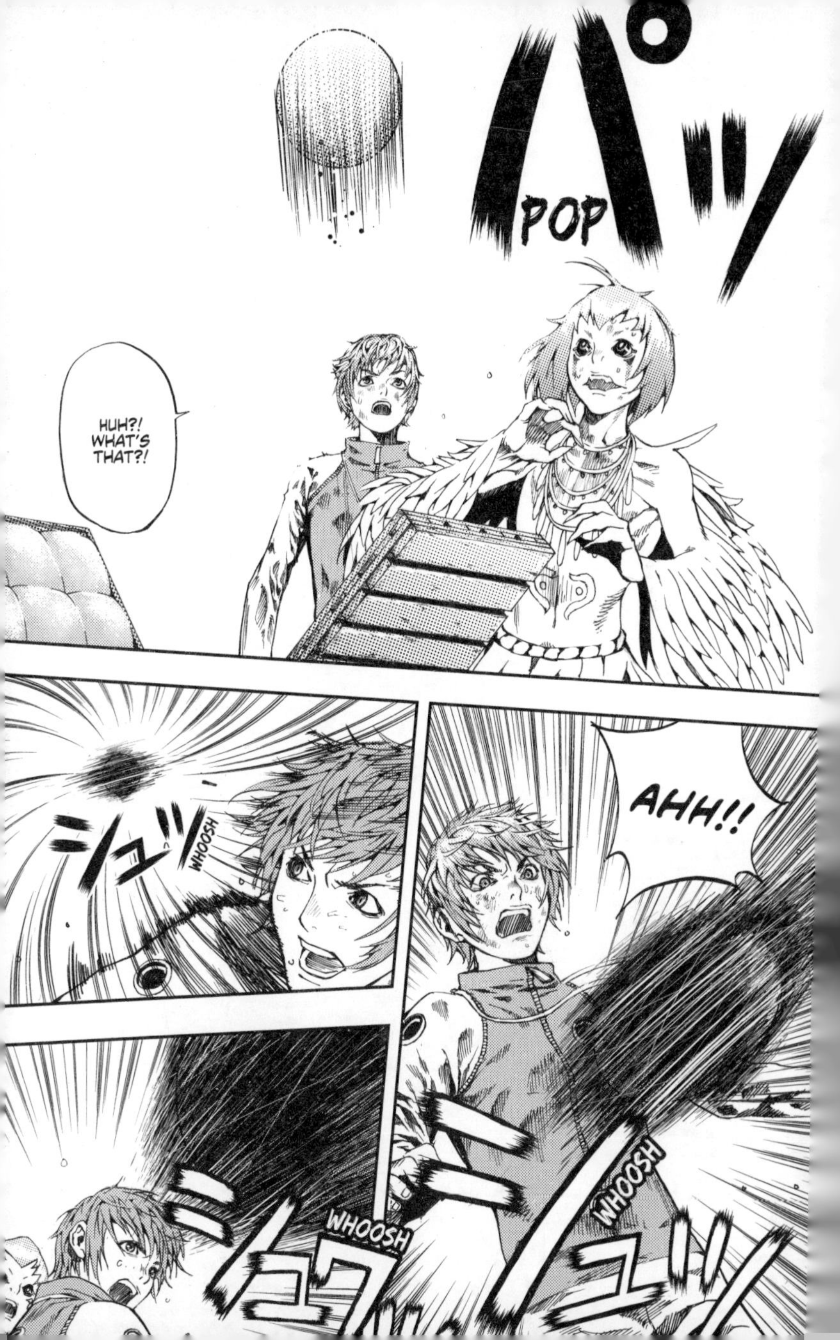
パッ
POP
HUH?! WHAT'S THAT?!
AHH!!
WHOOSH
WHOOSH
WHOOSH

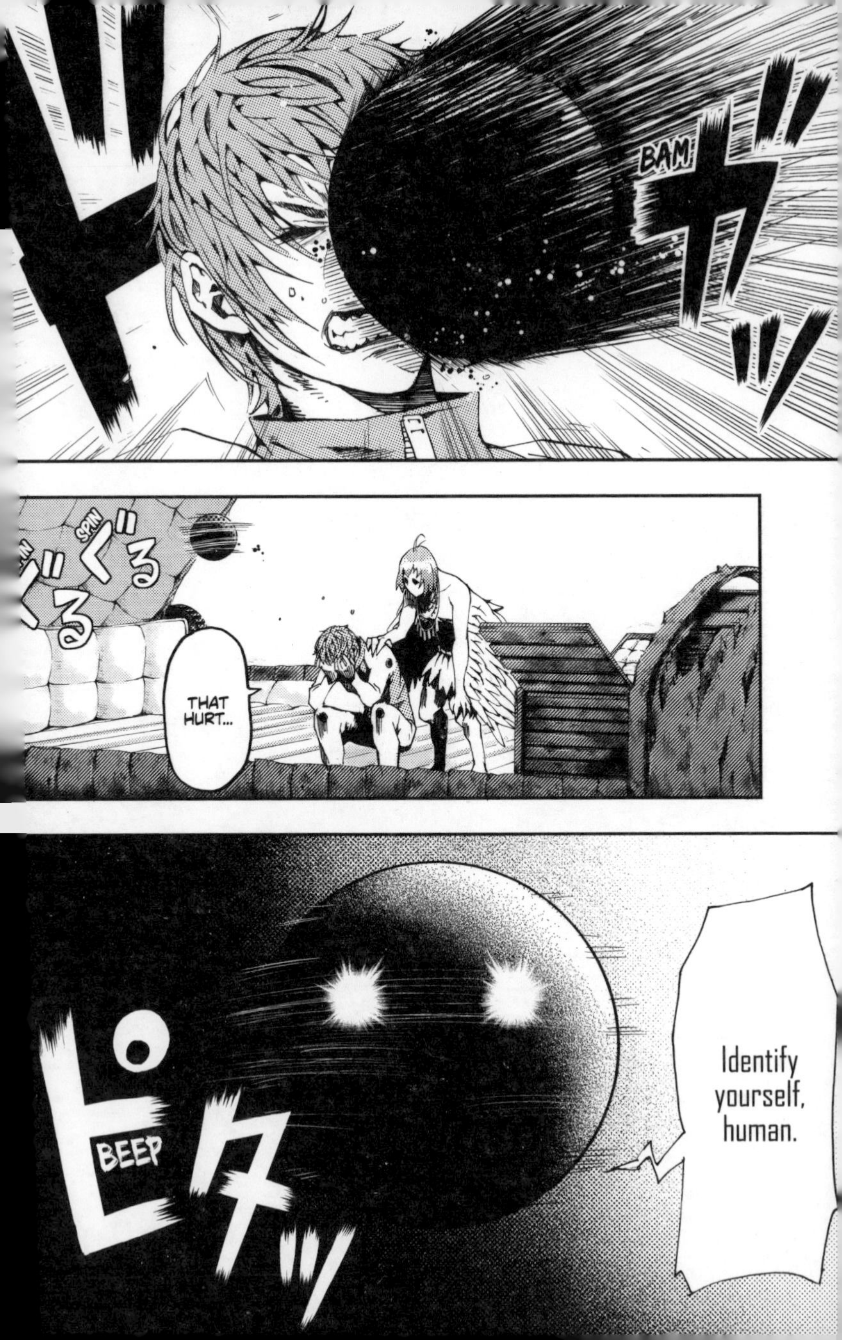
BAM
SPIN
ぐるぐる
THAT HURT...
Identify yourself, human.
BEEP

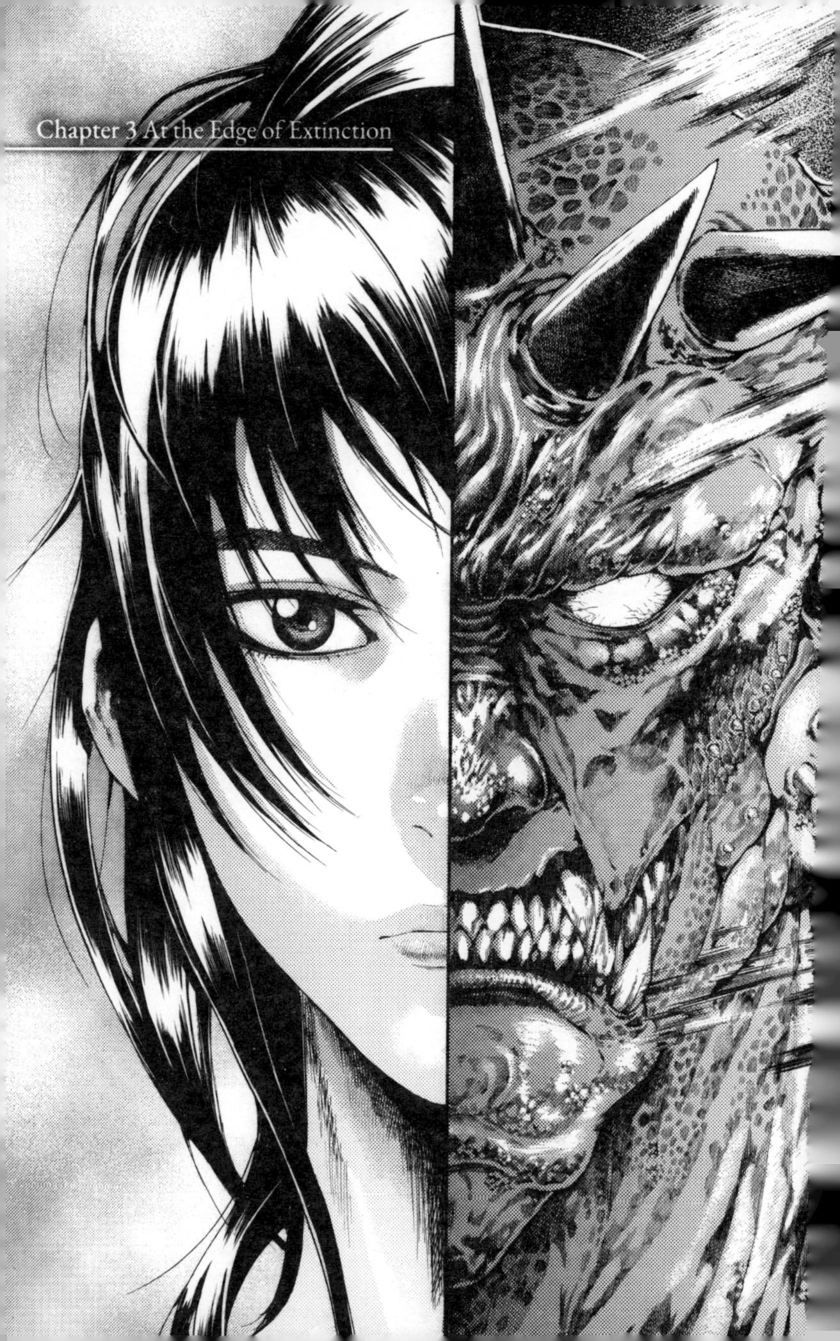
Chapter 3 At the Edge of Extinction

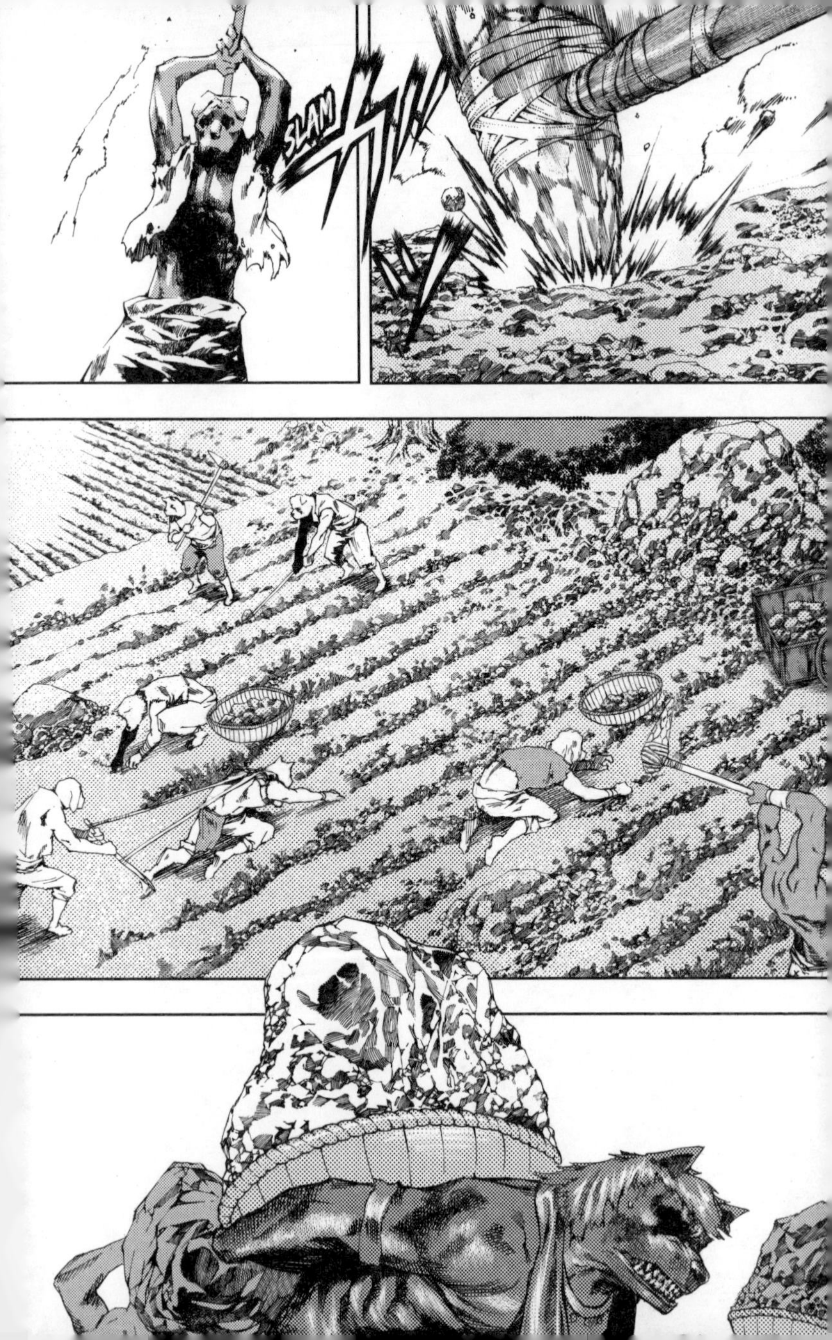
SLAM

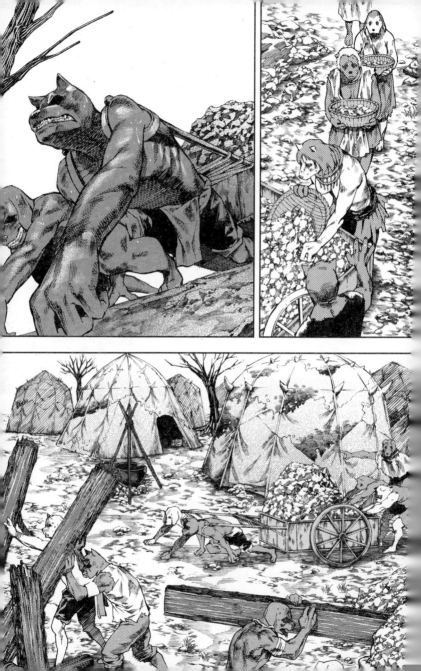

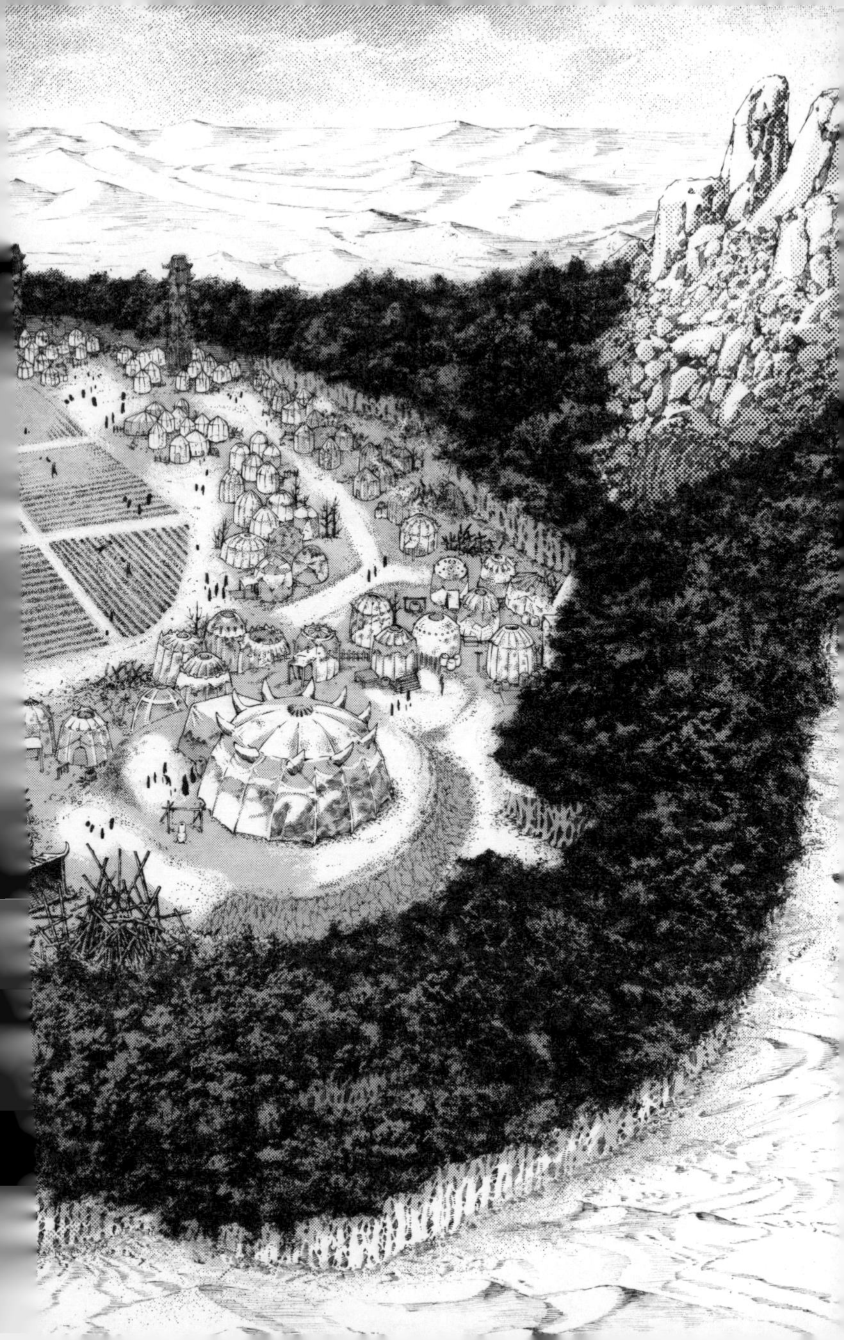

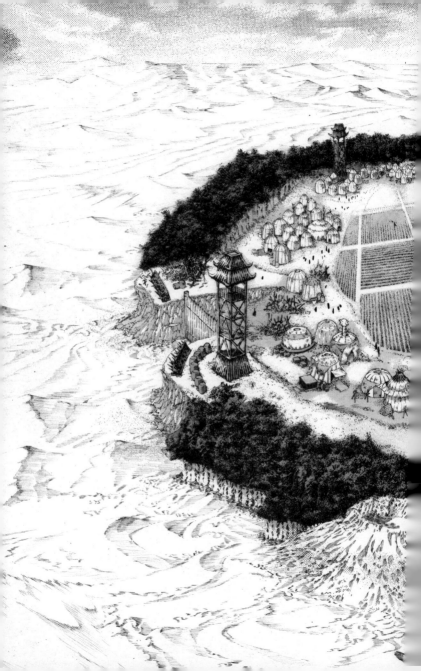

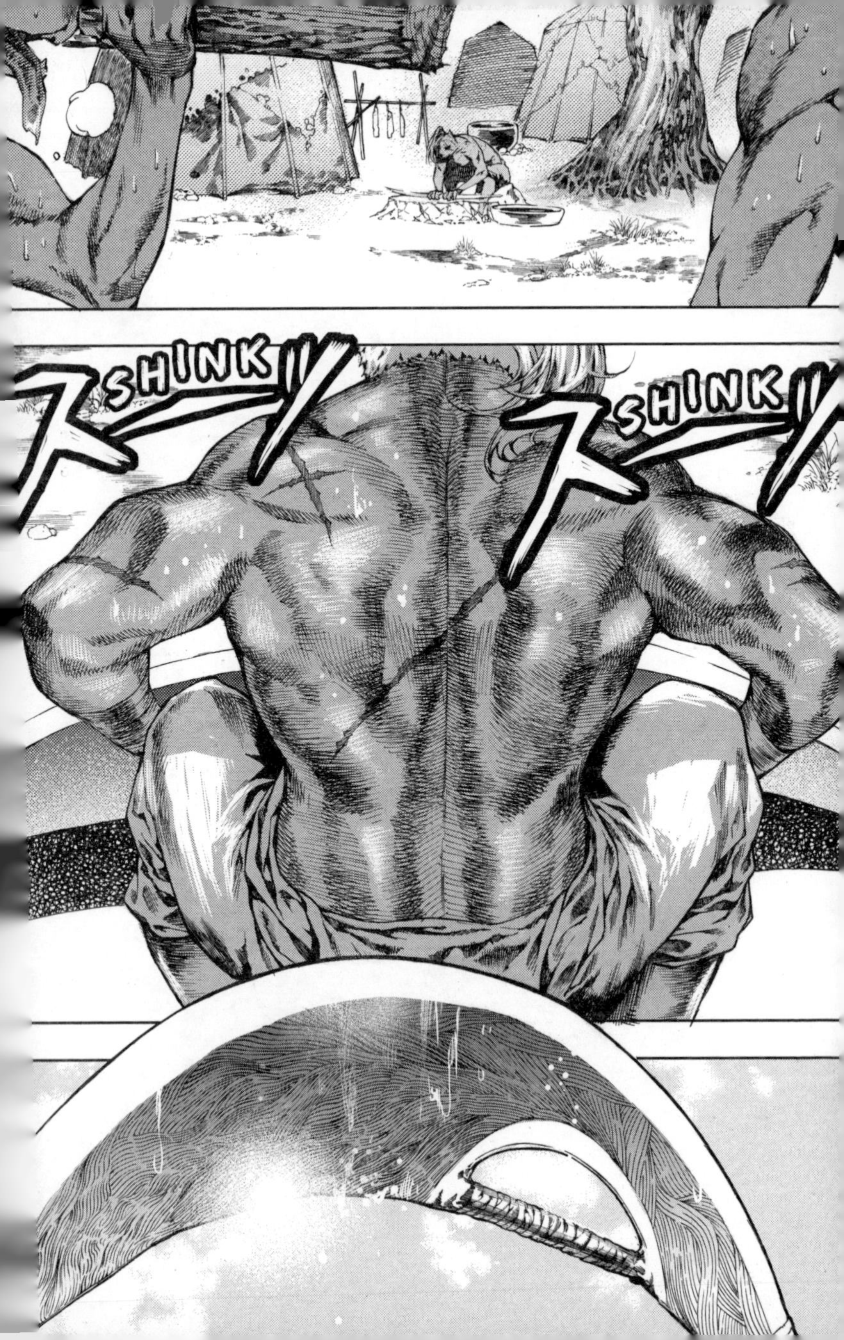
ス SHINK
ス SHINK

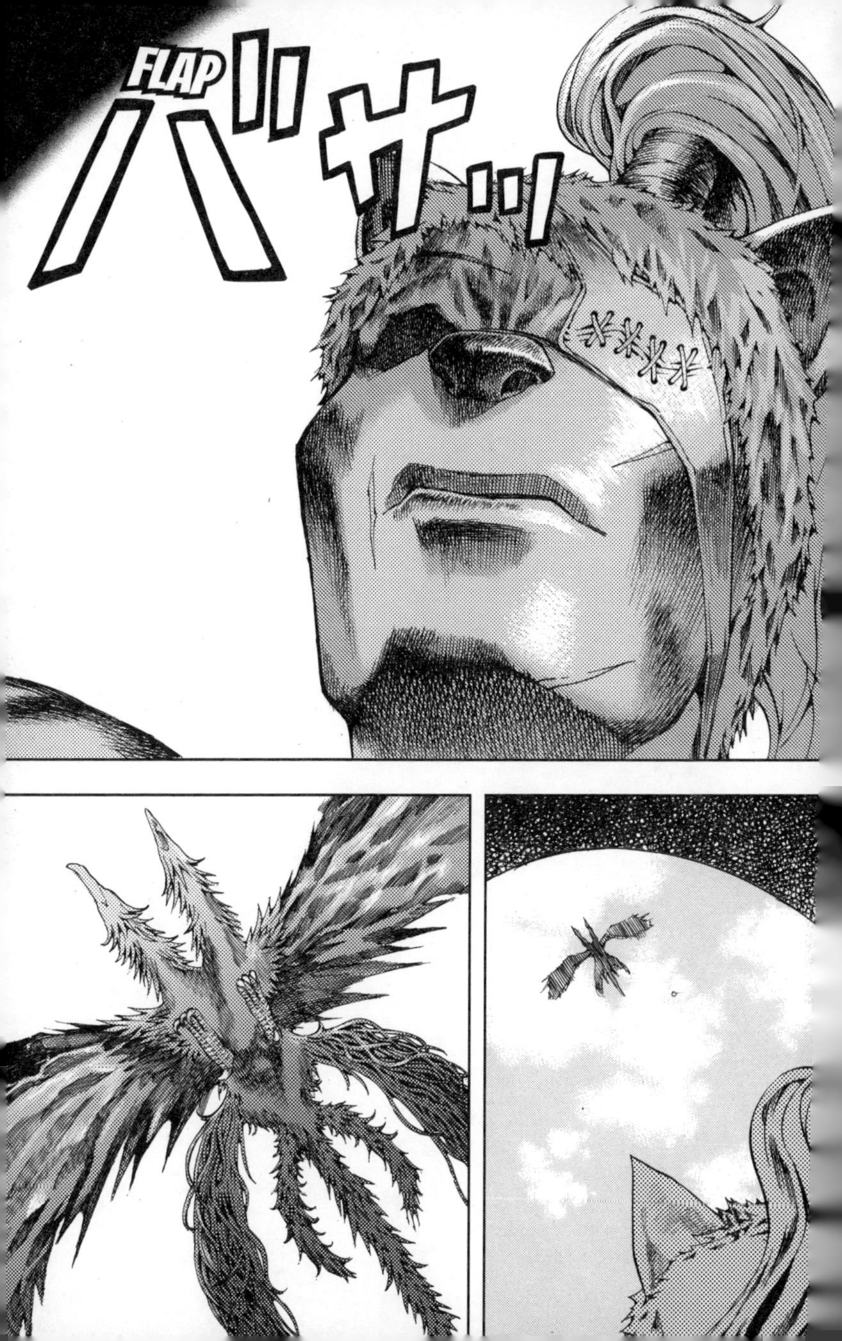
FLAP
バサッ

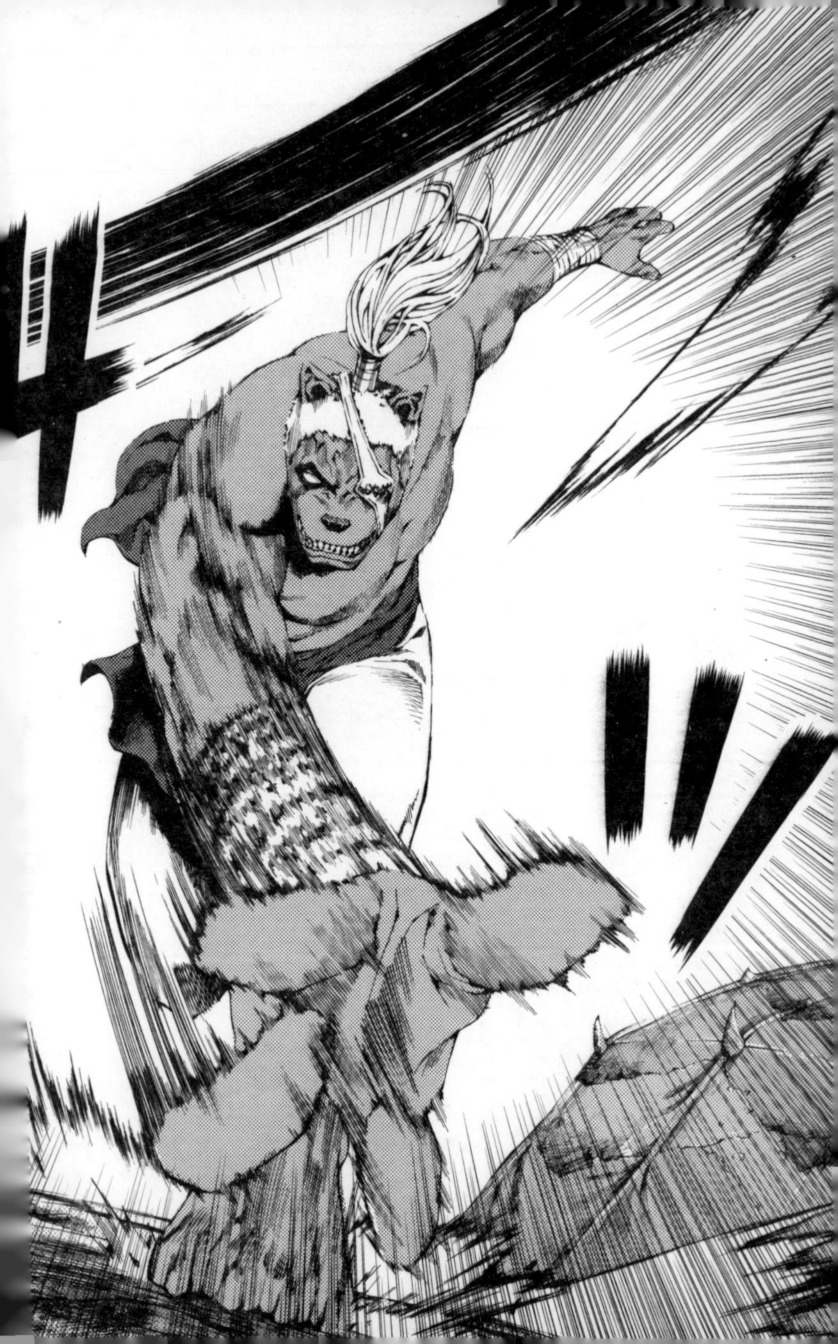

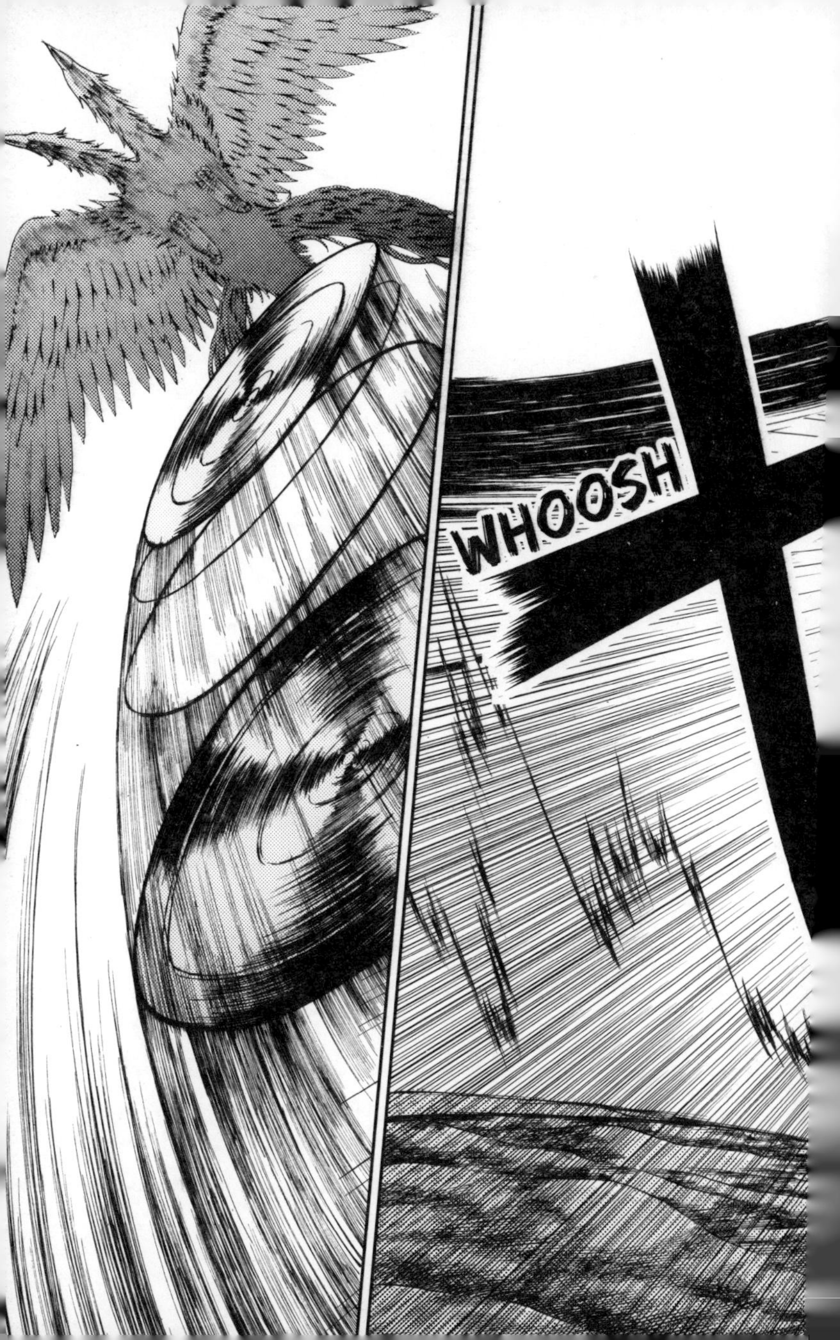
WHOOSH

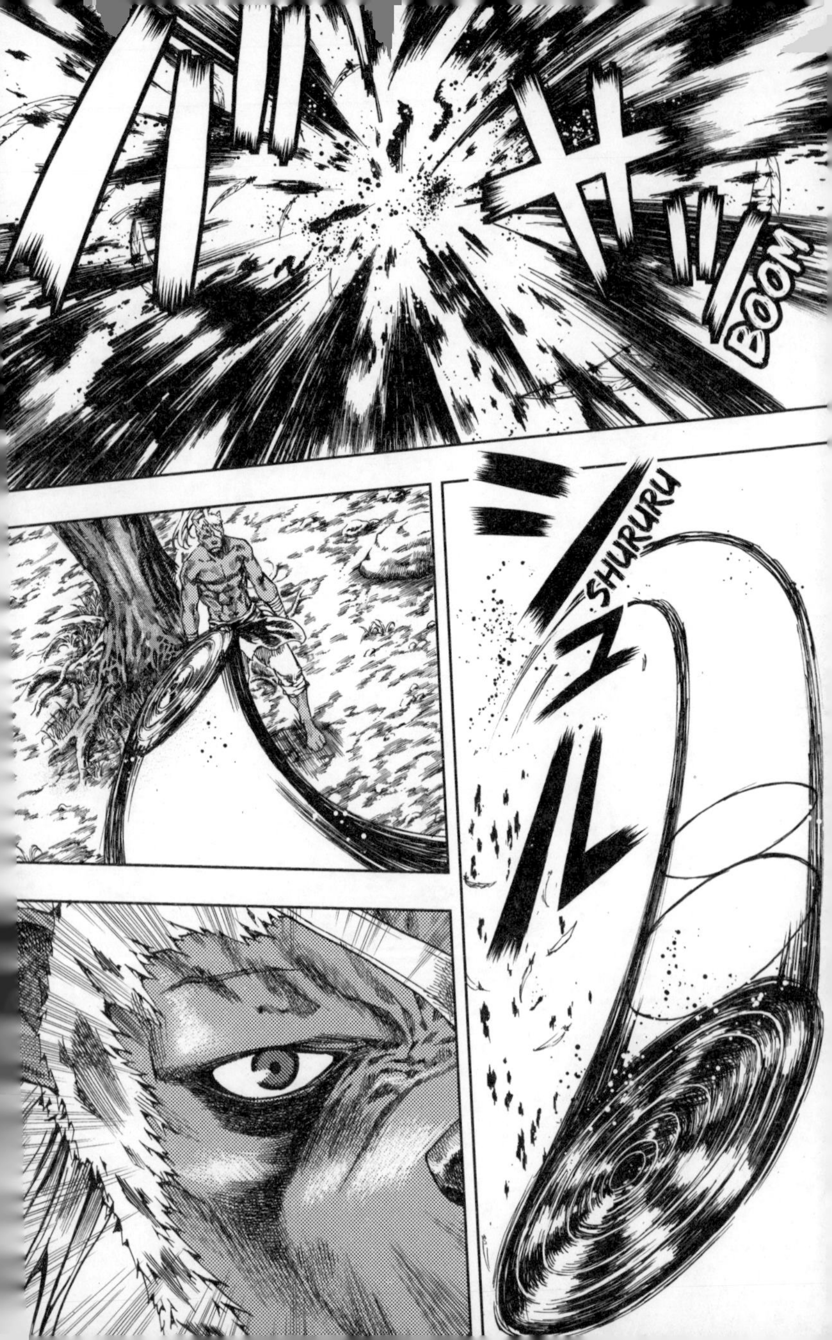
BOOM
SHURURU

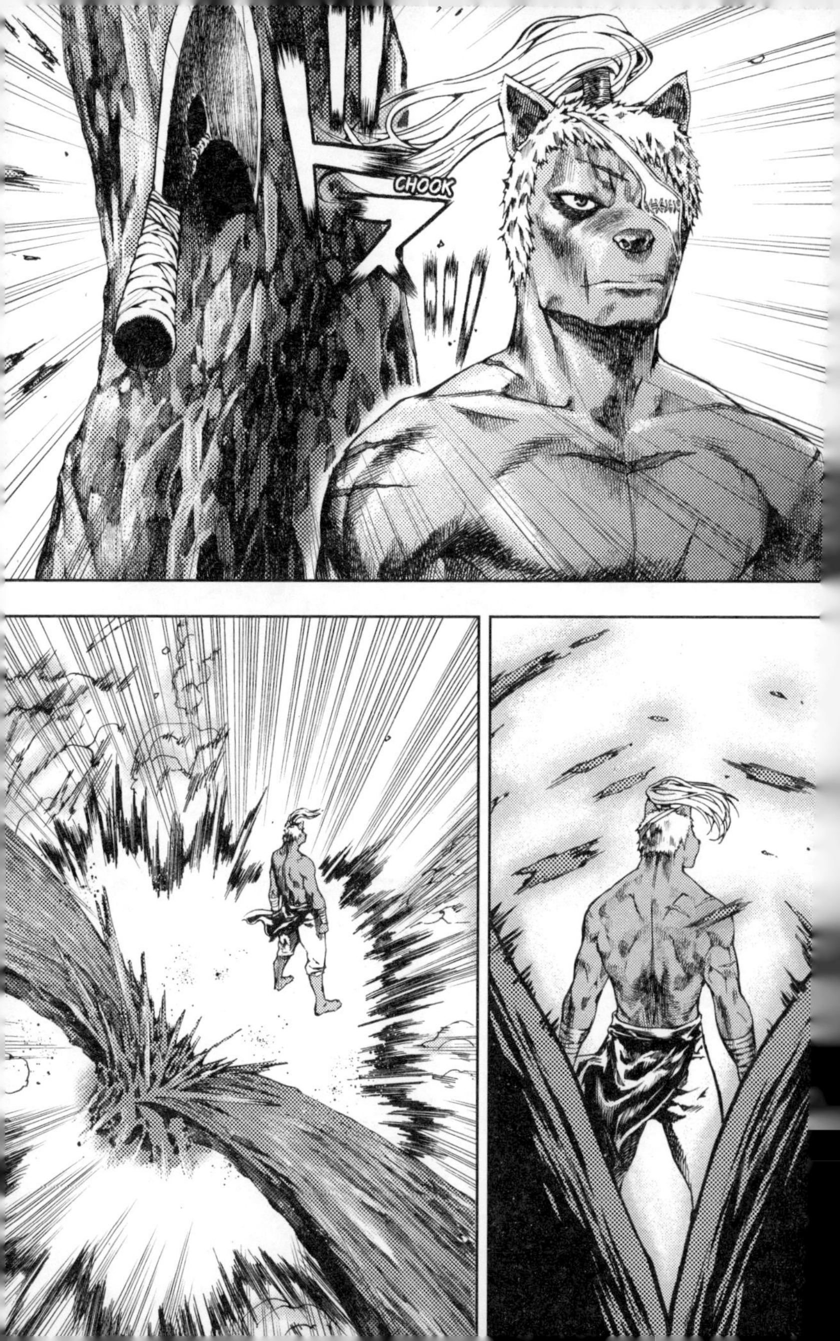
CHOOK

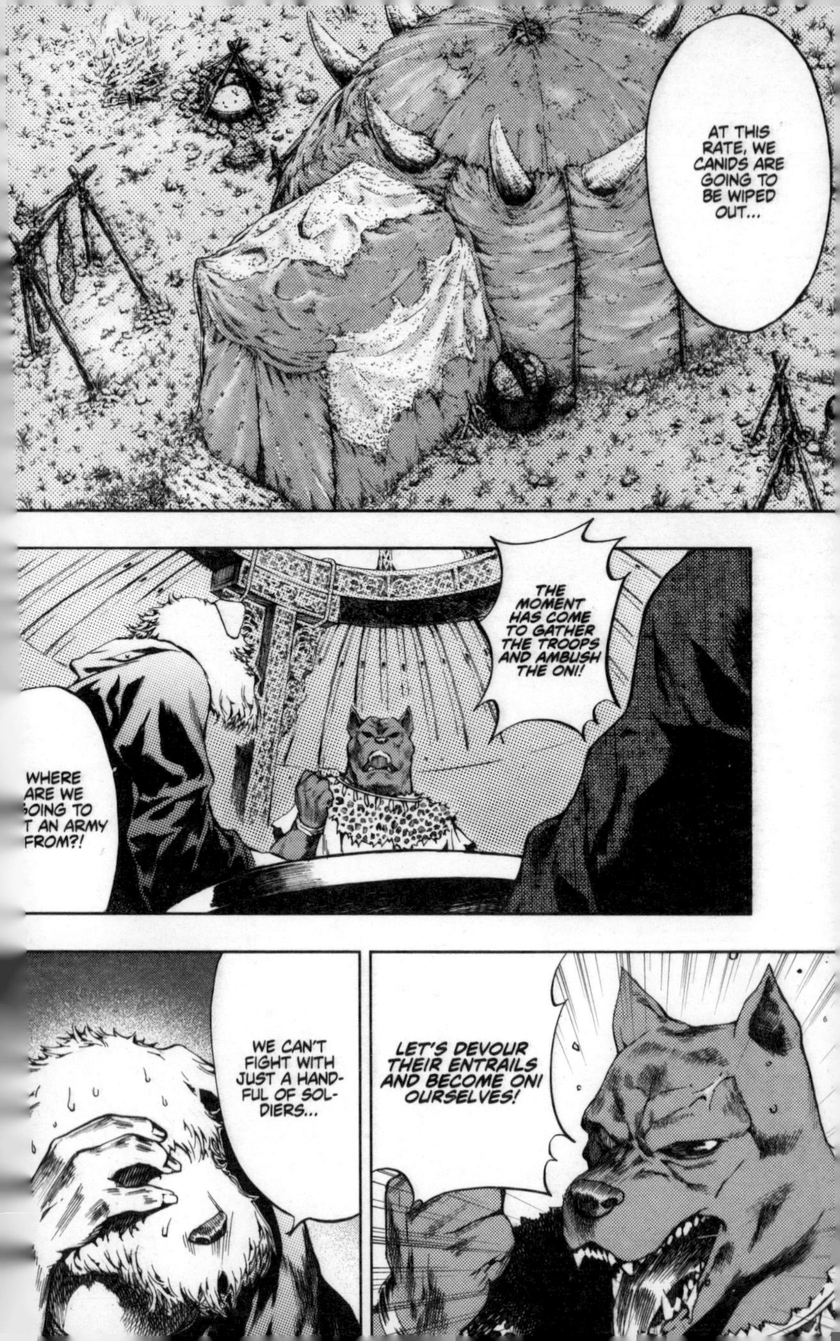
AT THIS RATE, WE CANIDS ARE GOING TO BE WIPED OUT...
THE MOMENT HAS COME TO GATHER THE TROOPS AND AMBUSH THE ONI!
WHERE ARE WE OING TO T AN ARMY FROM?!
LET'S DEVOUR THEIR ENTRAILS AND BECOME ONI OURSELVES!
WE CAN'T FIGHT WITH JUST A HAND-FUL OF SOL-DIERS...

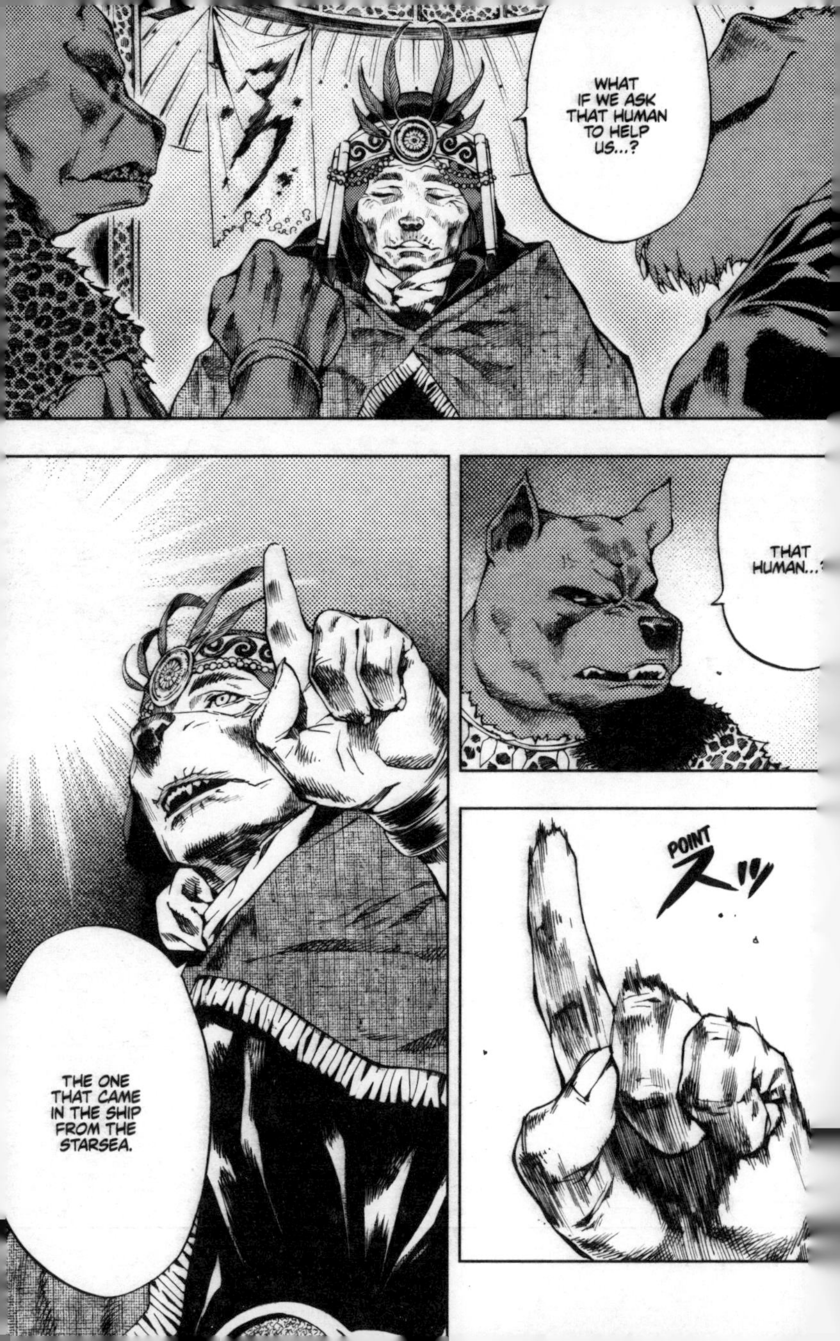
WHAT IF WE ASK THAT HUMAN TO HELP US...?
THAT HUMAN...
POINT
スッ
THE ONE THAT CAME IN THE SHIP FROM THE STARSEA.

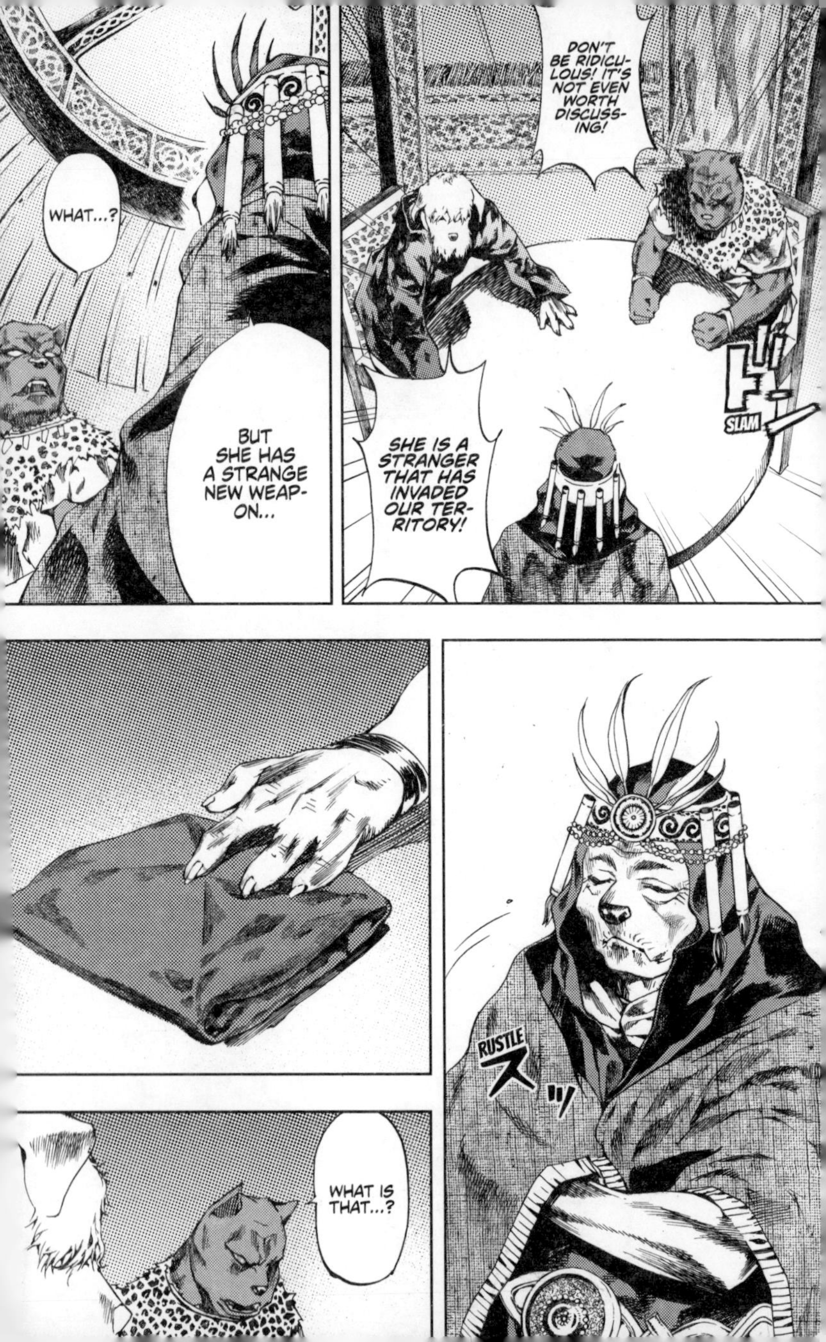
DON'T BE RIDICULOUS! IT'S NOT EVEN WORTH DISCUSSING!
SLAM
SHE IS A STRANGER THAT HAS INVADED OUR TERRITORY!
WHAT...?
BUT SHE HAS A STRANGE NEW WEAPON...
RUSTLE
WHAT IS THAT...?

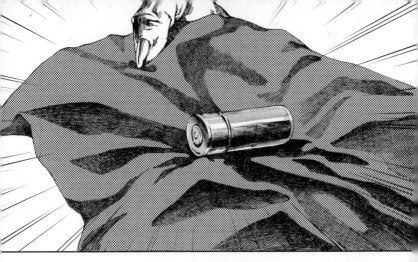

ピク SNIFF
ピク SNIFF
ピク SNIFF

A SINGLE ONE OF THESE OBJECTS WAS ENOUGH TO KILL A STRONG ONI.

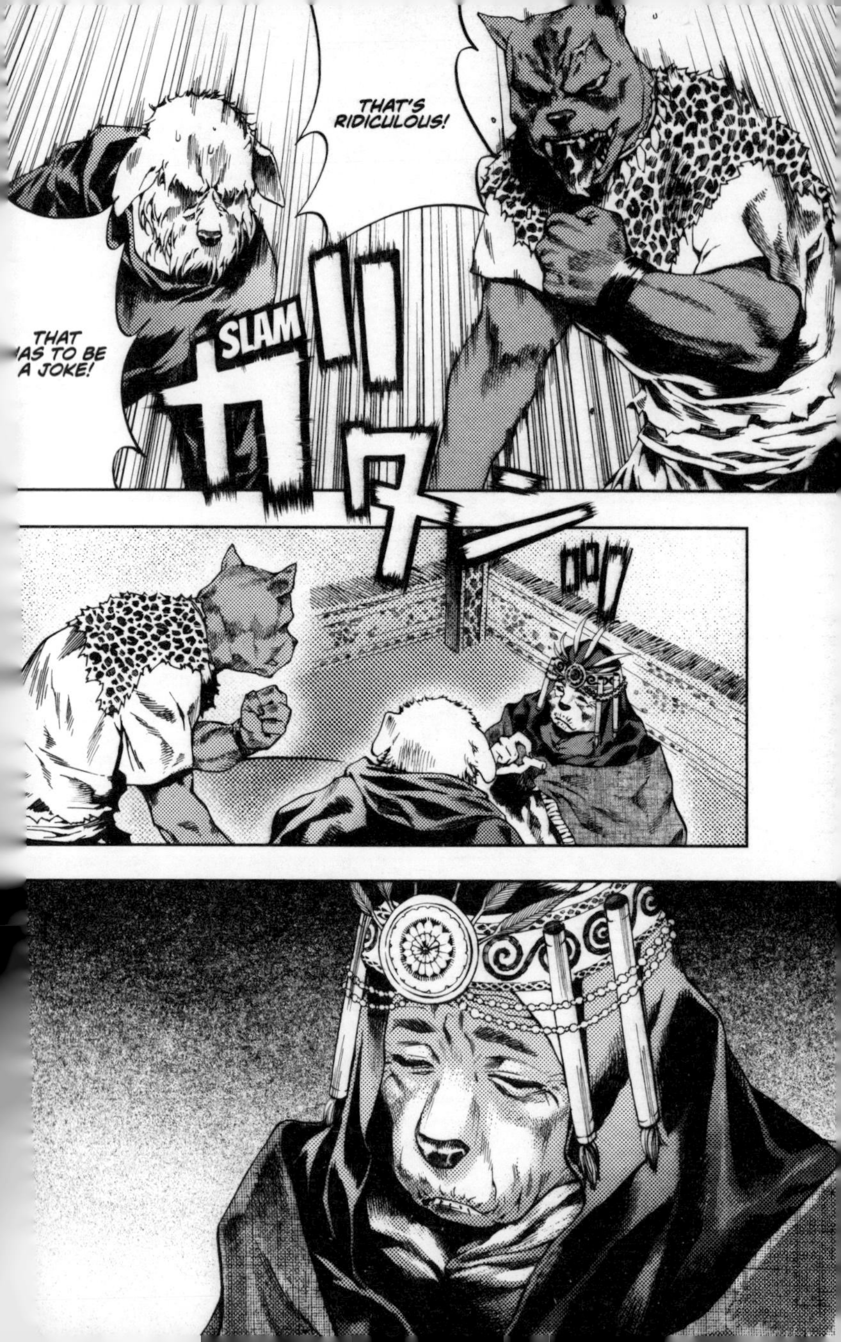
THAT'S RIDICULOUS!
THAT
AS TO BE
A JOKE!
SLAM

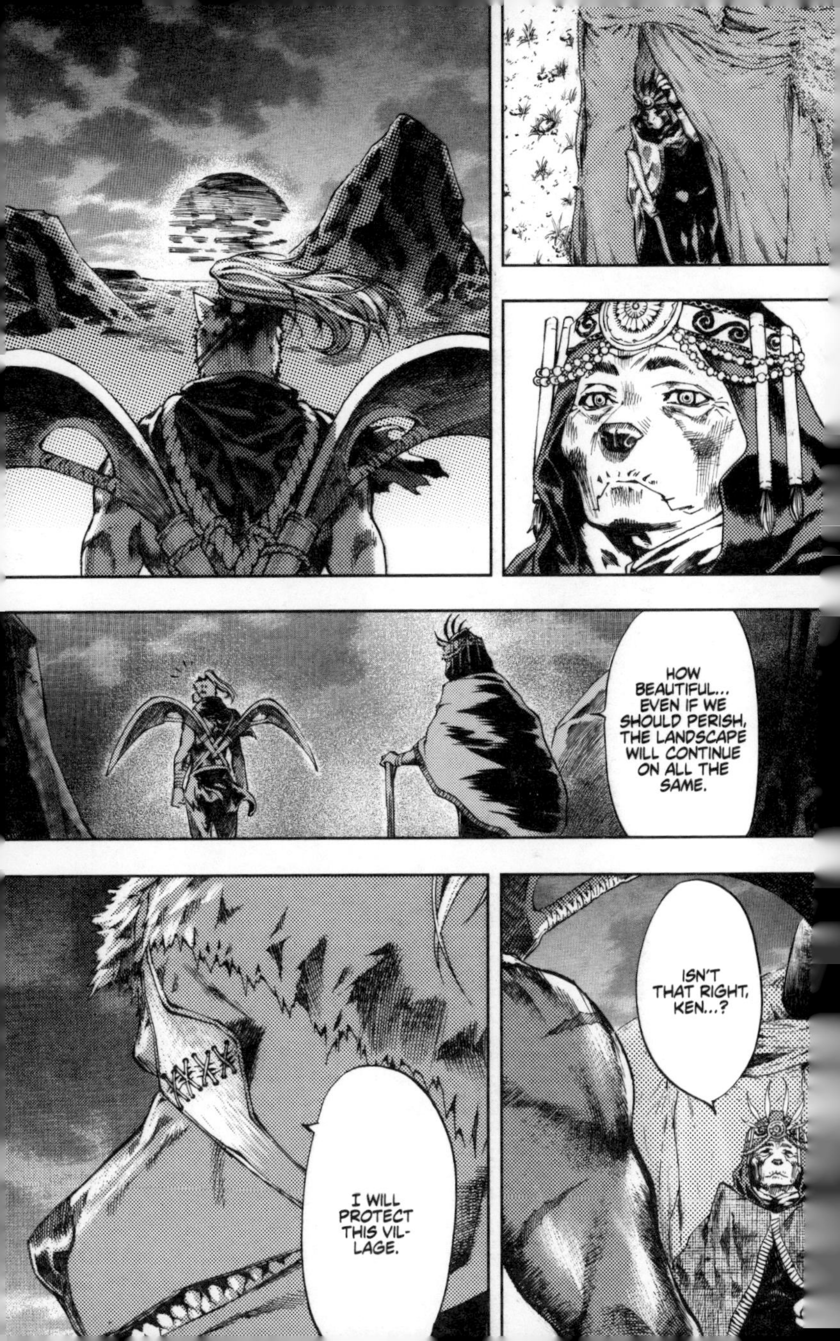
HOW BEAUTIFUL... EVEN IF WE SHOULD PERISH, THE LANDSCAPE WILL CONTINUE ON ALL THE SAME.
ISN'T THAT RIGHT, KEN...?
I WILL PROTECT THIS VIL-LAGE.

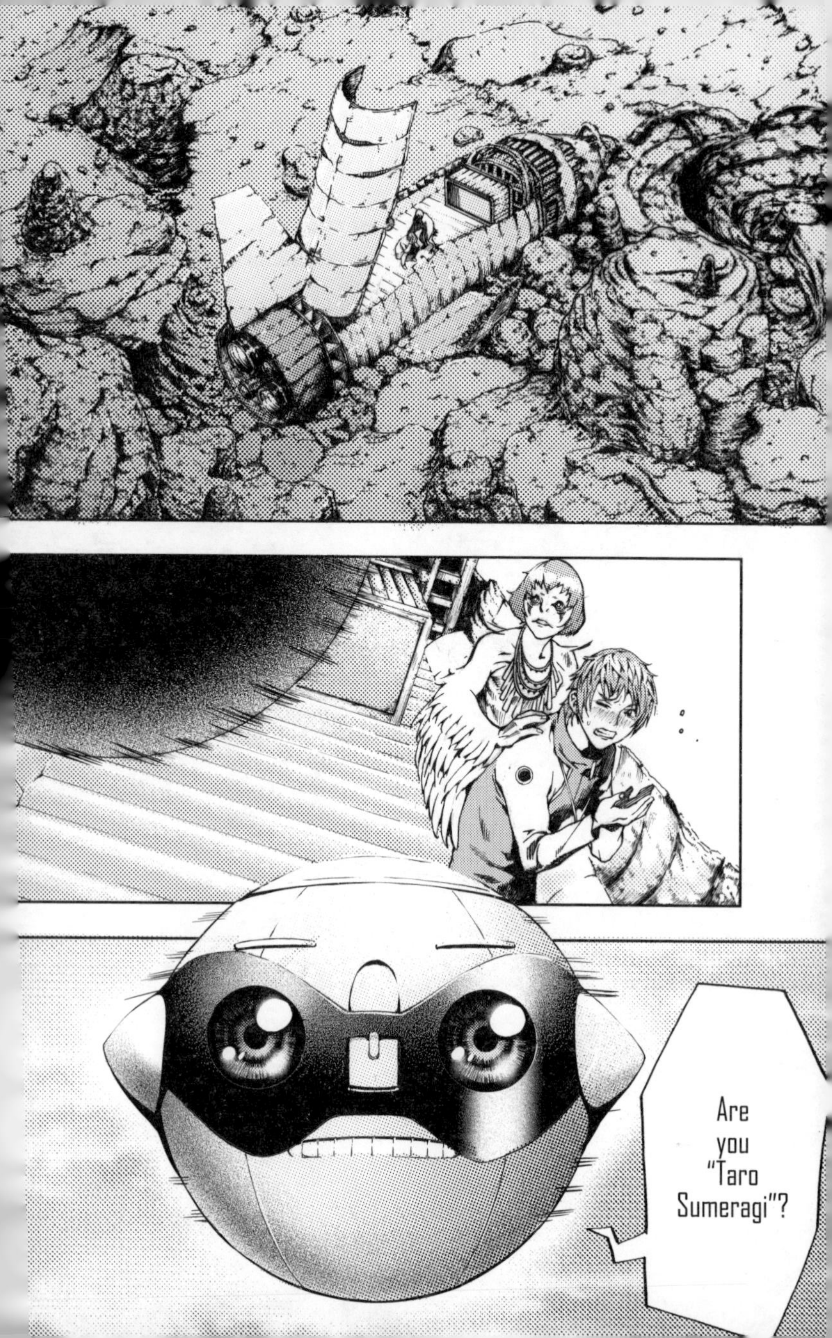

Are you "Taro Sumeragi"?

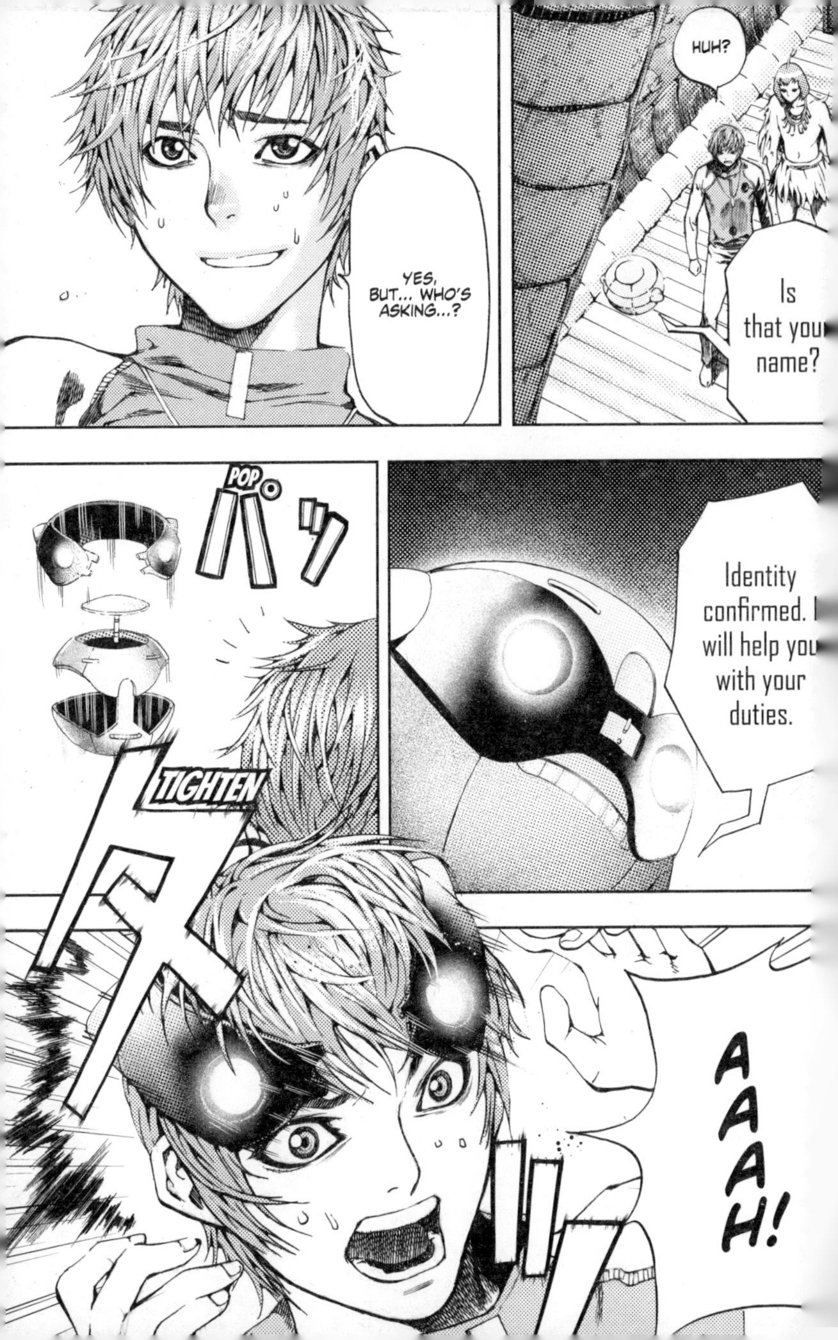
HUH?
Is that your name?
YES, BUT... WHO'S ASKING...?
Identity confirmed. I will help you with your duties.
POP
TIGHTEN
AAAAH!

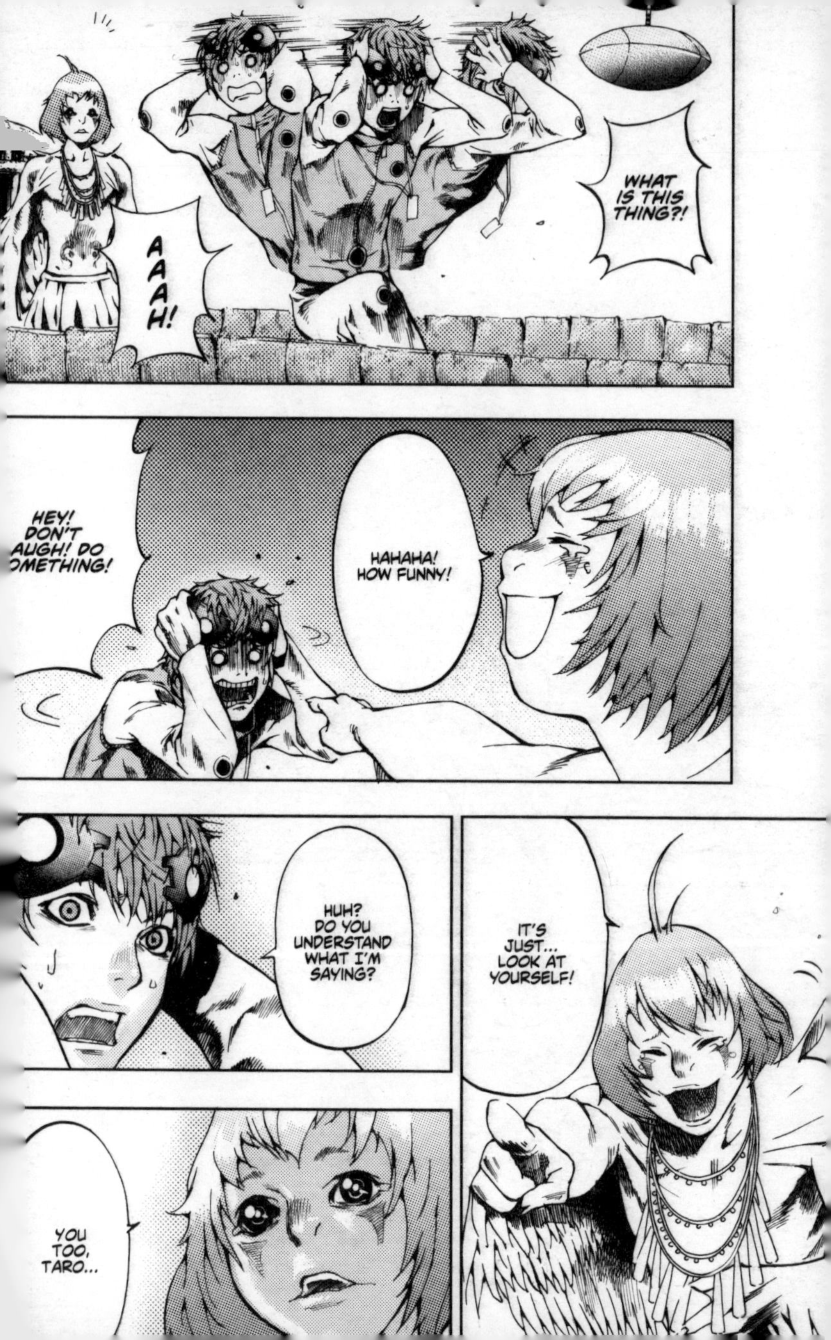
WHAT IS THIS THING?!
AAAAH!
HAHAHA! HOW FUNNY!
HEY! DON'T AUGH! DO OMETHING!
IT'S JUST... LOOK AT YOURSELF!
HUH? DO YOU UNDERSTAND WHAT I'M SAYING?
YOU TOO, TARO...

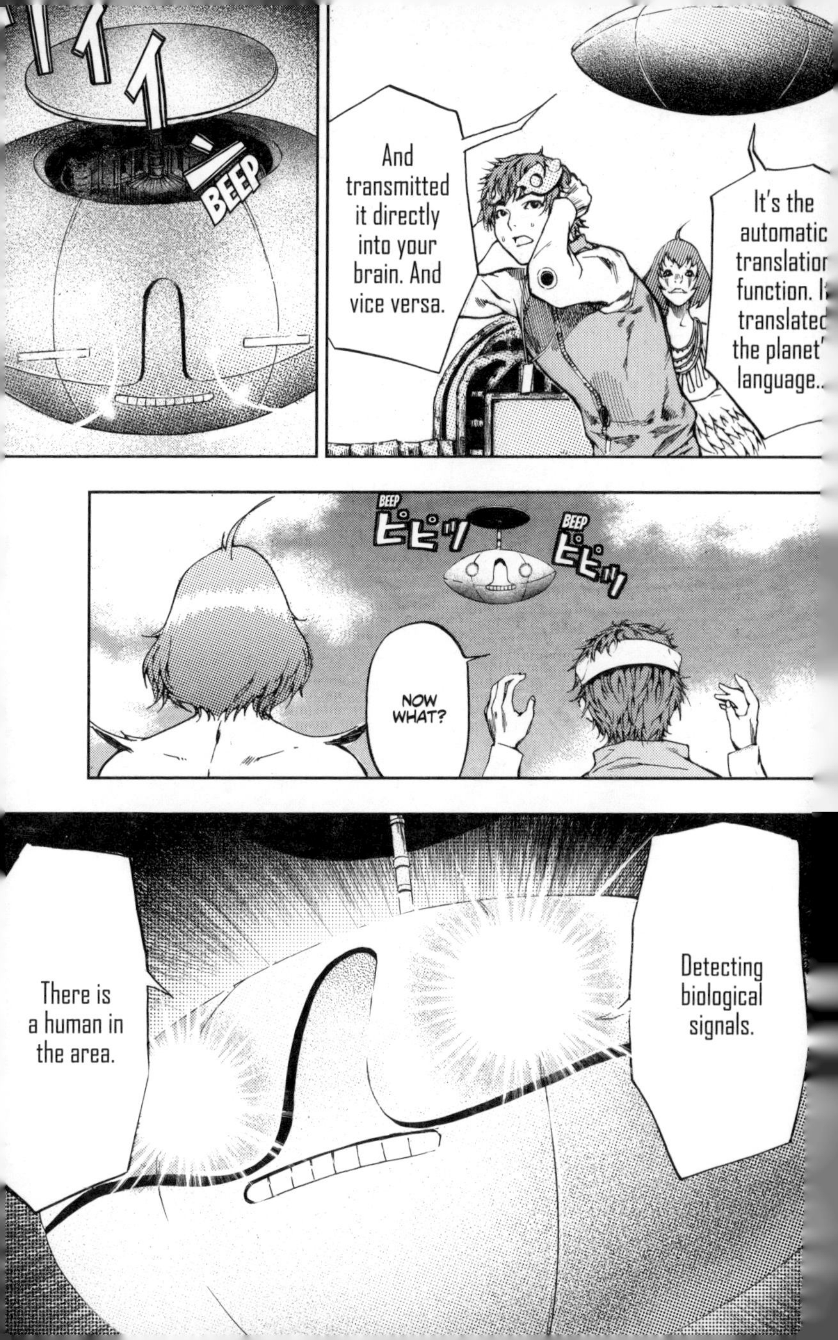
It's the automatic translatio function. I translate the planet' language..
And transmitted it directly into your brain. And vice versa.
BEEP
BEEP ピピッ
BEEP ピピッ
NOW WHAT?
Detecting biological signals.
There is a human in the area.

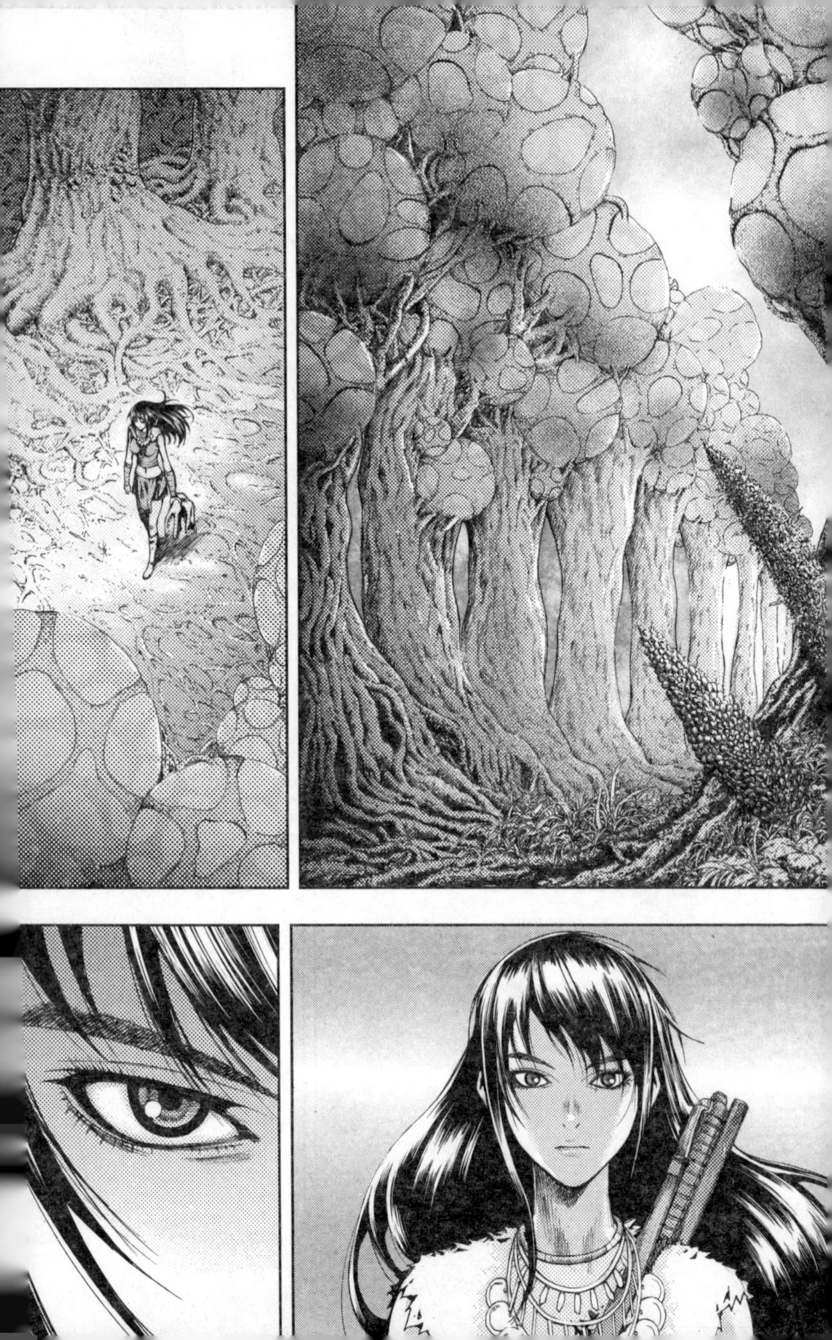

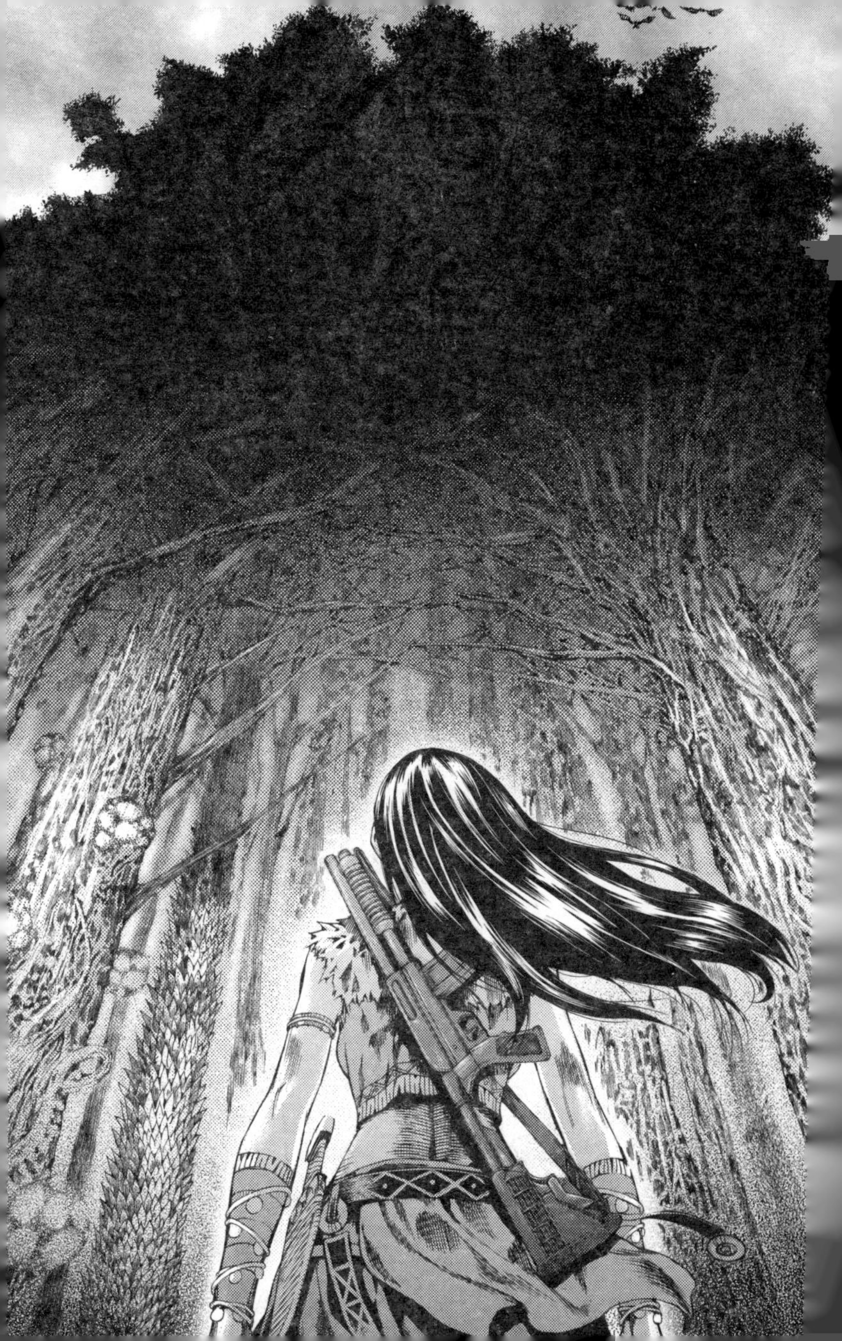

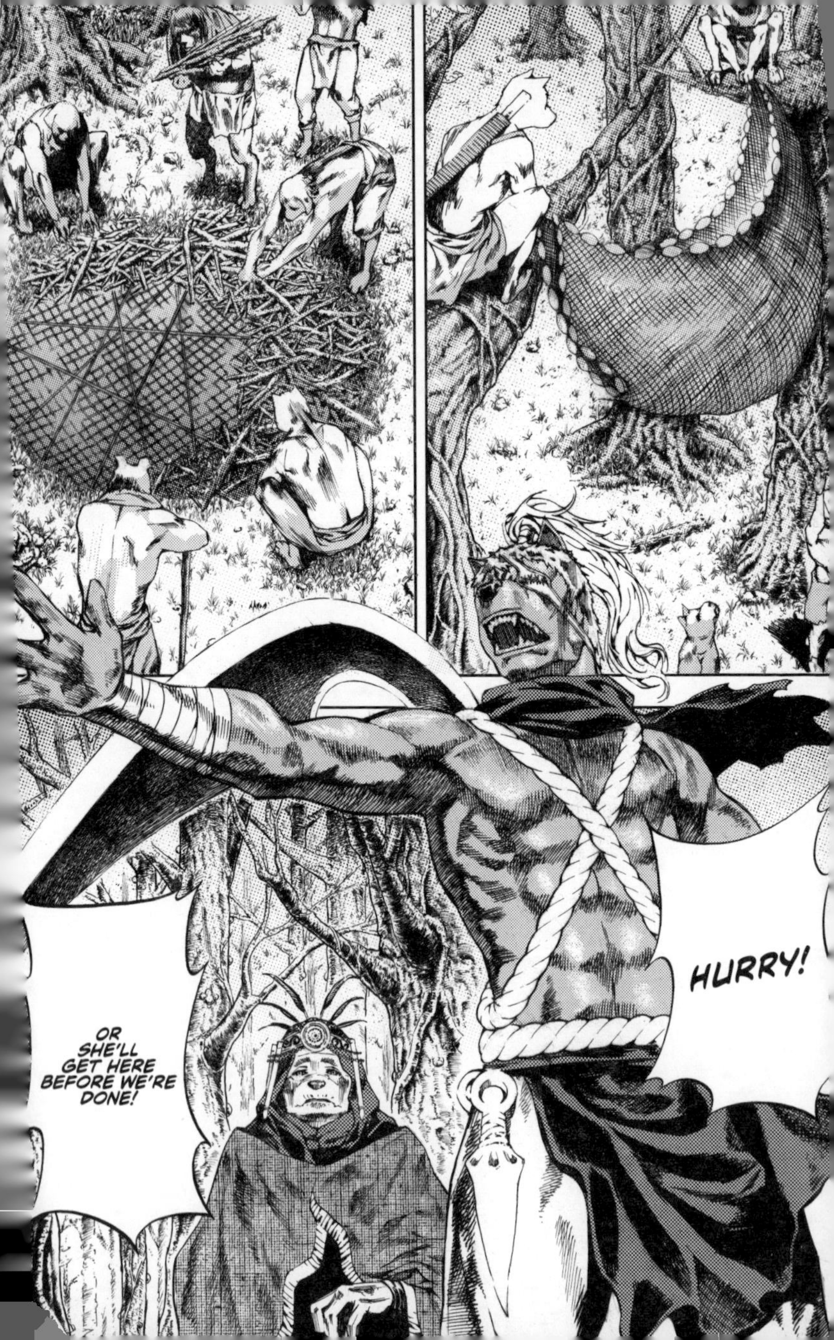
HURRY!
OR SHE'LL GET HERE BEFORE WE'RE DONE!

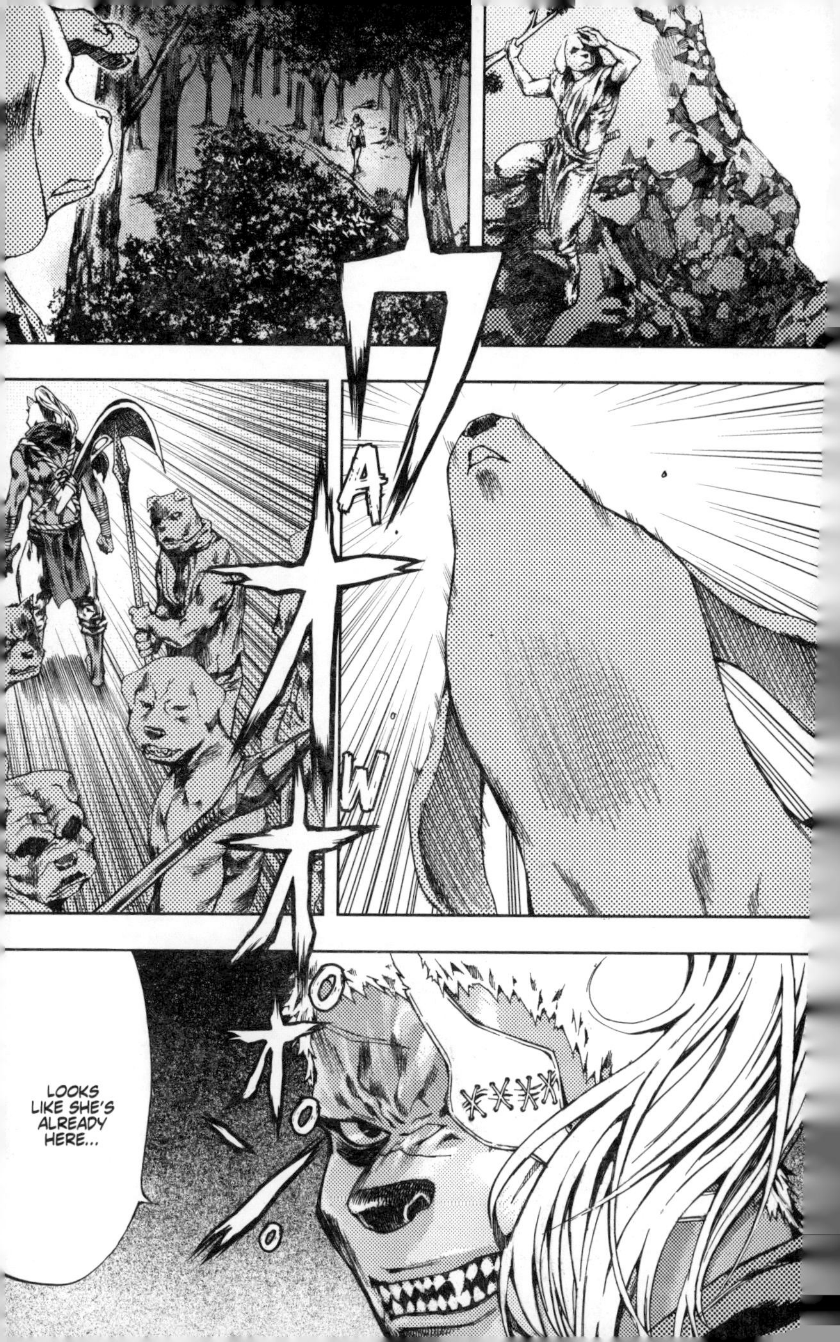
AWOOO
LOOKS LIKE SHE'S ALREADY HERE...

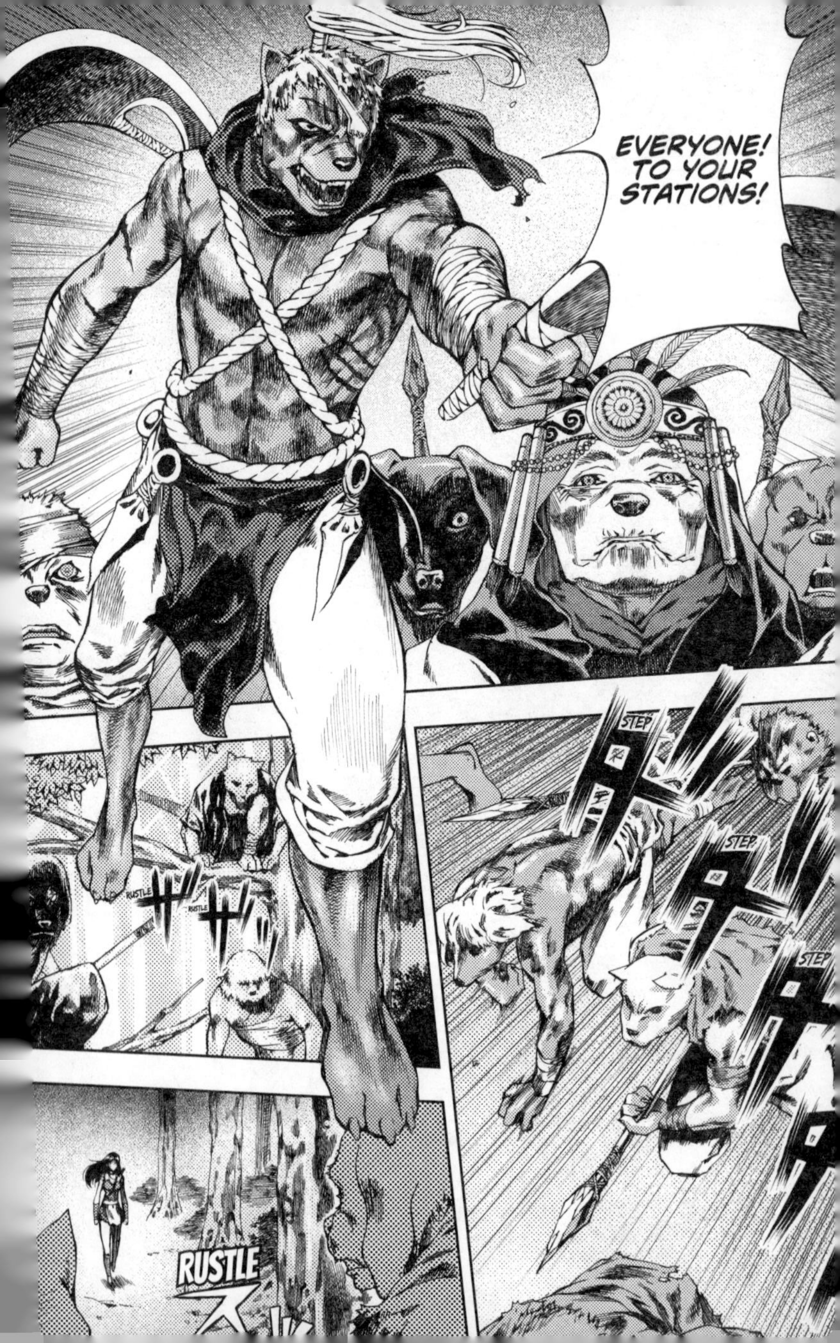
EVERYONE! TO YOUR STATIONS!
STEP
STEP
STEP
RUSTLE
RUSTLE
RUSTLE

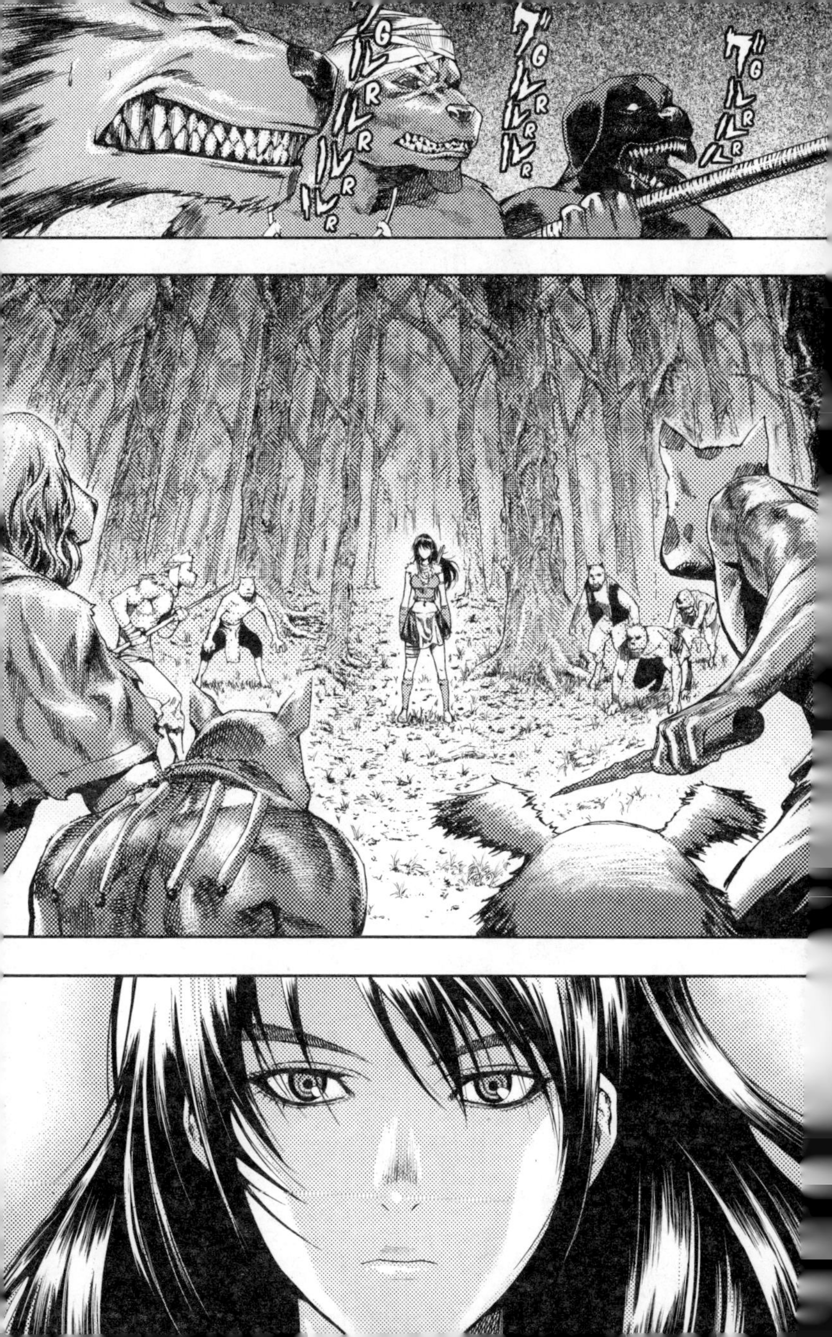
ヴルルル GRRR
ヴルルル GRRR
ルルルル GRRRR

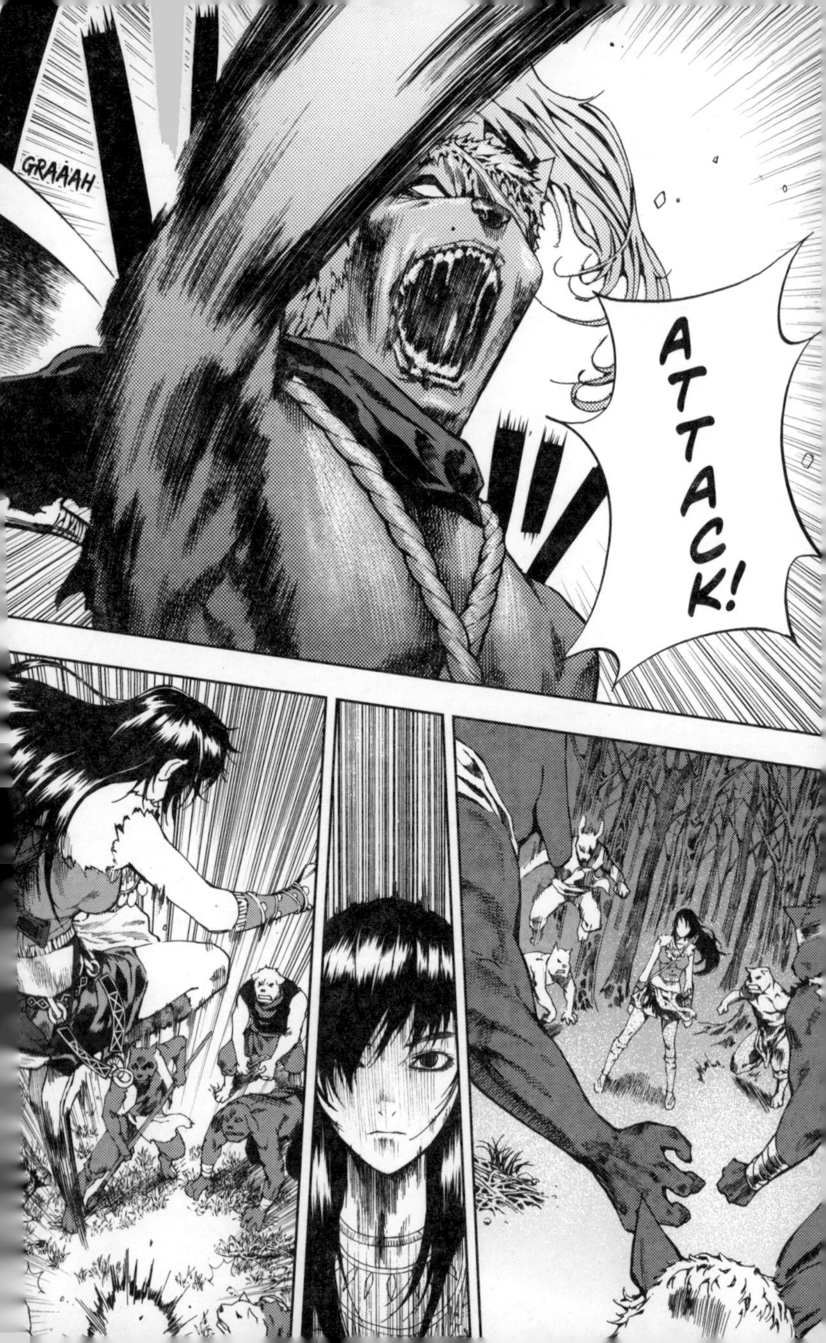
ATTACK!
GRAAAH

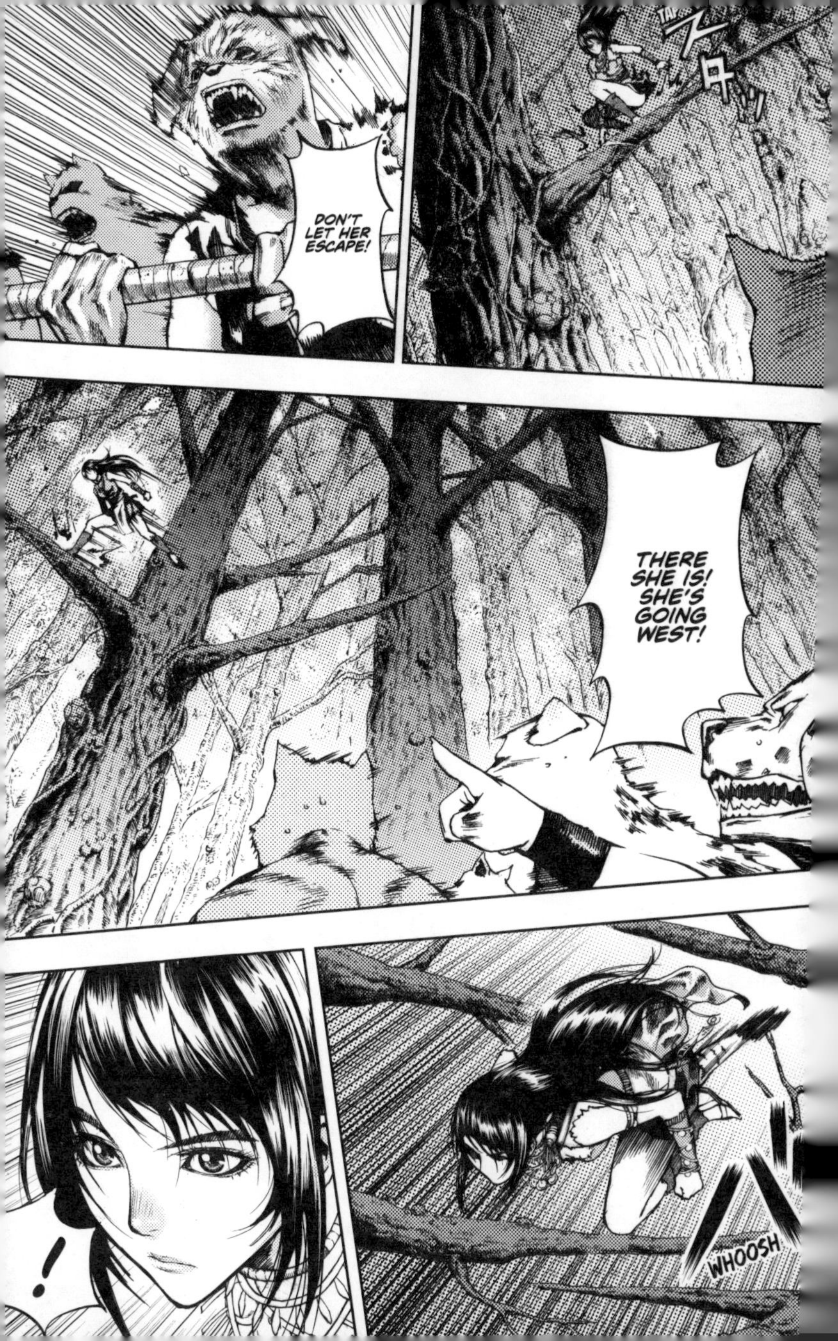
TAP
DON'T LET HER ESCAPE!
THERE SHE IS! SHE'S GOING WEST!
WHOOSH
!

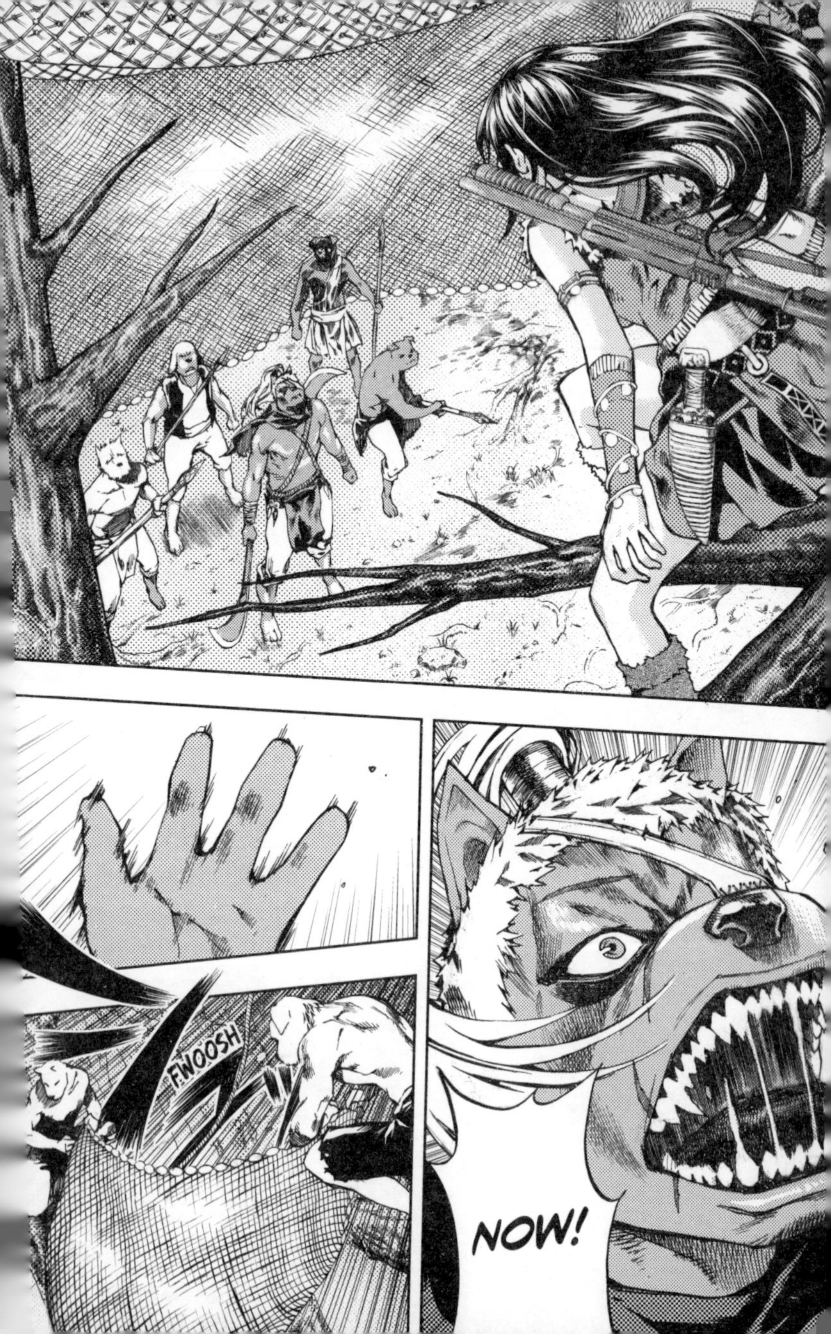
NOW!
FWOOSH

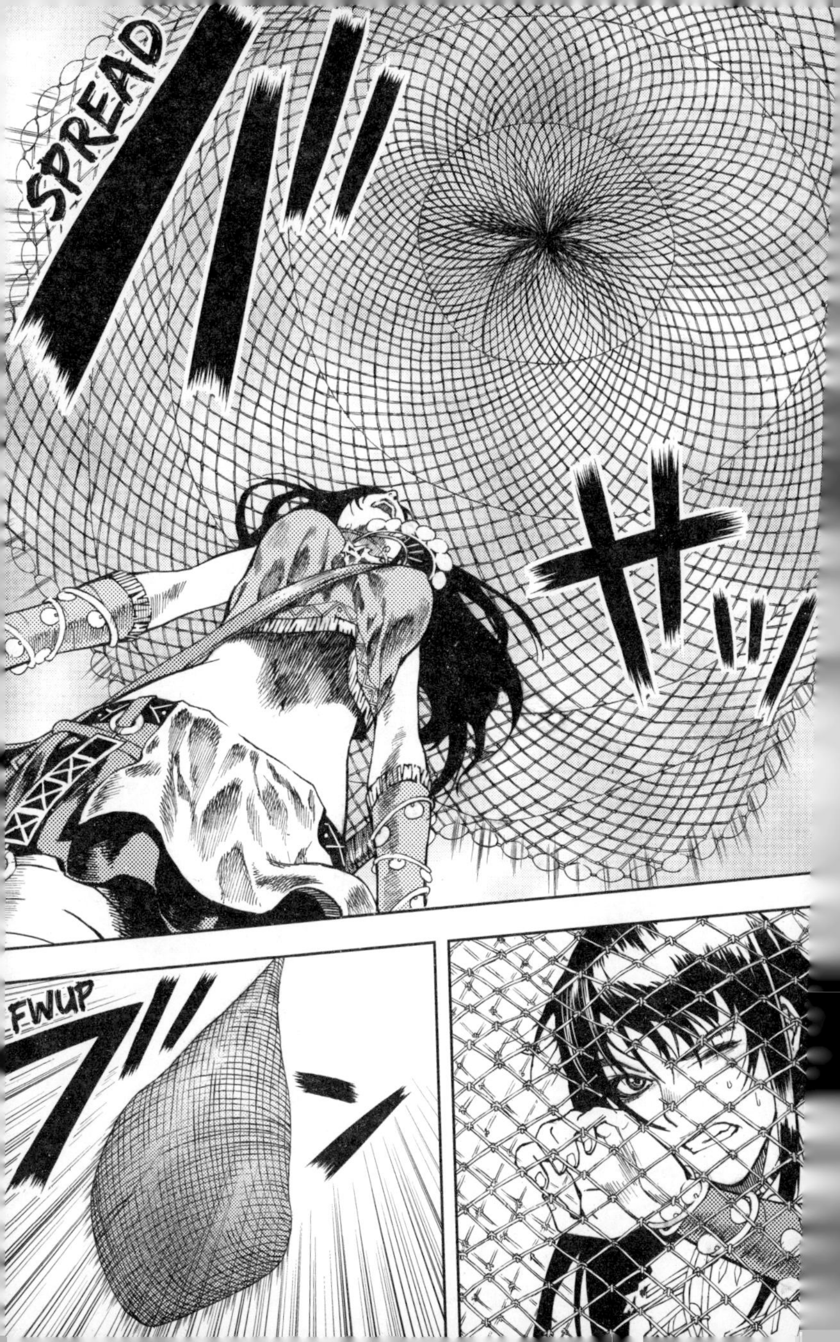
SPREAD
FWUP

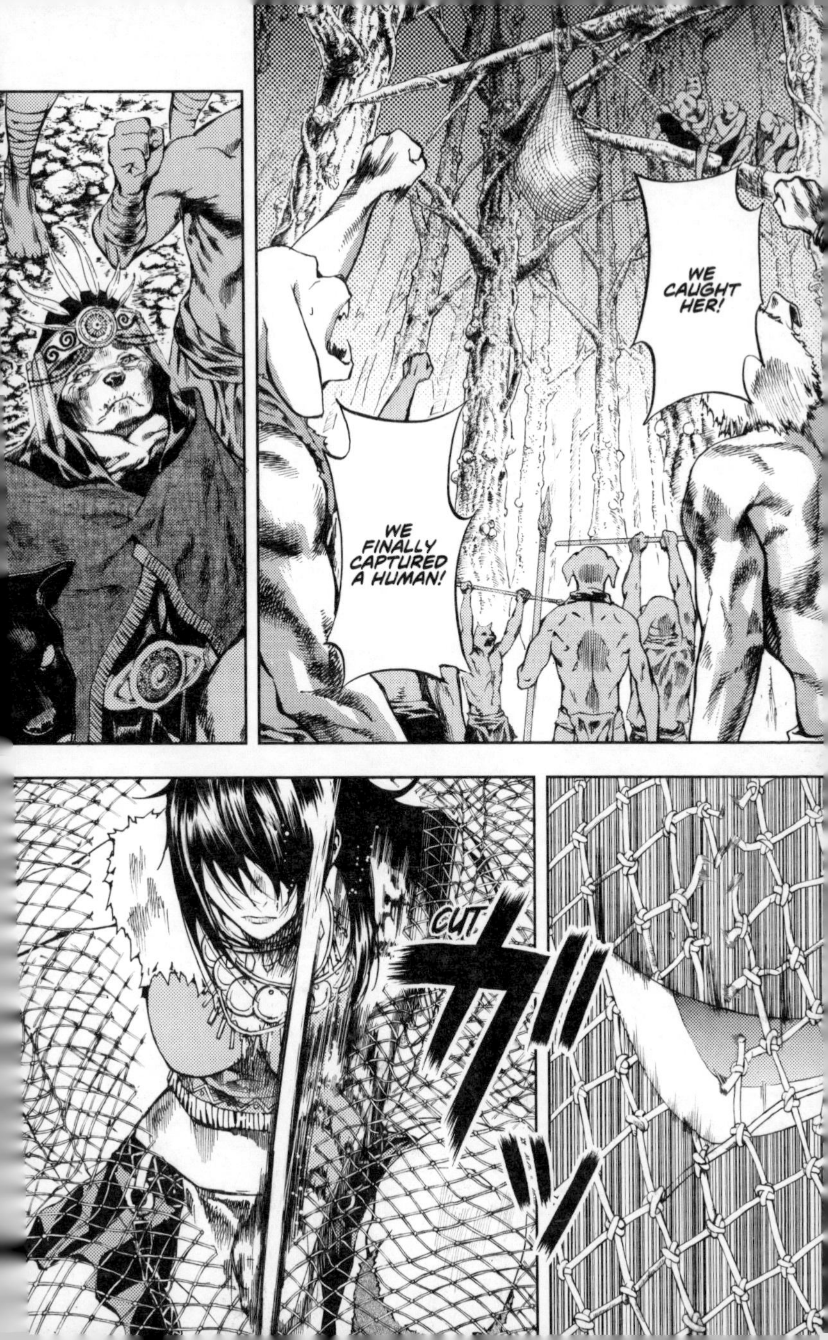
WE CAUGHT HER!
WE FINALLY CAPTURED A HUMAN!
CUT

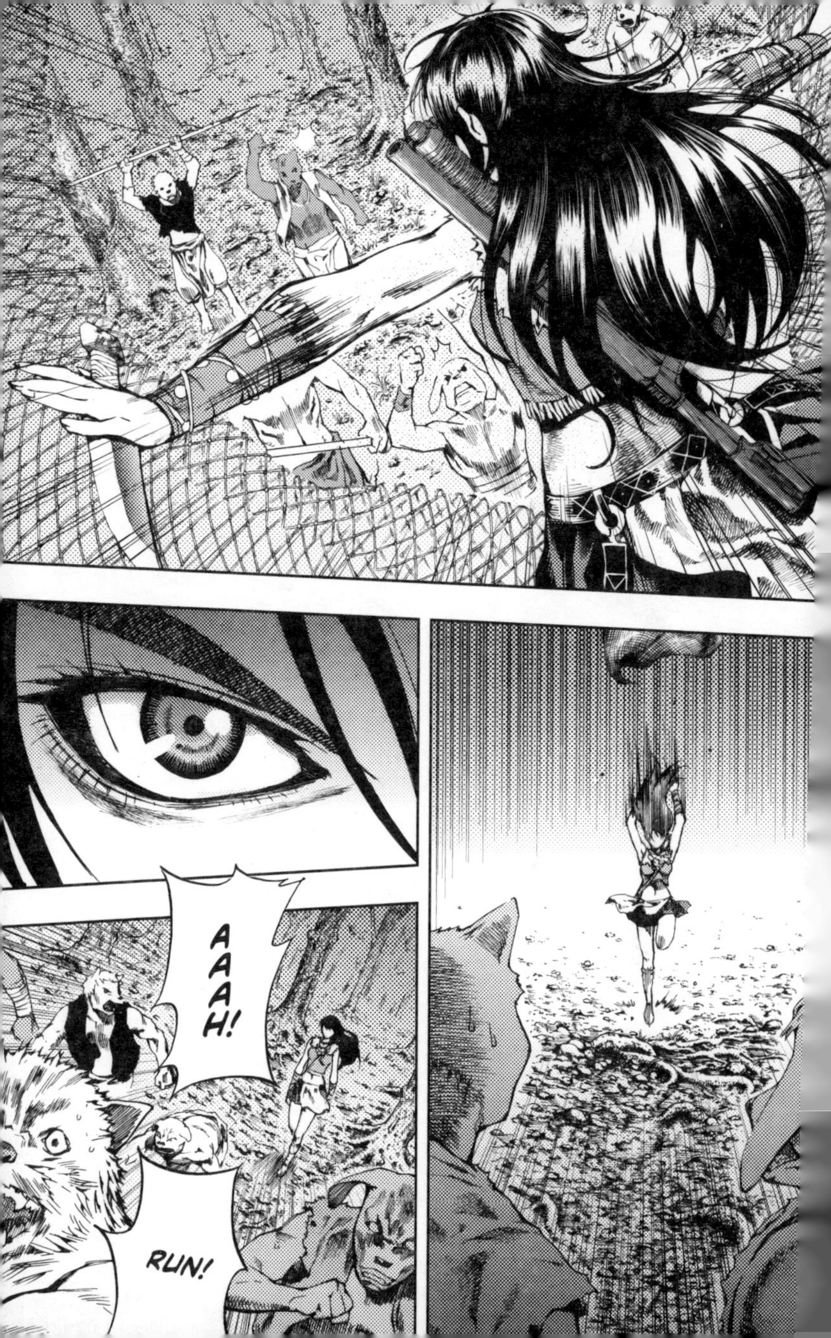
AAAAH!
RUN!

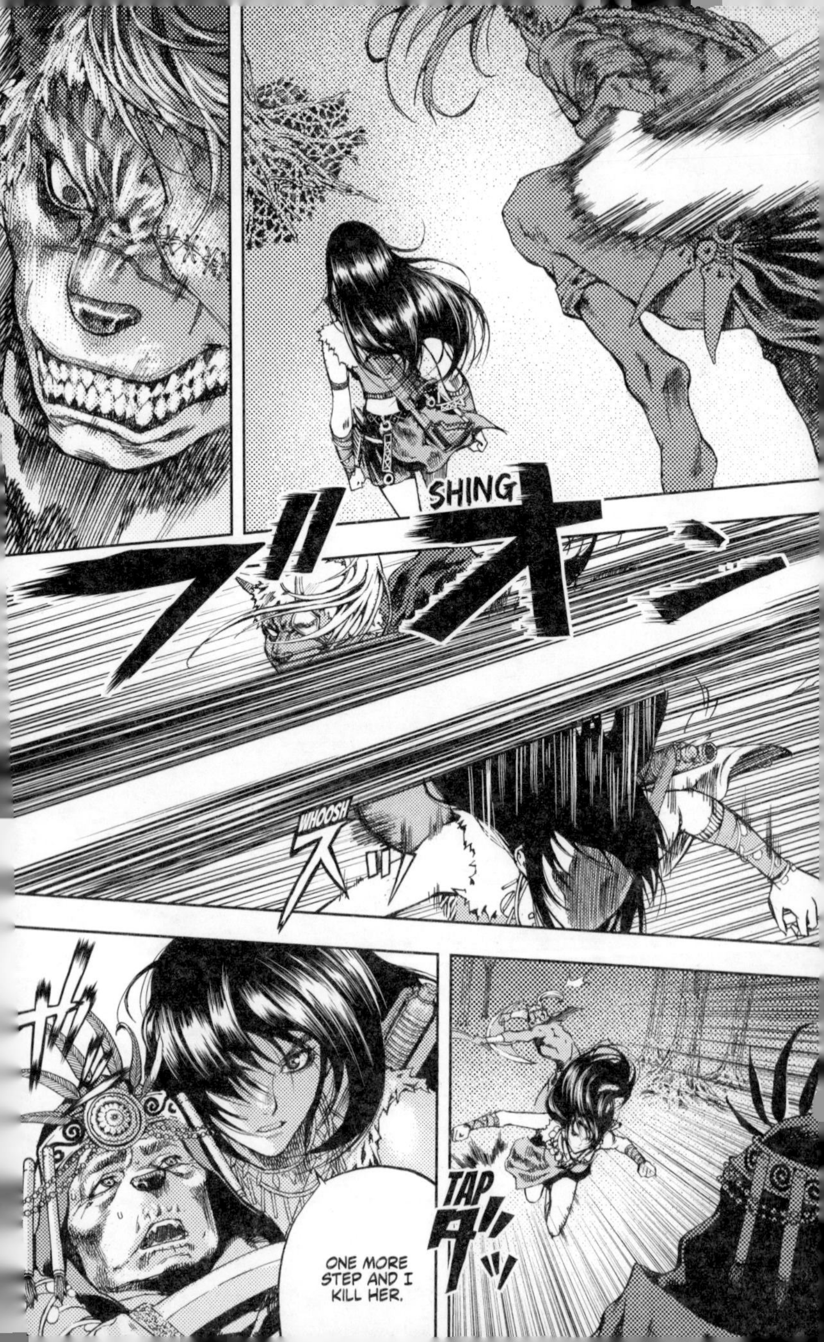
SHING
WHOOSH
TAP
ONE MORE STEP AND I KILL HER.

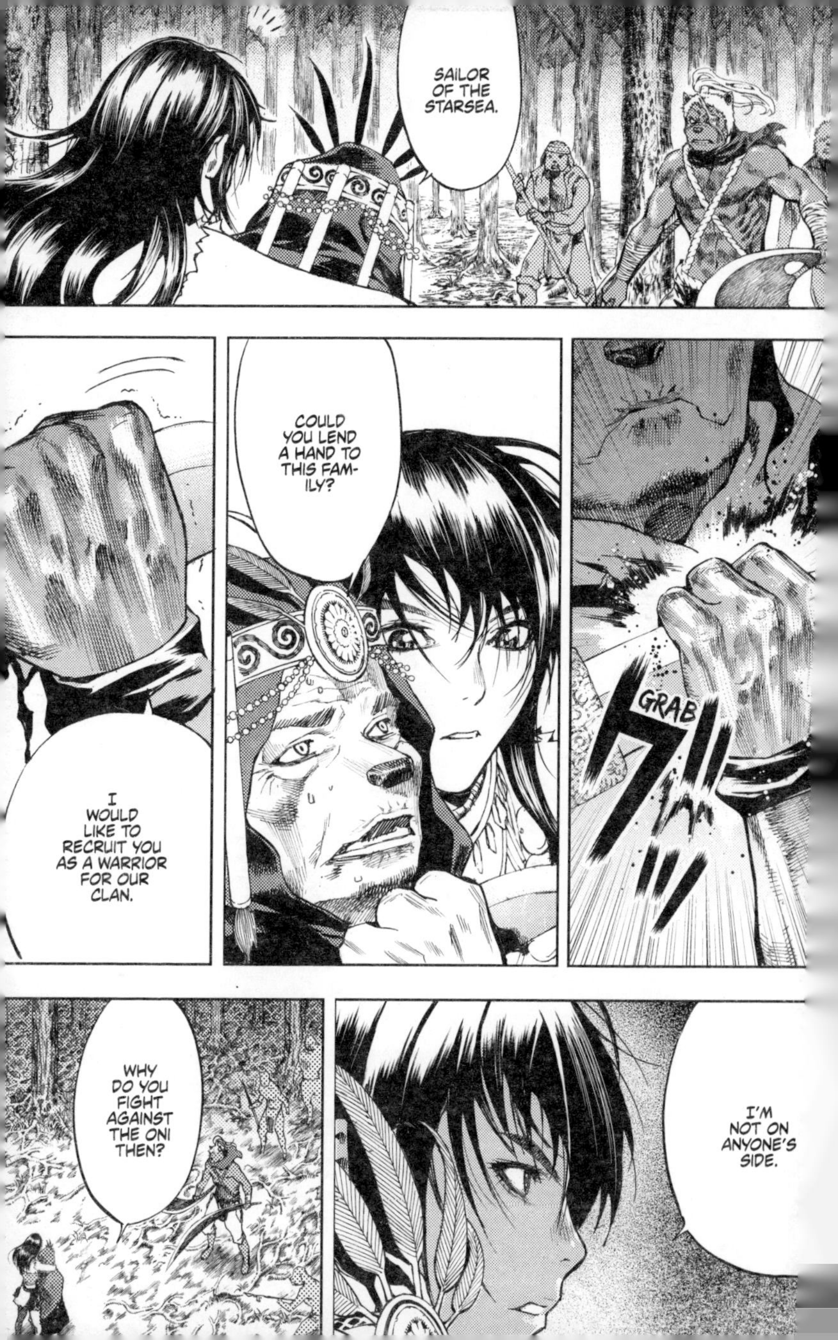
SAILOR OF THE STARSEA.
GRAB
COULD YOU LEND A HAND TO THIS FAMILY?
I WOULD LIKE TO RECRUIT YOU AS A WARRIOR FOR OUR CLAN.
I'M NOT ON ANYONE'S SIDE.
WHY DO YOU FIGHT AGAINST THE ONI THEN?

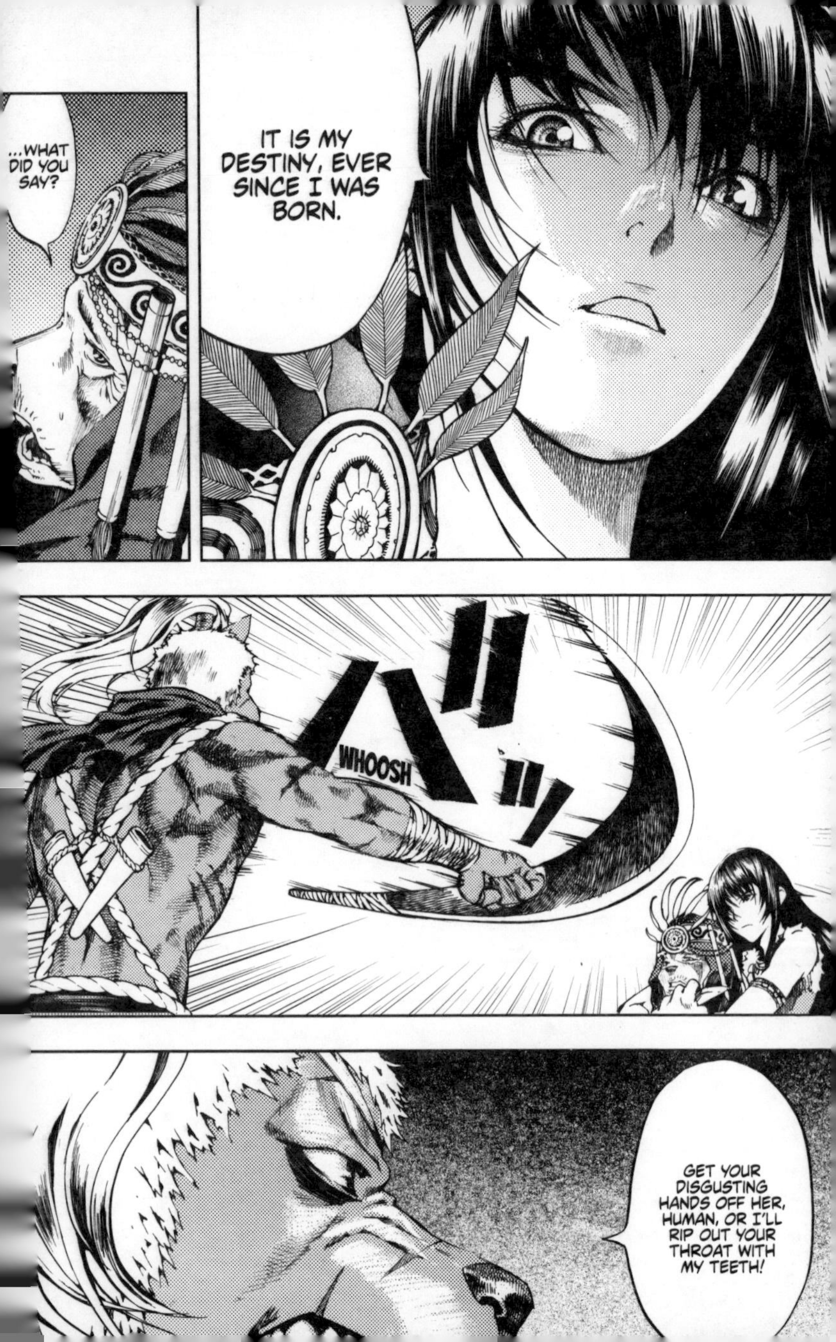
IT IS MY DESTINY, EVER SINCE I WAS BORN.
...WHAT DID YOU SAY?
WHOOSH
GET YOUR DISGUSTING HANDS OFF HER, HUMAN, OR I'LL RIP OUT YOUR THROAT WITH MY TEETH!

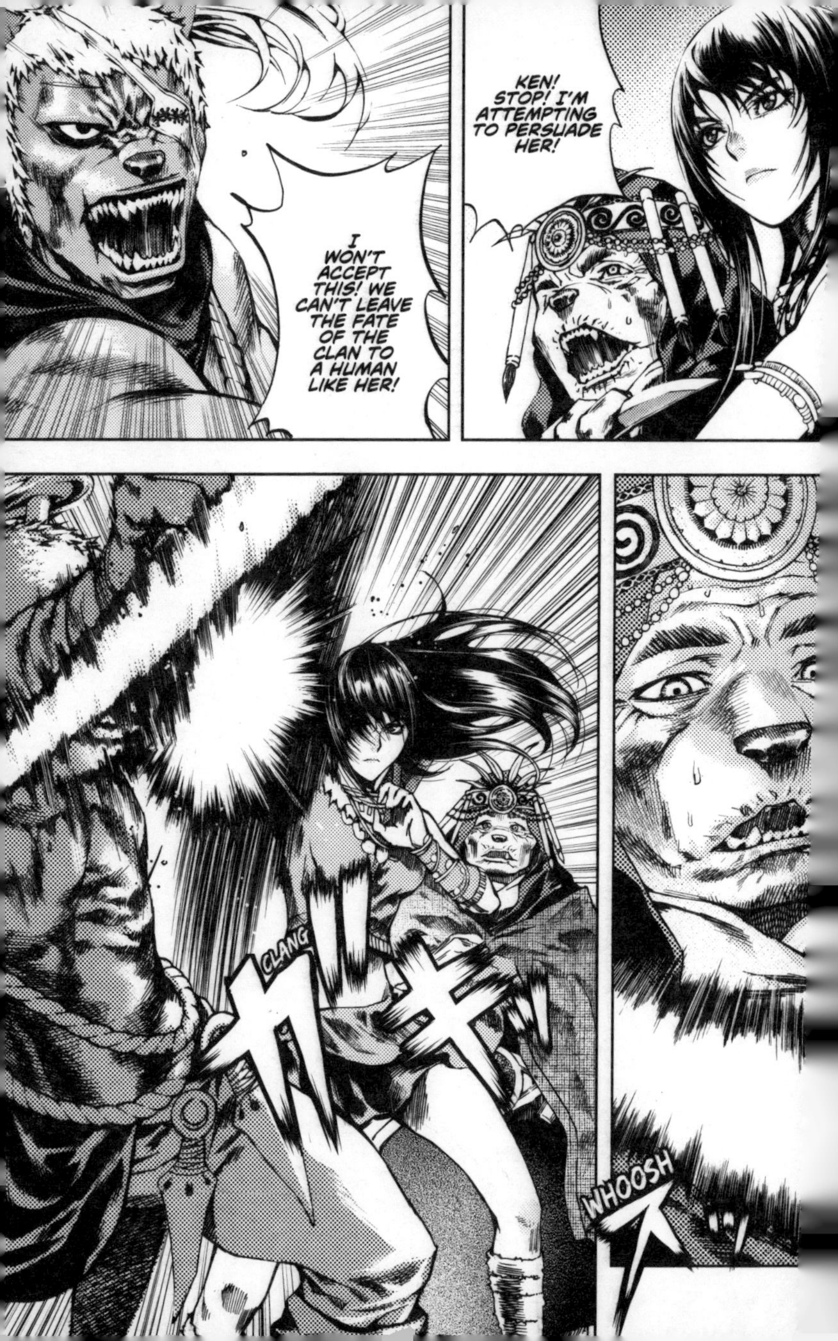
KEN! STOP! I'M ATTEMPTING TO PERSUADE HER!
I WON'T ACCEPT THIS! WE CAN'T LEAVE THE FATE OF THE CLAN TO A HUMAN LIKE HER!
WHOOSH
CLANG

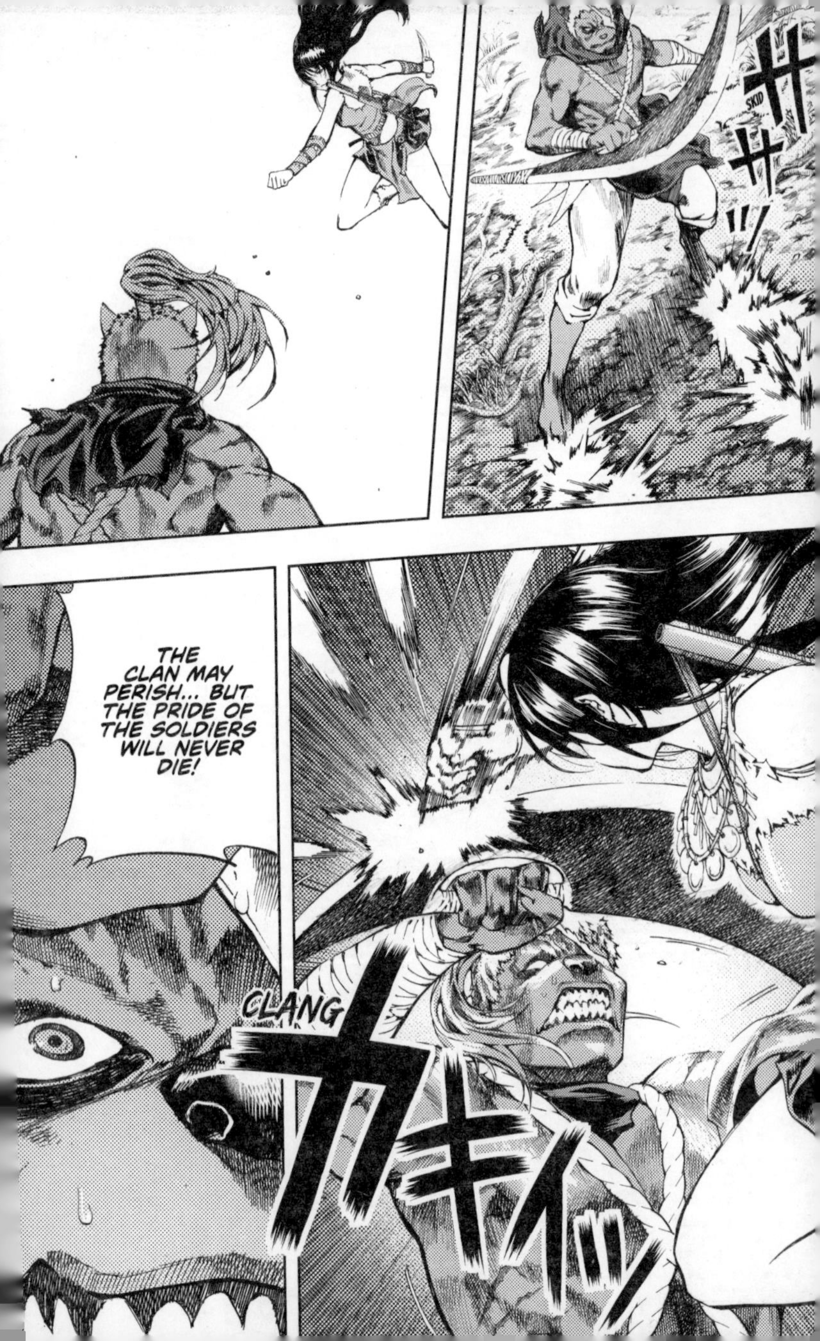
SKID
CLANG
THE CLAN MAY PERISH... BUT THE PRIDE OF THE SOLDIERS WILL NEVER DIE!

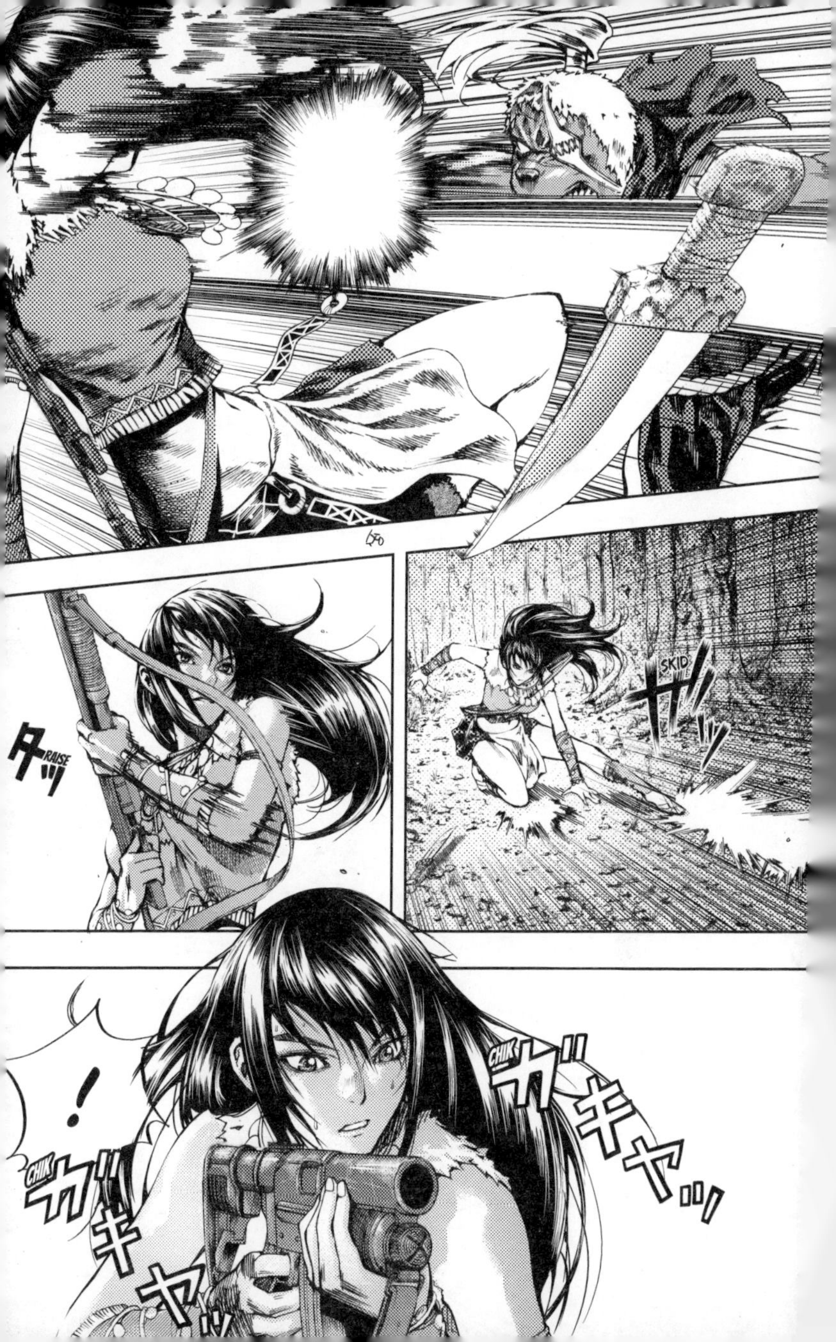
SKID
RAISE
CHIK
!
CHIK

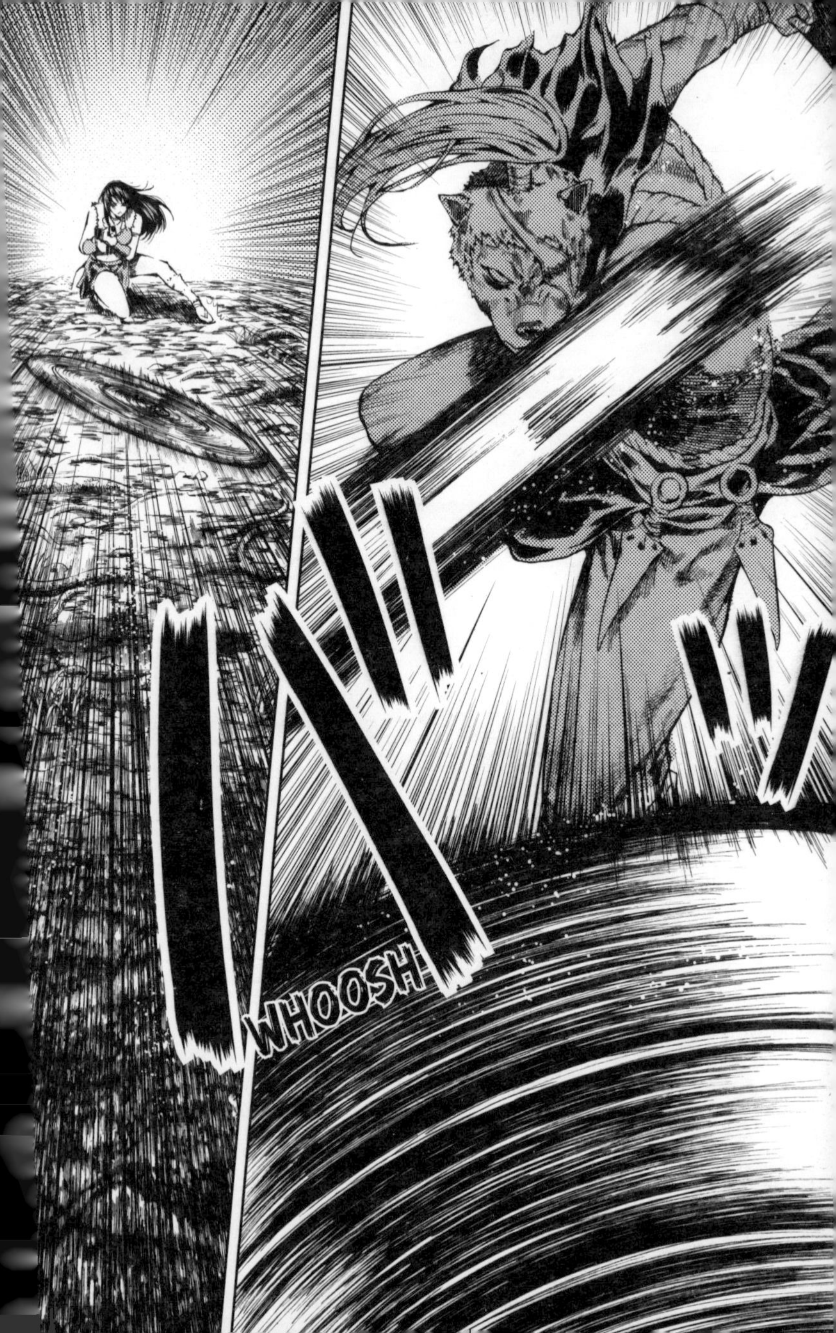
WHOOSH

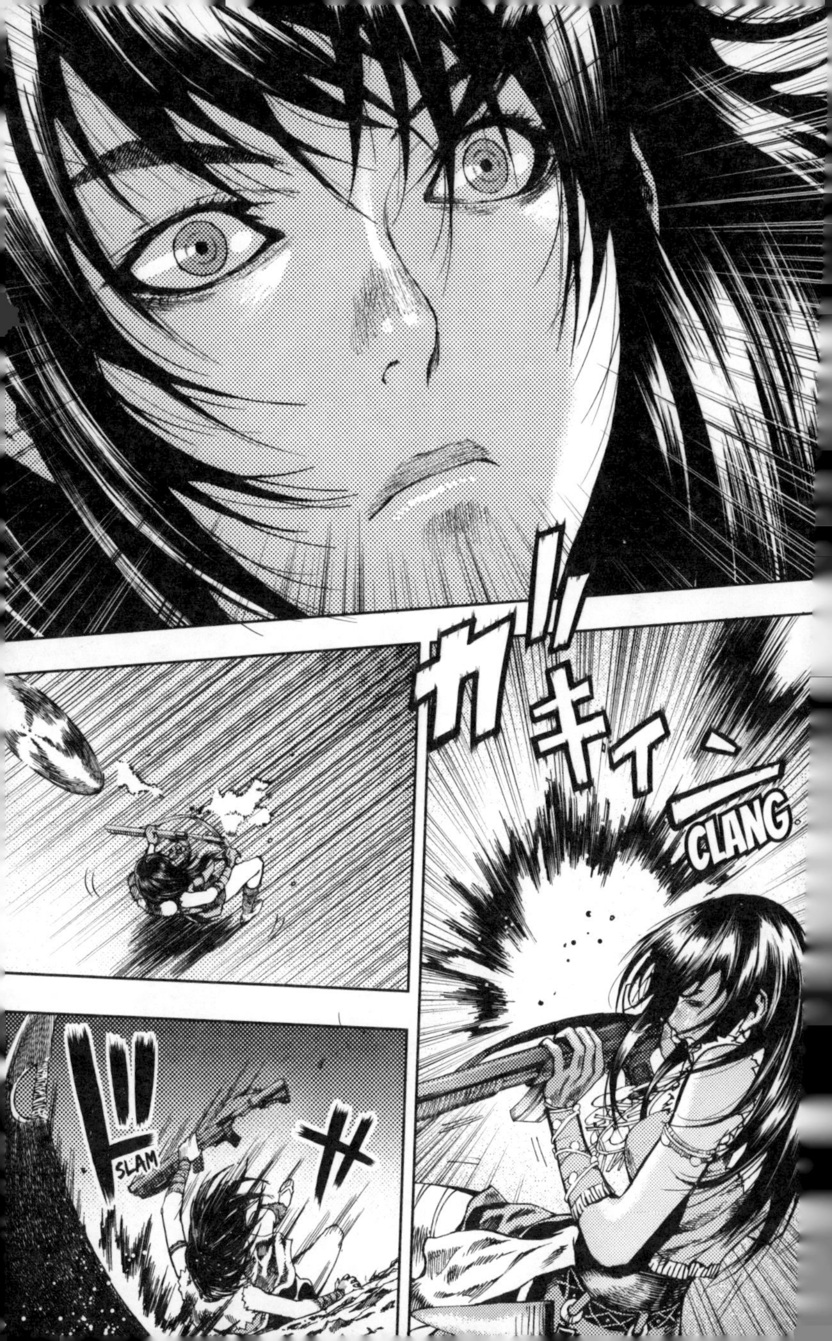
カキィー
CLANG
ド
SLAM

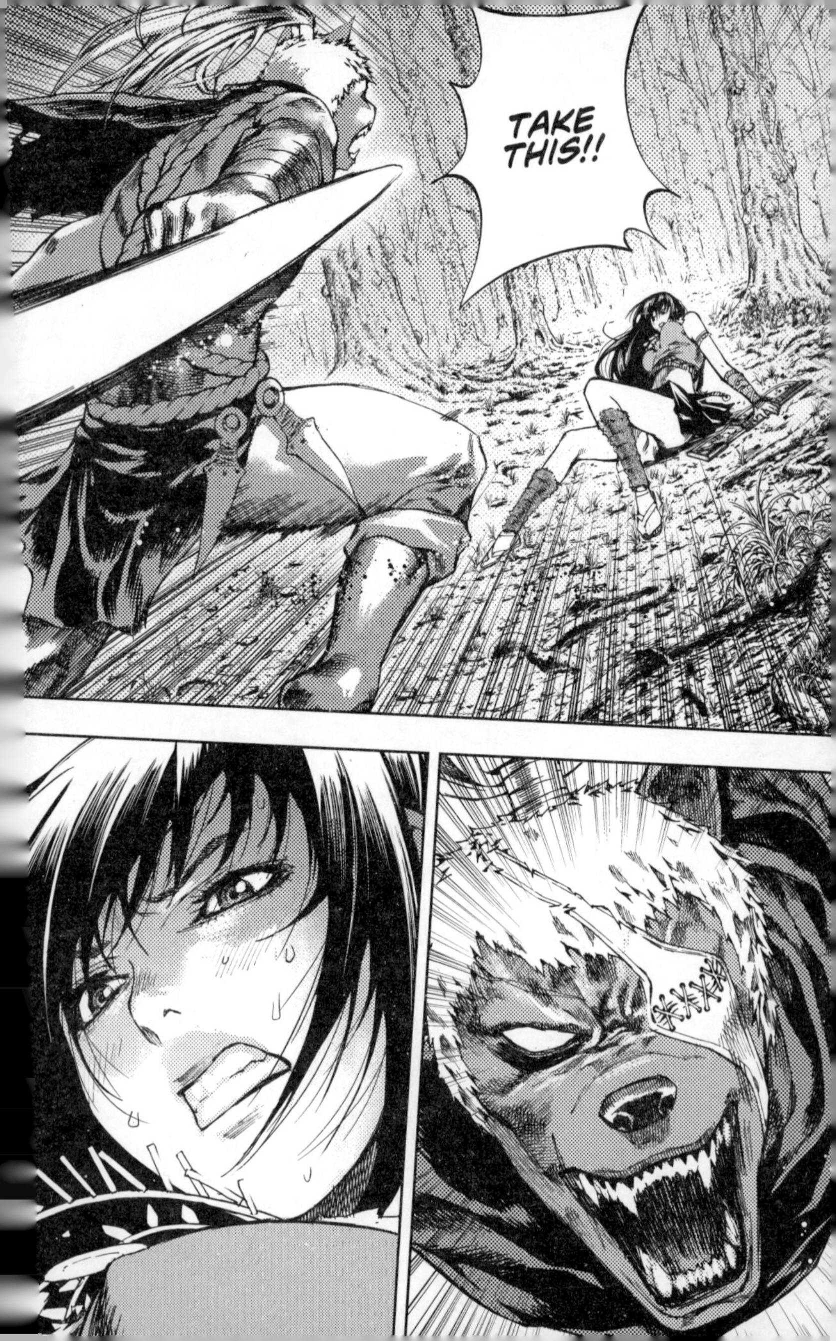
TAKE THIS!!

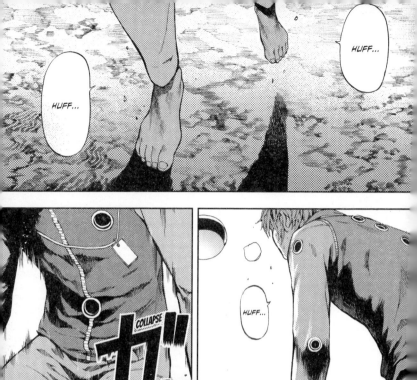

HUFF...

HUFF...

HUFF...

COLLAPSE

W-WAIT!

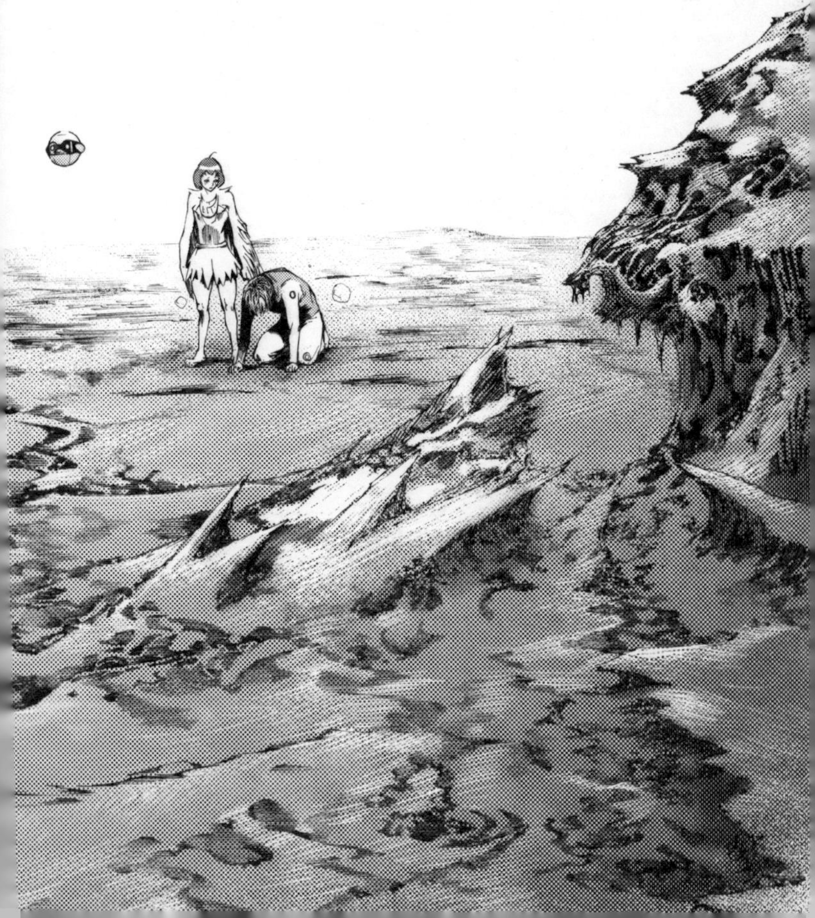

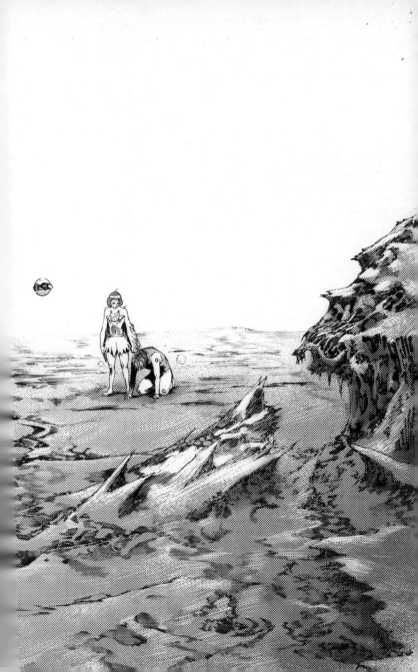

Chapter 4 Memories of Earth

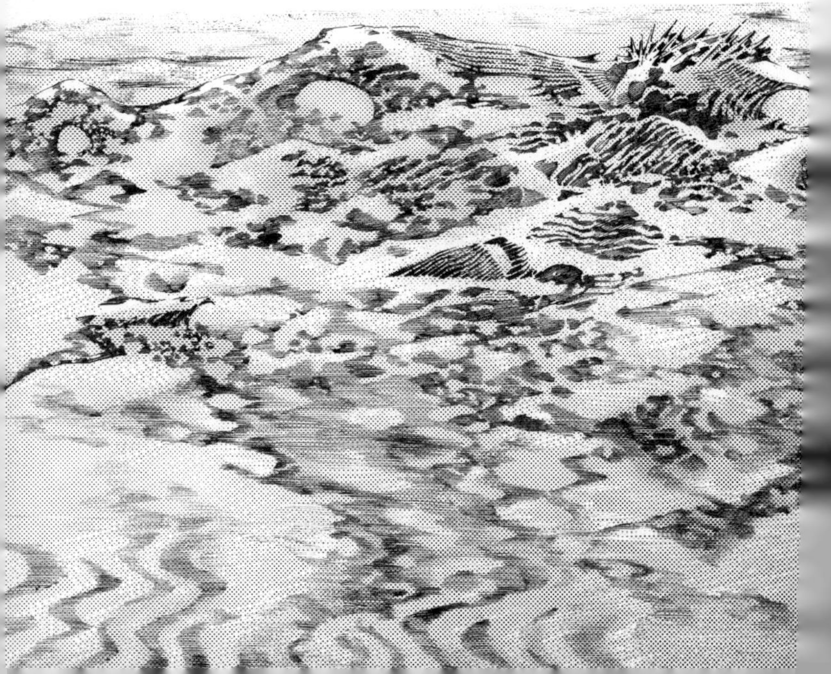

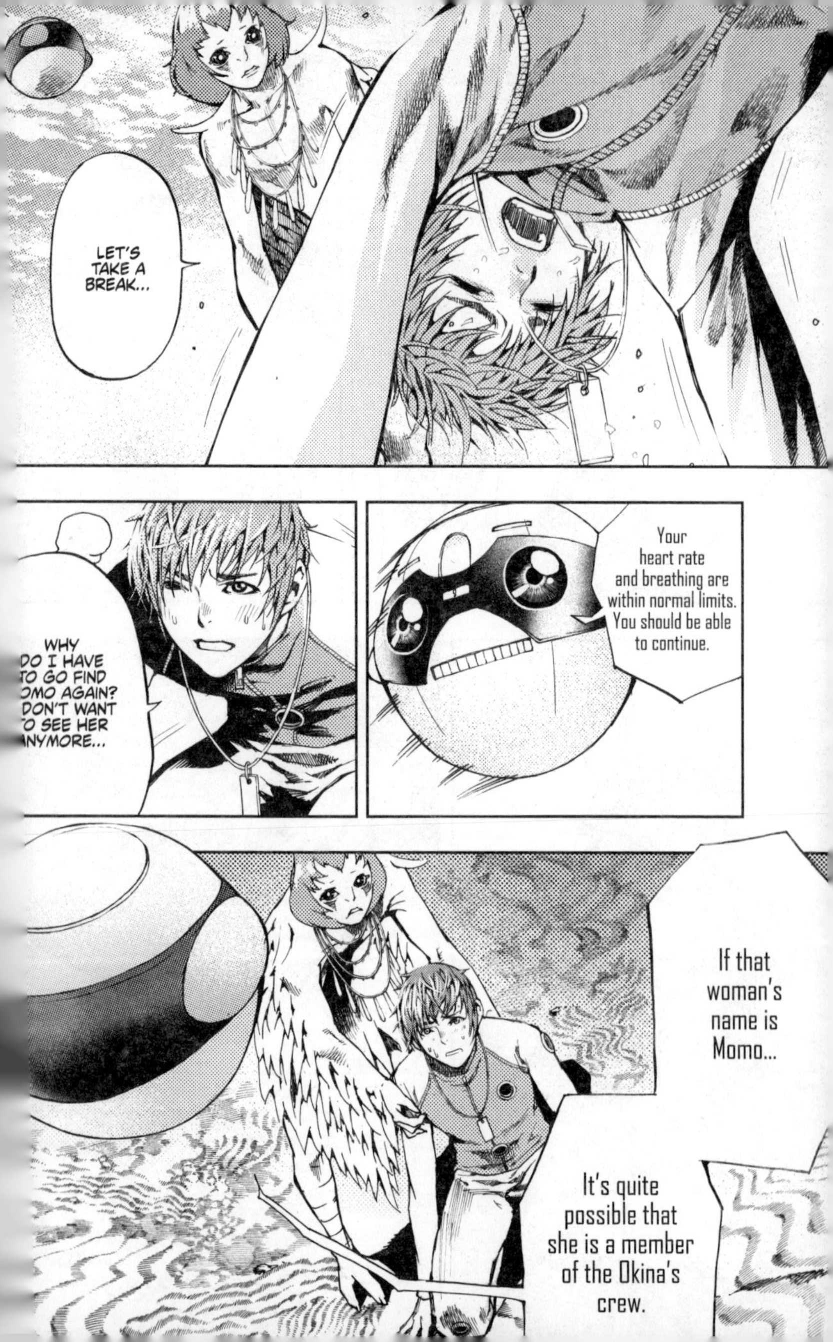
LET'S TAKE A BREAK...
Your heart rate and breathing are within normal limits. You should be able to continue.
WHY DO I HAVE TO GO FIND MOMO AGAIN? I DON'T WANT TO SEE HER ANYMORE...
If that woman's name is Momo...
It's quite possible that she is a member of the Okina's crew.

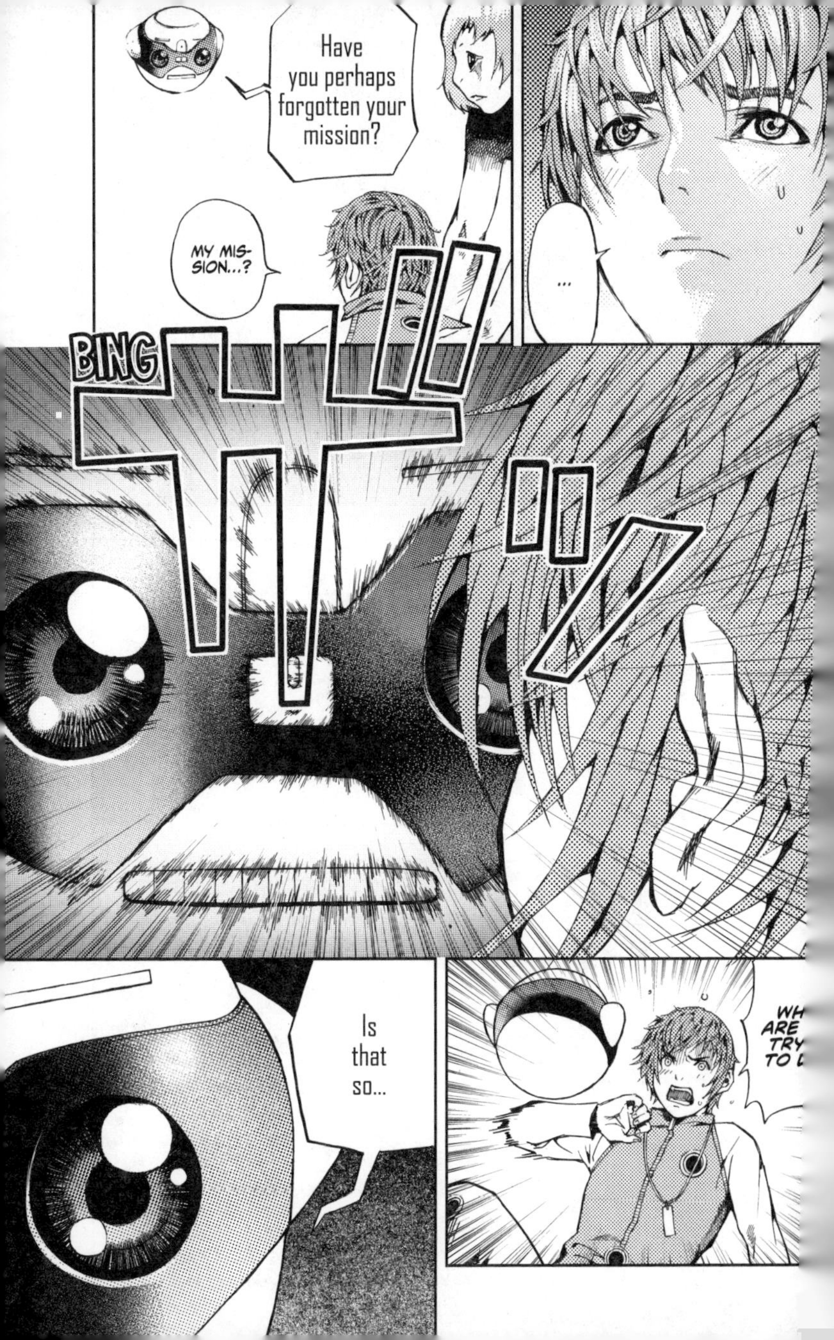
...
Have you perhaps forgotten your mission?
MY MIS-SION...?
BING
WH ARE TRY TO
Is that so...

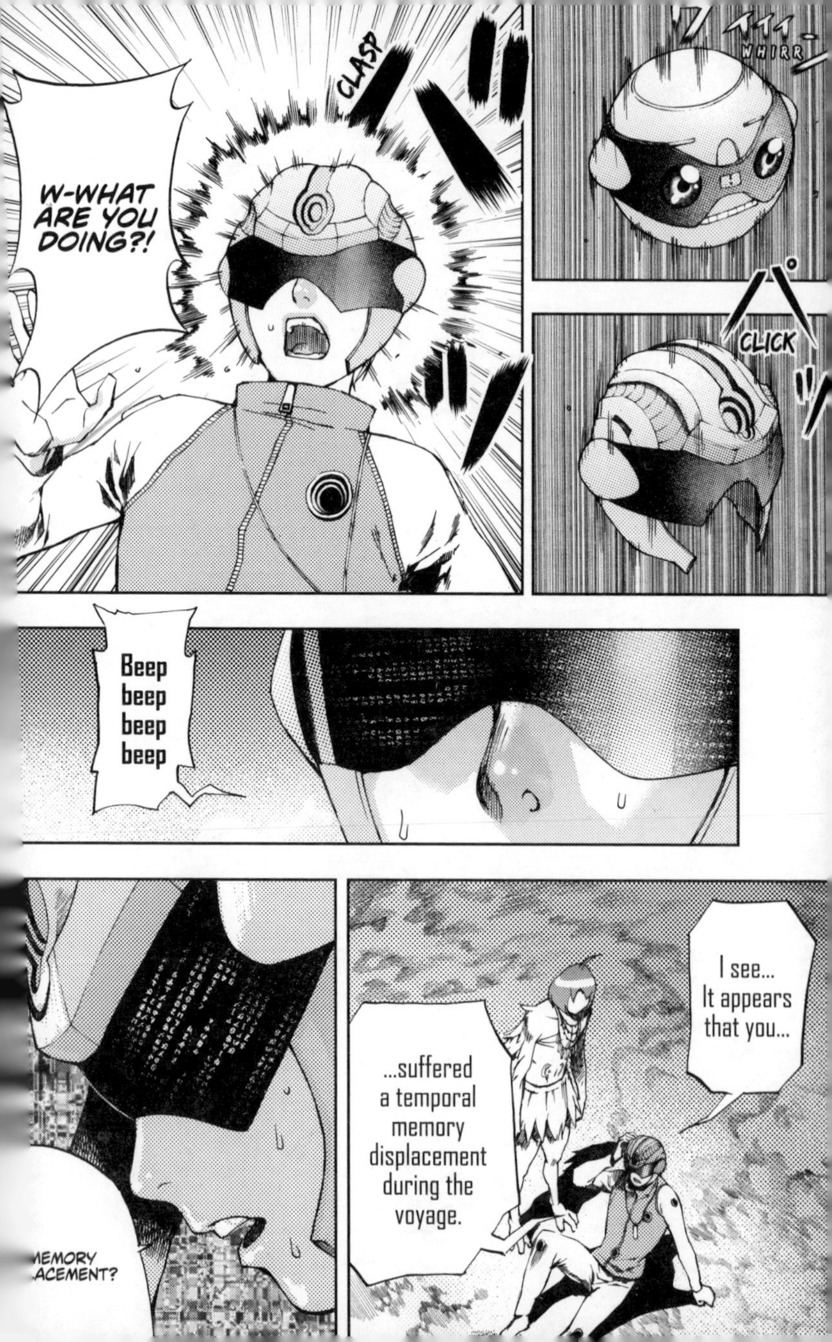
イイー
WHIRR
CLICK
CLASP
W-WHAT ARE YOU DOING?!
Beep beep beep beep
I see... It appears that you...
...suffered a temporal memory displacement during the voyage.
MEMORY
ACEMENT?

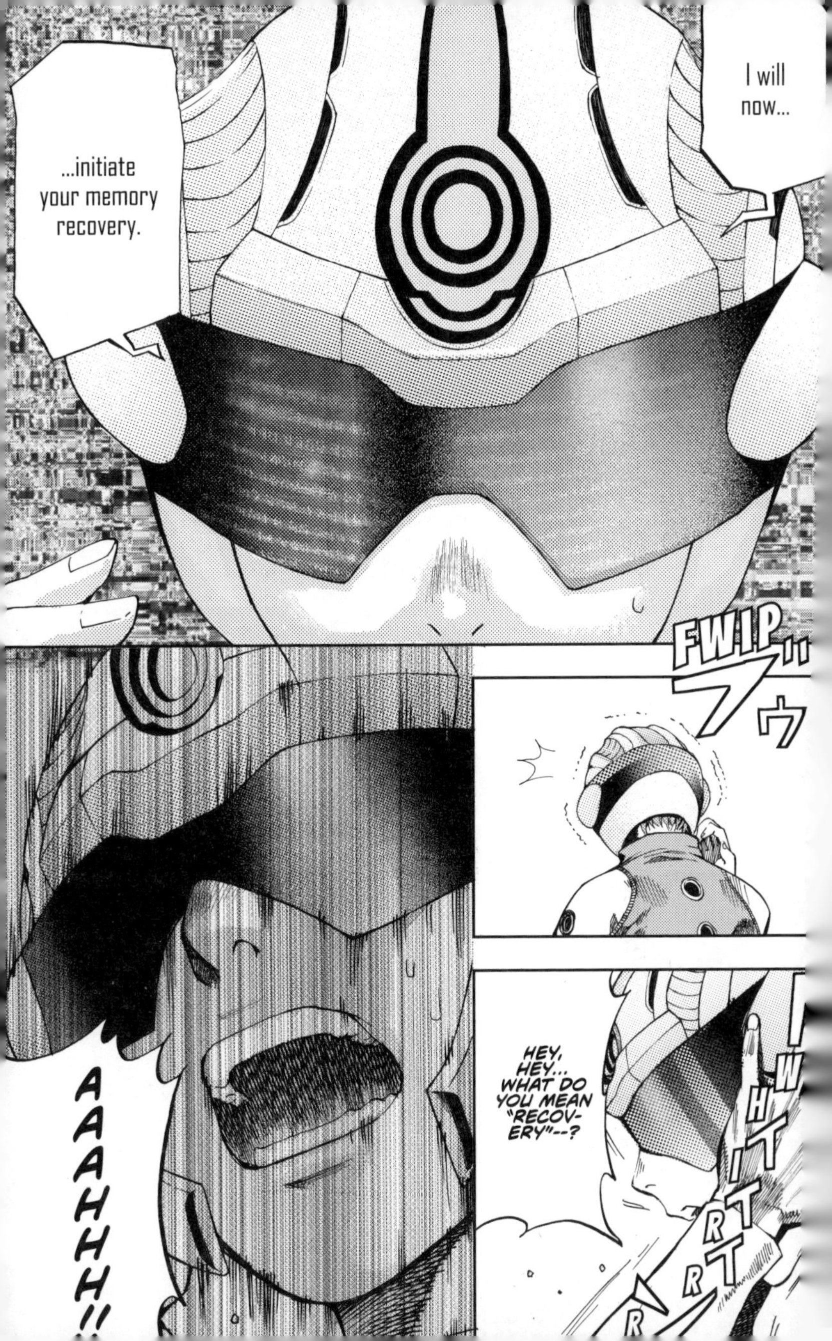
I will now...
...initiate your memory recovery.
FWIP
HEY, HEY... WHAT DO YOU MEAN "RECOV-ERY"--?
AAAAHHHH!!

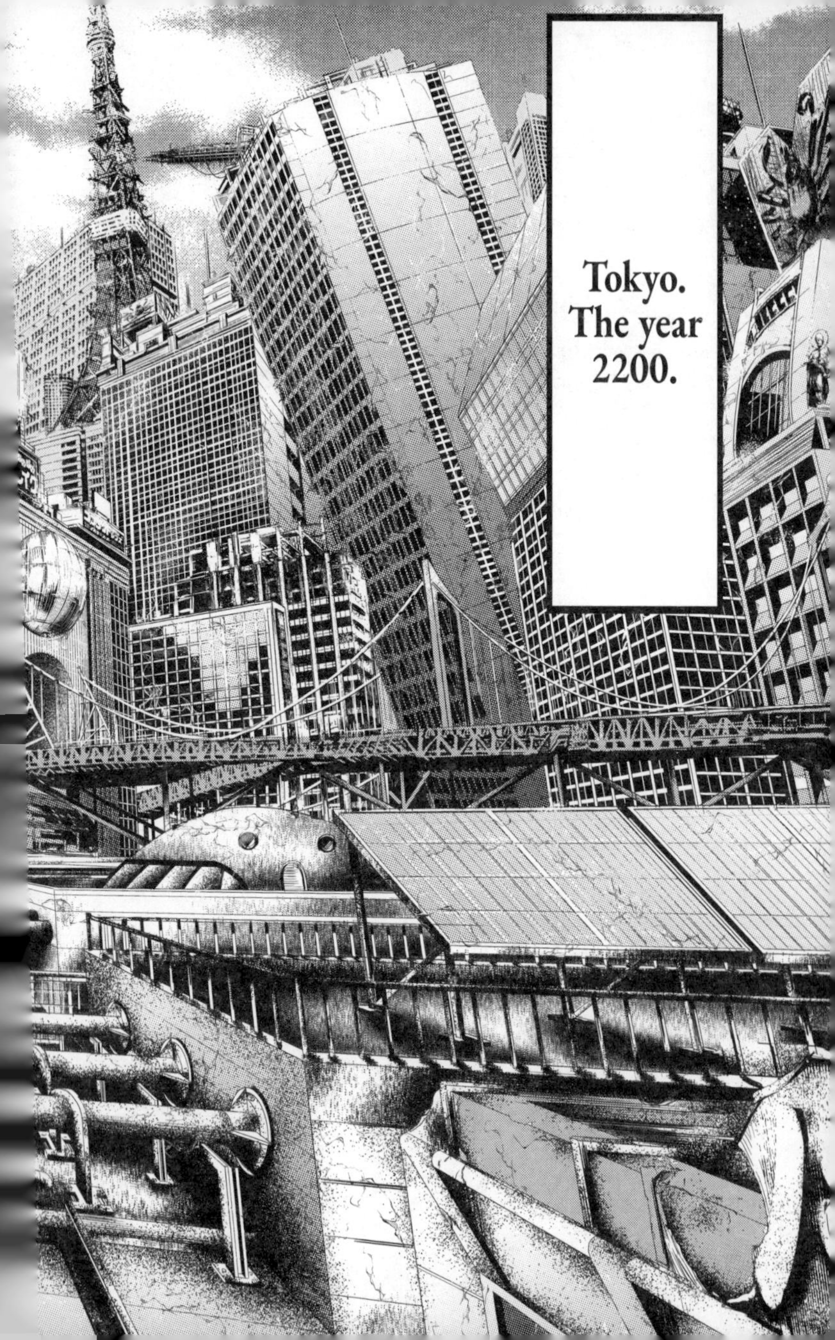
Tokyo.
The year
2200.

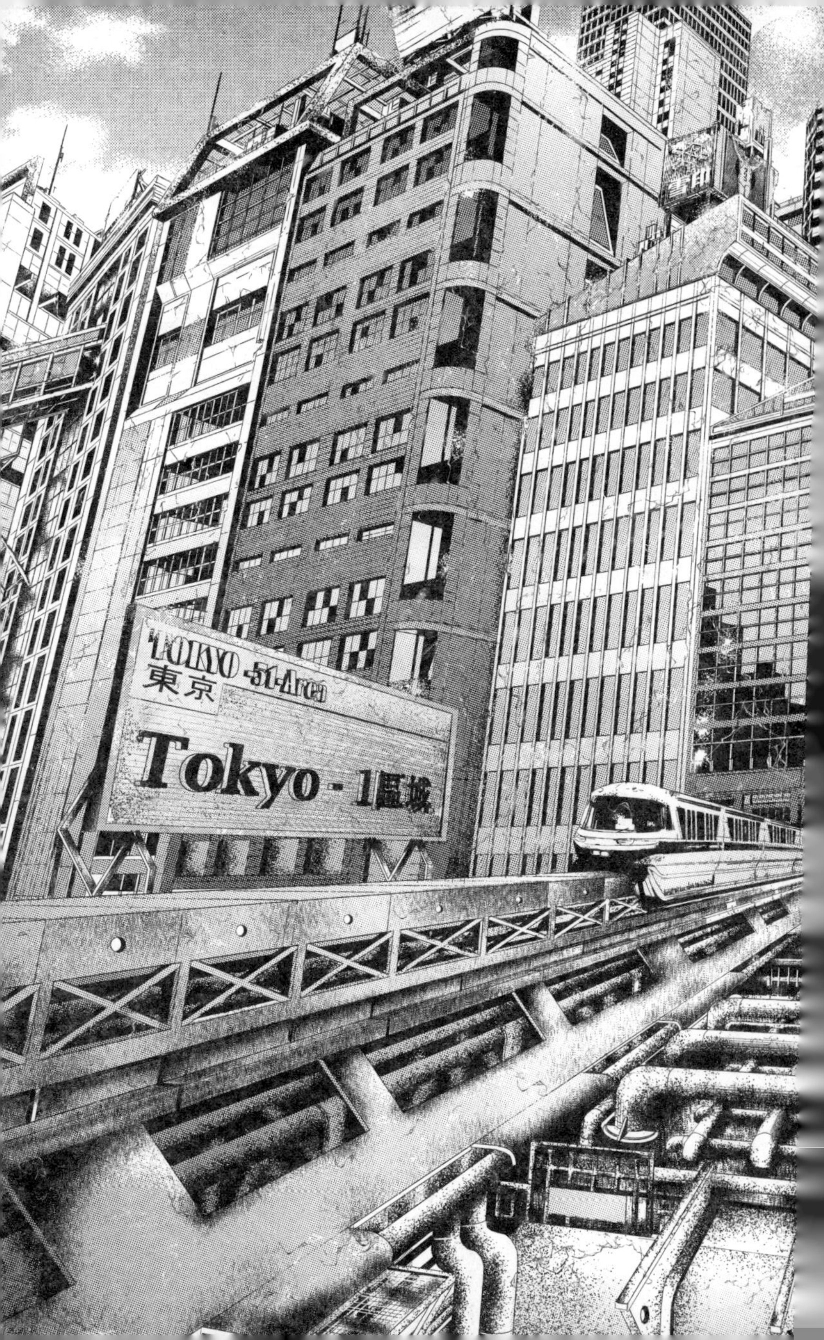
TOKYO -51-Area
東京
Tokyo - 1區域

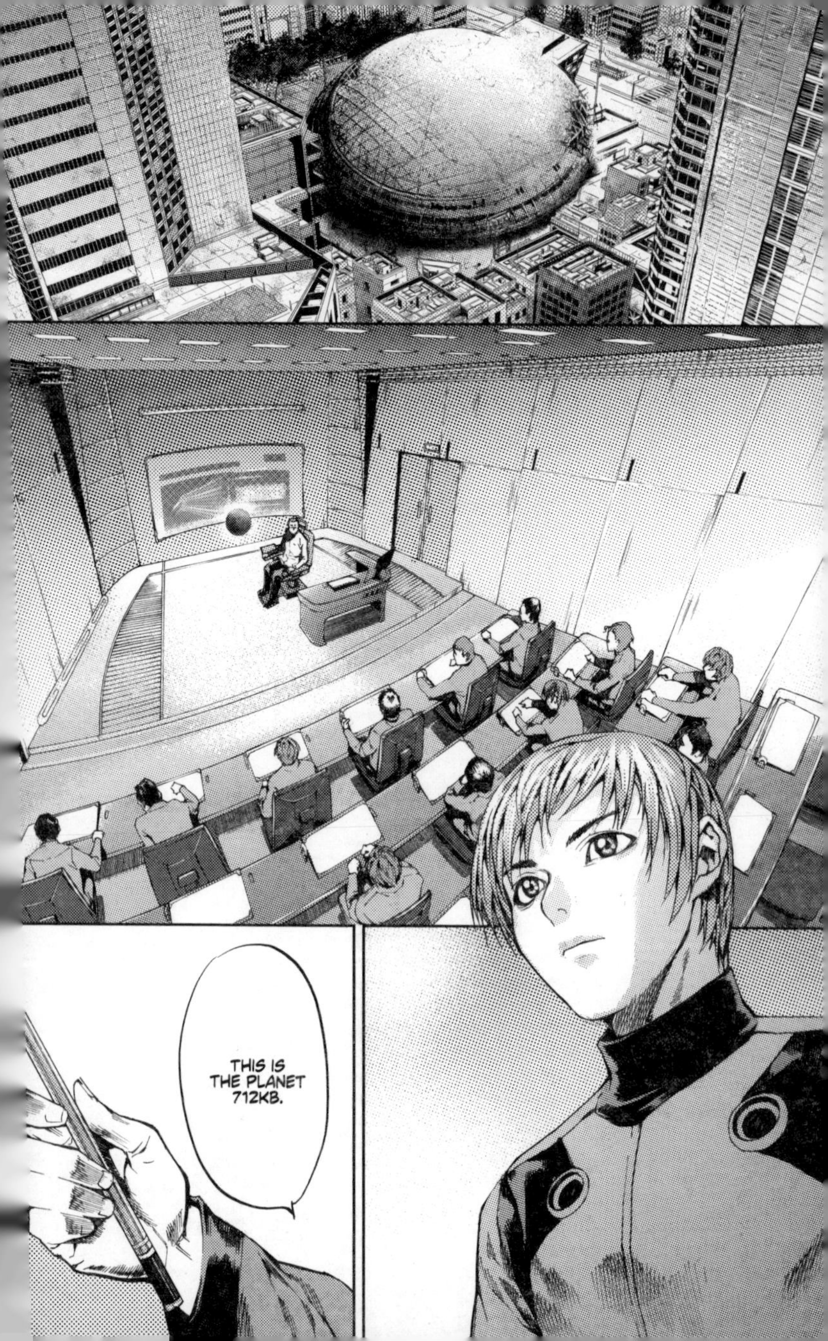
THIS IS THE PLANET 712KB.

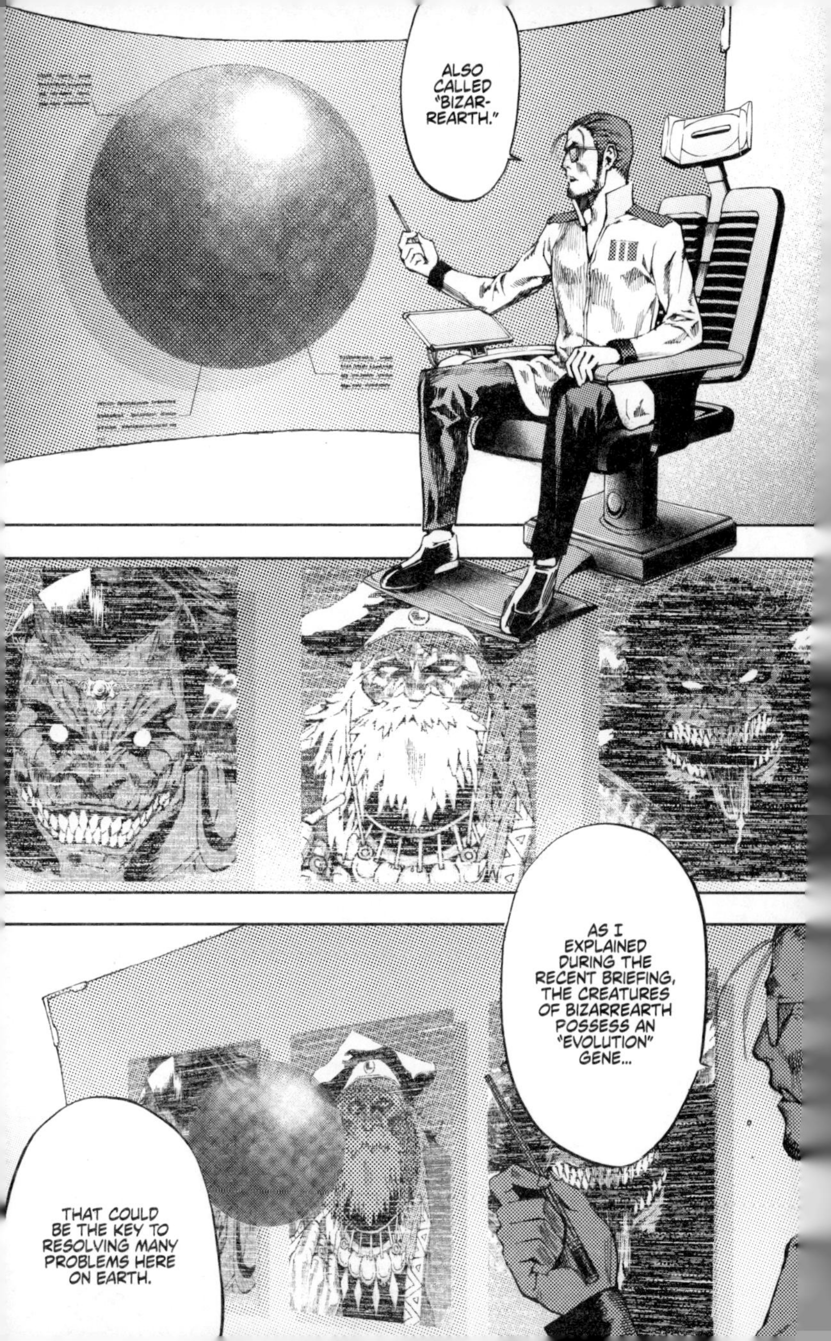
ALSO CALLED "BIZAR-REARTH."
AS I EXPLAINED DURING THE RECENT BRIEFING, THE CREATURES OF BIZARREARTH POSSESS AN "EVOLUTION" GENE...
THAT COULD BE THE KEY TO RESOLVING MANY PROBLEMS HERE ON EARTH.

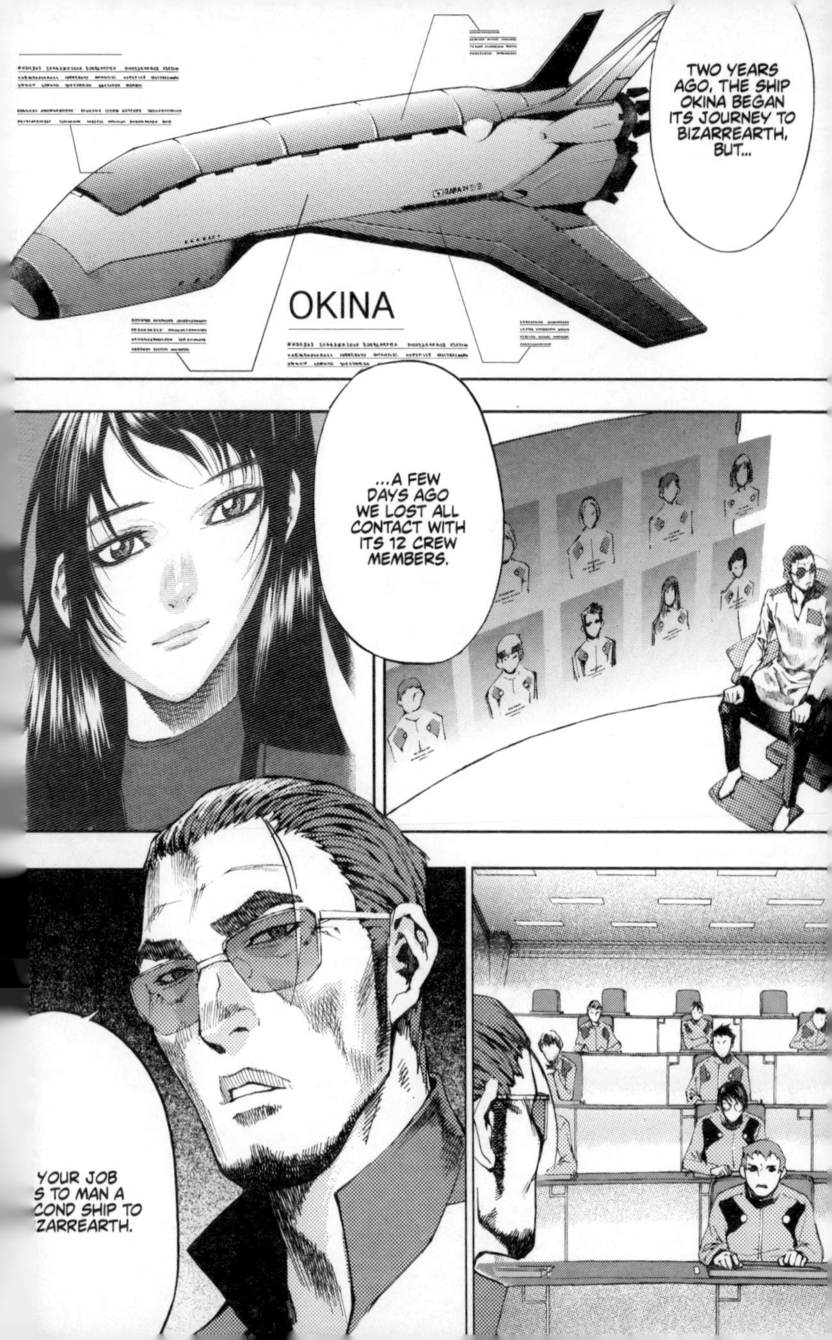
TWO YEARS AGO, THE SHIP OKINA BEGAN ITS JOURNEY TO BIZARREARTH, BUT...
OKINA
...A FEW DAYS AGO WE LOST ALL CONTACT WITH ITS 12 CREW MEMBERS.
YOUR JOB S TO MAN A COND SHIP TO ZARREARTH.

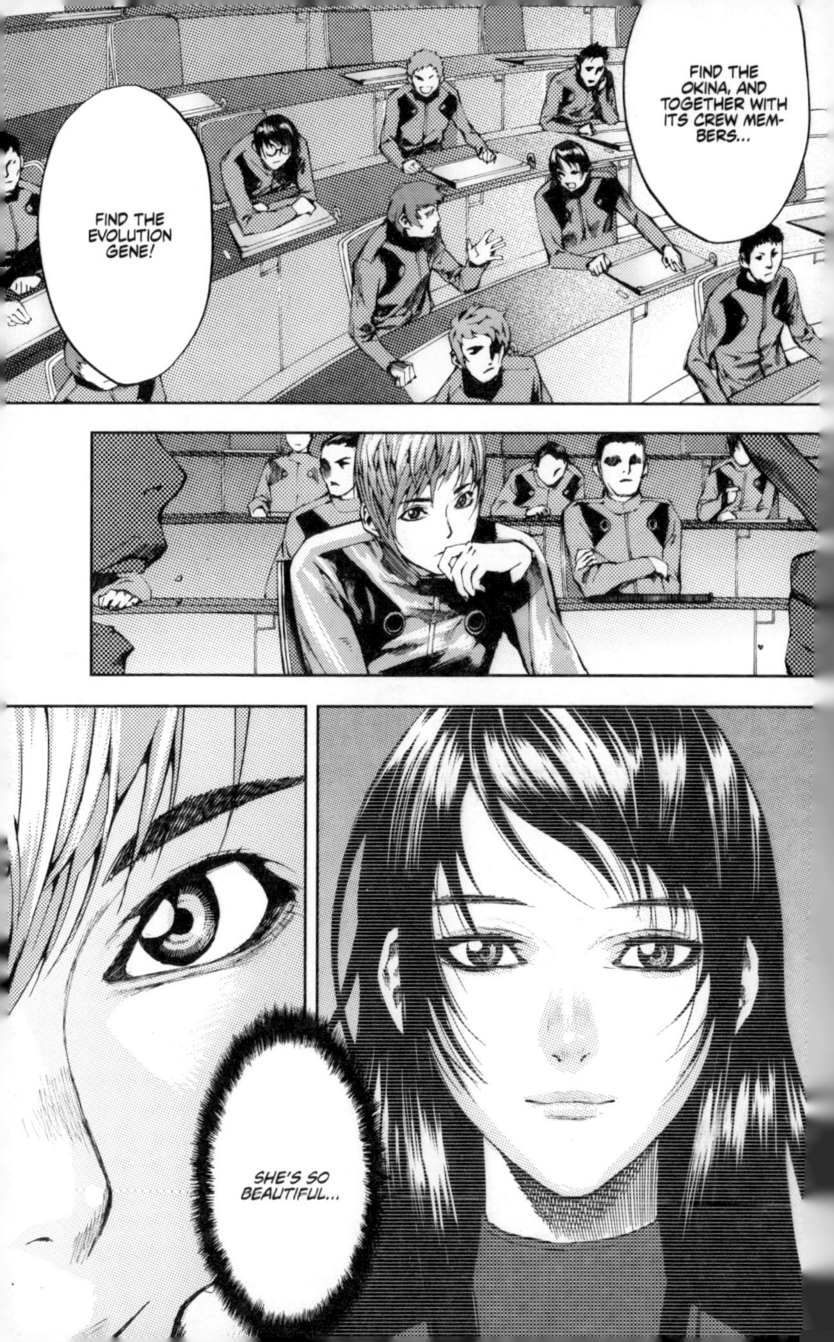
FIND THE OKINA, AND TOGETHER WITH ITS CREW MEM-BERS...
FIND THE EVOLUTION GENE!
SHE'S SO BEAUTIFUL...

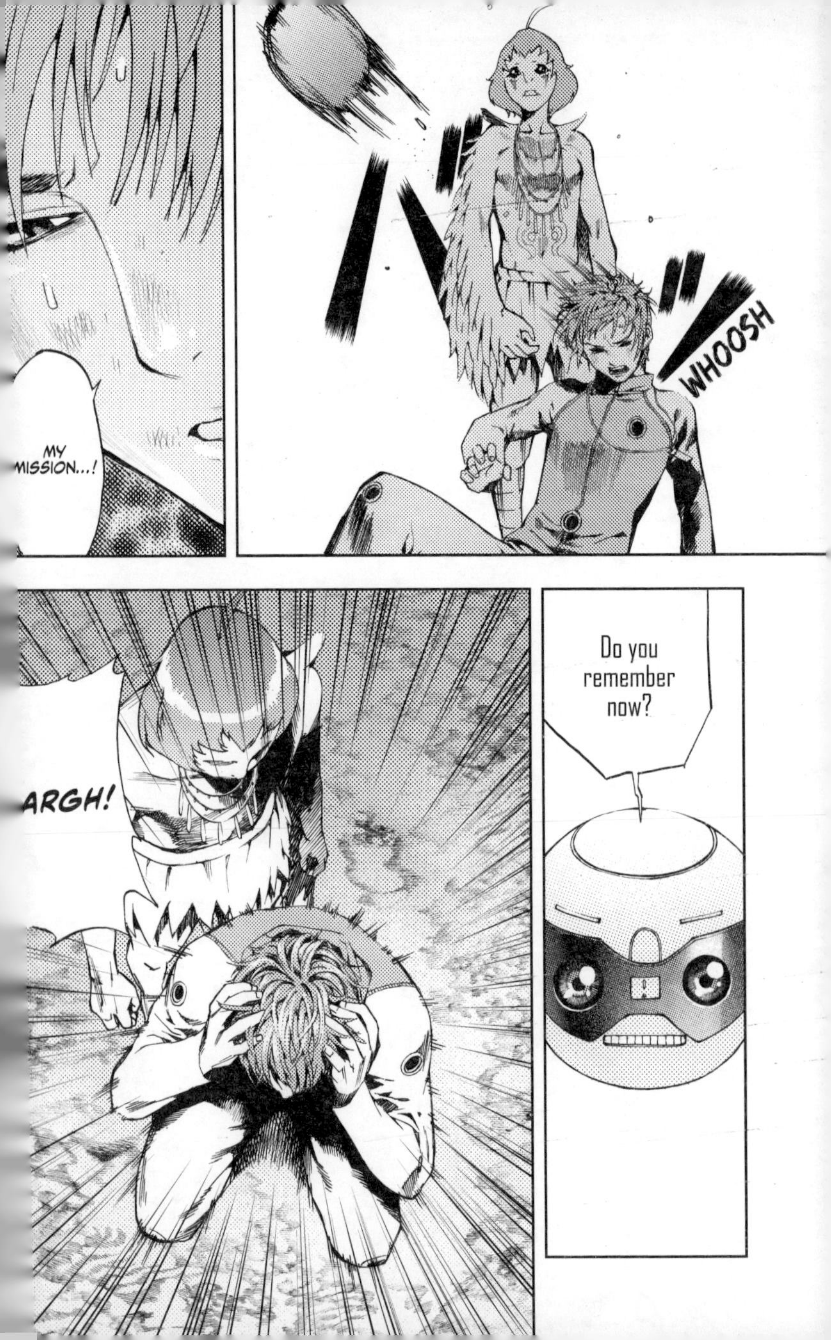
WHOOSH
MY MISSION...!
Do you remember now?
ARGH!

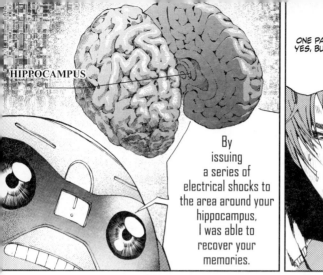

HIPPOCAMPUS

ONE PART, YES, BUT...

By issuing a series of electrical shocks to the area around your hippocampus, I was able to recover your memories.

Going any further than this could end up harming your body.

MOMO...

In time, you should recover the rest of your memories.

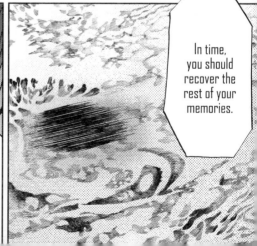

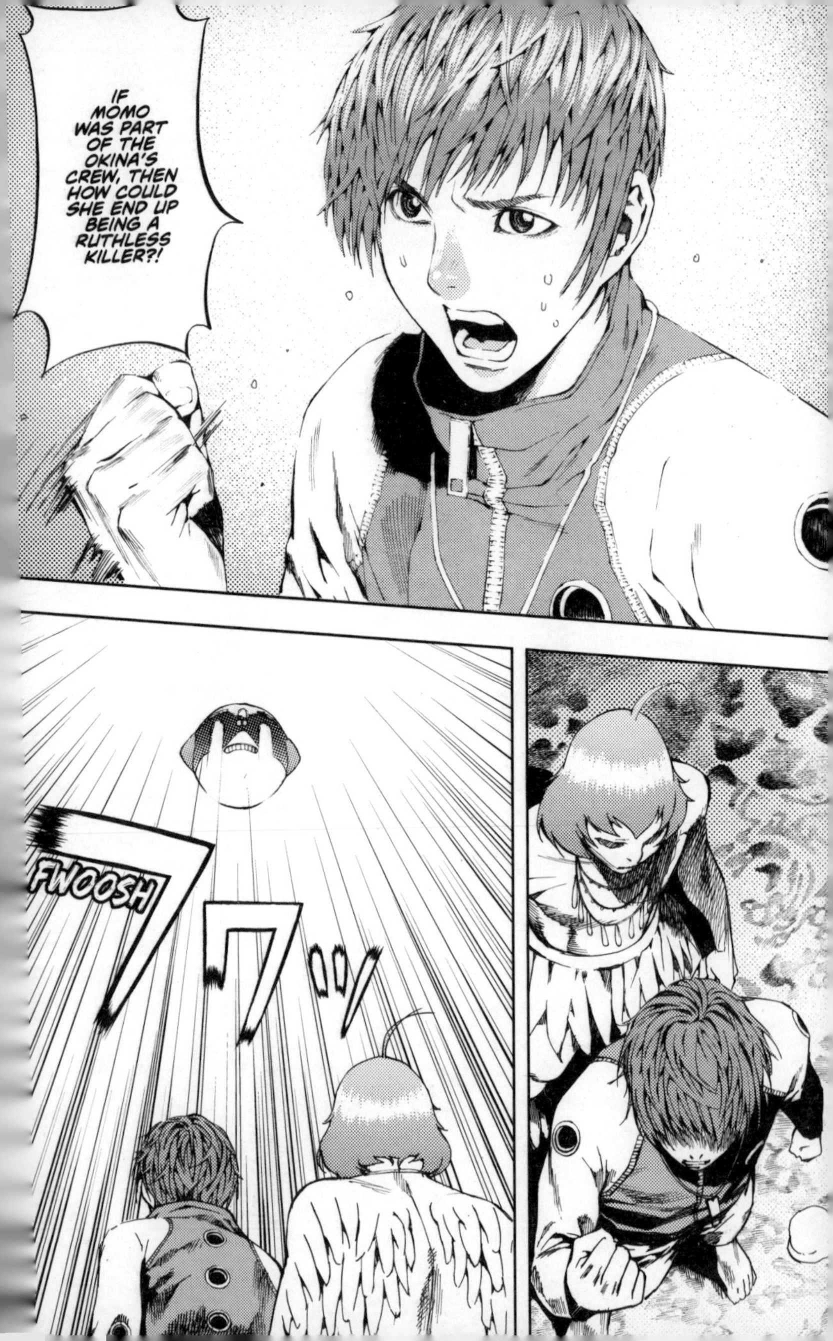
IF MOMO WAS PART OF THE OKINA'S CREW, THEN HOW COULD SHE END UP BEING A RUTHLESS KILLER?!
FWOOSH

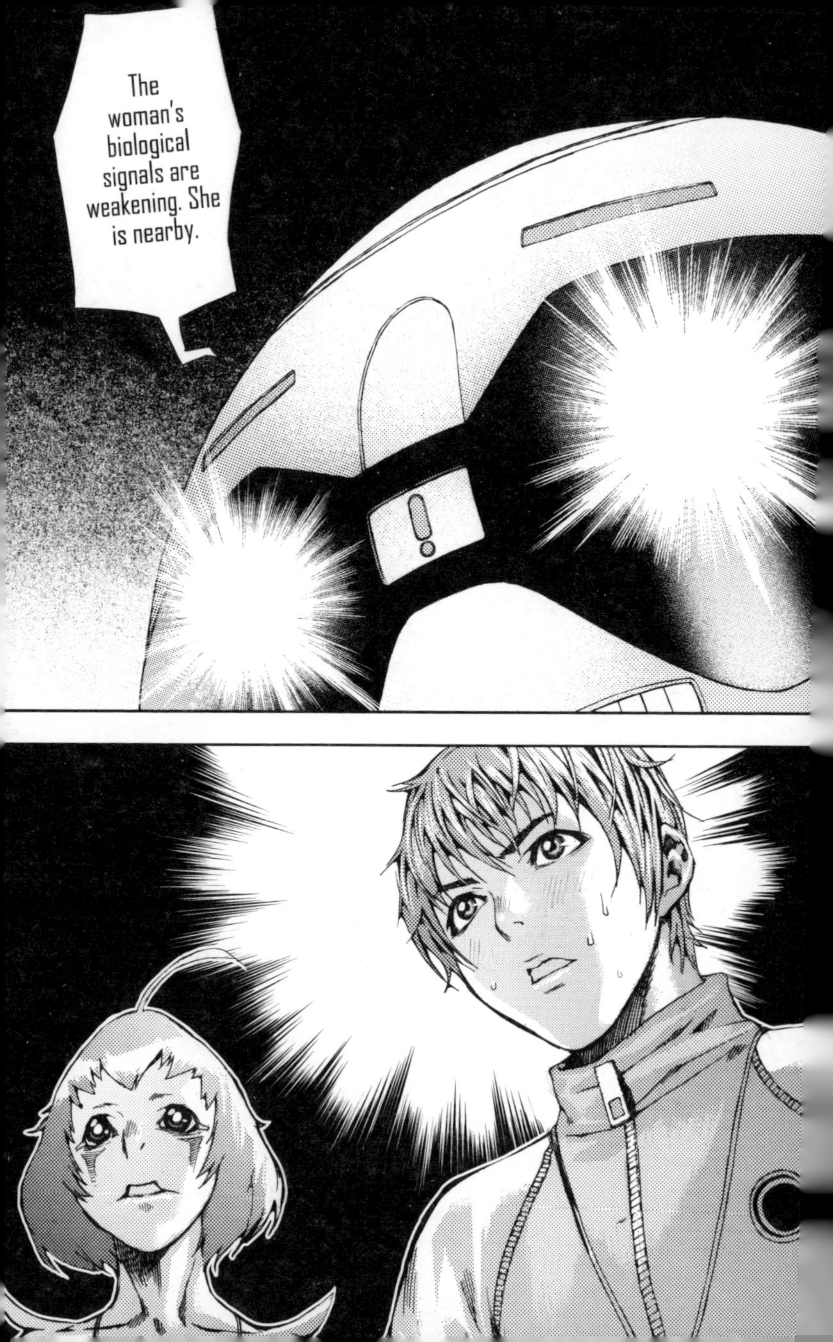
The woman's biological signals are weakening. She is nearby.

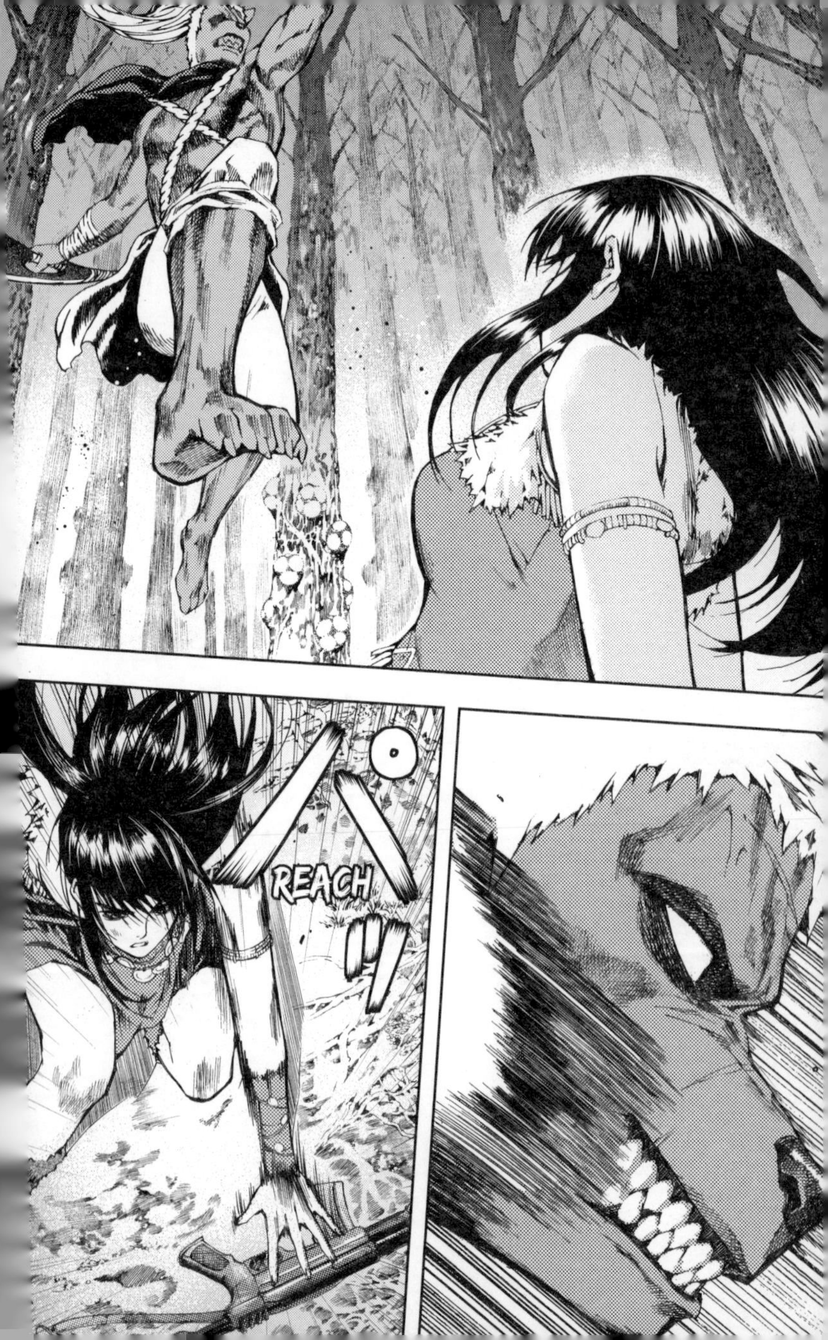
REACH

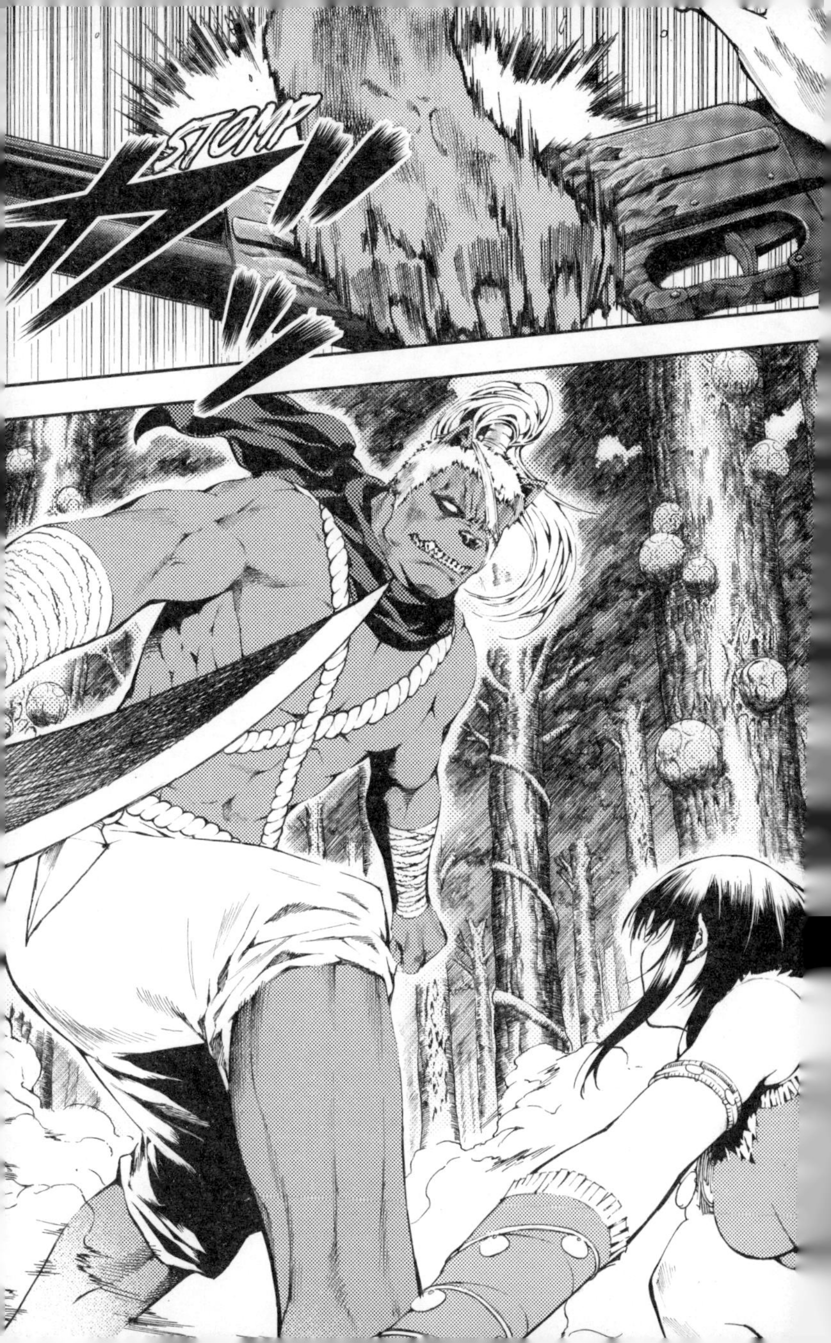
STOMP

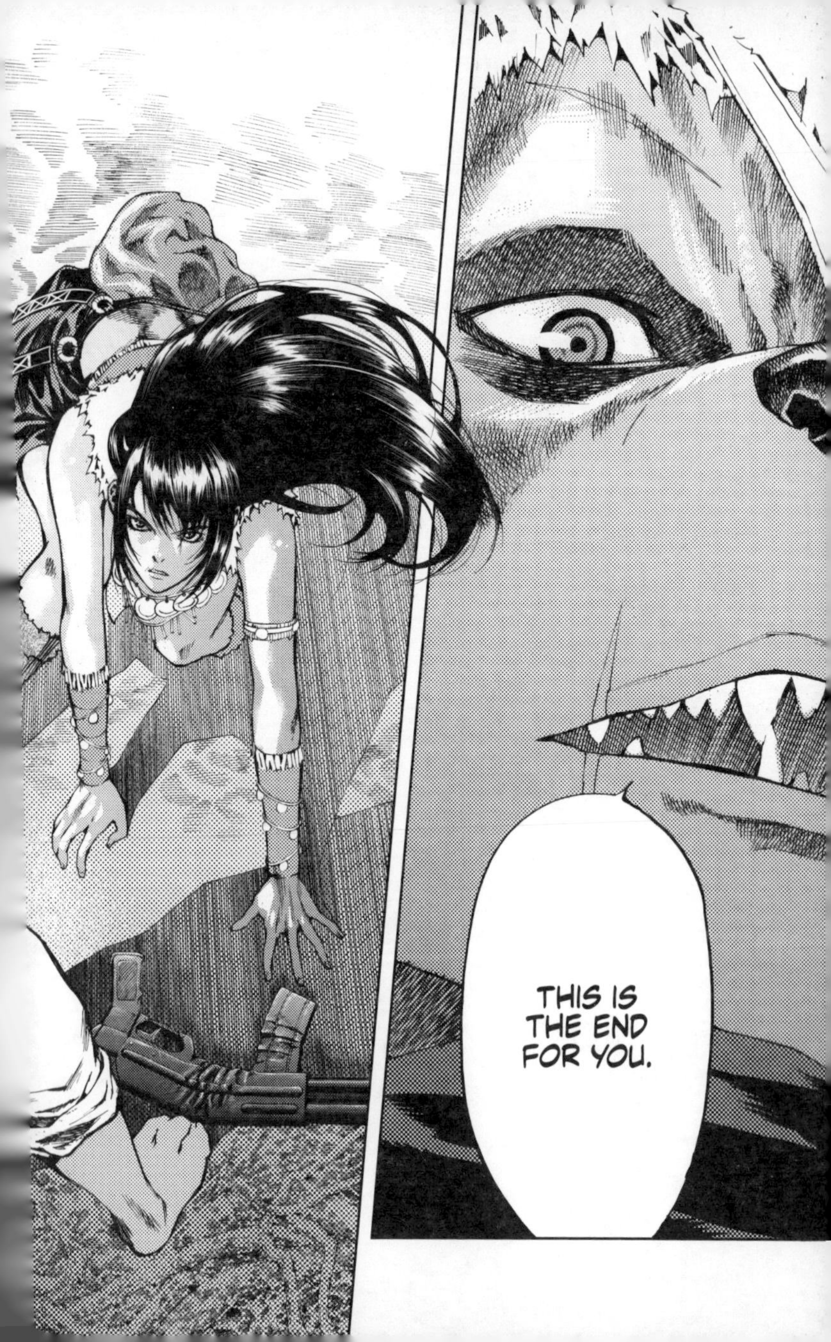
THIS IS THE END FOR YOU.

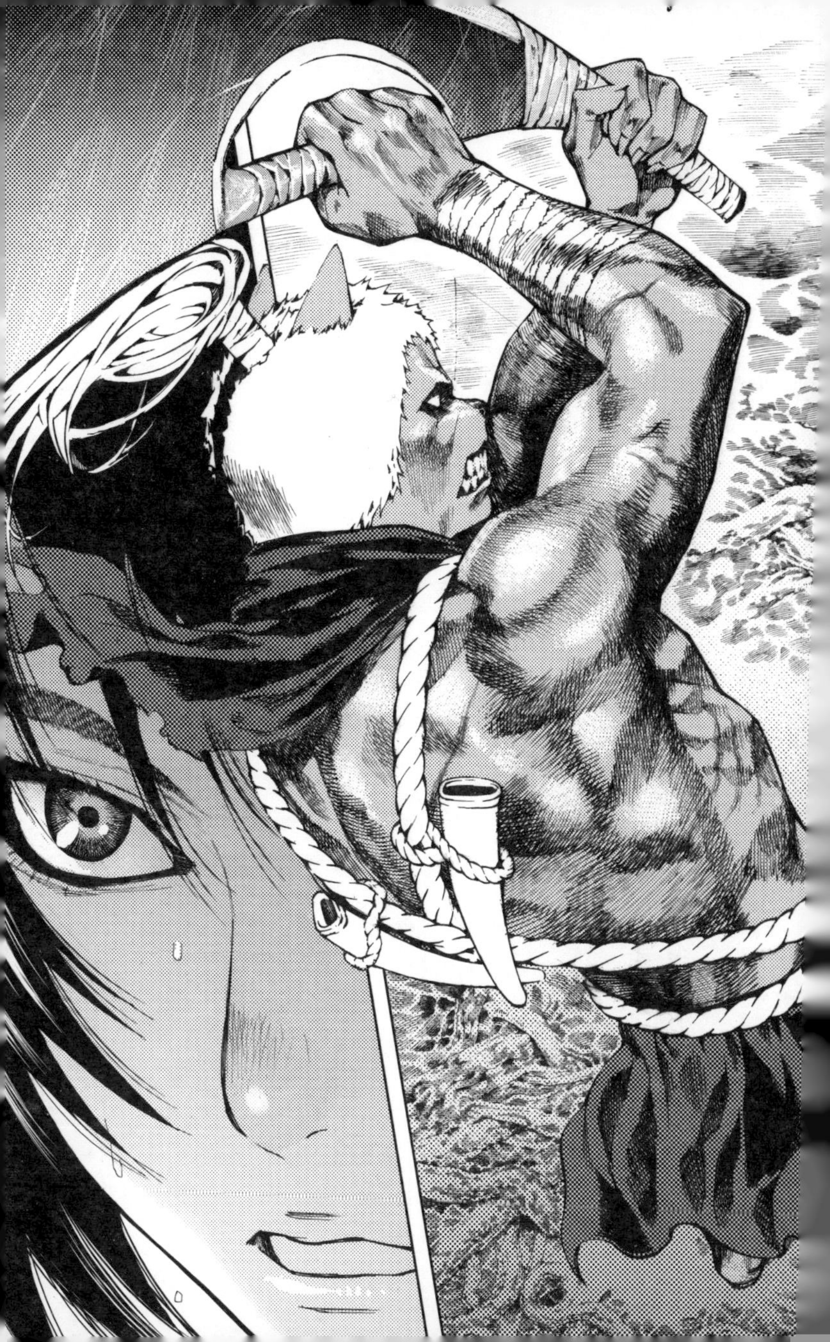

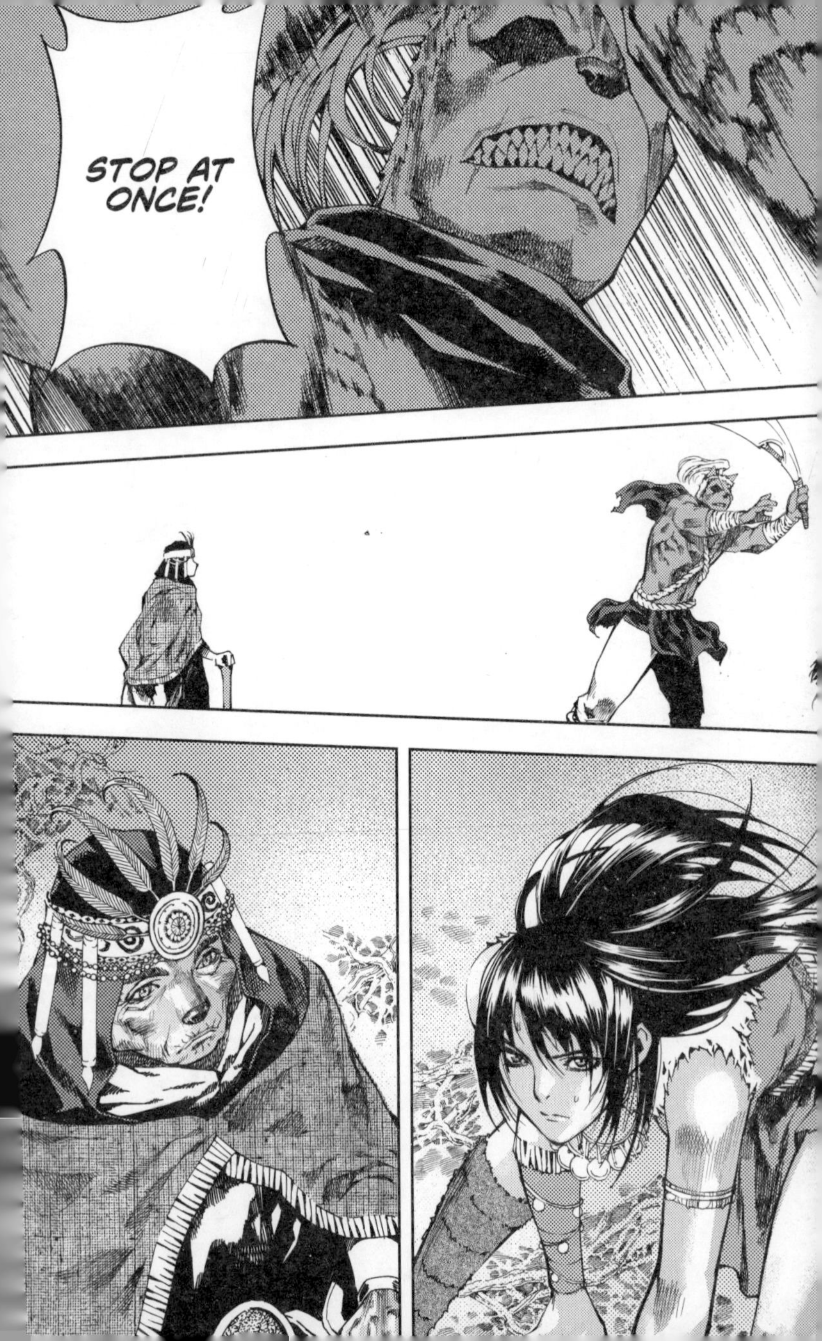
STOP AT ONCE!

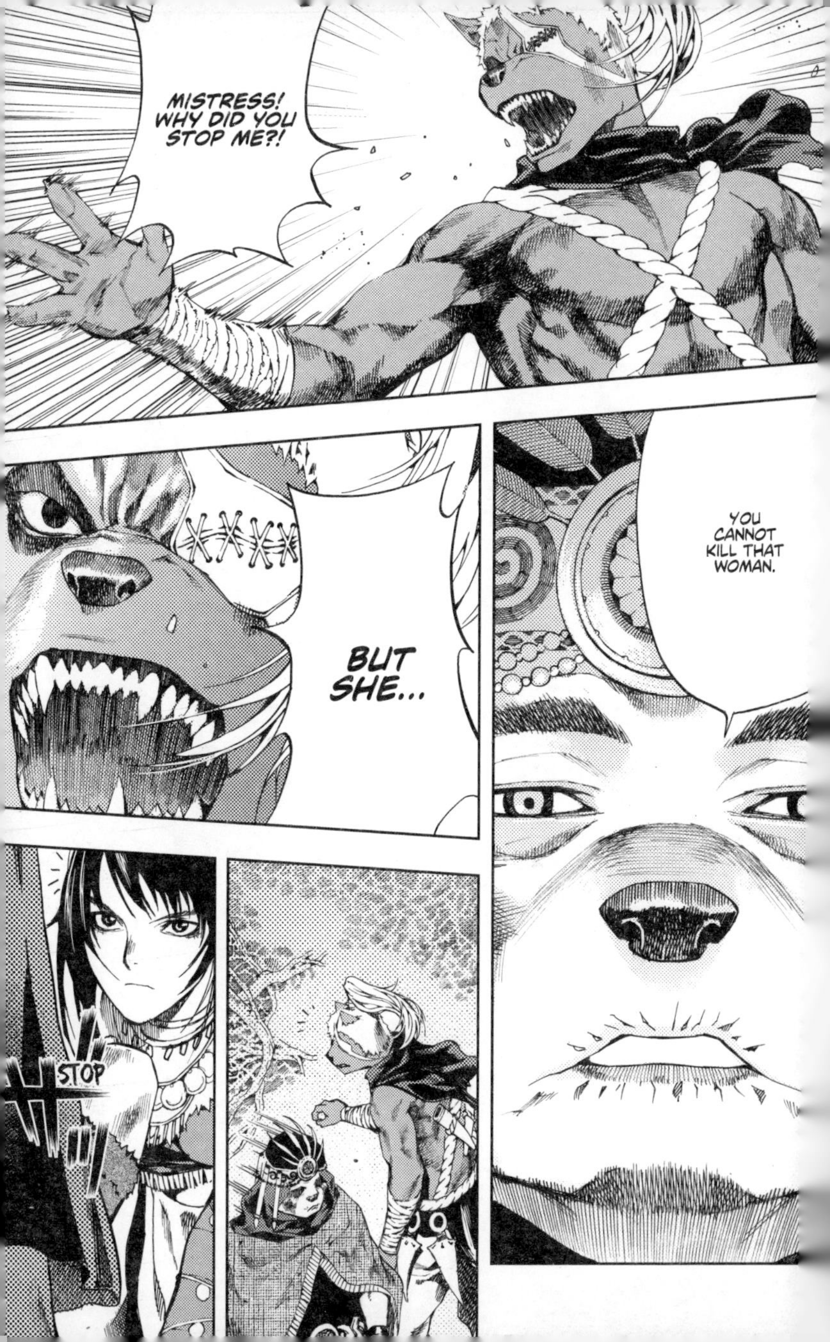
MISTRESS! WHY DID YOU STOP ME?!
YOU CANNOT KILL THAT WOMAN.
BUT SHE...
STOP

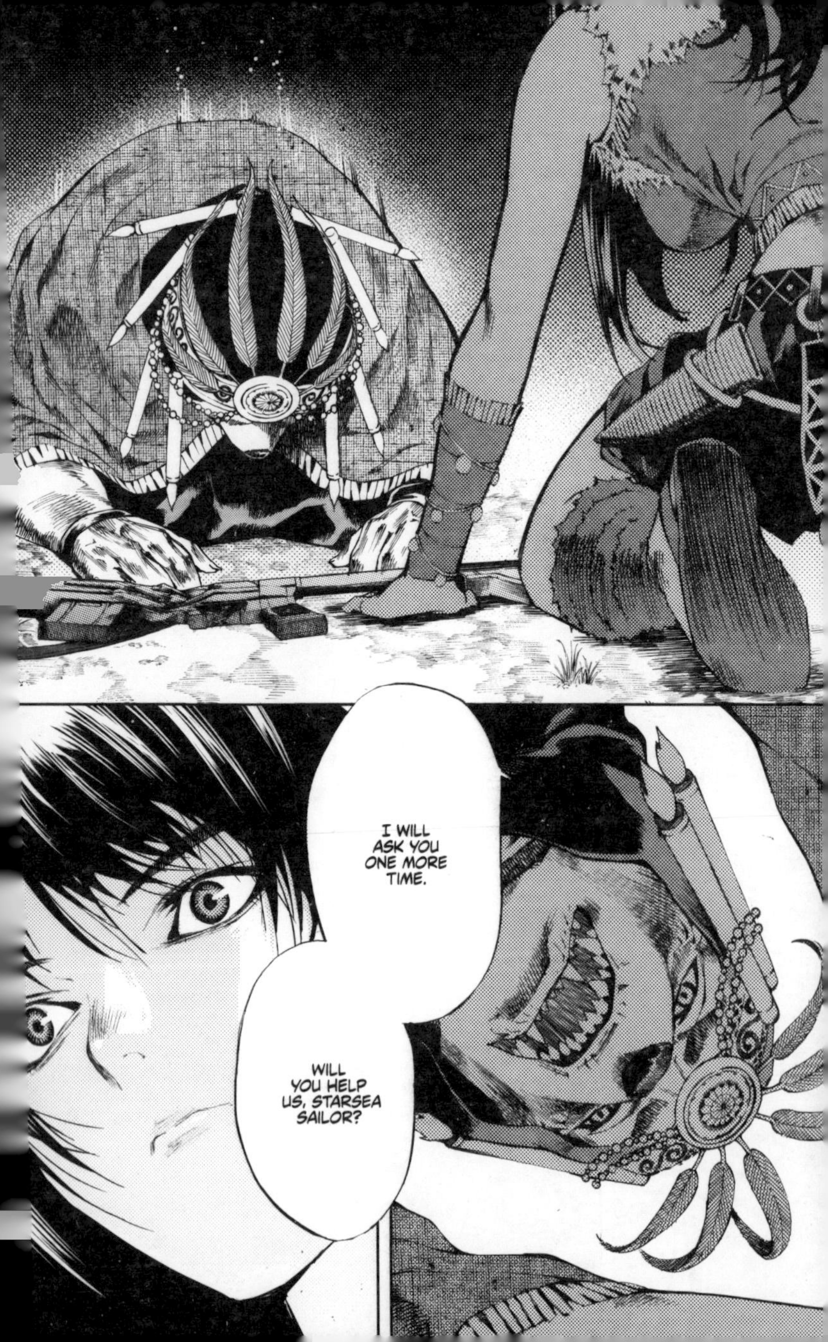
I WILL ASK YOU ONE MORE TIME.
WILL YOU HELP US, STARSEA SAILOR?

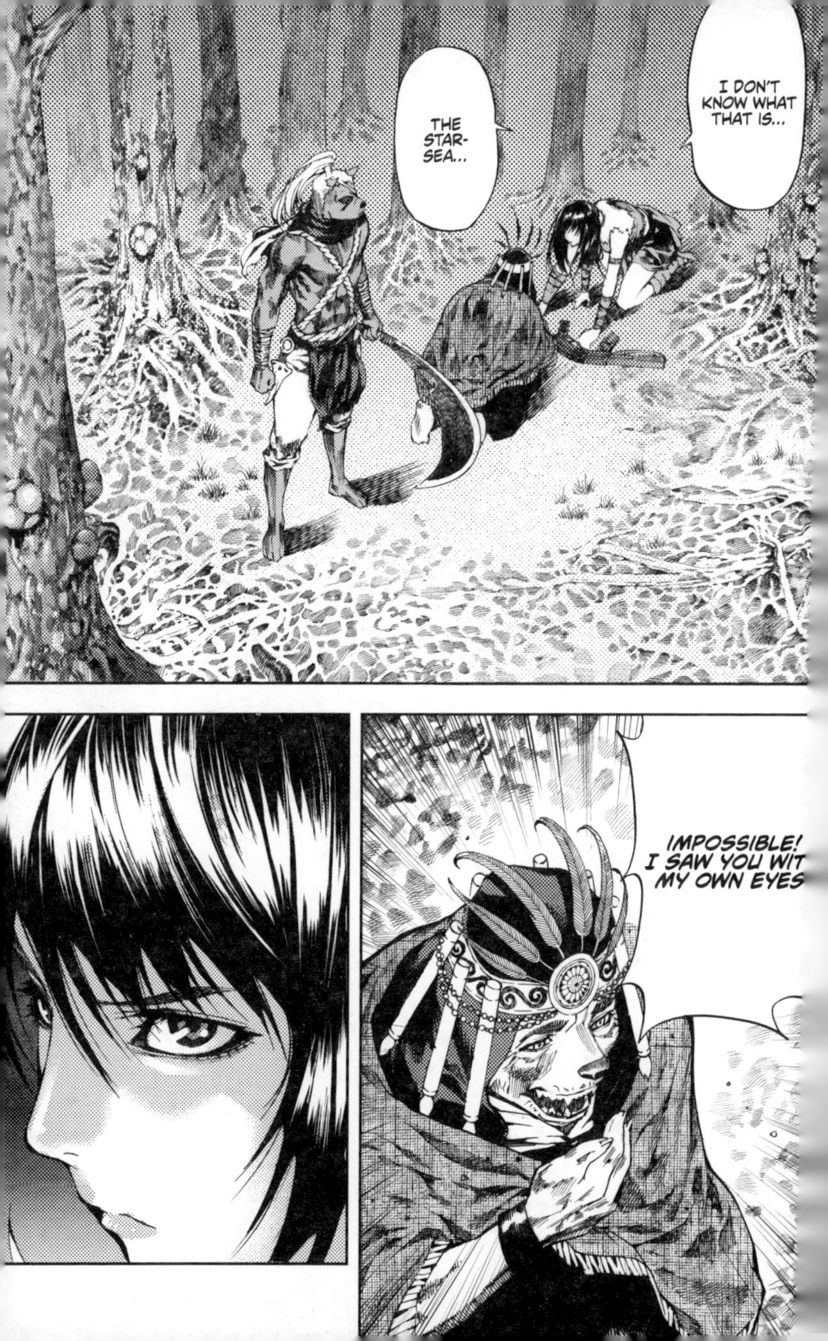
I DON'T KNOW WHAT THAT IS...
THE STAR-SEA...
IMPOSSIBLE! I SAW YOU WIT MY OWN EYES

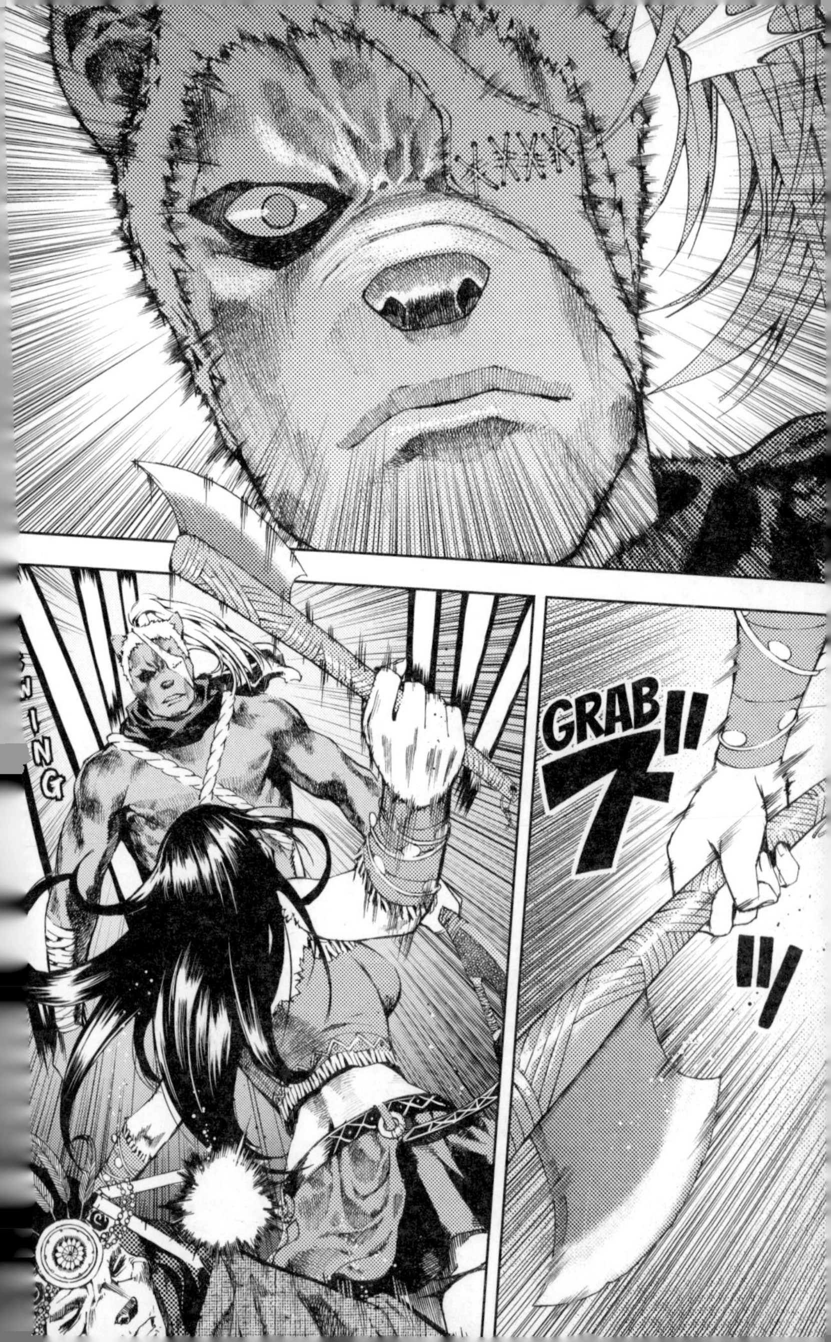
GRAB
SWING

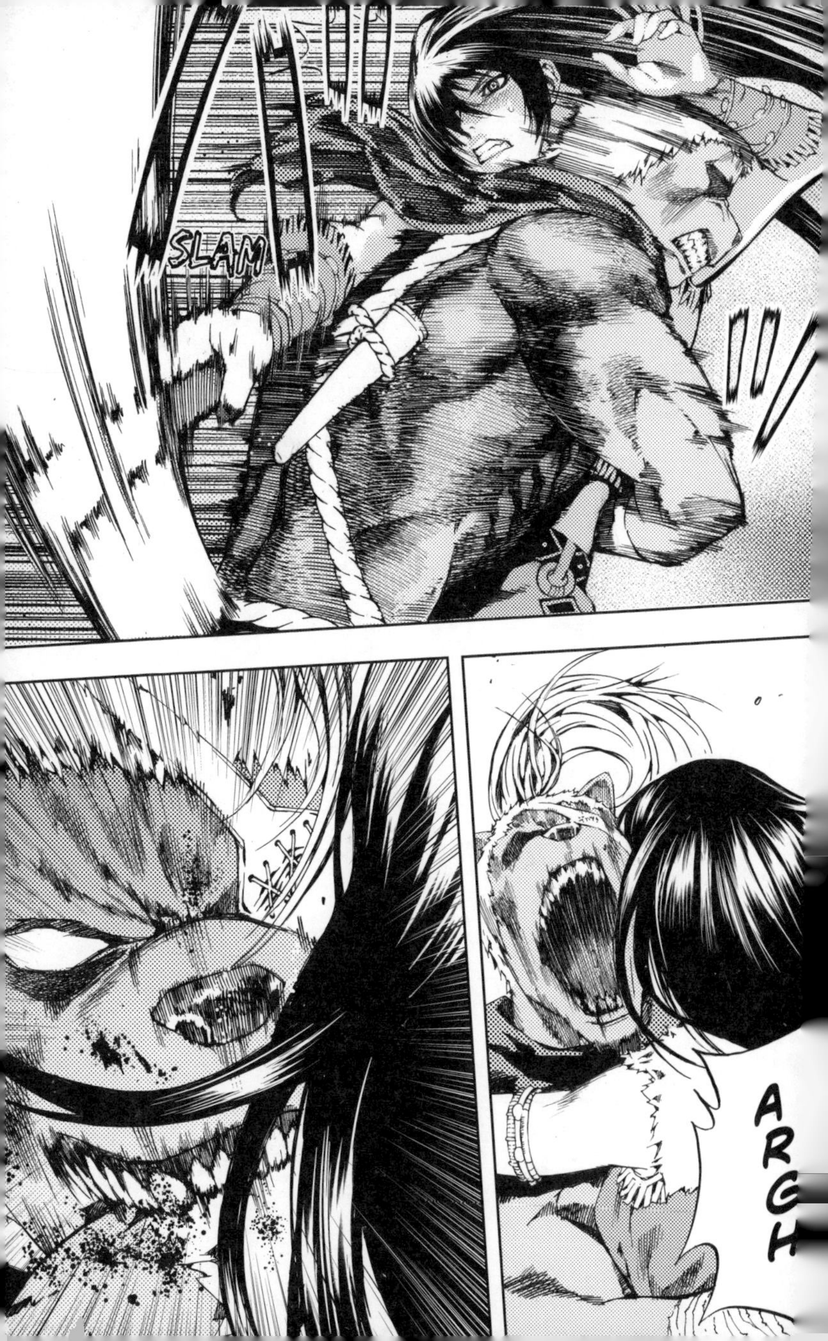
SLAM
ARCH

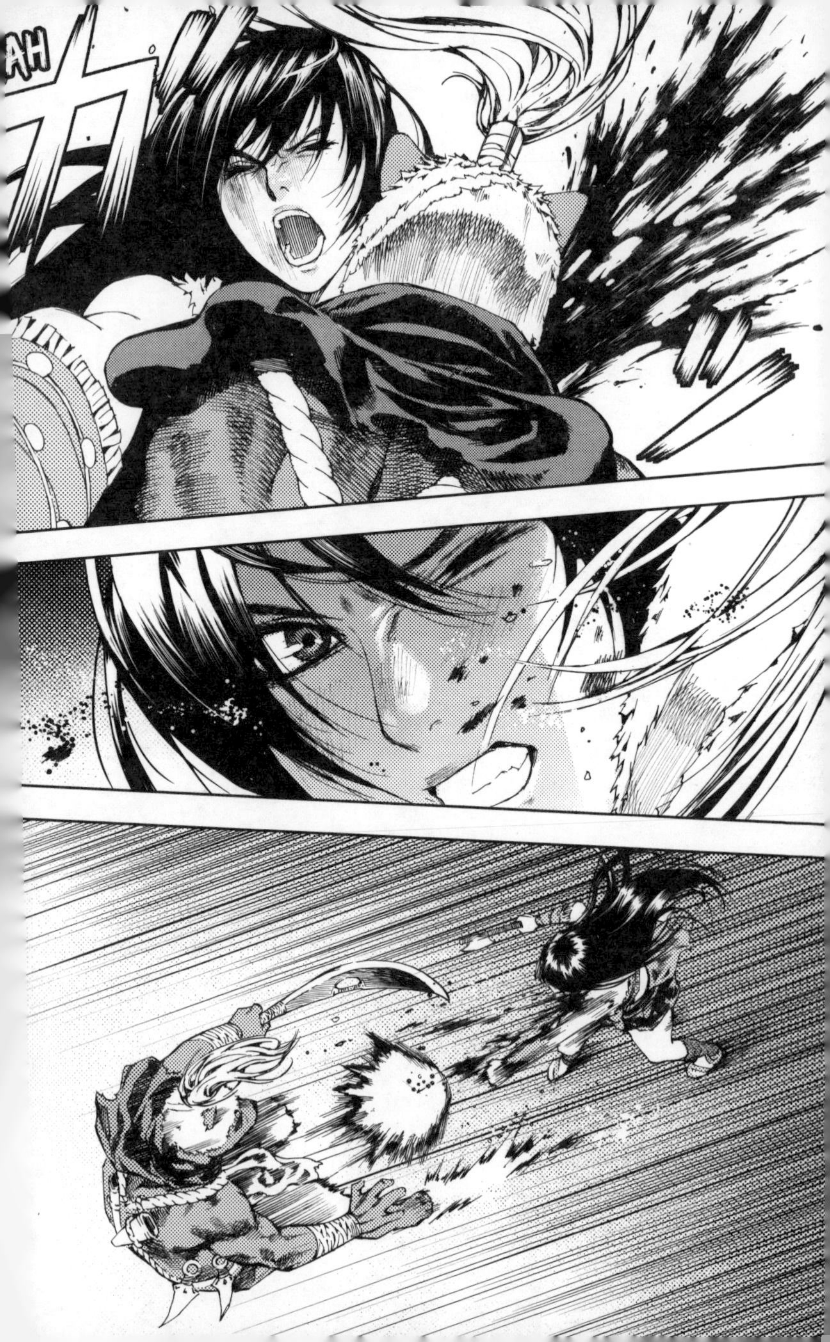
AH

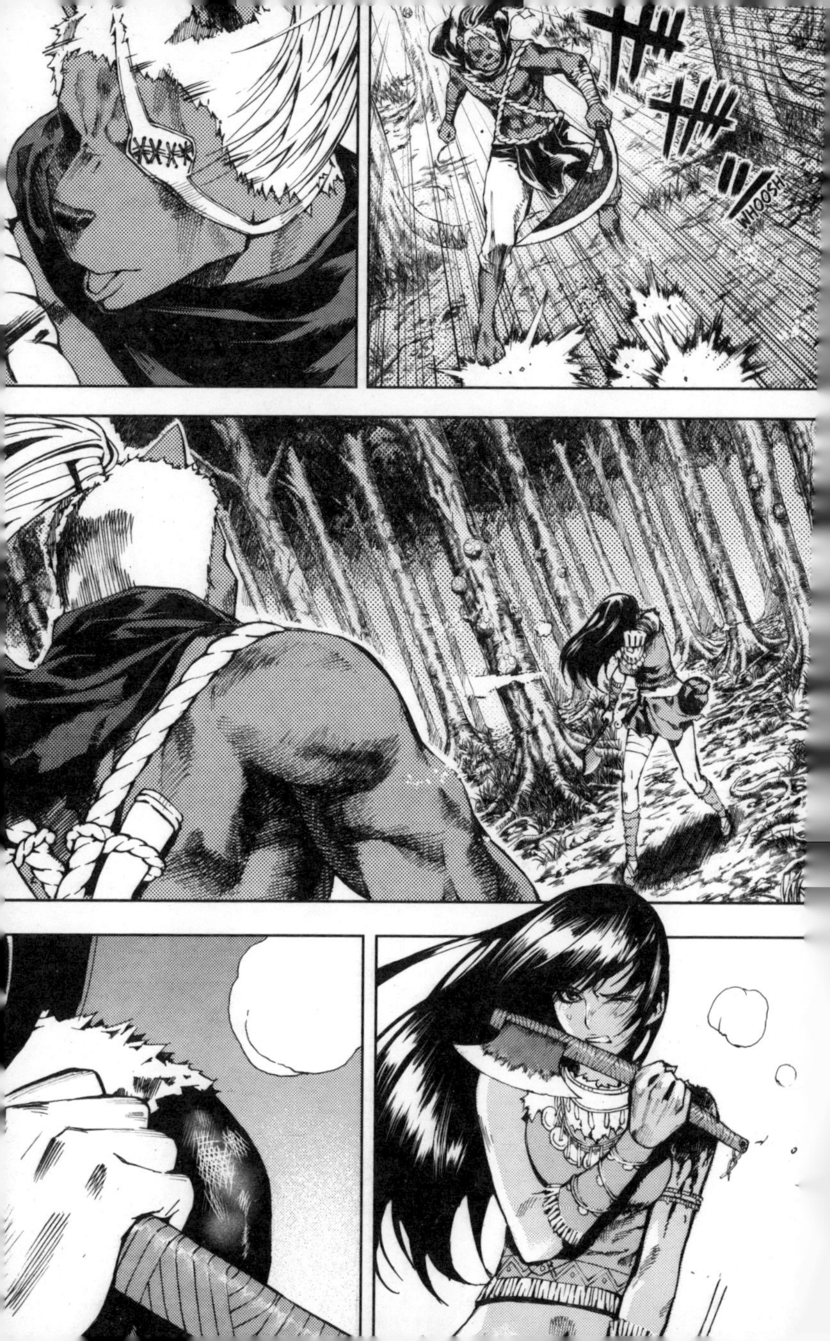
WHOOSH

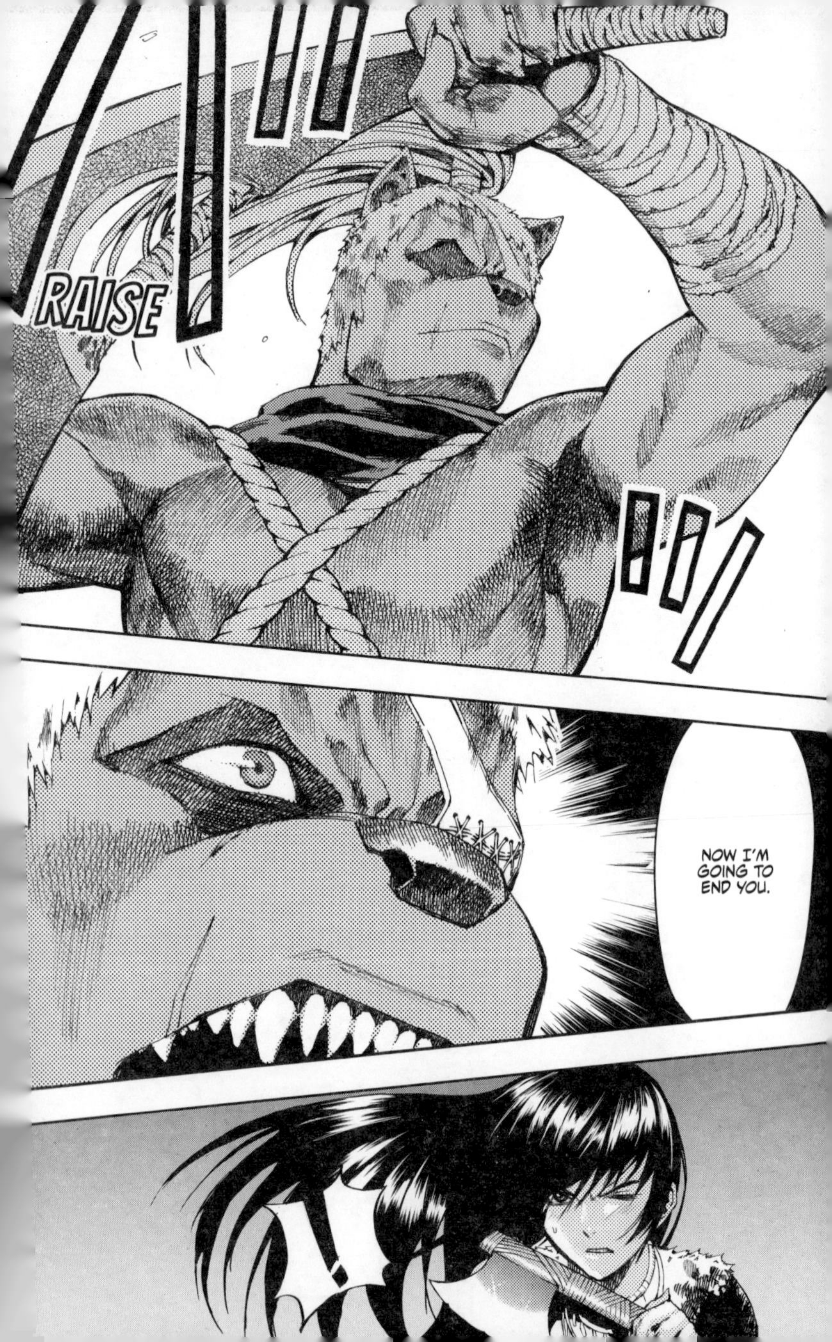
RAISE
NOW I'M GOING TO END YOU.
!

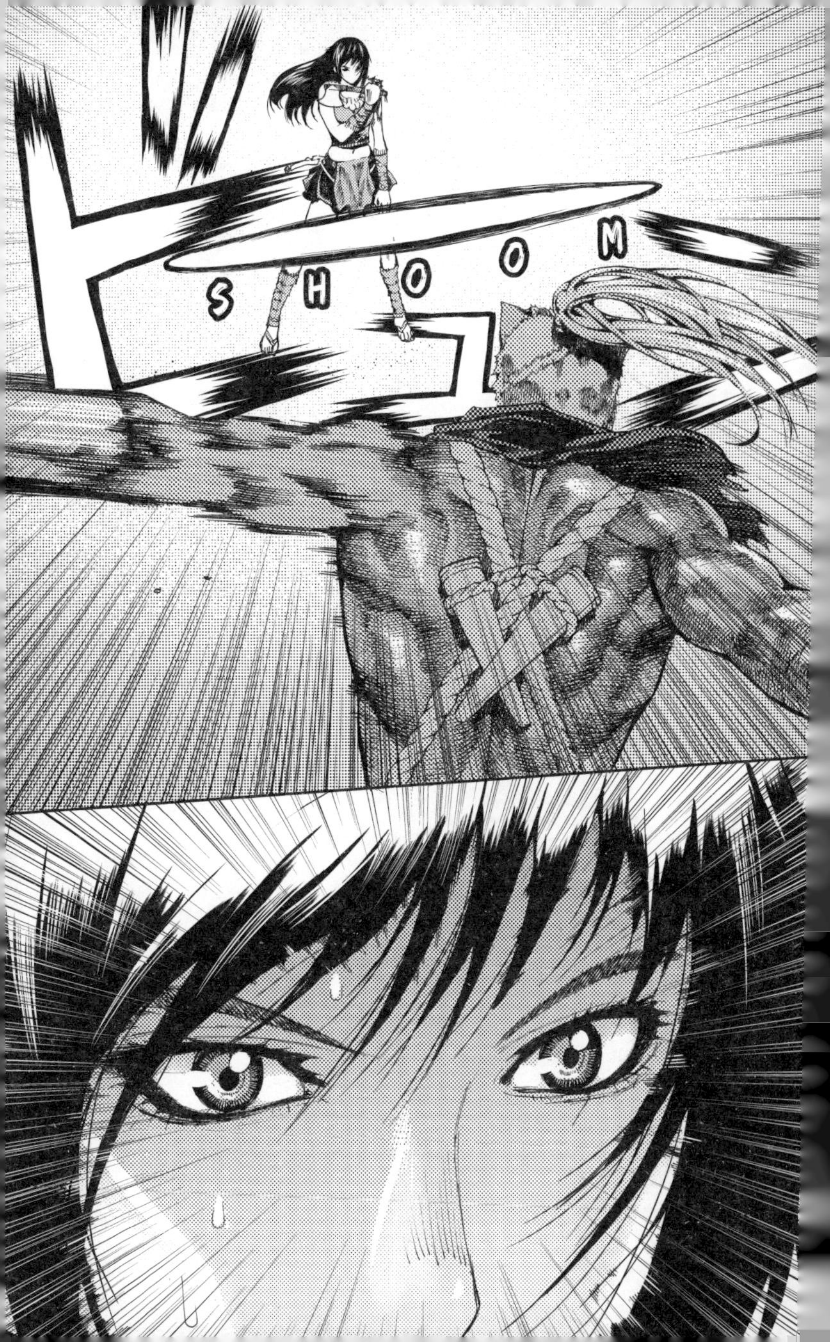
SHOOM

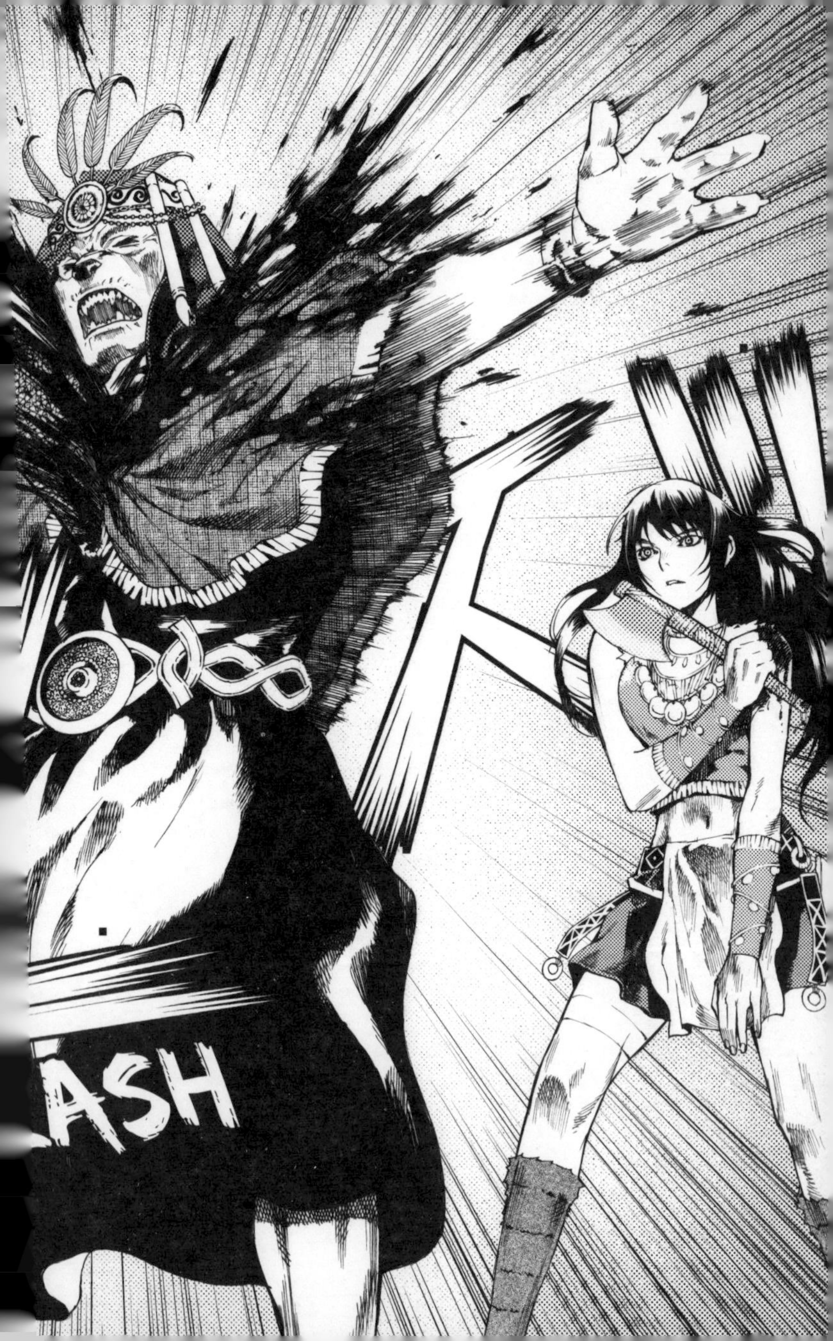
ASH

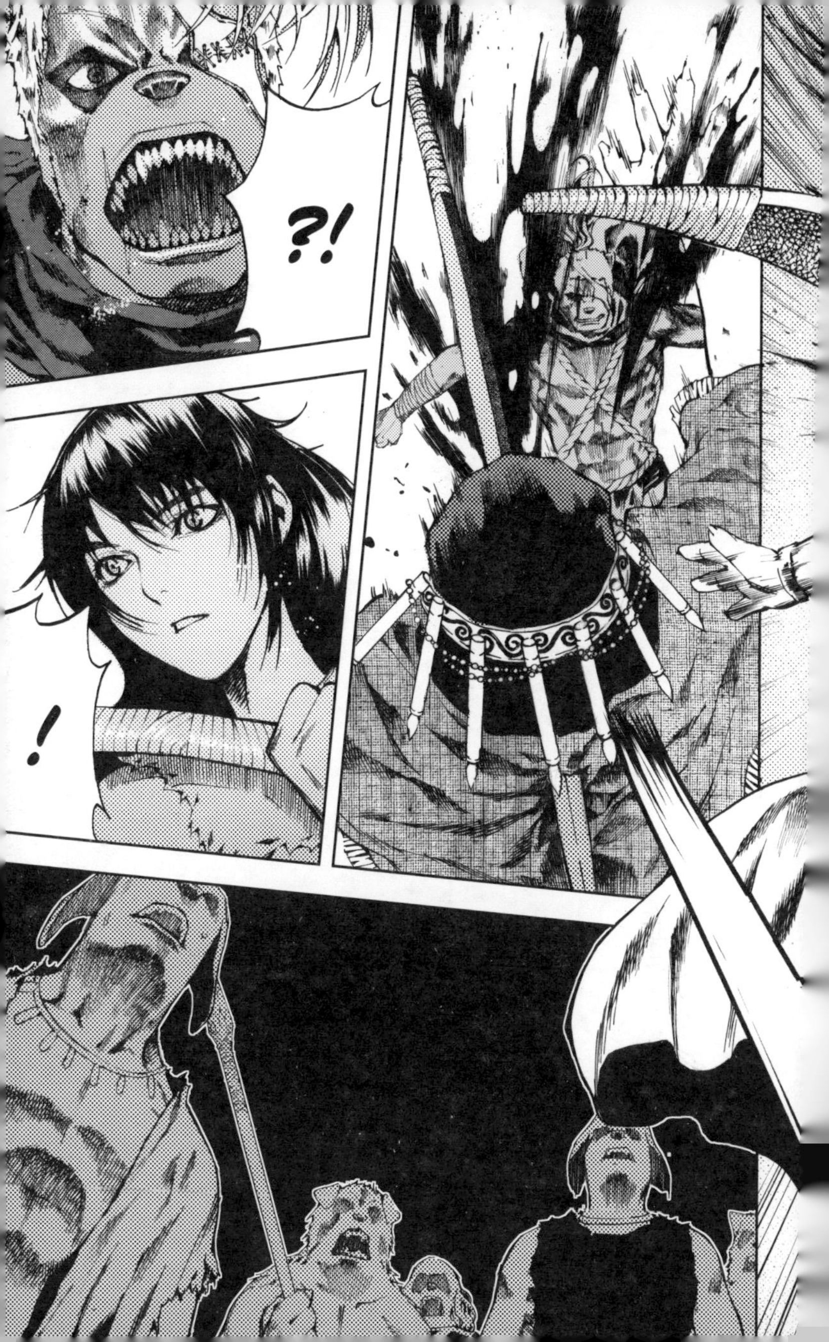
?!
!

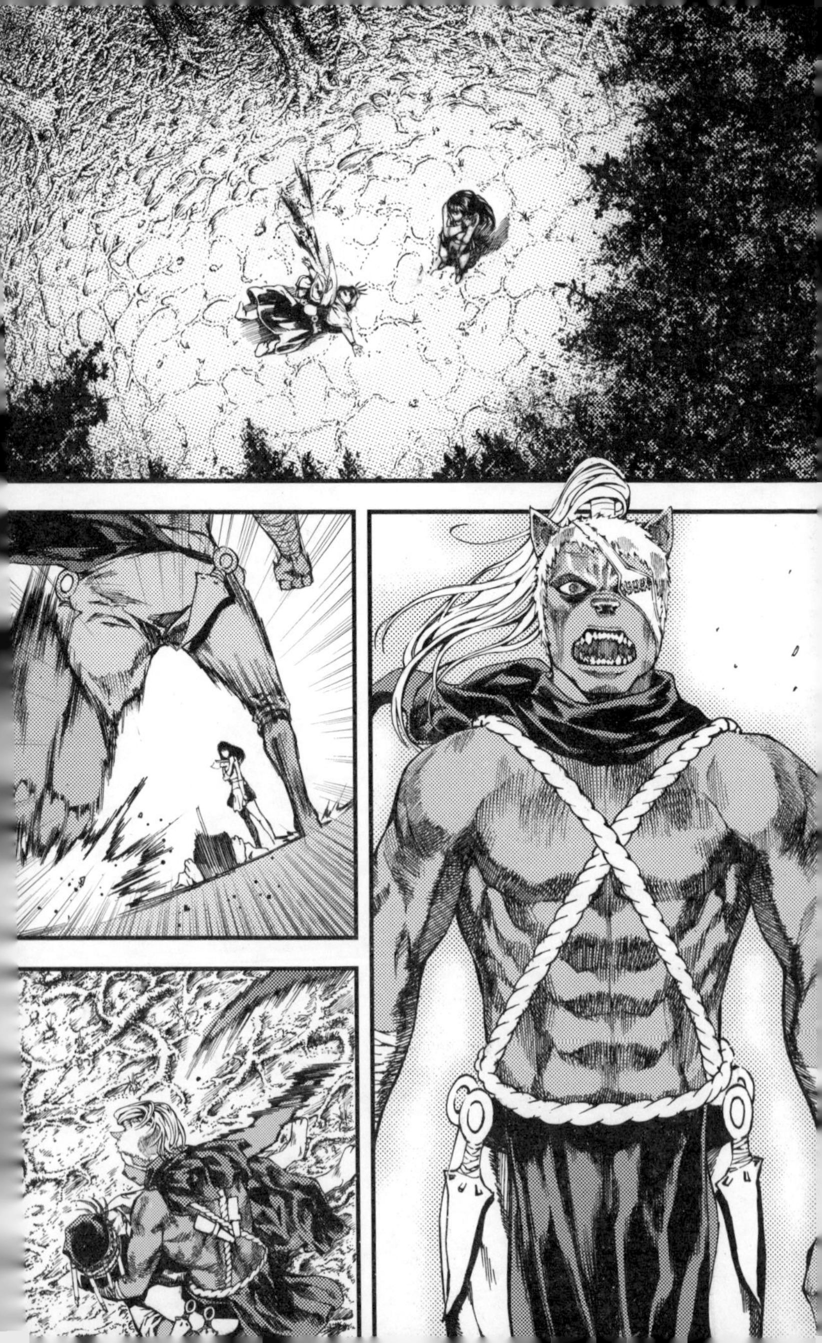

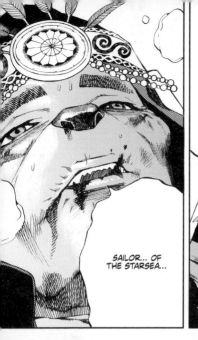

MOTHER...
WHY?! WHY
DID YOU DO
THAT?!

SAILOR... OF
THE STARSEA...

YOU WILL END
THIS EVIL... AND
BRING PEACE...
TO THIS LAND...

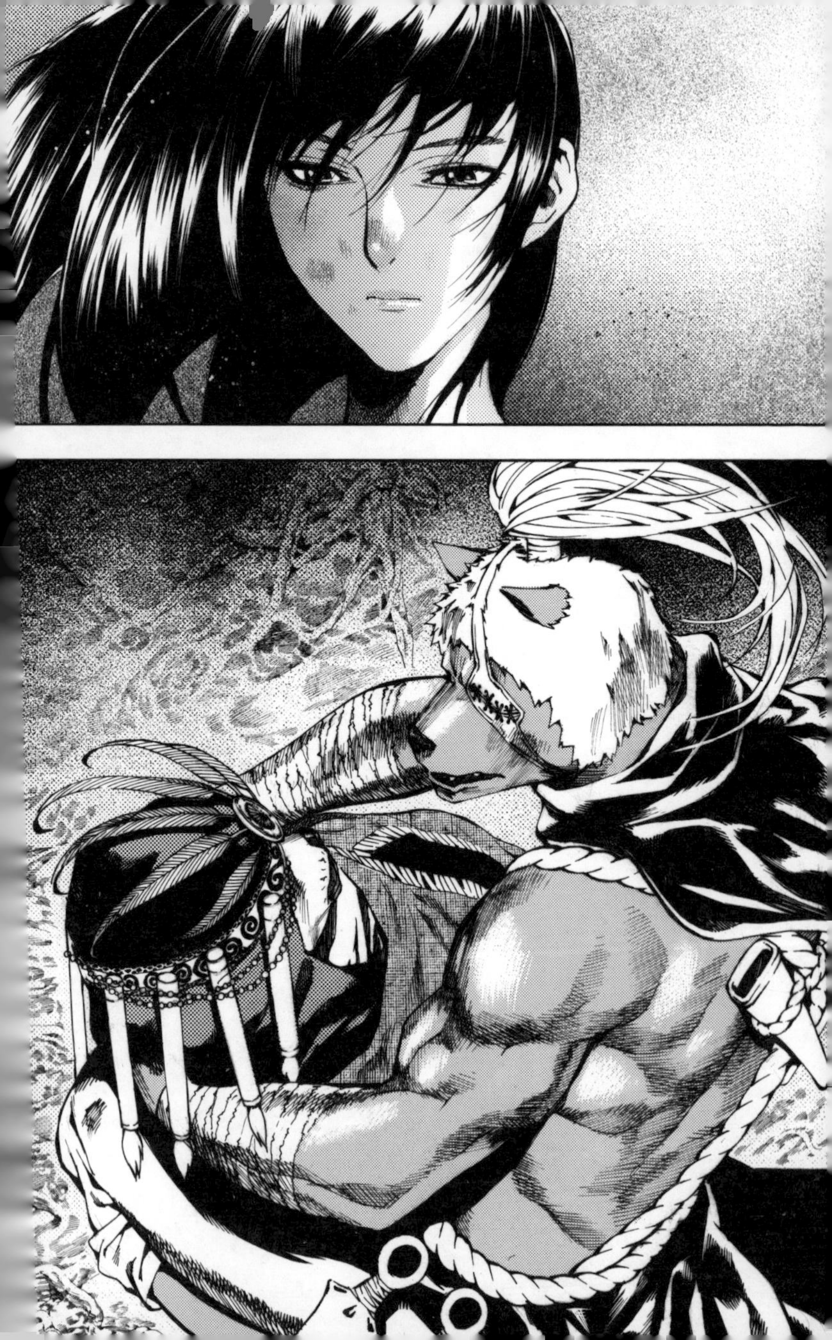

MOMO

LEGENDARY WARRIOR

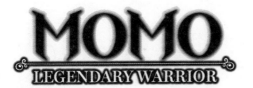

Epilogue ~The Hero of the Z-ONE Home~

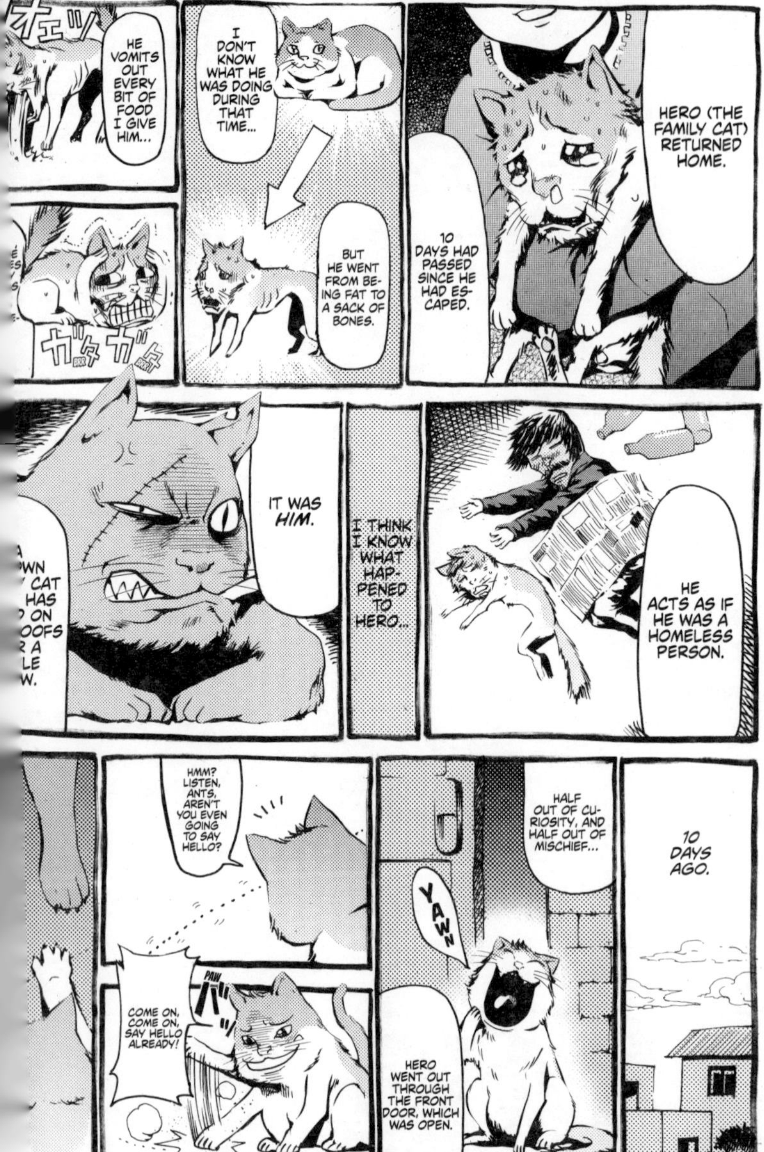
HERO (THE FAMILY CAT) RETURNED HOME.
10 DAYS HAD PASSED SINCE HE HAD ES-CAPED.
I DON'T KNOW WHAT HE WAS DOING DURING THAT TIME...
BUT HE WENT FROM BE-ING FAT TO A SACK OF BONES.
HE VOMITS OUT EVERY BIT OF FOOD I GIVE HIM...
BRR
BRR
HE ACTS AS IF HE WAS A HOMELESS PERSON.
I THINK I KNOW WHAT HAP-PENED TO HERO...
IT WAS *HIM.*
10 DAYS AGO.
HALF OUT OF CU-RIOSITY, AND HALF OUT OF MISCHIEF...
YAWN
HERO WENT OUT THROUGH THE FRONT DOOR, WHICH WAS OPEN.
HMM? LISTEN, ANTS, AREN'T YOU EVEN GOING TO SAY HELLO?
PAW
COME ON, COME ON, SAY HELLO ALREADY!

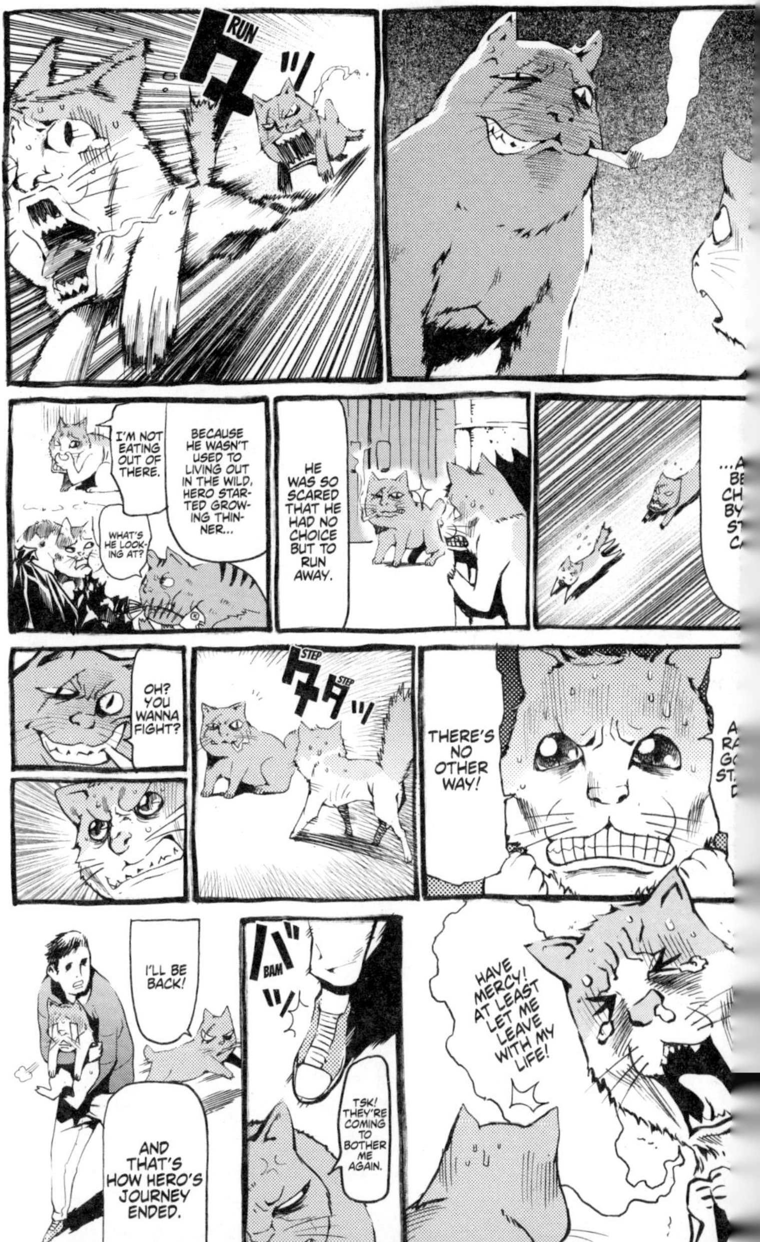
RUN
HE WAS SO SCARED THAT HE HAD NO CHOICE BUT TO RUN AWAY.
BECAUSE HE WASN'T USED TO LIVING OUT IN THE WILD, HERO STARTED GROWING THINNER...
I'M NOT EATING OUT OF THERE.
WHAT'S HE LOOKING AT?
THERE'S NO OTHER WAY!
STEP STEP
OH? YOU WANNA FIGHT?
HAVE MERCY! AT LEAST LET ME LEAVE WITH MY LIFE!
BAM
TSK! THEY'RE COMING TO BOTHER ME AGAIN.
I'LL BE BACK!
AND THAT'S HOW HERO'S JOURNEY ENDED.

MOMO

LEGENDARY WARRIOR

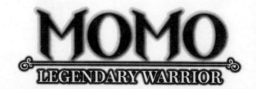

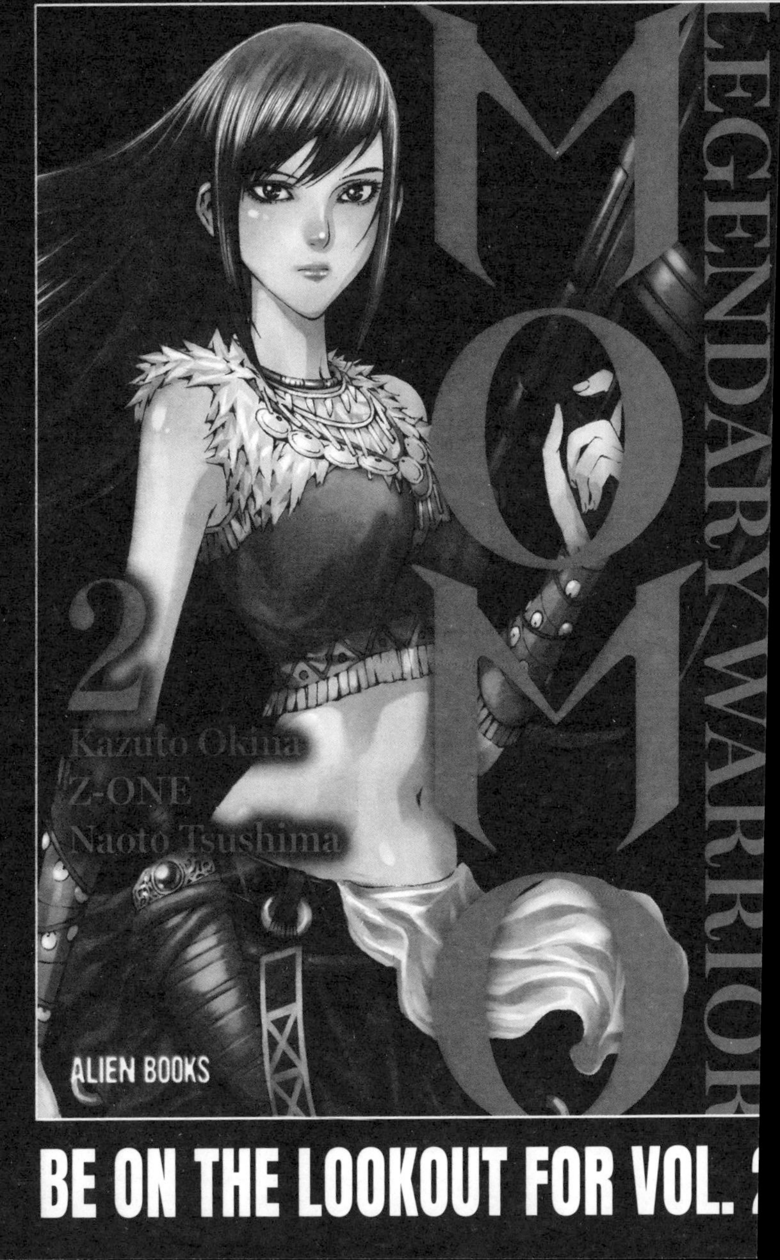
MOMO
LEGENDARY WARRIOR
2
Kazuto Okima
Z-ONE
Naoto Tsushima
ALIEN BOOKS

BE ON THE LOOKOUT FOR VOL. 2

WAIT!
YOU'RE GOING THE WRONG WAY!

TRADITIONAL JAPANESE MANGA IS READ FROM RIGHT TO LEFT! MAKE SURE YOU FOLLOW THE DIRECTIONS BELOW WHEN READING PAGES, PANELS, BALLOONS AND SOUND EFFECTS!

PANEL READING ORDER

BALLOON READING ORDER

TOR IN CHIEF: **Matias Timarchi**

IOR EDITOR: **Lysa Hawkins**

TOR: **Matias Mir**

ISTANT EDITORS: **Martin Casanova & Clara Bartolozzi**

ES & OPERATIONS: **Danielle Ward**

NSLATION: **Lourdes Saez & Ignacio Gonzalez**

TERING: **Eugenia Arnodo**

SOCIAL MEDIA: **Rodrigo Molina**

HIN DENSETSU MOMO VOL. 1

2 Yuji Kobayashi, Z-ONE Originally published in Japan in 2012 by HERO'S INC., Tokyo.
sh translation rights arranged with HERO'S INC. through Tuttle-Mori Agency, Inc., Tokyo.

ALIEN BOOKS

 aliencomicbooks aliencomicbooks alien_books
aliencomicbooks   www.alienbooks.com / info@alienbooks.com